The Which? Guide to
Scotland

The Which? Guide to
Scotland

ANDREW LESLIE

CONSUMERS' ASSOCIATION

Which? Books are commissioned and researched by
Consumers' Association and published by
Which? Ltd, 2 Marylebone Road, London NW1 4DF
Email address: books@which.net

Distributed by The Penguin Group:
Penguin Books Ltd, 27 Wrights Lane, London W8 5TZ

First published April 1992
Revised editions April 1994, June 1996
This edition March 2001

British Library Cataloguing in Publication Data
A catalogue record for this book is available from the British Library

ISBN 0 85202 852 0

The author and publishers would like to thank the following for their assistance: Alison Cunningham and David Minns (RSPB Scotland), Anne
Harvey, Steven Murray, Valerie Strachan

Cover photograph by Chris Walsh/Britstock–IFA
Typographic design by Julie Martin
Line illustrations by Paul Saunders
Maps by European Map Graphics Ltd

For a full list of Which? books, please write to Which? Books,
Castlemead, Gascoyne Way, Hertford X, SG14 1LH
or access our web site at *www.which.net*

Typeset by Saxon Graphics Ltd, Derby
Printed in England by Clays Ltd, St Ives plc

Contents

Introduction

'Stands Scotland where it did?' asks the exiled Macduff in Shakespeare's *Macbeth*. To this perennial question of the expatriate longing for news of home, the short answer is no. Scotland is on the move, although the precise direction it is taking is far from clear. The seminal event of the last decade has been the re-establishment of a Scottish Parliament with extensive, if limited, powers over the country's destiny. In its first years of operation the Parliament has, perhaps inevitably, suffered from accusations of parochialism and ineffectiveness, but there are signs that it is going to make a real difference. Already, Scotland has regained a political energy that she has not seen for centuries, and this is bound, eventually, to create a different, more exciting country.

Why come to Scotland on holiday? Because it is is a beautiful, largely unspoilt place, and still uncrowded. Because it has a long history which is shot through with both light and darkness, and has left the country sprinkled with monuments, from prehistoric burial cairns to stately homes. Because its thinkers, explorers, writers, inventors and engineers have had such an impact on the rest of the world. Because hospitality here is less moribund than in many other areas. Most of all, because here it is possible to enjoy the outdoors properly, without being shepherded or corralled.

In fine weather, Scotland is one of the loveliest countries in the world. The quality of the light which illuminates its ancient, ice-gouged mountains and its turquoise sea-lochs is not to be matched further south. At every season of the year, except in bleakest November or March, the Scottish landscape is a blend of subtle colours. Blues predominate – in the sea and the lochs, or in the distant hills. Green and white add their shades in spring, lilac and purple in summer, and, perhaps most magnificent, the tans, caramels and russets of autumn, garnished by the intense orange of the seaweed on the banks of western lochs. A frosty winter's day in sharp black, white and grey shows a landscape less subtle, more magnificent. The way in which these colours blend and change over a patch of hillside is worth taking time to contemplate. It is a landscape to provoke despairing wonder in the most skilled of artists.

Scotland is an ideal country for outdoor activities of almost any kind. Walkers and hillwalkers have the best of it, for there is scarcely an area of the country lacking access to magnificent, lonely landscape. Walks can vary from less-than-strenuous strolls to hard days on knife-edge ridges where only the experienced should venture. Golfers and fishermen are also spoilt for choice, as are those in pursuit of birds to watch, prehistoric remains to track down, or interesting geological outcrops to investigate. Opportunities for surfers, divers, cyclists, sailors and riders abound.

It is not a place for fair-weather hobbyists, however. The weather can be sluicing wet, damply misty or bitingly windy. Waterproof clothing is essential, as is a decent alternative plan for when the weather is too awful for outdoor pursuits. That said, Scotland can bask in temperatures more typical of the Mediterranean, at which times it seems lunacy to holiday anywhere else.

All these reasons to visit Scotland may not, however, be enough. In an era of ever-cheaper flights to the European sun, Scotland can be a very expensive alternative. It is true that there are some amazingly cheap airfares from London to Edinburgh or Glasgow these days, but if you want to get any further afield, flights begin to look very pricey in comparison to those you can get to Europe. The Orkney Islands may be wonderful for a spring break, but if a return flight there from London costs £137.50 before tax (as it did in early 2001), while a flight to the palm trees and restaurants of Nice in the French Riviera costs only £36 at the same time, it makes the decision rather easy, and not to Scotland's advantage.

To this price disadvantage, you must add the fact that travel to the most scenic parts of Scotland can be time-consuming and frustrating. Should you, for example, wish to visit the isolated, beautiful island of Colonsay for the day, you can currently do it only in summer, on a Wednesday. Otherwise, you will have to spend at least two nights on the island. This kind of timetabling was all very well in an era of stay-put, fortnight-long holidays. Now that time is at a premium and more frequent but shorter holidays are the norm, it means that visitors who want to see the most beautiful parts of Scotland may miss out.

This is not all that visitors to Scotland may miss out on. There is a definite buzz to Scottish culture at the moment, inspired partly by the success of films such as *Trainspotting*, partly by the revival of traditional music in the new guise of Celtic Rock, and partly by the growing interest in Gaelic as a language and a culture. There is the ongoing excellence and excitement of the art pouring out of Glasgow, the love-affair that much of Central Scotland has with Country and Western music, the Highland delight in shinty (how many tourists get to a game?) and much more, including an increasingly eclectic and interesting cuisine.

Much of this is poorly marketed to visitors, if at all. Scotland has, thank goodness, moved on from selling itself on the back of tartan, shortbread, haggis and Nessie, but it is still relying too much on traditional images – the lonely loch, the friendly landlady, whisky and heather. Even the proud, defiant warrior figure, first popularised by Sir Walter Scott almost two centuries ago, has had a runaround in the shape of Mel Gibson's portrayal of William Wallace in *Braveheart*.

There is much more to Scotland than you might think from the tourist literature. Luckily you can find most of it on the World Wide Web instead. This book can be used in conjunction with the Internet for planning a holiday to Scotland and for finding all the hidden corners and characters which you might otherwise pass by. But in the end, the Internet can offer only virtual Scotland.

The real version deserves to be seen for itself.

Scotland on the Internet

The advent of the Internet has transformed the business of planning a Scottish holiday. It is now possible for anyone to take a virtual tour of a chosen area, look up timetables, search for and book accommodation, order goods, pick up gossip from local communities or drop in on a particular sight to see if it is likely to appeal. Hundreds of sites cater for special interests from fishing to cycling, with hints, tips and links to local clubs or businesses. Equally, a multitude of sites exist where ordinary people have recorded their experiences of holidays in Scotland, or have left their photographs for others to look at. There are even 'webcams' – continually live cameras – positioned at strategic places such as Edinburgh Castle, or overlooking Loch Ness.

This book breaks new ground in recognising this change. Throughout, we have attempted to give URLs (web site addresses) for as many sights and areas as possible. We don't claim always to have found the best, and the nature of the Web means that we shall have missed some, but we have at least provided starting points. By using the addresses given under the 'Key web sites' section at the beginning of each chapter, you will rapidly find yourself in touch with your chosen area. There is masses more to discover and to enjoy than we can possibly guide you to.

Key web sites

Between them, these four sites will provide you with information about almost anything you could possibly wish to know concerning Scotland. Each of them has a massive collection of links to a whole variety of specialist sites, including many of those listed elsewhere in this book.

www.electricscotland.com Excellent for culture, history and general news and gossip. Links all over the place, with a good section on genealogy

www.rampantscotland.com Over 9,000 links, with most subjects covered somewhere

www.scran.ac.uk A distinctive cultural resource site, designed to be of especial value to educationalists, with a huge collection of well-organised links

www.scotlands.com/tp The 'tartan pages' site, with a good directory of Scottish links

---

Scottish web sites

So how is Scotland doing when it comes to telling the electronic world about itself? Not too badly, if the hours we have spent online are anything to go by. Two things are noteworthy: the first is that some of the bodies with responsibility for many of the top sights, such as Historic Scotland and the National Trust for Scotland, have uninteresting, scanty web sites which make no attempt to link you to better ones. The area tourist boards (with a few golden exceptions) are just as bad, content to reproduce the gush of their brochures without a glimmer of understanding that they are working in a different medium. In general, the bigger the organisation, the worse its web site.

In contrast, and equally noteworthy, the smallest and most isolated communities seem to have adopted the electronic age with enthusiasm and understanding. Visit the tiny islands of Colonsay or Eigg on the Web or trawl the communities in the far north-west, and you will find sites where the design and quality of information for the visitor far outrank those of much bigger places.

The web sites for individual attractions (listed after the opening times and telephone number for each sight) vary enormously. Privately owned stately homes, new, purpose-built attractions, museums and art galleries often have excellent sites. Those for gardens and ancient monuments are less good, on the whole.

We have not attempted to give URLs for the many businesses that cater for tourists. But they are there to be found. Networks of local businesses, often via the Chamber of Commerce or the local Enterprise sites, exist for most areas. Tour operators for walking holidays, craft shops by the dozen, mills, specialists in smoked meats or fish, purveyors of kilts and organisations who will help you trace your ancestors all have a presence on the Web. In many cases you can buy on-line – but take the precautions outlined below.

Protect yourself on-line

- Look for a logo that indicates that the trader complies with a code of good practice, such as the Which? Web Trader logo or the TrustUK 'e-hallmark' (see below).

- Don't do business through a web site which does not give you real-world contact details (address and telephone number).

- Make sure the site explains how it will handle personal data you supply. If you are not happy with the arrangement, don't give any personal information.

- Before sending personal details or debit or credit-card numbers, move to a secure link. This may be indicated by a key or closed padlock on your browser toolbar or the letter 's' for secure in the Internet address after the 'http' prefix.

- Don't send confidential information such as your card number via email. Protect your card number from 'sniffer programs' (used by fraudsters to detect card-like strings of digits) by writing it in words or splitting it over more than one email.

- Keep any order numbers and other reference information. Check credit-card and bank statements if you suspect discrepancies or other problems.

The Which? Web Trader logo and TrustUK e-hallmark

Searching the Internet with this book

We are assuming here a little knowledge of how computers and the Internet work. To get to grips with the basics, read *The Which? Guide to Computers* and *The Which? Guide to the Internet*. Alternatively visit a library or Internet café, or, best of all, get a child or grandchild to show you.

The bugbear of the Internet is the complexity of the address system. To avoid having to type in the lengthy string of obscure symbols often needed to reach an individual web site, we have chosen URLs which are relatively easy to type in, putting 'via' if you then need to make further connections (easily done by a click of the mouse) to reach the precise place you want to go. Sometimes you may have to choose from a menu – often 'attractions', 'local links' or 'things to do' will get you there. Occasionally, you may have to exercise some skill and judgement. This is especially true of university web sites, many of which have useful information or guides hidden away behind course details.

The 'Key web sites' section at the start of each chapter takes you to sites which we have found to be a useful introduction to the region, or which provide useful links to follow up. They are good starting points for a general trawl. Additionally, some excellent general guides to the country exist on-line. Currently the best is the Internet Guide to Scotland *www.scotland-inverness.co.uk* which is packed with information and links. There are also useful sites (but not enough of them) which compile as many links and as much information as possible for a chosen subject. For example, *www.scottishculture.about.com* is almost infallible when it comes to Scottish castles, and we have listed it frequently.

If you want to do some searching of your own, use three or four different search engines if you can. They are all structured differently and throw up different results. In general, we have found Excite and Alta Vista to be useful. When searching, remember that Scottish towns often have much larger counterparts on other continents. Searching for 'Perth' or 'Banff', for example, may throw up large numbers of sites on the other side of the world.

If you can't find what you want, it is worth trying a random fling, typing in 🖱 *www. (area or town name)* where the name is all in one word, and adding *.net, .com, .co.uk,* or *.org.uk* at the end. Much of the time, this method will return 'Server not found', but we have known it to give results where search engines failed us.

The Web is constantly changing as users create new web sites, change their location, update (or fail to update) and simply disappear. Not every site we mention will continue to exist, and new, better, ones will continue to appear.

The Internet can be very slow, and service providers' machines get clogged up, refusing to answer, or, even worse, disconnecting you in mid-browse. Early birds have the best of it, clocking on before most of the country is at work and when much of America is still asleep. Avoid times when children have just got back from school, wet weekends and early evenings. After midnight, the lines usually clear again.

Practical Directory

The information sources listed here should come in handy for helping you to plan your trip. We have included guidance on useful organisations as well as pointers on getting around and accommodation. To find out about activities in Scotland and the cultural background, see 'Distinctive Scotland' on page 509.

TOURIST INFORMATION

The Scottish Tourist Board (STB) is in the process of rebranding itself as VisitScotland at the time of writing. It currently oversees a network of fourteen area tourist boards, which carve up the country between them (see box overleaf). Reorganisation may change this pattern in the near future. More than 150 tourist information centres (TICs) in towns and villages provide the lowest, and most useful, level of the hierarchy. A wide variety of literature is available from the area tourist boards, some of it extremely useful, such as *The Complete Guide to Fishing in the Scottish Borders* (available from the Scottish Borders Tourist Board), some of it mere purple prose. Accommodation guides are also available. In local offices you will often find town trail leaflets or descriptions of walks in the area in addition. The size and efficiency of the local TICs varies, but in general they are excellent.

The STB's web site (see overleaf) contains a search engine for accommodation throughout Scotland. This is useful, although only the barest details of the character of the accommodation are given. An ambitious project is under way to provide availability details and a booking facility for all the accommodation listed, although at the time of writing it has only reached pilot stage, and it will probably be some time before everywhere is on-line. See also the recommendations on where to stay at the end of each chapter for lists of establishments inspected by *Holiday Which?* and its sister publications.

Tourist board offices

Scottish Tourist Board
Head office
23 Ravelston Terrace
Edinburgh EH4 3TP
☎ 0131-332 2433
📠 0131-343 1513
🖱 *www.visitscotland.com*

Aberdeen and Grampian
Tourist Board
St Nicholas House
Broad Street
Aberdeen AB10 1DE
☎ (01224) 632727
📠 (01224) 620415
🖱 *www.agtb.org*

Angus and City of Dundee
Tourist Board
21 Castle Street
Dundee DD1 3AA
☎ (01382) 527527
📠 (01382) 527551
🖱 *www.angusanddundee.co.uk*

Argyll, the Isles, Loch Lomond,
Stirling and Trossach
Tourist Board
7 Alexandra Parade
Dunoon
Argyll PA23 8AB
☎ (01369) 701000
🖱 *www.scottish.heartlands.org*

Ayrshire and Arran
Tourist Board
15 Skye Road
Prestwick
Ayr KA9 2TA
☎ (01292) 262555
📠 (01292) 471832
🖱 *www.ayrshire-arran.com*

Dumfries and Galloway
Tourist Board
64 Whitesands
Dumfries DG1 2RS
☎ (01387) 245550
📠 (01387) 245551
🖱 *www.galloway.co.uk*

Edinburgh and the Lothians
Tourist Board
3 Princes Street
Edinburgh EH2 2QP
☎ 0131-473 3800
📠 0131-473 3881
🖱 *www.edinburgh.org*

Greater Glasgow and Clyde
Valley Tourist Board
11 George Square
Glasgow G2 1DY
☎ 0141-204 4400
📠 0141-221 3524
🖱 *www.seeglasgow.com*

Highlands of Scotland
Tourist Board
Peffery House
Strathpeffer
Ross-shire IV14 9HA
☎ (01997) 421015
📠 (01997) 421168
🖱 www.host.co.uk

Kingdom of Fife Tourist Board
70 Market Street
St Andrews
Fife KY16 9NU
☎ (01334) 472021
📠 (01334) 478422
🖱 www.standrews.com

Orkney Tourist Board
6 Broad Street
Kirkwall
Orkney KW15 1NX
☎ (01856) 872856
📠 (01856) 875056
🖱 www.orkney.com

Perthshire Tourist Board
Lower City Mills
West Mill Street

Perth PH1 5QP
☎ (01738) 627958
📠 (01738) 630416
🖱 www.perthshire.co.uk

Scottish Borders Tourist Board
Tourist Information Centre
Murray's Green
Jedburgh TD8 6BE
☎ (01835) 863435
📠 (01835) 864099
🖱 www.scot-borders.co.uk

Shetland Tourist Board
Market Cross
Lerwick ZE1 0LU
☎ (01595) 693434
📠 (01595) 695807
🖱 www.shetland-tourism.co.uk

Western Isles Tourist Board
26 Cromwell Street
Stornoway
Isle of Lewis
☎ (01851) 703088
📠 (01851) 705244
🖱 www.witb.co.uk

THE SUPPORT SYSTEM

In addition to the tourist boards, other organisations exist which manage popular sights or provide services and information for the visitor to Scotland. The most useful are listed below.

Heritage and history

Historic Scotland (HS)

Longmore House
Salisbury Place
Edinburgh EH9 1SH
☎ 0131–668 8600
📠 0131–668 8789
💻 *www.historic-scotland.gov.uk*

This is a government agency (the equivalent of English Heritage), responsible for the care of Scotland's historic buildings and monuments. Most of Scotland's prehistoric sites, ruined castles, abbeys and cathedrals are looked after by Historic Scotland. Its custodians are often experts on the buildings in their care, and while they manage not to be obtrusive they are well worth chatting to, especially if you want to know something obscure that is not in the guidebook. They keep the lawns round their monuments in first-class condition, too.

In recent years, Historic Scotland has taken to running a substantial events programme – mostly historical re-enactments, falconry displays and musical events at many of its more popular sights, notably Stirling Castle. You will find details on the web site.

If you are going to visit a number of ancient buildings, the discounted 'Explorer' pass is worth buying. This gives the holder entrance to all HS properties. The 3-day pass costs £9 and £12 (child and adult rates); the 7-day pass costs £12.50 and £17; and the 14-day pass costs £16.50 and £22 (2001 prices).

The National Trust for Scotland (NTS)
Wemyss House
28 Charlotte Square
Edinburgh EH2 4ET
☎ 0131–243 9300
📠 0131–243 9301
🖱 *www.nts.org.uk*

Like its sister organisation in England, the NTS is a charity that is independent of government support and is charged with the preservation of the properties in its care. It looks after over 100 of these, which include castles, historic sites, gardens and tracts of Scottish land. Among its many responsibilities, the NTS is particularly good at maintaining and running its gardens. Opening hours for its historic properties can be frustratingly short in some areas, especially out of season.

NTS houses gleam with polished furniture, and guides are enthusiasts if not experts. However, despite attempts to give them a lived-in feeling, the houses are inclined to lack the personal touches or downright eccentricity you may find when visiting those which are still privately owned.

NTS membership allows you free entry to its properties in Scotland, and to those of its sister organisations in England and Ireland. NTS also organises conservation holidays, working in such places as Fair Isle or St Kilda.

Conservation, walks and wildlife

Forestry Commission
231 Corstorphine Road
Edinburgh EH12 7AT
☎ 0131–334 0303
📠 0131–334 3047
🖱 *www.forestry.gsi.gov.uk*

The Forestry Commission manages over 500,000 hectares of woodland in Scotland through its commercial arm, Forest Enterprise. Visitors are allowed to walk on forest roads, and there are trails for cyclists and horses too. The Forestry

Commission picnic site, with its wooden benches, is a common occurrence throughout the country.

Individual Forest Districts publish leaflets with details of walks and facilities (contact the Commission office). Several other charitable bodies and trusts are working to restore Scotland's native woodland. For more information look up ✓🖱 *www.scotweb.co.uk/environment/wildwood* and ✓🖱 *www. millenniumforest.com*

Scottish Wildlife Trust (SWT)

Cramond House
Kirk Cramond
Cramond Glebe Road
Edinburgh EH4 6RB
☎ 0131–312 7765
📠 0131–312 8705
✓🖱 *www.swt.org.uk*

The SWT runs over 100 wildlife reserves in Scotland. They have an open access policy, subject to occasional restrictions during the breeding season. Visitors are advised to contact local wardens for advice on best times to visit. There are visitor centres at Loch of the Lowes and Dunkeld (ospreys), the Falls of Clyde and New Lanark (badgers, woodland), and at Montrose Basin (migratory birds). The Edinburgh office can put you in touch with the regional centres.

John Muir Trust

41 Commercial Street
Leith
Edinburgh EH6 6JD
☎ 0131–554 0114
📠 0131–555 2112
✓🖱 *www.jmt.org*

The trust, which is named after the Scots-born conservationist who founded America's National Park system, is increasingly involved in buying land in Scotland with the purpose of promoting the conservation of some of the country's outstanding natural wildernesses. It owns, or part-owns, sites from Knoydart to Ben Nevis.

Disabled travellers

Disability Scotland
Princes House
5 Shandwick Place
Edinburgh EH2 4RG
☎ 0131–229 8632
📧 enquries@disabilityscotland.org.uk

Holiday Care
Second Floor
Imperial Building
Victoria Road
Horley
Surrey RH6 7PZ
☎ (01293) 774535
📠 (01293) 784647
minicom: (01293) 776943
📧 holiday.care@virgin.net

Both these organisations are useful points of contact for visitors with disabilities, and can supply information on services as well as accessible accommodation and attractions. Readers can write to Holiday Care for information packs on Scotland, visitor attractions, and holiday centres and caravan parks (enclose an s.a.e.).

TRANSPORT

By air

From south of the border you can fly direct to Aberdeen, Edinburgh, Glasgow, Inverness and Prestwick. Flights depart from London (Heathrow, Luton, Gatwick and Stansted) and several regional airports. At the time of writing, several no-frills airlines were offering some very reasonably priced deals between London and Edinburgh or Glasgow.

Further connections will take you to Inverness, Wick, Shetland, Orkney, the Western Isles, Campbeltown, Tiree and Islay. These routes, by contrast, tend to be horribly expensive. Good additional connections are in place between the islands in Orkney, Shetland and the Western Isles.

The airlines that fly to Scotland are listed on ✆ *www.visitscotland.com*, and this web site provides further contact details. For details of internal flight times and fares on British Airways look up ✆ *www.britishairways.com*

By rail

Frequent and fast connections from south of the border take you to Edinburgh and Glasgow or further north. The current cross-border operators are GNER on the east coast [☎ *(0345) 225225;* ✆ *www.gner.co.uk]* and Virgin on the west coast [☎ *(08457) 222333;* ✆ *www.virgintrains.co.uk]*. A variety of advance tickets, fares and promotional offers are usually available.

Scotrail [☎ *(08457) 550033;* ✆ *www.scotrail.co.uk]* operates most of the services within Scotland. It also runs its 'Caledonian Sleeper' overnight service to and from London Euston.

The most scenic rail journeys in Scotland are those from Inverness to Kyle of Lochalsh, from Inverness to Wick and from Fort William to Mallaig. The 'Jacobite' steam excursion run by the West Coast Railway Company [☎ *(01542) 732100;* ✆ *www.home.clara.net/vickphil/wchome]* during summer brings some extra spice to the Fort William–Mallaig route.

By bus

Scottish Citylink [☎ *(0870) 5505050;* ✆ *www.citylink.co.uk]* is the first port of call for coach travel between Scottish towns. They also have connections south of the border.

A variety of different bus companies operate local networks

in Scottish towns and regions. Most tourist information centres will have timetables for their local operators.

Competing companies in the cities can make life very confusing for the visitor, especially in Glasgow. For assistance contact the relevant tourist board. In the remote areas of the Highlands, post-buses connect the small communities. Details of their networks are available through the area tourist boards listed above.

Although it is possible to get to most places in Scotland by bus, it can be very time-consuming. Worse, there is no guarantee of a return connection the same day. To visit the famous gardens of Inverewe by public transport, for example, is impossible unless you are prepared to stay overnight in the area.

By car

The vast majority of visitors to Scotland come by car or hire one when they arrive. To go anywhere at all remote, a car is a necessity.

If you do not bring your own car, hiring is easy from all main towns and airports, where there are branches of all the main chains such as Avis, Budget, Europcar and Hertz. Out on the islands (where a combination of flying and hiring is often the most efficient way to see them in a short time), cars are equally easily hired from local operators (often the island's garage), although it is advisable to book in advance, via the tourist offices, if you can.

Road connections from Scotland to southern England via the M6 or A1 seem to get slower every year, thanks to traffic congestion. Within Scotland, motorways are less crowded, although the M8 between Edinburgh and Glasgow regularly clogs up in rush hour. The spinal north–south A9 route between Perth and Inverness can be very frustrating when the caravans are out in force, and has dangerous sections at the best of times. The main roads to the west vary in quality and traffic density, but travelling on them is still usually a pleasure.

In much of the Highlands and Islands, local roads are single track with passing places. Such routes are often very twisty and usually unfenced. Driving on these roads takes concentration if you are not used to them. It is inadvisable to look at the scenery at the same time. Additional hazards are posed by the sheep, who enjoy lying on the warm tarmac and are reluctant to move, and by the locals, who usually drive a lot faster than the visitors.

Passing places should be used to allow overtaking, and it is only courteous to let drivers behind you pass whenever possible. Equip your car with a tow rope before you set off, in case you need to rescue another driver or be pulled out of a ditch yourself. It is forbidden, for obvious reasons, to use passing places for overnight stops in camper vans or caravans.

Unleaded petrol is available everywhere, as is diesel, but petrol prices in remote areas are usually far higher than close to the towns. In the Western Isles and in parts of Sutherland, it can be a long drive between filling stations.

By sea

Scotland has no external ferry connections, apart from a service between Shetland and Norway. This may change if Rosyth, near Edinburgh, beomes a ferry port as planned. Within the country however, most inhabited islands are linked by ferry routes (although not all take cars), and travelling by sea between the islands is an experience not to be missed. Bear in mind that ferry sailings are easily disrupted by the weather – the waters of the Minch and Pentland Firth in particular can be very rough. Less than hardy sailors may want to take sea-sickness precautions.

The chief ferry operator on the west coast of Scotland is Caledonian MacBrayne, universally known as Calmac [☎ (0990) 650000; ☜ www.calmac.co.uk]. As we went to press their routes were being put out to tender under European law, and the situation may change. Calmac's web site is excellent, with full timetables, booking information and a clear description of the discounted tickets on offer. Advance booking is vital in high season, if you are taking a car.

P&O Scottish Ferries [☎ (01224) 572615; ☜ www.poscottishferries.co.uk] run services between Aberdeen, Orkney and

Shetland. The journey can be long and sometimes rough, but it may be preferable to the drive north to catch P&O's shorter (but equally rough) crossing from Scrabster, near Thurso, to Stromness on Orkney.

An independent passenger ferry, John O'Groats Ferries, runs between John O'Groats and Orkney [☎ (01955) 611353; ✆ www.jogferry.co.uk].

Inter-island ferries on Orkney are run by Orkney Ferries [☎ (01856) 872044; ✆ www.orkneyferries.co.uk] and on Shetland by the local council [☎ (01957) 722259; ✆ via www.shetland-tourism.co.uk].

ACCOMMODATION

There is usually no shortage of accommodation for holiday-makers in Scotland. The only exceptions are Edinburgh during the summer Festival or at Hogmanay, and some of the smaller towns (notably Dunoon) during their annual Highland Games or other festivals.

Hotels and bed and breakfasts

Many good hotels now exist in most regions of Scotland, even the most remote, although their prices can put severe strain on holiday budgets. Cheaper bed and breakfast establishments are thick on the ground however, and using them as a base for touring holidays remains a popular choice. To help you plan your holiday this book contains lists of establishments that have been independently inspected (see 'How to use this book' pages 28–9).

The Scottish Tourist Board (STB) grades accommodation providers which are members. Note that some establishments are not STB members, among them some very good places to stay. The STB has broken away from English and Welsh practice when it comes to grading accommodation and awards places to stay between one and five stars based entirely on quality: instead of facilities, hotels are assessed on criteria such as warmth of welcome, service, food, cleanliness and condition. Additionally, the STB breaks down accommodation into different categories such as small hotel, guest house, and so forth. For a full explanation of the scheme, write to the Scottish Tourist Board (see page 16), or look up ✒ *www.visitscotland.com*

Youth hostels

Scottish Youth Hostels Association (SYHA)
7 Glebe Crescent
Stirling FK8 2JA
☎ (01786) 891400
📠 (01786) 891333
✒ *www.syha.org.uk*

The SYHA runs 83 hostels ranging from cottages to Highland castles, and organises various activity holidays including skiing, sailing, walking and pony-trekking (ask for the Breakaway Holidays leaflet). Their main handbook is *The Scottish Hosteller*, obtainable from the address above.

Self-catering

Self-catering properties range from traditional croft cottages to chalet complexes and caravans, and are found everywhere. Having a place of your own to return to for drying your clothes and relaxing in can make a lot of sense, but remember that the local shops in remote areas will probably only stock essentials. The Scottish Tourist Board publishes a book entitled *Where to stay: Self-Catering [☎ (08705) 511511 to order a copy],* and the regional tourist boards listed on pages 16–17 can provide lists of properties.

Caravanning and camping

There are caravan sites in abundance in Scotland, many of them well positioned on the coast. Do not expect every site to have ample facilities; some may simply be a field which is put to other uses out of season. The Scottish Tourist Board publishes *Where to stay: Camping and Caravanning* which gives details of sites throughout the country *[to order a copy call* ☎ *(08705) 511511],* or, if you are a member of the following organisations, you can contact the Camping and Caravanning Club *[*☎ *(02476) 694995],* the AA *[*☎ *(0990) 500600; to join* ☎ *(0990) 444444],* the RAC *[*☎ *(0345) 333222; to join* ☎ *(0800) 550550]* or the Forestry Commission *[*☎ *0131-334 0303].*

Campsites with full amenities do exist, but they are few and far between, due, perhaps, to the climate and the seasonal nature of camping. Rough camping is the preferred norm in Scotland, and numerous farmers and crofters informally turn a patch of ground over to campers in the summer. Rough camping in the mountains is possible if you exercise some tact and ask permission. Some estates forbid it; others ask you not to camp in certain areas. The local tourist offices should be able to provide contact numbers and advice.

How to use this book

The Which? Guide to Scotland splits the country into 13 separate geographical areas, including the cities of Edinburgh and Glasgow. Within each chapter, we pick out the best of the many things to see and do in the region and also recommend accommodation and places to eat (see box opposite). The 'Scotland for everyone' section (see page 481) contains themed touring routes featuring sights of special interest throughout Scotland and provides suggestions for activity holidays.

At the start of each chapter, we give some suggestions for towns or villages which may make suitable bases for exploring an area. Further descriptions follow later under 'Towns and villages to explore'.

Our 'Top sights' for each area are the best attractions to visit if you do not have much time. If you want to explore a region further, we also recommend the sights on our 'Next Best' list. People who enjoy small or specialist sights and are prepared to track down out-of-the-way places may wish to follow up some of the suggestions we give under 'Also in the area'.

Throughout the book we also pick out some routes to follow for pleasant excursions by car, indicate worthwhile trips and expeditions and note a few interesting walks. In the chapters on the North-West and the Central and Northern Highlands, we concentrate on where to find the best of the scenery and list some interesting things to see or do nearby.

Using our recommendations on where to stay and eat

At the end of each chapter you will find details of places to stay. Our recommended hotels have all been inspected by *Holiday Which?* or its sister publications, *The Which? Hotel Guide* and *The Which? Bed and Breakfast Guide*. The price categories are based on the cost, per night, of a double or twin-bedded room in 2001, including VAT and breakfast. Tariffs quoted by hotels sometimes include dinner – check when booking.

£ – under £70 per room per night
££ – £70 to £110 per room per night
£££ – over £110 per room per night

Each chapter also includes recommended places to eat. Entries were compiled with the help of *The Good Food Guide* and *The Which? Guide to Country Pubs* (both published by Which? Books), and establishments featured in this section offer notably good food. It is advisable to phone in advance as opening hours may change.

Useful contacts to help you plan your trip are listed at the front of the book, while 'Distinctive Scotland' on page 509 provides background reading on Scotland's history and culture to enhance your stay.

Opening times, telephone numbers and web sites for the tourist attractions covered are given in square brackets. HS means that the sight is run by Historic Scotland and NTS indicates that it is cared for by the National Trust for Scotland. For more about these organisations, see pages 18–19.

All contact details and admission times are correct at the time of going to press. However, opening times for sights can change from year to year, as can phone numbers and web addresses. We advise checking with the regional tourist offices listed on pages 16–17 for the latest information.

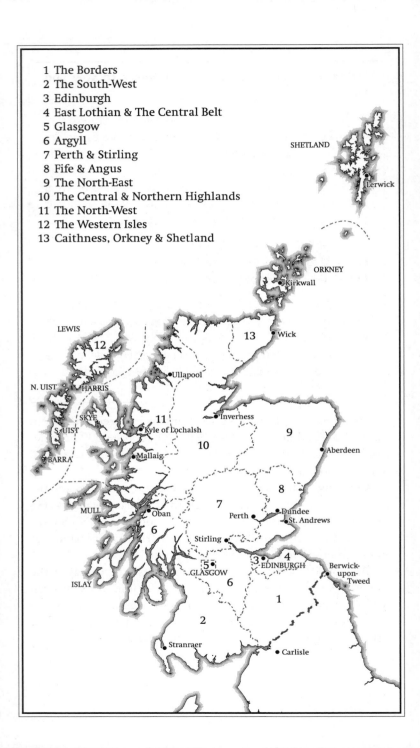

1 The Borders
2 The South-West
3 Edinburgh
4 East Lothian & The Central Belt
5 Glasgow
6 Argyll
7 Perth & Stirling
8 Fife & Angus
9 The North-East
10 The Central & Northern Highlands
11 The North-West
12 The Western Isles
13 Caithness, Orkney & Shetland

The Scottish Borders

Jedburgh Abbey

- An exceptionally varied landscape, ranging from windswept sheep pasture to fertile woodland and rocky coast
- A rich folk tradition and a violent history
- Ruined castles and abbeys, stately homes and country walks
- Compact, small towns, all different
- Excellent fishing, walking and cycling

THE SCOTTISH BORDERS

At a glance

✓ Good for three- or five-night short breaks

✓ Suited to outdoor holidays, especially for walkers

✓ Fishing holidays

✓ Touring

✗ Not much for small children

✗ Limited public transport

It is surprising to anyone who knows the area that the Borders are among the least-visited regions of Scotland. If you choose to go against the trend, you will find your enterprise well rewarded.

The region's pleasures are subtle, for the hills are lonely rather than dramatic, the towns quirky but unassuming, the coastline rugged but not wild, and the people hospitable but reticent. Yet in all of Scotland there are few other regions with such a mixture of landscapes; bleak moorland lies only a few minutes' road journey from thick beech woods and lush pasture. The character of the countryside changes with a peculiar rapidity, often between one river valley and the next.

In the Borders it pays to become a little obsessive about the past, for the region is rich in history and mythology, and traces of bygone times lie everywhere. Tracking down old castles will lead you from end to end of the region, but you can equally well pursue Roman remains, old churches, drove roads, Iron Age settlements, eighteenth-century bridges or the relics of the once-magnificent railway network, whose stark embankments and broken bridges bear witness to the vandalism inflicted on the region.

There is a final consideration: in foul weather the Scottish Borders are much less depressing than the wilderness areas north of the Highland Line. There is more to be seen under cover; you do not suffer the frustration of being unable to see magnificent landscape and, if the worst comes to the worst, Edinburgh and Glasgow are within easy reach.

Key web sites

www.scot-borders.co.uk The tourist board's web site has some useful information

www.northumbria-tourist-board.org.uk Good for exploration south of the border

www.galloway.co.uk The Dumfries and Galloway tourist board. Useful for the western half of the Borders

www.bordernet.co.uk A very useful site for information on towns and local businesses

www.tweedalepress.co.uk Publisher of most of the local newspapers. News, gossip, events

www.reivers.com A good site from which to learn something about Border warfare

Good bases in the Borders

Berwick-upon-Tweed
✓ *Market town of character*
✓ *Ideal for coastal exploration*

The town has been English since 1482, but Scotland laps up to its doorstep. Once an important port, now a quiet river-mouth town, old Berwick is enclosed by sixteenth-century ramparts and has streets lined by elegant eighteenth-century buildings. You will find old coaching-inns within the walls and plenty of guesthouses outside. Berwick is a logical base for exploring the east coast up as far as Edinburgh, or down into Northumbria.

Kelso
✓ *Attractive market town*
✓ *Good location on River Tweed*
✓ *Fine base for walkers*
✗ *Limited range of accommodation*

The most appealing of all the Border towns, thanks to its graceful square, the ruined abbey and the River Tweed which flows round it. Kelso is well placed for exploring the central Borders, especially the abbeys and stately homes. The Cheviot

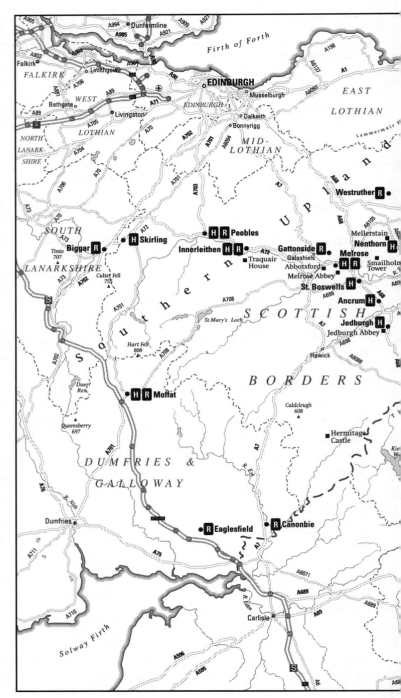

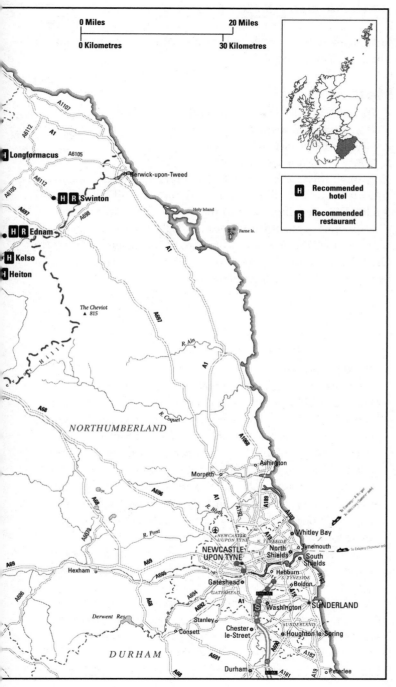

0 Miles   20 Miles

0 Kilometres   30 Kilometres

H Recommended hotel

R Recommended restaurant

A1107

A6112

A1

H Longformacus

A6105

A6112

A6105

Berwick-upon-Tweed

A697

H **R** Swinton

A698

Holy Island

A1

Farne Is.

H **R** Ednam

H Kelso

H Heiton

The Cheviot
▲ 815

A697

R. Aln

A1

A68

R. Coquet

NORTHUMBERLAND

A1068

Ashington

Morpeth

A696

A1

A192

A189

A19

A68

R. Blyth

A1079

R. Pont

Whitley Bay

NEWCASTLE UPON TYNE

N. TYNESIDE

Tynemouth

A69

Hexham

A69

A695

NEWCASTLE UPON TYNE

North Shields

South Shields

Hebburn

A194

A68

Gateshead

GATESHEAD

S. TYNESIDE

Boldon

A694

A1

S Washington

SUNDERLAND

A692

Stanley

SUNDERLAND

A691

Chester le-Street

Houghton le-Spring

A182

Consett

DURHAM

A693

Durham

A181

A19

Peterlee

Derwent Res.

A68

Hills, with their intricate valleys and fine walks, are about 20 minutes' drive away.

Moffat

✓ *Pleasant small town in steep hill country*
✓ *Wide range of accommodation*
✓ *Good for walkers and wildlife enthusiasts*
✗ *A little remote from the main sights*

This small town was once a spa, and retains the atmosphere of an early Victorian hill resort. Poised between hill country and the lowlands leading down to the Solway Firth, it is in an ideal position for exploring the western edge of the Borders, for touring into Dumfries and Galloway, or for travelling up to the Clyde Valley and Glasgow. There is plenty of accommodation here, mostly bed-and-breakfast.

Border warfare

For three centuries, between the first invasion by Edward I of England in 1296 and the union of the crowns of England and Scotland in 1603, the Borders were the battleground for two warring nations. Those 300 years of invasion, counter-invasion, siege, burning and plunder have shaped the land and its people more significantly than anything that has happened since. They left the countryside scattered with ancient fortresses, with the ruins of once-great abbeys, and with small towns which were frequently burned. They also left an obsession with riding, a fierce local pride and a vivid folk-culture – the ballads.

For the inhabitant of those times, nothing was worth possessing which was not portable. Horses, weapons and cattle were the currency of the Borders, and 'gear' was accumulated by raiding, not by trade. This was the age of the reiver – the horseman with his lance and his steel bonnet riding secret hill routes by night, descending in a flurry of violence on village or farmstead, driving his slow, mooing plunder homewards.

Peebles

✓ *Excellent location in pretty country*
✓ *Numerous attractions in the area*
✓ *Good base for cyclists*
✓ *Wide range of accommodation*

An ancient royal burgh, fortuitously placed among some of the best Tweed Valley scenery, Peebles is a thriving one–time county town and a bustling centre for day excursions from Edinburgh and Glasgow. The best sights in the Tweed Valley are only a few minutes away by car, and good walks abound.

Top sights

Abbotsford

✓ *Will interest Sir Walter Scott fans*
✓ *Intriguing collection of historical jumble*
✓ *Pleasant gardens*

The house that the novelist Sir Walter Scott built (most of it

---

The predation was not a simple question of Scots against English. Constant feuding between families, cross-Border connivance, protection rackets and bribery by the agents of one or other government meant that the Borderer was accustomed to putting his own interest before that of his neighbour, and was as ready to steal the cattle next door as to rustle those across the frontier. The frontier provided an easy refuge for those on the run and, for both the Scottish and English authorities, attempts to impose order were a nightmare. Over the years a whole canon of frontier law involving a degree of cross-Border co-operation came into being. It was enforced by the six Wardens of the Marches, three on each side of the frontier, with varying degrees of success. Yet it never stopped the raiding; it took the Union of the Crowns in 1603 to do that. Sixty hours' hard riding brought Robert Carey from London to Edinburgh with Queen Elizabeth's coronation ring to hand to her successor, James VI, King of Scotland, and the frontier disappeared for ever.

around 1822) is an eccentric one. Few would call its turreted, corbelled and battlemented exterior pretty, but it appealed to Scott's eclectic taste. Inside, Abbotsford is less a literary shrine than a high-class junk shop. Few people would have built a door used by condemned criminals into their own house, or hung the skull of an elk dug out of a Roxburgh bog in their entrance hall, but Scott loved curiosities such as these. The whole house is stuffed with a jumble of objects, many of them reputedly once owned by the most famous figures in Scottish history. On show is a model of Robert the Bruce's skull, the sword of James Graham, Marquess of Montrose, Rob Roy's sporran purse, a pocket book belonging to Flora Macdonald, plunder from the battlefields of Waterloo and Culloden and more.

Scott drew sightseers during his lifetime, but in nothing like the numbers that flock to his house today. Abbotsford was not constructed with coach parties in mind, and you can feel like a herring in a barrel if you go round when visitors are at their thickest. But there is ample space in the gardens (which contain their own curiosities). See the box on pages 58–9 for more on Scott's life. *[Mar to May and Oct, Mon–Sat 10–5, Sun 2–5; June to Sept, Mon–Sat 10–5, Sun 10–5;* ☎ *(01896) 752043;* 🖱 *via www.melrose.bordernet.co.uk]*

Hermitage Castle (north of Newcastleton)

✓ *Grim ruin in isolated setting*
✓ *The most menacing castle in Scotland*

This great square lump of virtually windowless masonry, pierced by flying arches like sharks' mouths, was once the stronghold of the Keeper of Liddesdale. The massively thick walls are stained algae-green where the light does not penetrate and nothing in the interior suggests comfort, least of all the horrible pit prison.

Throughout most of its early history the castle changed hands between Scots and English, with plenty of plotting and cross-border treachery revolving round it. One of its earliest lords, William de Soulis, supposedly dabbled in demonology within the walls. A later overlord, Sir William Douglas, starved his rival Sir Alexander Ramsay to death in the pit prison. In

1566 Mary Queen of Scots rode the 40 miles from Jedburgh and back again in a single day when her future husband James Hepburn, fourth Earl of Bothwell, was lying wounded at Hermitage after a tangle with a local villain.

Hermitage Castle was restored in the early nineteenth century, extremely effectively in view of its current air of nastiness. Although it has played no part in history since the union of the Scottish and English crowns, it is one of those places you sense to be dormant, not extinct. *[HS; Apr to Sept, daily 9.30–6.30; Oct and Nov, Mon–Wed and Sat 9.30–4.30, Thur 9.30–12.30, Sun 2–4.30; ☎ (01387) 376222; ᥱ via www.scottishculture.about.com]*

Jedburgh Abbey

✓ *The best preserved of the famous border abbeys*
✓ *Good interpretation*

Jedburgh is an austere ruin, with none of the immediate beauty of Melrose. However, enough remains of the tall abbey church for it to be an impressive place, much aided by Historic Scotland's excellent interpretation, which provides clear insights into the life led by the black-robed Augustinian canons in medieval times. Jedburgh, like other Border abbeys, was founded on the initiative of King David I in 1138, and, like the others, suffered the depredations of English invaders. Few of the surrounding buildings have survived above their foundations, but it is easy to see their position and how they related to each other. *[HS; Apr to Sept, daily 9.30–6.30; Oct to Mar, Mon–Sat 9.30–4.30, Sun 2–4.30; ☎ (01835) 863925]*

Mellerstain House (near Kelso)

✓ *Outstanding Adam house*

Mellerstain is the most beautiful Adam house in Scotland. It was started by William Adam, who was responsible for the wings, and finished by his son Robert in a style which approaches the perfection of neoclassicism. The exterior of Mellerstain is severe and uncompromising, but the interior, with its sequence of breathtaking ceilings, its fireplaces, its Adam-designed side tables, mirrors and cupboards, is a place of light and harmony, created for gracious family living rather than for stately processions. The library is the most perfect of the public rooms, where the eighteenth-century bindings on the shelves are complemented by the figures of Teaching and Learning.

After the splendour of the ground floor the bedrooms seem distinctly ordinary, though the main staircase is memorable. At the very top of the house, Adam designed a ceiling for the magnificent long gallery, but unfortunately it was never put into execution.

Do not become so engrossed in the architecture that you overlook the family portraits. The strength of the Baillie-Hamiltons (Earls of Haddington) lay in the women they married – you can see it in their dignity and power. One in particular – Grisell Baillie – spent her childhood dodging government forces to help her covenanting father. She later became mistress of Mellerstain and left meticulous household records from the early eighteenth century, some of which are on display. *[Mid-Apr to Sept, Sun–Fri 12.30–5;* ☎ *(01573) 410225;* 🖥 *http://muses.calligrafix.co.uk/mellerstain]*

Melrose Abbey

✓ *Ruined abbey with fine stonework*
✓ *The most beautiful of the border abbeys*

Melrose Abbey is widely agreed to be Scotland's finest Gothic building, with stone carving to rival the best in the United Kingdom. The first impression the ruins give is of delicate precariousness. Flying buttresses, reduced to a single course of stone, hang perilously between ruined masonry, while the east window, its internal tracery missing, is divided by pencil-thin columns of stone, ready to be blown down by the slightest wind.

The interior is blemished by the hideous remains of the parish kirk which was built inside the nave after the Reformation. Where there was once soaring vaulting, there is now a tunnel like a stone Nissen hut. Luckily, in the presbytery and the north transept some of the vaulting has survived the fall of the tower. Under the east window an embalmed heart in a casket was discovered in 1920 – perhaps that of Robert the Bruce.

The best views are from the outside. The remains of the old cloisters (copied by Scott for the Abbotsford garden) are especially worth spending time on. *[HS; Apr to Sept, daily 9.30–6.30; Oct to Mar, Mon–Sat 9.30–4.30, Sun 2–4.30; ☎ (01896) 822562; ✆ via www.aboutscotland.com]*

Smailholm Tower (west of Kelso)

✓ *Well-preserved fortress-tower in photogenic setting*
✓ *Excellent place to recall the violent past*

Of the many simple sixteenth-century fortresses known as pele towers which litter the Border landscape, Smailholm is the best preserved. It has the advantage of a superb setting on a craggy outcrop above a small loch, and is frequently photographed. The interior has been extensively restored by Historic Scotland with modern flooring, atmospheric music and displays of dolls and tapestries illustrating the Border ballads (see box overleaf). These do not spoil the strong sense of the past with which the fort is imbued. From the guard-post on the roof there are views down to the Eildons and the Cheviots, and you can readily imagine the raiders from Tynedale storming the crags and making away with the cattle. *[HS; Apr to Sept, daily 9.30–6.30; Oct and Nov, Mon–Wed and Sat 9.30–4.30, Thur 9.30–12.30, Sun 2–4.30; ☎ (01573) 460365; ✆ via www.scottishculture.about.com]*

Traquair House (near Innerleithen)

✓ *Ancient house, full of curiosities*
✓ *Friendly atmosphere*
✓ *Good for families*

Traquair is the oldest continuously inhabited house in Scotland, possibly dating back to the tenth century. Twenty-seven monarchs are said to have visited over the centuries, and there are connections with many of the best-known figures of Scottish history, such as Mary Queen of Scots and Bonnie Prince Charlie, who was made welcome by the staunchly Jacobite household. The Bear Gates on the main avenue were

The Border Ballads

We can only guess at the reasons why the bloodstained Borderland produced the stirring poetry it did. Sir Walter Scott, who first started collecting the old ballads which had been handed down for generations, put it down to a link between a wild society and the wild violence of poetry. Whatever the case, reading the ballads while touring the Borders gives immediacy to the history. Among them you will find the tale of Thomas Rhymer's journey into fairyland, the rescue of Tam Lin from enchantment, the battle of Otterburn where Douglas and Percy met in a fierce night-time encounter, the slaying of Lord Douglas and his seven sons, and the lament of the Border Widow. Four of the best ballads come from Liddesdale, among them the tale of Kinmont Willie's rescue from Carlisle Castle, and the raid suffered by Jamie Telfer in the Fair Dodhead and how it was avenged.

A compact edition of the ballads is *Border Ballads* (edited by James Reed), published by the Spredden Press.

closed as he left, and they will not reopen until a Stuart sits on the throne again.

This is an ancient house, not a stately home. The steep stone stairs, thick walls and small rooms are tortuous rather than elegant, and though grand do not distance the visitor. Everywhere lies an array of objects, some ancient, some mysterious, others merely endearing.

The cleverness of the Traquair style is to recognise that museum-pieces are not all that visitors want to see. The objects on display vary from items of great rarity to everyday things such as letters and bills. Each has its place in the tale of the house and its family, and visitors are encouraged to speculate as well as to admire (and occasionally have their leg gently pulled too). *[Apr to May and Sept to Oct, daily 12.30–5.30; June to Aug, daily 10.30–5.30;* ☎ *(01896) 830323;* ✆ *www.traquair.co.uk]*

The next best sights

The Barracks (Berwick-upon-Tweed)

These are the earliest purpose-built barracks in the United Kingdom, dating from 1721. They are home to the Berwick local museum, a display about the life and times of the British infantryman, and the regimental museum of the King's Own Scottish Borderers. The most surprising thing in the museum is Berwick's very own Sir William Burrell collection. It is hardly a rival to the one in Glasgow (see page 192) but well worth a visit. The wealthy art collector lived in Berwickshire for much of his life and made a number of gifts from his collection to the museum. *[Apr to Oct, daily 10–6; Nov to Mar, Wed–Sun 10–4;* ☎ *(01289) 330933]*

Dawyck Botanic Garden (south-west of Peebles)

This arboretum is an outstation of the Royal Botanic Garden in Edinburgh. Among the redwoods, Nootka cypresses and Douglas firs are many specimens over a century old. Most of the older planting runs along a small burn, where rhododendrons, azaleas, meconopsis and rodgersias lend colour in spring and autumn. It makes a lovely walk. *[Mar to Oct, daily 9.30–6;* ☎ *(01721) 760254;* 📞 *via www.rgbe.org.uk]*

Dryburgh Abbey (near St Boswells)

This is the best positioned of the Border abbeys, virtually surrounded by a bend of the Tweed and set round with fine old trees. There is little left of the abbey church, apart from the transepts, but the surrounding buildings are well preserved – the remnants of painted walls in the chapter house are visible. Like Melrose, Dryburgh was more or less destroyed in 1545. Since then its buildings have been used as a house, a cow byre and as a romantic folly. Sir Walter Scott is buried here, squeezed into the north transept among other Scotts. Earl Haig, the British Commander-in-chief on the Western Front from 1915–18, lies here too. *[HS; daily 9.30–6.30;* ☎ *(01835) 822381;* 📞 *via www.aboutscotland.com]*

Eyemouth Museum

Housed in the Old Kirk near the harbour, this is an excellent local museum, centred around the tapestry stitched locally to commemorate the tragedy of 1881, when 129 local fishermen were drowned within sight of land. There is also much well-displayed information about Eyemouth's fishing connections. *[Apr, June and Sept, Mon–Sat 10–5, Sun 1–5; July and Aug, Mon–Sat 10–6, Sun 11.30–4.30; Oct, Mon–Sat 10–4;* ☎ *(01890) 750678]*

Fast Castle (north of Eyemouth, off A1107)

The remains of the castle are fragmentary, but the site is spectacular. Twenty minutes' walk from the car park brings you to the cliff's edge with the sea rolling beneath. A path across a narrow isthmus, barely protected by some very ancient chains, takes you to the rock on which Fast Castle was constructed. It is a splendid, rather scary spot, and there is a legend of buried treasure to go with it (one of those who searched was John Napier, inventor of the logarithm). It is not a place for children or those who cannot stand heights. *[HS; access at all times]*

Neidpath Castle (Peebles)

This is an atmospheric ruin with massively thick walls, tiny windows and a gloomy pit prison, in which you are invited to deposit your children. It stands above a dark and swirly part of the Tweed, and there is a lot of it left to explore, even up to roof level. *[Easter to Sept, Mon–Sat 11–5, Sun 1–5;* ☎ *(01721) 720333;* 🖱 *via www.scottishculture.about.com]*

Old Blacksmith's Shop Centre (Gretna Green, off M74 north of Carlisle)

It was an eighteenth-century legal difference between the marriage laws of Scotland and England that made Gretna famous as a haven for eloping couples. Perhaps it is the popularity of romantic fiction, and the continuing triumph of hope over experience that draws half a million visitors a year to this sight. For, in comparison to an old house or a great castle, there is virtually nothing historic to be seen. A small walk-through exhibition outlines the history of Gretna marriages and there is a splendid collection of coaches and carriages, but that is all. Sightseeing, however, is not really the point of the place. The point is better summed up by the thousands people for whom a wedding or renewal of vows at Gretna Green is an act of self-evident importance. The floor space devoted to shopping easily outstrips that in most other sights in Scotland, and you can pick up souvenirs of every kind. Gretna Green is certainly a tourist trap, but a well-managed and friendly one. *[All year, daily, winter 9–5, Apr to May and Oct–Nov 9–6; June and Sept 9–7, July and Aug 9–8;* ☎ *(01461) 338224;* 📱 *www.gretnagreen.com]*

Priorwood Gardens (Melrose)

This small garden specialises in flowers suitable for drying, and for anyone interested in the hobby it is a fascinating place, the actual flowerbeds complemented by a shop and a display of dried flowers and preserving techniques. Beyond the garden, a quiet orchard, ideal for a picnic, is laid out to show the history of apple-growing from Roman times. *[NTS; Apr to Sept, Mon–Sat 10–5.30, Sun 1.30–5.30; Oct to Xmas, Mon–Sat 10–4, Sun 1.30–4;* ☎ *(01896) 822493;* 📱 *via www.nts.org.uk]*

Robert Smail's Printing Works (Innerleithen)

This little family business was saved with all its antiquated equipment and business records intact in1986. Imaginative work by the National Trust for Scotland has recreated the life of a jobbing printer from the early nineteenth century onwards. The machines still run and you can practise setting type by hand or simply leaf through the books packed with advertisements, announcements of concerts, business cards, hymn sheets, menus and postcards. *[NTS; Easter and May to Sept, Mon–Sat 10–1 and 2–5, Sun 2–5, also weekends in Oct;* ☎ *(01896) 830206;* 📱 *via www.nts.org.uk]*

Border castles

Half-crumbled into the fields, hidden by trees, or restored and converted into homes, the old Border fortresses are every-where. The biggest, such as Roxburgh or Jedburgh, were too vulnerable to being taken and held by the English and were often demolished by the Scots themselves, so the ruins that remain are usually simple rectangular towers or 'peles', mostly dating from the sixteenth century. They are simple structures, usually with a vaulted ground-floor room, the main hall directly above, and a further one, or perhaps two, storeys. Entrance was on the first floor. Much of the life went on outside the tower in the surrounding enclosure called the 'barmkin', where cattle could be sheltered in times of trouble. Pele towers were designed to hold off small raids. They did not catch fire easily and could act as a rallying point and defensive centre.

Most of the ruined towers are still on private land, and you should obtain permission before exploring. The ruins are often precarious, so you venture into them at your own risk. As well as the castles mentioned in the text, look out for:

Cessford (near Jedburgh), stronghold of the Cessford Kerrs, now a riven hulk of red stone, easily visible from a nearby road. St Cuthbert's Way passes close by.

Gilknockie (near Langholm), now restored, may have been the stronghold of Johnnie Armstrong, the notorious raider. There are guided tours [Easter to Oct, 10 and 2.30 or by appointment; ☎ (01387) 371876].

Whitton (near Morebattle), a ruin in a farmyard, surrounded by hens.

Stately homes of the Borders

The prosperity of the farmland and the beauty of the land-scape has left the Borders dotted with great houses. Some are the lavish creations of the descendants of the notorious reiving families, such as Bowhill (the Scotts) or the Hirsel (the Homes). Others are elegant houses built after border warfare had died out, when new dwellings were needed to replace the old fortresses, or are the creations of the eighteenth-century taste for elegant country living. Some of the wealth behind the great houses was accumulated after the Reformation, when the great Border families took over the extensive land once owned by the abbeys.

The architecture of the Borders' stately homes ranges from the Palladian elegance of Paxton to the florid pinnacles of Floors Castle. Most have extensive grounds, often with marked walks, play areas or other attractions. Particularly good in this respect are Bowhill, Floors, Paxton and the Hirsel. For paintings, go to Bowhill or Paxton; for plasterwork to Thirlestane. The unique silver staircase at Manderston is worth seeing on its own account. To help you choose which to visit, we have highlighted the main attractions.

Bowhill (west of Selkirk) Not the most elegant of houses, but the quality of what lies inside makes it essential visiting for lovers of art, furniture and porcelain. Look out for the portrait of Sir Walter Scott with Hermitage Castle in the background, the painting of George IV in Highland dress and the portrait of Lady Caroline Scott by Reynolds. The most intriguing object in the house is the Pittenweem-made clock of 1775, which plays tuneful airs six days a week, but ceases on Saturday and does not start again until the Sabbath is over. *[House: July only, daily 1–4.30; grounds: May to Aug, Sat–Thur 12–5, also Fris in July;* ☎ *(01750) 22204;* ⬤ *via www.aboutbritain.com]*

Floors Castle (Kelso) This huge palace-like house has an amazing roofscape of turret caps and chimneys, resembling a pinball table in the sky. The interior is on a more human scale, with views down to the Tweed, and to a yew tree which marks the spot where James II was killed by a bursting cannon while besieging Roxburgh.

Not many rooms are open, but you can see some fine tapestries, post-Impressionist paintings and Chinese porcelain. Best of all are the strange collections – stuffed birds, snuff-boxes, minerals, coins, robes, potties and carriages – which you encounter on the way out. The grounds are good for a walk, with open parkland down by the river. *[mid-Apr to Oct, daily 10–4.30;* ☎ *(01573) 223333;* 🖥 *www.roxburghe.bordernet.co.uk]*

Grounds of The Hirsel (Coldstream) Lord Home's woods and parkland are open daily and make a good spot for Sunday walks or dalliance beside the lake. An old steading has been turned into a craft centre and estate museum. Dundock Wood – reached from the A697 – is generously endowed with rhododendrons and azaleas and is extremely colourful on a bright spring day.

Manderston House (Duns) The house bills itself as the swansong of the Edwardian country house. Most of the ideas for this twentieth-century statement of wealth came from an earlier age – imitations of Adam work in particular. However, the silver staircase (which must be dismantled and polished now and again) is unique to Manderston. Keep an eye open for the collection of biscuit tins – the present owner is a member of the Huntly and Palmer dynasty. *[May to Sept, Thur and Sun 2–5.30;* ☎ *(01361) 883450;* 🖥 *www.manderston.co.uk]*

Paxton House (near Berwick) A compact and charming Palladian house, built by the Adam family (there's a romantic history to its construction). It is completed by a picture gallery hung with paintings from the collection of the National Galleries of Scotland. See wonderful furniture by Chippendale and others, or explore the pleasant grounds. *[Apr to Oct, daily; house: 11–4.15, grounds: 10–sunset;* ☎ *(01289) 386291;* 🖥 *www.paxtonhouse.com]*

Thirlestane Castle (Lauder) The pinnacles, turrets and ogee-roofed tower of Thirlestane stand strategically over the River Leader, looking like something from a peaceful French landscape. The old keep was transformed in the 1670s, and added to in Victorian times. It's a friendly place to visit with helpful guides and lots of family mementoes. *[mid-Apr to Oct, Mon–Fri and Sun 11–4.15;* ☎ *(01578) 722430;* 🖥 *via www.great-houses-scotland.co.uk]*

Literary museums

Carlyle's Birthplace (Ecclefechan, south-east of Lockerbie) Thomas Carlyle, one of Scotland's graver Victorian sages, was born in this quiet village of trees and harled cottages. The Arched House was built by his father and now holds a small museum and many family mementoes. *[NTS; May to Sept, Fri–Mon 1.30–5.30;* ☎ *(01576) 300666;* 🖰 *via www.nts.org.uk]*

John Buchan Centre (Broughton) This excellent museum celebrates the extraordinary career of the author of *The Thirty-Nine Steps*. Buchan was not only a novelist but Governor-General of Canada too, and the museum has photographs, mementoes and books aplenty, as well as knowledgeable curators happy to answer all questions. *[Easter and May to Sept, daily 2–5;* ☎ *(01899) 221050]*

James Hogg Exhibition (Ettrickbridge) Aikwood tower, restored by Sir David Steel (at the time of writing the Presiding Officer of the Scottish Parliament), has an exhibition about the poet, a contemporary of Sir Walter Scott called the 'Ettrick Shepherd' who is better known today for his psychological novel *Confessions of a Justified Sinner* than for the poetry that originally made him famous. There is a memorial to him in the hamlet of Ettrick, further up the glen. *[Apr to Sept, Tue, Thur and Sun, 2–5;* ☎ *(01750) 52253]*

Also in the area

Johnnie Armstrong Memorial (Teviothead, on A7) Johnnie Armstrong was a notorious reiver, who was convicted of common theft and strung up by James V. 'What wants yon knave that a king should have?' asked James, seeing Armstrong's finery. Legend rapidly turned Johnnie into the betrayed patriot, and the headstone in the churchyard here reflects this.

The Chambers Institute (Peebles) Drop in to see the Chambers Room, an unusual survival of the Victorian idea that a museum should uplift and enlighten its visitors. Quiet greys and clarets are the background to two large classical friezes – one a copy of a section from the Parthenon, the other the Alexander Frieze, done in similar heroic style by the nineteenth-century Danish sculptor Bertil Thorvaldsen. *[All year, Mon–Fri 10–12 and 2–5, also Sats from Apr–Oct, 2–5;* ☎ *(01721) 724820]*

Jim Clark Memorial Room (Duns) Even if you are not a keen motor-racing fan, this small museum dedicated to the former farmer turned world champion is extensive and moving. There are 122 trophies on the shelves, and photographs and letters from all over the world. *[Easter to Sept, Mon–Sat 10.30–1 and 2–4.30, Sun 2–4; Oct, Mon–Sat 1–4;* ☎ *(01361) 883960]*

The Cornice (Peebles) The fascinating Scottish Museum of Ornamental Plasterwork is a tiny plasterer's workshop from the early 1900s. There is a jumble of patterns for flowers, fruits, geometrical abstracts and faces of nymphs or cupids, as well as some explanation of the techniques. *[Mon–Thur 10.30–12 and 2–4, Fri 10.30–12 and 2–3.30, closed weekends and hols;* ☎ *(01721) 720212]*

The Debateable Land (around Canonbie) Head east from Gretna on the back roads towards Canonbie and you enter one of the bloodiest parts of the Borders. For more than 300 years it was a no man's land between the Scots and English, claimed by both but subject to the rule of neither, a haven for outlaws. In 1552 it was divided, with the French ambassador acting as referee. A dyke was dug, cutting the land in half. Its line is still clearly marked by a plantation of trees.

Harestanes Visitor Centre (off A68 north of Jedburgh) A converted farm acts as an information centre for walks, nature trails and exhibitions. Most walks are flat, so it's good for families. There's a play area and an indoor games room with wood puzzles. *[Apr to Oct, daily 10–5;* ☎ *(01835) 830306]*

Jedforest Deer and Farm Park (south of Jedburgh, at Mervinslaw) A big, friendly and unpatronising rare breeds farm with masses to see and do. Good for families with small children. *[May to Aug, daily 10–5.30; Sept and Oct 11–4.30;* ☎ *(01835) 840364]*

Kagyu Samye Ling Tibetan Centre (Eskdalemuir) Behind an old shooting lodge, where prayer flags flutter in the breeze, lies the largest Tibetan temple in Europe. In this high, bleak landscape it is an astonishing burst of colour; inside, the red and the gilt dazzle, while rows of Buddhas gaze contemplatively down at you. The centre runs residential courses on aspects of Buddhism. *[Daily 9–10pm (temple 6–10pm);* ☎ *(01387) 373232;* ⬛ *www.samyeling.org]*

Kershopesfoot (near Newcastleton) The junction of burn and river at this isolated spot was one of the meeting places for the English and Scottish Wardens of the Border Marches. On designated days of truce, both sides would meet at places like this to settle cross–border disputes. They were tense occasions, more than once degenerating into fights. It is curious to think, sitting on the peaceful banks of the Liddel, that this place was once a hair-trigger frontier.

Leaderfoot Viaduct (east of Melrose) The structure which once carried the railway across the Tweed is one of the most delicate bridges to be found in the Borders, and is much photographed. You can see it from the A68.

Legerwood Church (Legerwood, off A68) One of the best-hidden sights in the Borders, the tiny church lies behind a farm east of the village. The pink sandstone Norman archway which frames the chancel is a thing of sensuous magnificence in an otherwise bare kirk. Its colour, its carving and its warmth have the intriguing quality of a revealed secret, and indeed the arch was hidden behind a wall for centuries.

Hugh MacDiarmid Memorial (east of Langholm) On the edge of the moors above Langholm, a piece of sculpture, shaped like an open book pierced by cutouts, stands in memory of

Scotland's greatest modern poet, whose childhood was spent in Langholm. The memorial's appearance, its siting and its very existence aroused huge local controversy, and the fact that it ended up in this little-travelled spot in the moors says a lot about MacDiarmid's reputation in Langholm.

Rhymer's Tower (Earlston) Just behind the filling station on the southern outskirts of the village, a crumbling, ivy-clad heap of stone is all that remains of the tower said to have been the home of Thomas of Ercildoune, or True Thomas, the Border country's best-known prophet-poet. Taken into fairyland after boldly kissing the queen of the fairies, Thomas returned gifted with second sight, prophesying, among other intuitions, that 'Kelso Kirk would fall at its fullest'.

Towns and villages to explore

Berwick-upon-Tweed

If you have been touring the Scottish Border towns, Berwick may not seem very different until you notice that the banks are English, and the tourist literature carries a rose on the front cover. For 400 years of its history the town belonged to Scotland, and was a Scottish royal burgh while Glasgow was still a village. It is a measure of Berwick's importance that, when Edward I of England decided to make an example of it, he found 12,000 inhabitants to massacre.

During the wars between Scotland and England, Berwick changed hands 12 times and was finally seized for England in 1482. The loss of Berwick was a disaster for Scotland, and it also turned the town from a flourishing port into an isolated frontier fortress; the massive Elizabethan fortifications show how much England felt it to be under threat. These fortifications are the only complete sixteenth-century example in Britain. The ramparts make a magnificent walk round the perimeter of Berwick, with glimpses of the Tweed, the sea, the Scottish hills and of lovingly tended back gardens.

Berwick makes an excellent base for exploring the eastern half of both the Scottish and the English Border country, and it is an attractive town into the bargain. Behind the ramparts the buildings are eighteenth- and nineteenth-century, with some fine Georgian houses. The modern developments at Berwick are all outside the ramparts, so in the centre you feel that you are in a small, rather old-fashioned county town. There are plenty of places to stay, ranging from town-centre coaching-inns to bed-and-breakfasts on the outskirts. For information about the town on-line see ⁓🖱 *www.berwick.org.uk*

Coldstream

The regiment of guards which now bears the town's name marched south from here to aid in the restoration of Charles II. Away from the main road which runs through it, Coldstream is a quiet place, and it is easy to find your way down to the river bank and gaze at the dark swirls of the Tweed. A **museum** [*Easter to Sept, Mon–Sat 10–4, Sun 2–4; Oct, Mon–Sat 1–4;* ☎ *(01890) 882630*] outlines the history of the famous regiment, and of the town.

Eyemouth

The coastal A1107 north of Berwick brings you to this mixture of fishing port and seaside resort. Eyemouth was once a notorious smuggling town. Kegs of contraband liquor came straight into the harbour and were stored in the warren of caverns lying beneath Gunstone House, an innocent-looking Georgian building standing on its own above the fishing boats. Ploughs have been known to vanish from the fields as the roofs of old underground passages caved in. The higgledy-piggledy layout of the old town was ideal for smugglers on the run; much of it has been rebuilt in modern fishing village vernacular style. A respectable semicircle of sand fringes the bay beneath the sea front.

Galashiels

Gala, as it is known, is home of the Scottish College of Textiles, centre of the tweed industry and the largest town in the area, with a rash of housing estates and light industry extending towards Melrose. Galashiels is one of the few towns in Britain that is worth visiting just to see the war memorial: under the clock-tower, a Border reiver astride his horse seems to shout brave defiance across the centuries. Information about the sculptor, Thomas Clapperton, is on view at Old Gala House, on the hill behind the High Street. There is an excellent little historical display about the woollen industry in the **Lochcarron Cashmere and Wool Centre**, where you can also see the modern machines at work. *[June to Sept, Mon–Sat 9–5, Sun 12–5;* ☎ *(01896) 751100;* ✆ *www.galashiels.bordernet.co.uk]*

Hawick

This is a busy town, with none of the gentility of Melrose or the county-town atmosphere of Kelso. It is grey, grainy, and has enough mills left to remind you that textiles, especially stockings, have long been its speciality. There are several different mill shops with bargain bins or end-of-line offers.

In Wilton Park, the local **museum** has plenty of fascinating material about the hosiery industry and the working conditions of a previous century *[Apr to Sept, Mon–Fri, 10–12 and 1–5, weekends 1–7; Oct to Mar, Mon–Fri 1–4, Sun 2–4;* ☎ *(01450) 373457]*. In the High Street, one of the few old buildings left in Hawick, **Drumlanrig's Tower**, has been restored as a modern museum bringing the town's history to life. *[Mar to Oct, Mon–Sat 10–5, Sun 12–5 (5.30 in June, 6 in July and Aug);* ☎ *(01450) 377615]*.

Find out more about the town at ✆ *www.hawick.org.uk*

Jedburgh

Only ten miles from the frontier and in the heart of Teviotdale, Jedburgh has seen plenty of violence in its time; its inhabitants gained a reputation for playing football with Englishmen's heads – the streamers attached to the ball in today's festive version represent the hair. Growing up around its abbey, Jedburgh later became a textile town. These days all the industrial dereliction has been swept away.

At the top of the steep hill on which the town is built, the **Castle Jail and Museum** shows what life was like for prisoners in the early nineteenth century. Displays also show how

Jedburgh developed. *[Mon–Sat 10–4.30, Sun 1–4;* ☎ *(01835) 863254]*. A short distance from the town centre, **Mary Queen of Scots' House** is a lovely building in which Mary may have stayed during a visit to Jedburgh. Displays are a little thin, but you can see the watch which she may have dropped on her journey. *[Easter to Oct, Mon–Sat 10–4.45, Sun 10–4.30;* ☎ *(01835) 863331]*. For more on the town see ⌁ *www.injedburgh.freeserve.co.uk*

Kelso

Kelso is the most attractive of the Border towns thanks to its eighteenth-century square, which gives it a distinctly French air. The ruins of the abbey, the sweep of the Tweed past the backs of houses and Rennie's elegant bridge contribute to the easy atmosphere. It is worth exploring the strange octagonal parish church, the old Cross Keys coaching-inn, and the small streets running down to the Tweed. There's a good range of shops, especially for ceramics and fishing tackle. Little is left of Kelso Abbey, probably once the largest of the great Border Abbeys, which was so comprehensively destroyed that only part of a tower remains.

Melrose

The town rivals Kelso as the most attractive in the Borders, for, despite the ruin of its abbey, it still has some of the atmosphere of a quiet, contemplative place. Solid red sandstone buildings, generously interspersed with old coaching inns, line the central streets, and there are several small craft and clothes shops to explore. As well as the abbey and Priorwood gardens, which can be seen nearby, the teddy-bear museum, **Teddy Melrose**, has a fine collection which should please both adults and children *[Daily 10–5;* ☎ *(01896) 823854]*.

Melrose *[⌁ www.melrose.bordernet.co.uk]* lies in the shadow of the Eildon Hills, a triple-peaked volcanic plug visible from all over the central Borders, and the focus of many legends. Michael Scott, the wizard who lies buried at Melrose, instructed the Devil to split the hill into three, and King Arthur's knights are said to sleep beneath them. The Roman fortress of Trimontium was built beneath the Eildons and there is a good display of finds at the **Trimontium Exhibition** in town *[Apr to Oct, daily 10.30–4.30;* ☎ *(01896) 822651]*.

Moffat

Where the Southern Uplands close in on Annandale lies Moffat, reached in a couple of minutes from the M74 *[www.moffattown.com]*. It was once a spa resort, and even had the distinction of its own branch railway line from Beattock. Its huge hydro hotel burned down early in the century, but it is still possible to visit the two mineral springs where Moffat's health-seeking visitors used to gather before breakfast. Today, Moffat is bed-and-breakfast land – its sedate Victorian villas are thick with signs. It has everything you need for a couple of days – good walks close by, a broad, sedate High Street with shops selling woollens, antiques and sweeties (especially the renowned Moffat toffee), a little local **museum** *[Easter and May to Sept, Mon–Sat 10.30–1 and 2.30–5, Sun 2.30–5, closed Wed pm;* ☎ *(01683) 220868]* and the best of the sun if there is any. It also claims the narrowest detached hotel in Britain. Where most towns have statues of local worthies, Moffat's High Street boasts a huge sculptured ram, symbolising the links between the town and the woollen trade.

Peebles

King James V wrote a poem about Peebles, describing the bustle and raucous excitement of the town's Beltane festival, which still takes place in mid-June. Peebles is now a popular place for a day trip from Edinburgh. Its pleasures are gentle ones – golf, fishing, walking, and above all excursions into the scenery, for it is well situated in the best of Tweed Valley countryside.

The High Street fills up fast at weekends: buyers of gifts, antiques and woollens contend with people in town to do the Saturday shopping. There are craft shops, and old weavers' cottages beyond the ancient Cuddy's brig. There is no shortage of hotels, of which there is a good range, though they have to live in the shadow of the enormous Peebles Hotel Hydro, a vast, much-altered nineteenth-century spa hotel which sits in cheery splendour on the edge of town, host to family holidays and conferences alike.

Selkirk

The long High Street in Selkirk has a statue of Walter Scott at one end and one of Mungo Park, the explorer of the Niger, at the other. Here, too, is the fierce Flodden Memorial by Thomas Clapperton. Of all Border towns, Selkirk seems to have taken the terrible battle of Flodden in 1513 most to heart. **Halliwell House** is one of the best local museums in the Borders, with a complete ironmonger's shop and much well-presented information on the growth of the town; here you can see the Flodden flag, brought home by the town's sole survivor of the disaster *[Apr to Oct, Mon–Sat 10–5, Sun 2–4; July and Aug 1 hr longer in evenings;* ☎ *(01750) 20096].* The old **courtroom** where Sir Walter Scott once dispensed justice as Sheriff of Selkirk is open as a small museum, commemorating Scott and Park *[Apr and May, Mon–Sat 10–4; June to Sept, Mon–Sat 10–4, Sun 2–4; Oct, Mon–Sat 1–4;* ☎ *(01750) 20054].* The town web site is ⬚ *www.selkirk.bordernet.co.uk*

Scenery and touring routes

Beaches Two sandy beaches worth considering for a sunny day are to be found at Coldingham (north of Eyemouth) and at Pease Bay (south of Cockburnspath).

The Devil's Beef Tub (north of Moffat) This is a huge and gloomy declivity in the bleak rounded hills above Moffat, and the best-known of many such sanctuaries where stolen cattle could be hidden and easily guarded. You can drive and then walk from Moffat, or gaze down into it from the A701 *[⬚ via www.moffattown.com].*

Ettrick Valley A drive up the Ettrick takes you through the whole range of Borders scenery. From Selkirk, you travel through rich farmland. The river is wide and alluring, with hardly a bridge. Ettrickbridge, a tiny village, marks the start of the sheep country, the river narrowing and flowing faster through defiles, or flattening into shingly stretches, the haunt of oyster-catchers. The road becomes single-track and the hills close in, forming barriers so that it is hard to see where the valley is going to turn next. At the head of Ettrick the road stops, but you can walk on if you choose.

The Grey Mare's Tail (north-east of Moffat on A708) This splendid waterfall, dropping down from a hanging valley, is a popular spot for outings, though the crowds seldom reach oppressive numbers [⌁ *via www.aboutscotland.com*]. Beware of

---

Sir Walter Scott (1771–1832)

If one man can be said to be responsible for starting tourism to Scotland, it is Sir Walter Scott. At the height of the early nine-teenth-century passion for the Romantic, his poems (especially 'Lady of the Lake' and 'Marmion') thrilled readers with their tales of passion and legend among stirringly described scenery. When he gave up poetry (recognising the superior talent of Byron) and turned to writing novels drawn from Scottish history – *Waverley*, his first, was published in 1814 – the impact was just as great. The novels were at first published anony-mously, though many guessed Walter Scott to be the author.

In his childhood, staying with his grandparents in the Borders, Scott became infected with the passion for history and legend which informs his writing. Called to the Bar in 1792, he travelled extensively through Scotland, and there is scarcely a sight on today's tourist trail that he does not seem to have visited. From the valleys of the Borders, where his work as Sheriff of Selkirkshire took him, he collected the songs and ballads which had been handed down over the centuries and published them as *Border Minstrelsy*. With the money from his poems and novels he bought land by the Tweed and built Abbotsford, for Scott, a Tory by inclination, loved playing the country gentleman. Prosperous, admired, granted a baronetcy and at the centre of a legal and literary circle, Scott's happiness seemed assured until the sudden bankruptcy of his publisher in

coaches on the narrow road. To see the waterfall, you must walk a short distance from the car park on a slightly vertiginous track. Alternatively, a longer, steeper walk on the northern side of the Tail Burn leads you to the top of the fall, and eventually to Loch Skeen above it, set in some of the wildest country in the Borders. There are usually feral goats in the area, and peregrine falcons breed here. Watch out for the local sheep, which have learned that tourists are a soft touch.

Kale Valley From the village of Morebattle (south of Kelso), follow the narrow country roads deep into the Cheviots, to the

---

1826 left him with debts of £116,000. Determined to pay these off, he flung himself into his writing and eventually succeeded in doing so, but at a cost in mental and physical health which is only too well charted in his Journal. He was 61 when he died.

How his contemporaries felt about him is best symbolised by the magnificence of the Scott monument in Edinburgh. He had single-handedly restored the nation's pride by pointing out and popularising the richness of its past. He was responsible for the rediscovery of the long-forgotten crown jewels of Scotland, had stage-managed the first royal visit to Scotland (George IV in 1822) since Charles II, and had created, in the historical novel, a new literary form.

It is difficult, even today, to escape the influence of Sir Walter Scott. His poetry may remain largely unread and his novels be too tortuous and prosy for today's taste, but the Romantic Scotland he created, with its fierce passions, its unyielding scenery and its gallery of noble or villainous characters, is still happily sold to the modern visitor. He left a more solid legacy, too, for he was assiduous in encouraging the preservation of the past. It is largely thanks to him that Melrose Abbey is not more ruinous, that the Border Ballads are not lost and that Mons Meg draws visitors to Edinburgh Castle.

hamlet of Hownam. Here you can drive west to Oxnam and Jedburgh, partly along the line of the old Roman road, or continue into the wild hills, eventually joining the A68 south of Jedburgh.

Lammermuir Hills From Chirnside follow the valley of the Whiteadder up to the small village of Abbey St Bathans, deep in a wooded dell. Continue north to Oldhamstocks and Innerwick, and return over Moneynut Edge. There's a good variety of scenery on this route, and you should see plenty of wildlife.

Liddesdale What was once the most piratical of all Border valleys is now quiet green farmland. The B6357 runs beside the Liddel water to **Newcastleton**, an attractive planned village with a tiny heritage centre. From here a road leads west to Langholm over the beautiful bleak moorland of the Tarras Moss. Alternatively, continue north to visit Hermitage Castle and then drive west on another beautiful road across the moors.

Moorfoot Hills If driving to or from Edinburgh, the B709, which links Innerleithen to the A7, takes you through moorland scenery of steeply rounded hills covered with heather or dotted with sheep.

St Abbs Head (north-west of Eyemouth) St Abbs is a nature reserve, one of the few seabird cities on the mainland of south Scotland. In breeding season, the sheer cliffs echo to the raucous shouts of nesting gulls. A half-mile walk from the car park takes you to the clifftops and the network of paths. The views from the cliffside paths are splendid and the flowers varied. The visitor centre *[Apr to Oct, daily 10–5;* ☎ *(01890) 771443]* has remote camera links and other displays if you do not wish to walk. The offshore **St Abbs and Eyemouth Voluntary Marine Reserve** has a special car park for divers.

St Mary's Loch (north-east of Moffat) This is a well-known beauty spot at the head of the Yarrow valley, apt to become crowded on fine weekends. Sailors and windsurfers frequent it, as do walkers. The centre for most of the activity is Tibbie Shiel's Inn, once a convivial meeting place for Sir Walter Scott, James Hogg and fellow writers, and equally convivial, if not quite so literary, today.

Scott's View (north of St Boswells on B6356, signed) Sir Walter loved this view of the Tweed, and his horses stopped here out of habit during his funeral procession.

Tweed Valley The run down the Tweed from the watershed north of Moffat is the classic Border tour. The landscape is gentle, with heather replacing grass on many of the hills; the castles and houses are grand or imposing, the towns prosperous and sunny. The river itself, moving from upland shingle runs to deep salmon pools, is consistently lovely. The main (A72) road between Peebles and Galashiels can be busy with traffic. Follow roads on the southern bank for this stretch.

Suggested walks

Two long-distance walks thread their way through the prettier parts of the Borders; short sections can be easily accessed from nearby roads. All tourist centres will give guidance and provide leaflets.

St Cuthbert's Way The walk runs from Melrose to Lindisfarne (62 miles in total). From Melrose it passes the Eildon Hills and Dryburgh Abbey, then runs through the unfrequented fringes of the Cheviot Hills before crossing into England and heading for Holy Island [⌐ *www.stcuthbertsway.fsnet.co.uk*].

Southern Upland Way This route runs right across southern Scotland from Cockburnspath in the east to Portpatrick in the south-west, a total distance of 212 miles. The sections in the Borders take in much of the best countryside, including the Lammermuirs and the high country west of Ettrick [⌐ *www.southern-upland-way.com*].

Suggested cycle routes

These two routes are waymarked. For more see the leaflet *Cycling in the Scottish Borders*, available from tourist offices.

Four Abbeys cycle route A circular tour taking in the ruined abbeys of Jedburgh, Melrose, Dryburgh and Kelso.

Tweed Cycleway This route runs from Biggar to Berwick on unfrequented roads.

Information about both routes is accessible via ⛑ *www.scot-borders.co.uk* or ⛑ *www.scottishcycling.co.uk*

WHERE TO STAY

£ – under £70 per room per night, incl. VAT

££ – £70 to £110 per room per night, incl. VAT

£££ – over £110 per room per night, incl. VAT

ANCRUM
Ancrum Craig
Ancrum TD8 6UN
☎ (01835) 830280
📠 (01835) 830259
⛑ www.ancrumcraig.clara.net
Handsome Victorian bed and breakfast in pleasant grounds, with superb views. Good-sized, comfortable bedrooms and welcoming hosts; evening meals by arrangement.
£ All year exc Christmas and New Year

EDNAM
Edenwater House
Ednam, Kelso TD5 7QL
☎ /📠 (01573) 224070
Comfortable former manse, with an unpretentious atmosphere and lovely views across the neat garden to the Eden Water. Three large, comfortable rooms and fine food – including an unusual four-course dinner with a choice of main course.
££ All year exc first two weeks of Jan; dining-room closed Sun to Wed eves (exc by arrangement). (See Where to Eat)

HEITON
The Roxburghe
Heiton, Kelso TD5 8JZ
☎ (01573) 450331
📠 (01573) 450611
⛑ www.roxburghe.net
Country-house hotel with golf course plus fishing, shooting, tennis and croquet in the 200-acre grounds. Rooms in this mock-Jacobean mansion are comfortably furnished, and the menu includes plenty of local salmon, game, lamb and beef.
£££ All year exc Christmas

INNERLEITHEN

Caddon View Guest House

14 Pirn Road, Innerleithen EH44 6HH

☎ (01896) 830208

Rambling house with original wood panelling, set in mature gardens and offering bed and breakfast accommodation. Packed lunches and evening meals are available; guests can also enjoy a free sauna.

£ *All year exc Christmas*

JEDBURGH

Hundalee House

Jedburgh TD8 6PA

☎ /📠 (01835) 863011

Bed and breakfast in a handsome Georgian house set in ten acres of beautiful grounds. Bedrooms are attractive and there is a sitting room for guests' use, as well as outdoor picnic benches and tables. Hearty breakfasts.

£ *Closed Nov to March*

The Spinney

Langlee, Jedburgh TD8 6PB

☎ (01835) 863525

📠 (01835) 864883

Consistently high standards at this modern bed and breakfast with a magnificent garden, well shielded from the main road. Pretty bedrooms and hearty Scottish breakfasts.

£ *Closed Dec to Feb*

KELSO

Ednam House

Bridge Street, Kelso TD5 7HT

☎ (01573) 224168

📠 (01573) 226319

🖥 www.ednamhouse.com

Well-run fishing hotel on the banks of the River Tweed. Bedrooms in this rambling Georgian house are well equipped and the varied menu uses local fish and game.

££ *Closed Christmas and New Year*

LONGFORMACUS

Eildon Cottage

Longformacus, Nr Duns TD11 3PB

☎ (01361) 890230

Welcoming bed and breakfast in a moorland setting, offering good home cooking in a comfortable and well-furnished house. Guests can use a pleasant lounge.

£ *All year exc Christmas and New Year*

MELROSE

Dunfermline House

Buccleuch Street, Melrose TD6 9LB

☎ /📠 (01896) 822148

Welcoming family home offering comfortable bed and breakfast accommodation in the centre of Melrose. Breakfasts are substantial, with kedgeree, scrambled eggs and smoked salmon, haggis, neeps and tatties all on the menu.

£ *All year; credit cards not accepted*

The Gables

Darnick, Melrose TD6 9AL

☎ /📠 (01896) 822479

Bright and attractive house in a quiet, pretty village. Simple yet comfortable bedrooms, and a wide range of walking guides and local history books. Varied breakfast choices.

£ All year exc Christmas

MOFFAT
Alba House

20 Beechgrove, Moffat DG10 9RS

☎ / ☎ (01683) 220418

Georgian bed and breakfast on the edge of Moffat, with an attractive terraced garden overlooking the Annan Valley. A warm welcome and spacious bedrooms; breakfast is served in the splendid dining-room.

£ All year exc Christmas

Beechwood Country House

Harthorpe Place, Moffat DG10 9RS

☎ (01683) 220210

📠 (01683) 220889

✓ www.beechwoodhousehotel.co.uk

Friendly and agreeable hilltop hotel, secluded in 12 acres of woods. Bedrooms are well equipped; public rooms include a conservatory, bar and restaurant with hill views. Food ranges from straightforward Scottish dishes to more unusual fare.

££ Closed 2 Jan to 18 Feb

Ericstane

Moffat DG10 9LT

☎ (01683) 220127

Traditional farmhouse offering every modern comfort in the Annan Valley, with lovely views from the two bedrooms; breakfast with home-baked bread is served in the sitting/dining-room overlooking the lawned garden.

£ All year

Well View

Ballplay Road, Moffat DG10 9JU

☎ (01683) 220184

📠 (01683) 220088

Compact and well-kept small hotel with comfortable rooms. Special arrangements made for children's teas.

££ All year (See Where to Eat)

NENTHORN
Whitehill Farm

Nenthorn TD5 7RZ

☎ / 📠 (01573) 470203

✓ www.whitehillfarm.freeserve.co.uk

A warm welcome at this working farm with attractive gardens. The four spacious bedrooms are attractively decorated. Food uses local ingredients wherever possible.

£ All year exc Christmas and New Year; credit cards not accepted

PEEBLES
Whitestone House

Innerleithen Road, Peebles EH45 8BD

☎ / 📠 (01721) 720337

A former manse, five minutes from the town centre. The six bedrooms are a reasonable size and simply furnished.

£ All year exc Christmas

ST BOSWELLS
Dryburgh Abbey Hotel

St Boswells TD6 0RQ

☎ (01835) 822261

📠 (01835) 823945

✓ www.dryburgh.co.uk

Large and comfortable hotel, well located for exploring the central Borders, with an indoor swimming pool

and attractive restaurant serving
straightforward Scottish food. Bedrooms
are fair-sized and well-equipped.
££ *Closed 1 to 10 Jan*

SKIRLING
Skirling House

Skirling, By Biggar ML12 6HD
☎ (01899) 860274
🖷 (01899) 860255
🖰 www.skirlinghouse.com
Hotel designed and built in 1908 in the
Arts and Crafts style, with a beautiful
Florentine ceiling in the drawing room.
Bedrooms are characterful and well-
furnished, with garden views. 'First-class'

four-course dinners are served in the
dining-room or conservatory.
£ *Mar to 2 Jan*

SWINTON
Wheatsheaf Hotel

Main Street, Swinton, Duns TD11 3JJ
☎ (01890) 860257
🖷 (01890) 860688
A comfortable small hotel with an
excellent conservatory restaurant and
refurbished bedrooms. Lunch and dinner
both offer an unusual and flavoursome
range of gourmet food.
££ *Closed 25 December and 1 to 7 Jan*
(See Where to Eat)

WHERE TO EAT

BIGGAR
Culter Mill

Coulter Village, Biggar ML12 6PZ
☎ (01899) 220950
Ancient converted mill offering a varied
menu. A range of Mediterranean and
European dishes are served alongside
traditional game, fish and poultry dishes.
Desserts are likewise unusual.
Wed–Sun

CANONBIE
Riverside Inn

Canonbie DG14 0UX
☎ (013873) 71295
Attractive seventeenth-century pub-
cum-hotel with restaurant. The split-
level, copper-hung bar shares much the
same food as the dining-room, and
offers a fixed-price menu with soups,
game, roasts and fish, plus blackboard
specials. Extensive wine list.

*Bar open all week L and D; restaurant
open all week L 12–2 (bookings only),
Tue–Sat D 7–9*

EAGLESFIELD
Courtyard

Eaglesfield DG11 3PQ
☎ (01461) 500215
Relaxed and welcoming front bar, with
bar meals served elsewhere; a separate
restaurant is strong on sauces and fruit.
Inventive menus include game, pork, and
home-made puddings. The wine list is
almost exclusively from the New World.
*Tue–Sun 12–2.30, all week 6.30–12;
bar food and restaurant 12–2 and 7–8.30*

EDNAM
Edenwater House

Ednam, Kelso TD5 7QL
☎ /🖷 (01573) 224070

Small, relaxed dining-room with four-course menu. Food combinations are good and occasionally unusual; dishes include fish, game, and flavoursome desserts. A house *vin de pays* is £11.
Thur–Sat D only (residents all week), 8–8.30 (See Where to Stay)

GATTONSIDE
Hoebridge Inn
Gattonside, Melrose TD
☎ (01896) 823082
Coaching inn on the banks of the Tweed with a monthly-changing menu featuring local and seasonal produce such as rare-breed beef, pork and lamb. The daily specials, blackboard and menu offer a wide selection of both traditional and contemporary fare.
Tue–Sun, D only

INNERLEITHEN
Traquair Arms
Traquair Road, Innerleithen EH44 6PD
☎ (01896) 830229
Traditional, medium-sized hotel just off the main street, close to the Traquair House Brewery and famous Bear Gates (see pages 41–2). A pleasant bar and a formal dining area offer a wide selection of vegetarian options, as well as Aberdeen Angus beef, lamb and fish.
11–11, Sun 12–11; bar food and restaurant 12–9; closed 25 Dec, 1 and 2 Jan

MELROSE
Burt's Hotel
The Square, Melrose TD6 9PN
☎ (01896) 822285

Whitewashed eighteenth-century hotel with imaginative bar and restaurant menus incorporating both avant-garde choices and more traditional game, fish, lamb and desserts. Extensive wine list.
12–2.30 and 5–11; bar food and restaurant 12–2, 6–9.30; closed 26 Dec

MOFFAT
Well View
Ballplay Road, Moffat DG10 9JU
☎ (01683) 220184
📠 (01683) 220088
The wide-ranging five-course set menu is augmented by canapés, a mid-meal sorbet, coffee and sweetmeats. House wines start at £12, with four of the wines of the day featured on the menu.
Mon to Fri L 12.30–1.25, D all week 6.30–8.30 (booking essential Sun L and D). (See Where to Stay)

PEEBLES
Cringletie House
Eddleston, Peebles EH45 8PL
☎ (01721) 730233
📠 (01721) 730244
🖳 www.cringletie.com
Modern *haute cuisine* in a luxurious setting. The 30-acre garden includes a walled kitchen garden that supplies vegetables and soft fruit in the summer. Extravagant and unusual menus include beef, game and seafood, and the wine list includes ten house wine recommendations.
All week, 12.30–2 and 7–9

SWINTON
Wheatsheaf Hotel
Main Street, Swinton, Duns TD11 3JJ
☎ (01890) 860257
📠 (01890) 860688
Food at this stone-built restaurant-with-rooms includes both local and organic produce offered in lunch, bar and dinner menus. Simply made beef, lamb, game and fish dishes, and a wide range of wine, with six by the glass.
Tue–Sun 12–2.15 and 6.30–9.30 (residents only Mon D, and Sun D Oct to Apr). (See Where to Stay)

WESTRUTHER
Old Thistle Inn
Westruther TD3 6NE
☎ (01578) 740275
Charming Victorian terraced cottage with traditional bar and coal fire. Food (served in the more formal dining-room) is mostly pub staples, with a good range of Aberdeen Angus steaks; four of the nine wines are served by the glass.
Mon–Fri 5–11, Sat and Sun 12.30–11; bar food Mon–Fri 6–9.30, Sat and Sun 12.30–9.30

The South-West

Statue of Robert Burns

- Burns Country – Most sights connected with the poet are here
- Golf on the famous courses of Troon and Turnberry
- Birdwatching, castles and gardens on the Solway Coast
- Forest park, watersports and some hillwalking inland
- Agricultural country; a few very small, attractive towns in the south
- Early Christian remains
- The islands of the Clyde estuary – easily accessible and popular

THE SOUTH-WEST

At a glance
- ✓ Good for isolated self-catering holidays
- ✓ Gentle touring
- ✓ Recommended for artists, birdwatchers and walkers

Except for a narrow strip by the Solway coast, the lowlands of south-west Scotland are separated from the rest of the country by the bulk of the Lowther Hills and the high ground south of Glasgow. Between these hills and the sea lie the fertile farm-lands of Ayrshire and Dumfries and the dairy country of Galloway. Another upthrust of moorland country culminates in the respectable-sized mountains of Glentrool, with Merrick, at 2,766ft, the highest peak.

The Ayrshire coast is fringed with small towns, many of which became resorts for the holidaying Glaswegians who travelled 'doon the watter' from the steamer piers of the Clyde in the early years of the twentieth century. Among them, Troon and Turnberry are especially famous for their golf courses. Inland Ayrshire has patches of coalfield dereliction, but much of the area remains as rural as in the days when Robert Burns immortalised its inhabitants in some of his best poetry.

The towns and villages of Dumfries and Galloway are small and quiet. Tiny places such as Kirkcudbright, Port William and Portpatrick once thrived on seaborne trade, but have now become attractive backwaters. Only Stranraer, the ferry port for Northern Ireland, retains some of its bustle.

Ruins of great abbeys and castles are witness to the region's importance in history, while it was to Galloway that St Ninian came on his mission to the southern Picts, leaving an area rich in early Christian remains. Gardens flourish in the mild, damp climate, birds flock to the Solway coast, and the fishing is good.

Off the Ayrshire coast, the mountainous island of Arran, often dubbed Scotland in minature, has long been a popular holiday destination, with some of the best hill-walking in the area, excellent views and a varied landscape. The small island of Great Cumbrae in the mouth of the Clyde estuary is easily relished on a day trip.

Robert Burns (1759–1796)

Scotland's most famous poet was born in Alloway, a village just south of Ayr, on 25 January 1759. Hailed in his lifetime as 'ploughman-poet', Burns' agricultural antecedents appealed to the eighteenth-century idea that the wellsprings of genius were the more intriguing for being found in a man of humble background.

In fact, Robert Burns, thanks to an intelligent and determined father, was an educated and well-read man. He read Ramsay, the Scottish poet, as well as Pope, Locke and Shakespeare. By the time he was 22, he had already worked in several agricultural jobs, without much success. Emigration to Jamaica seemed to be the solution to his problems. Though he had circulated manuscripts of his poems, none of his work was published until he was 27, but *Poems, Chiefly in the Scottish Dialect*, published in Kilmarnock in 1786, was an instant success.

He exchanged a pledge of marriage with Mary Campbell (Highland Mary), but in fact remained loyal (though far from faithful) to Jean Armour, whom he first declared his common-law wife at the age of 26. His womanising got him into trouble with the Presbyterian Kirk – a constant theme of Burns' best poetry is one of protest against the restrictions placed on mankind's freedom by artificial distinctions of birth, morals or custom.

He next published in Edinburgh, where he stayed and was fêted as literary hero for two winters, thereafter flinging himself into collecting, editing and writing the *Scottish Songs* which form such a large part of his work. In 1788, he moved, with his family, to Ellisland Farm north of Dumfries. A year later, after another failed attempt at agriculture, he moved to Dumfries and became a customs officer.

Burns hated hypocrisy and pomposity in all their forms, and there is little doubt that his most successful poems are the biting satirical pieces in Scots, such as 'Holy Willie's Prayer', though it is by such classic songs as 'Auld Lang Syne' and the sanitised version of 'Comin' Thro' the Rye' that he is often remembered. The cult of Burns – marked by Burns suppers held in his honour in Caledonian societies throughout the world – is often mawkish and sentimental. In fact, he was a tough, no-nonsense poet who loved sensual pleasures in the best tradition of his predecessors Ramsay and Fergusson.

He died at Dumfries in 1796 at the age of 37.

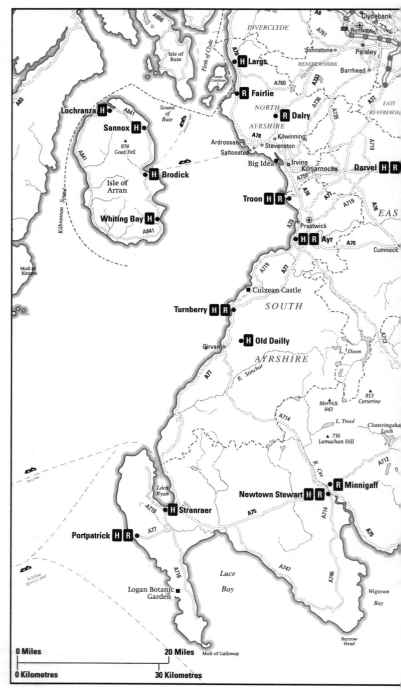

Good bases in the South-West

Ayr

✓ *A useful base for those on the Burns trail*

✓ *Good golf courses within striking distance*

✓ *Well located for trips to Arran (from Ardrossan) or to Ailsa Craig (from Girvan)*

✓ *Reasonable transport links, especially northwards*

✗ *Takes time to get in or out of*

The biggest town in the region offers access to a host of sights connected with Robert Burns in nearby Alloway and the surrounding country (see pages 77–8). Not much remains of the medieval town, but the coast offers attractions such as The Big Idea to the north and Culzean Castle to the south (see page 76), while the town centre is lively. There is a wide range of accommodation and shops, a seafront esplanade, and the thirteenth-century Auld Brig across the River Ayr.

Dumfries

✓ *Easy access from M74 or by rail*

✓ *Good base for touring the Solway coast*

✓ *Comparatively large choice of accommodation and shops*

Built from the characteristic local red sandstone, and with a riverside setting, this ancient burgh has been much fought over since its foundation in the twelfth century. Robert the Bruce murdered his rival, John Comyn, in a church here (see box, pages 90–1), and Robert Burns spent the last years of his life in the town.

Kirkudbright

✓ *Peaceful, but big enough to avoid total isolation*

✓ *Centrally located for touring the coast or inland*

✓ *Fair range of crafts and antique shops*

A very attractive small town at the head of an estuary, with a fine range of Georgian buildings and a ruined castle. The place is something of an artists' colony and a one-time haunt of the author Dorothy Sayers. There is an excellent local museum and several galleries with the work of local artists on display.

New Galloway

✓ *Attractive place in an excellent location*

✓ *Good for activity holidays*

✗ *Not many facilities*

Barely larger than a village, but ideally situated for walks in the Galloway Forest Park or for watery activities on Loch Ken. Another haunt of artists.

Portpatrick

✓ *Attractive harbour and coastline*

✓ *Good for touring the extreme south and west*

✓ *Close to Stranraer – a handy stop on the way to or from Ireland*

✗ *A long, slow drive to get here, if coming from the east*

A tiny fishing port on the western side of the hammerheaded Rhins Peninsula. It has a lively atmosphere in season, with plenty of day visitors.

AYRSHIRE

The rolling hills and farmlands of Ayrshire have always been a place apart. Historically, these were the lands where Robert the Bruce had his base, and where he staged a comeback that was to end at Bannockburn in 1314. At a later period, Ayrshire was a stronghold of the radical presbyterian Covenanters (see box, pages 156–7). But today Ayrshire is known above all as the home of Scotland's national poet, Robert Burns, and many of the visitors who come here are on the trail of the poet.

Key web sites

www.ayrshire-arran.com The local tourist board's web site. Some useful links

www.ayrshire-online.co.uk A gazeteer of local web sites, including some of interest to visitors

www.ayrshire2000.co.uk Rudimentary on places to visit, but with a very useful section on Ayrshire golf courses

---

Top sights

The Big Idea

✓ *Recommended for children over seven*

✗ *Primary-school hotspot*

Billed as the world's first inventor centre, this purpose-built attraction inhabits a patch of barren sand dune on the outskirts of Irvine. The building, which looks like a half-buried aircraft hangar, is virtually on the site of the old ICI explosives factory, and this hands-on sight is centred around the story of Alfred Nobel, inventor of dynamite, gelignite and other substances that go bang. A place with strong child-appeal which embraces a 'pink-knuckle' ride on the history of explosions, the Big Idea contains numerous gadgets which demonstrate useful principles such as leverage or conductivity. In a quieter workshop area, visitors assemble kits (buggies, boats and rockets, for example) and try them out on test beds. It is rather too high-tech – the display screens flash up your own name whenever you activate them – but it is good fun with children of the right age (seven upwards). *[Daily exc 25 Dec and 1 Jan, 10–6 (last admission 4pm);* ☎ *(01294) 461999;* 🖰 *www.bigidea.org.uk]*

Culzean Castle

✓ *Excellent family day out*

✓ *Gentle walks*

✓ *Good selction of shops and restaurants*

This is the flagship property of the National Trust for Scotland: a huge country park stretching along a rocky shoreline, with an Adam mansion as its centrepiece. Visitor facilities are impressive, with several shops, two restaurants and very detailed information. The castle itself was remodelled by Robert Adam in the eighteenth century, turning a rather grim old fortress into an elegant home. The exterior is not especially beautiful, but the interior should be seen, primarily for the sake of the wonderful galleried staircase and the small circular salon, seemingly poised over breaking waves. Restored kitchens, a sequence of bedrooms and a hallway stuffed with old armaments fill out the rest of the castle. President

Eisenhower was given a wing of the house for his own use, and this is now the setting for a small exhibition, focusing on his achievements as Supreme Allied Commander during World War II.

The parkland is extensive enough for walks of varying distances. Paths along the seashore are popular; there are wonderful views across to Arran and the Kintyre peninsula, and several small coves to explore. Ranger activities take place in the grounds, and there is an open grassy area where children can run free. *[NTS; castle, walled garden, visitor centre, restaurants and shops: 1 Apr to 31 Oct, daily 10.30–5.30 (last admission 5); other times by appointment. Country Park: all year, daily 9.30–sunset;* ☎ *(01655) 884455;* ◌ *www.nts.org.uk]*

The next best sights

Bachelor's Club (Tarbolton)

The top floor of this former inn was the meeting place for the debating society started by Burns in 1780. The building is now preserved by the National Trust for Scotland and fitted out with period furnishings. Erudite guides do much to bring the place to life. *[NTS; Apr to Sept, daily 1.30–5.30; Oct, weekends only 1.30–5.30;* ☎ *(01292) 541940;* ◌ *www.nts.org.uk]*

Burns House Museum (Mauchline)

The cottage where Burns and Jean Armour lived for much of the poet's life, now restored. Along with Burns memorabilia, you can see a collection of curling stones and Mauchline boxware. Close by, **Poosie Nansie's Tavern** served as the setting for the poem 'The Jolly Beggars'. *[Easter and May to Sept, Tue–Sun;* ☎ *(01290) 550045;* ◌ *via www.robertburns.org]*

Burns National Heritage Park (Alloway)

✓ *Recommended for Burns lovers*
✗ *Large numbers of tour coaches*

This somewhat overblown title covers the combination of the Burns Cottage, where the poet was born, and the Tam o' Shanter

Experience, a purpose-built visitor centre with add-on videos. Alloway Auld Kirk, the Auld Brig and the Burns Monument are also included in the park [☞ *via www.robertburns.org*].

The **Burns Cottage** must look much neater now than it did in Burns' lifetime, when humans and farm animals inhabited the same building. Relics include the family bible and several manuscripts; figures and furniture bring the rooms to life. The **Tam o' Shanter Experience** shows two videos. One introduces the poet's life and works and fills in some of the Ayrshire background. The other is a dramatisation of the famous poem itself, complete with scolding wife, convivial company, witches and warlocks. It is cunningly filmed in places – although getting the horse to gallop seems to have been beyond the creators. The poem itself forms the narrative and is very well read. A shop and restaurant flesh out the entertainment.

Across the road stands the **Auld Kirk**, now a roofless ruin, where Tam o'Shanter gazed upon the 'warlocks and witches in a dance', and it is a short stroll to the **Auld Brig**, where his mare lost her tail to a pursuing witch. The **Burns Monument**, a formal Georgian memorial to the poet in the shape of a collonaded rotunda rising from well-maintained gardens, dates from 1823 and contains further relics of the poet, including the bible of his one-time fiancée Highland Mary and the wedding ring of Jean Armour (his wife). There are statues of some of the characters from Burns' poems too. *[Tam O' Shanter Experience: Apr to Oct, 9–6; Nov to Mar, 9–5; ☎ (01292) 443700; Burns Cottage: Apr to Oct, 9–6; Nov to Mar, 10–4, Sun 12–4; ☎ (01292) 443700]*

Crossraguel Abbey (near Maybole on A77)

A ruined Benedictine abbey, founded in 1244. The remains, especially of the church, chapter house and cloister, are well preserved. The impressive towered gatehouse and palatial lodging area demonstrate how prosperous the abbey became in the pre-Reformation years. Fine views are to be had from the gatehouse. *[HS; Apr to Sept, daily 9.30–6.30; ☎ (01655) 883113; ☞ www.historic-scotland.gov.uk]*

Dalgarven Mill Museum (near Kilwinning on A737)

A restored sixteenth-century grain mill, which houses a museum of country life and a costume gallery. The water wheel runs as often as possible. *[Apr to Oct, Tue–Sun 10–5; Nov to Mar, Wed–Sun 11–4;* ☎ *(01294) 552448;* ✆ *via www.aboutbritain.com]*

Dean Castle (Kilmarnock)

Surrounded by a country park full of things to do, Dean Castle is a venerable medieval fortress with a keep dating to the fourteenth century and a more refined adjoining fifteenth-century version. The castle was the seat of the Boyd family. Collections of musical instruments, armour and tapestries, combined with the approachability of the guides, give it much appeal. *[Apr to Sept, daily 10–5.30; Oct to Mar, 10–4.30, closed Fri;* ☎ *(01563) 522702;* ✆ *www.caledoniancastles.btinternet.co.uk]*

The Boyd Putsch

In medieval times, whenever the king was a minor, the road to power was open to any powerful family which could gain control of the young monarch. In 1466, the Boyds of Kilmarnock seized the young James III while he was out hunting, and immediately started accumulating power. One Boyd was created Earl of Arran and married to the King's sister. But since the King was already fifteen, they did not have long enough to consolidate their position. Their fall, in 1469, was swift, and their lands were forfeited.

Scottish Maritime Museum (Irvine)

Irvine was once an important port serving Glasgow, and still provides a suitable setting for an extensive collection of vessels (including an old coastal 'puffer'). It's always possible to board at least one of the ships, while the indoor exhibition is comprehensive and certain to interest anyone curious about the sea or engineering. Guided tours take you to parts of the museum other visitors do not reach. At the time of writing the museum was under threat of closure; call first before visiting. *[Apr to Oct, daily 10–5;* ☎ *(01294) 278283;* ✓▮ *via www.aboutbritain.com]*

Vikingar! (Largs)

At Largs the Scots defeated a Scandinavian force in 1263, putting an end to the Norse domination of the western seaboard. Vikingar! is a purpose-built attraction which brings Viking times to life in a sequence of well-conceived themes, using live actors, film and sound to good effect. Primarily aimed at children, this is nevertheless a good sight for adults too. *[Apr to Sept, daily 10.30–5.30; Oct and Mar, 10.30–3.30; Nov to Feb, Sat and Sun 10.30–3.30;* ☎ *(01475) 689777;* ✓▮ *www.vikingar.co.uk]*

Also in the area

Kelburn Country Centre (south of Largs) Extensive grounds surround an old castle, still lived in by the Earls of Glasgow. Many activities are available for children, and you can attempt some excellent short walks in fairly spectacular glens. *[Centre: Easter to Oct, daily 10–6; Oct to Easter, 11–dusk; Castle: Jul and Aug only;* ☎ *(01475) 568685;* ✓▮ *via www.aboutbritain.com]*

Nardini's (Largs) The most famous ice-cream emporium in the west of Scotland, housed in a huge art-nouveau building, and the best reason to visit Largs, according to many Scots. *[*✓▮ *www.nardini.co.uk]*

Skelmorlie Aisle (Largs) Behind the graveyard off the main street, this is a seventeenth-century conversion of part of a church into an elaborate mausolem with terrific carving and painting.

Suggested excursions

Boat trips round Ailsa Craig Ailsa Craig is a high, conical island off the Ayrshire coast, now a bird sanctuary with an enormous gannet colony. Several operators run trips from Girvan during the summer months. Early summer, during the breeding season, is the best time to go.

Trips to Great Cumbrae Regular ferries from Largs take ten minutes to do the crossing. Only eight square miles in area, the island has just one real settlement, the small town of Millport. Bike hire is available here. Visit the Cathedral of the Isles – the country's smallest, designed by William Butterfield in 1851 – and a small museum of marine life.

ARRAN

Tucked neatly between the sheltering arm of the Kintyre Peninsula and the mainland, Arran's landscape is much closer to the wild roughness of Argyll than to the fertility of Ayrshire. It is a big enough island to be worth taking more than a day over (though many people do make the day trip), especially if you intend to walk or spend time taking in the many magnificent views. The peak of Goatfell dominates the substantial mountains in the north of the island, where the land drops steeply to the sea. Further south, the landscape mostly consists of moorland and forest, with small fertile patches round the coast.

Arran has been a favourite holiday spot since Victorian times, so plenty of accommodation is to be found. Sandy beaches are few and far between, however.

Key web sites
www.arran-online.co.uk A general guide, with detailed descriptions of walks. You can also check on ferry details, including the Holy Island crossing
via **www.scotland-inverness.co.uk** Part of the *Internet Guide to Scotland*. Especially helpful on transport
www.arran.net A network of local sites, village by village

Local sights

Brodick Castle

A bulky baronial nineteenth-century creation, Brodick Castle was built for the Dukes of Hamilton, owners of Arran. The interior is fairly typical of the Scottish stately home of the period, with rows of stags' heads, a kitchen full of gleaming copper, and a sequence of elegant public rooms and bedrooms.

The gardens and grounds are more interesting than the house. Networks of paths weave between lush rhododendrons, leading to curiosities such as the Germanic summer house built by the eleventh Duke for his Bavarian wife. It is lined with images of pine cones worked into patterns. An extensive visitor centre caters for visitors to the castle and grounds and has information on the lengthy walks possible in the remoter parts of the grounds. *[NTS; Apr to June and Sept to Oct, daily 11–4.30; Jul and Aug, daily 11–5;* ☎ *(01770) 302202;* 🖥 *www.nts.org.uk]*

Machrie Moor

North of Blackwaterfoot, this lumpy moorland plateau is the setting for numerous relics from the Bronze Age, including burial chambers and five stone circles.

A rough (often wet) track leads uphill on to the moor, with the remaining uprights of the circles dotting the foreground and middle distance. With shower clouds blowing across the sky and the mountains brooding in the background, this is a peculiarly haunting place, where ancient history can feel very close. *[*🖥 *www.geocities.com/SoHo/2621/machrie]*

Also in the area

Holy Island The island is reached by ferry (frequency depends on season) from Lamlash or Whiting Bay. It is now a Buddhist retreat and a branch of the Kagyu Samye Ling foundation near Moffat (see page 51). *[*🖥 *www.holyisland.org]*

Home Farm Visitor Centre (north of Brodick) *[🖱 via www.arran-online.co.uk]* A collection of small factory and craft outlets including Arran Aromatics, where you can watch soap being made *[🖱 www.arran-aromatics.co.uk]* and Creelers Smokehouse, with excellent seafood.

Isle of Arran Distillers A new distillery, built in the glen just east of Lochranza. Visit, sample the whisky and eat at Harold's restaurant. *[Easter to Oct, daily 10–6;* ☎ *(01770) 830264;* 🖱 *www.arranwhisky.com]*

Isle of Arran Heritage Museum (north of Brodick) A proudly traditional museum of Arran life, with furnished interiors from the nineteenth century, an intriguing laundry, a smithy and a Bronze Age grave, not to mention the history of the Arran strains of potato. *[Easter to Oct, daily 10.30–4.30]*

Kildonan Castle An old ruin on a clifftop in the south of the island, beneath which lies one of the few good sandy beaches on Arran. Enjoy great views of Ailsa Craig.

Towns and villages to explore

Blackwaterfoot
On the western side of the island, this small, rural village has a unique twelve-hole golf course.

Brodick
The ferry terminal for the crossing from Ardrossan is the only settlement of any size on the island. It is not quite large enough to conceal the inevitable clutter caused by the need to supply the whole island by sea. There are several hotels, but the setting is not so fine as in the smaller villages. Brodick is the obvious base for climbing Goatfell up the comparatively gentle Glen Rosa route.

Lamlash

A very small-scale, gentle resort set in a shallow bay. It lacks a beach, but is blessed with views of Holy Island just offshore. Most of the guesthouses and hotels share this view.

Lochranza

Perfectly set in a mountain-ringed bay with an offshore ruined castle, this is the (seasonal) ferry terminal for the crossing to Kintyre. An ideal village for a quiet stay, but some distance from anywhere else.

Sannox

Squeezed beween the mountains and sea, this tiny place is held by some to be Arran's nicest village.

Whiting Bay

More exposed than Lamlash and with less character, although accommodation is plentiful.

DUMFRIES AND GALLOWAY

Scotland's south-western corner is a quiet countryside of fertile farmland, moorland and hills. The Gallowegians, in the early days of the country's history, took much pacifying before

---

Key web sites

www.dgvisitor.co.uk A small directory of sites in Dumfries and Galloway, organised by town

www.dumfries-and-galloway.co.uk A larger directory organised by subject, with many useful links

www.dalbeattie.com Of particular interest for its information on regional golf courses

www.dumfries.net Local news, gossip and a pub guide

www.southern-upland-way.com An exceptionally useful site for all walkers on this route, with suggestions to try out

www.galloway.co.uk The regional tourist board's web site

---

they were integrated into the new kingdom, and a certain independence of mind still rules down here. For the visitor, it can be ideal touring country, with a sprinkling of sights, some very attractive small towns, and good opportunites for walking in the forests or on the moors.

Top sights

Caerlaverock Castle (near Dumfries)

✓ *Extraordinary castle in marshland setting*

One of the most curious castles in Scotland, the building occupies a wonderful marshy setting south of Dumfries. The triangular shape of the moated stronghold is unique, and the double-towered gatehouse is extremely photogenic. The castle was a fortress for the Maxwell family, who disputed control of the western Borders with their Johnston rivals for much of the medieval period. First beseiged by Edward I of England in 1290, the castle was a focal point for much Border warfare, but suffered most severely from the Covenanters in 1640. Much still remains, including an elegant Renaissance building from 1634. A model siege engine stands before the walls. *[HS; Apr to Sept, daily 9.30–6.30; Oct to Mar, Mon–Sat 9.30–4.30, Sun 2–4.30;* ☎ *(01387) 770244;* ✆ *www.scottishculture.about.com]*

Drumlanrig Castle (by Dumfries)

✓ *Lots of activities for families*

✓ *Massive stately home with good grounds*

✓ *Notable paintings*

This is a massive seventeenth-century stately home, one of the seats of the Duke of Buccleuch and Queensbury, who traces his ancestry to two of the most famously piratical families in Scottish history, the Douglases and the Scotts. The huge wealth of the family is exemplified by the paintings at Drumlanrig, which include the last Leonardo da Vinci in private hands and Rembrandt's *Old Woman Reading*. The castle is surrounded by extensive grounds, and it is perhaps the many activities here that are the chief draw. They include demonstrations of birds of prey, craft workshops and an adventure playground. *[Castle: Easter to end Aug; Grounds: Easter to end Sept;* ☎ *www.drumlanrigcastle.org.uk]*

Logan Botanic Gardens (by Stranraer)

✓ *Botanical garden specialising in sub-tropical plants*
✓ *Recommended for keen gardeners*

One of the outstations of the Royal Botanic Gardens, Edinburgh, Logan specialises in tender plants, mostly from the southern hemisphere, which thrive in the virtually frost-free climate of the far west of Galloway. Tender rhododendrons are a speciality here, but tree ferns and palms flourish too. There are woodland and walled gardens, both planted with exotics, and a useful tea room in which to take a break from botany. *[Mar to Nov, 9.30–6;* ☎ *(01776) 860231);* ☎ *www.rgbe.org.uk]*

Threave Castle (near Castle Douglas)

✓ *Massive ruin on an island*
✓ *Enjoyable for all the family*

This castle has a magnificent setting on a flat island in the middle of the River Dee. A visit involves a ten-minute walk to the river bank followed by a ferry journey (ring the bell for the ferryman). This was a castle of the Black Douglas family and is immensely strong, with a five-storey tower house. It is still possible to scramble to the top for wonderful views. *[HS; Apr to Sept, daily 9.30–6.30;* ☎ *(01556) 502575;* ☎ *www.aboutscotland.com]*

Threave Garden (near Castle Douglas)

✓ *Good for garden lovers*

Threave serves as the training centre for the National Trust's gardeners, but it is a magnificent garden in its own right, with especially fine daffodil displays. It is a good place to pick up ideas on garden design, as the compositions created by shrubs and herbaceous plants are intriguing. Threave suffered badly from a blizzard combined with gales in the winter of 1997, but is now recovering. *[NTS; all year, 9.30–sunset;* ☎ *(01556) 502575;* ☎ *www.nts.org.uk]*

The next best sights

Burns sights in and near Dumfries

The **Robert Burns Centre** *[Apr to Sept, Mon–Sat 10–8, Sun 2–5; Oct to Mar, Tue–Sat 10–1 and 2–5;* ☎ *(01387) 264808]*, in a converted mill in the centre of Dumfries, is a good place to learn about the period the poet spent in and around the town. Of the nearby sights the best is the **Burns House**, where many of his most famous songs were written. There are lots of relics, including the bed in which Burns died, and his signature scratched on a window pane *[Apr to Sept, Mon–Sat 10–5, Sun 2–5; Oct to Mar 10–1 and 2–5;* ☎ *(01387) 255297]*. **Ellisland Farm**, north of the town, was leased by Burns for his last stab at farming in 1788 *[Easter to Sept, Mon–Sat 10–1 and 2–5, Sun 2–5;* ☎ *(01387) 74426]*. Now the working farm doubles up as a tourist attraction, with a good audio-visual display and period furniture. Keen Burns followers will want to see the **Mausoleum** in Dumfries, where the poet is buried. Look up information about all the Burns sights via *www.dumfriesmuseum.demon.co.uk*

Caerlaverock Wildfowl and Wetlands Centre (near Dumfries)

On the muddy flatlands and salt marshes of the Solway coast, Caerlaverock nature reserve is home to thousands of barnacle geese during the winter and a variety of wildlife during the summer months. It is a well-equipped place for birdwatchers, with marked trails, hides and a new visitor centre. *[All year, 10–5;* ☎ *(01387) 770200; via www.wwt.org]*

Castle Kennedy Gardens (near Stranraer)

Two castles (one ruined), two lochs and a two-acre lily pond form the framework of this ancient garden (which is eighteenth-century in origin). It is full of colour, but the layout is slightly rigid – possibly because it was constructed by soldiers for the Earl of Stair. *[Apr to Sept, 10–5]*

Dundrennan Abbey

The ruins of a Cistercian Abbey, tucked away by the coast in an isolated but very beautiful setting. What remains of the stonework shows some high-quality carving. Mary Queen of Scots spent her last night on Scottish soil here before crossing as a fugitive to England. *[HS; Apr to Sept, daily 9.30–6.30; Oct to Mar, Mon–Sat 9.30–4.30, Sun 2–4.30;* ☎ *(01557) 500262]*

Ruthwell Cross (near Dumfries)

The village of Ruthwell is home to one of the best-known early Christian relics in the country; an 18ft-high cross, elaborately decorated and engraved with the text of one of the earliest-known Anglo-Saxon poems, 'The Dream of the Rood'. It is found in the parish church and dates from the eighth century, when the Northumbrians ruled this part of the world. *[HS; access from key keeper – details at site;* ☎ *0131-668 8800;* ☙ *via www.dumfriesmuseum.demon.co.uk]*

Sweetheart Abbey (near Dumfries)

A lovely red ruined abbey dating from the thirteenth and fourteenth centuries, with the substantial remains of the abbey church dominating the complex. It was founded by Dervorguilla de Balliol in memory of her husband, and owes its name to the legend that she carried his heart around with her in a casket until the day of her death. *[HS; Apr to Sept, daily 9.30–6.30; Oct to Mar, Mon–Sat 9.30–4.30, Sun 2–4.30, closed Thur pm and Fri;* ☎ *(01387) 850397;* ☙ *via www.dumfriesmuseum.demon.co.uk]*

Whithorn Priory and Dig

Whithorn is where St Ninian, the earliest-known Christian missionary to Scotland, founded his *candida casa* or white house. An excellent visitor centre on the main street has many finds from the archaeological dig close to the priory, with excellent diagrams of how the Whithorn of the Dark Ages might have looked [‸❚ *via www.dumfriesmuseum.demon.co.uk]*. There are also guided tours of the dig. The priory is a comparatively small ruin, but atmospheric, and the nearby museum holds some very early Christian remains. Those on the trail of St Ninian should go to **Isle of Whithorn**, where the chapel that welcomed hosts of pilgrims stands isolated in a field. A cairn of stones is slowly being built by modern pilgrims. *[Easter to end Oct, 10.30–5]*

Also in the area

Gatehouse of Fleet, like Kirkudbright, is an attractive small town at the head of an estuary, with the **Mill on the Fleet Museum** and the ruins of **Cardoness Castle** to explore.

New Luce Abbey is not so well preserved as Sweetheart Abbey or Dundrennan Abbey (see above under 'The next best sights'), but is worth stopping for.

John Paul Jones Cottage (Kirkbean, near Dumfries) Tiny but charming birthplace of the founder of the United States navy.

Bruce's Stone(s) There are two in the area – one at Loch Trool where Robert the Bruce achieved his first victory over the English at the start of his comeback in 1307 (see box below for more detail). The other is by **Clatteringshaws Loch** (a bleak reservoir on the A712), where he is supposed to have rested after another victory.

Museums and galleries in Dumfries and Galloway

Numerous local museums are to be found in the small towns across the region, many of them intriguing places. Among the best are the **Stewartry Museum** in Kirkudbright (a local museum with some fascinating objects) [☎ *(01557) 331643]*, the **Tolbooth Museum** in Sanquhar [☎ *(01771) 622906]*, the **Museum of Leadmining** [☎ *(01659) 74387;* ⁀ *www.leadminingmuseum.co.uk]* high in the Lowther Hills at Wanlockhead and the **Dumfries Museum and Camera Obscura** [☎ *(01387) 253374]*. Among the castles and houses open to the public, **MacLellan's Castle**, a substantial sixteenth-century ruin [☎ *(01557) 331856]*, and the Georgian **Broughton House** (home of the artist E.A. Hornel) [☎ *(01557) 330437]*, both in Kirkudbright, are

---

Robert the Bruce (1274–1329)

'The Bruce' remains a revered half-legendary figure to many Scots, perhaps because of the fact that his ambition and persistence culminated in success against the odds, but more importantly because his reign marks the emergence of a distinctly Scottish patriotism from among the welter of Anglo-Norman and Celtic loyalties.

Robert the Bruce was grandson of that Robert Bruce whose claim to the Scottish throne Edward I of England had rejected. His behaviour during Edward's invasion of Scotland in 1296 had been ambiguous and indeed his name appears on the 'Ragman's Roll' of Scots who had sworn allegiance to Edward at Berwick. But in 1306 Robert Bruce killed his rival John Comyn in the church of Greyfriars at Dumfries, laying himself open to charges of murder and sacrilege. His reaction was to make a bid for power, and he had himself crowned King of Scots at Scone.

His revolt against Edward seemed doomed. He was defeated almost at once by the Earl of Pembroke near Methven; within a year three of his brothers were captured and executed, and his wife and daughter imprisoned. Bruce fled, possibly to Arran, spending the winter as an excommuni-cated outlaw. The spring of 1307 saw him back in Scotland, in Galloway. He won a skirmish with the English who were pinning him in Glen Trool, and beat them more thoroughly at

---

well worth seeing. The **Old Bridge House Museum** in Dumfries has a gruesome collection of dental instruments – if you care for that sort of thing *[☎ (01387) 256904]*. Details about all of the above are on the Net via ✆ *www.dumfries-museum.demon.co.uk*

Scenery and touring routes

This is an excellent area for touring by car, thanks to the variety of landscapes, which range from the pastoral to the

---

Ayr. But his real salvation in July of that year was the death of Edward I, who was already in Cumberland on his way north to flatten Bruce for once and for all. Edward II had no stomach for the Scottish campaign, and Bruce was left to himself.

He still had plenty of enemies within Scotland, but his greatest, the Comyns, were beaten at Inverurie and their lands of Buchan mercilessly harried. He then turned on the MacDougalls of the west while his supporters cleared south-west Scotland. The French King secretly recognised him and the clergy, despite his excommunication, gave him support. English-occupied castles fell one by one, and Bruce instigated the sensible policy of dismantling many of them so that they could not again be used against him.

With the Battle of Bannockburn in 1314, Bruce set the seal on his military success. Political success followed only some years later with a 13-year truce with England in 1323, the absolution of Bruce by the Pope in 1328 and the recognition by England of Scottish independence in the same year.

Bruce, increasingly ailing, was unable to go on crusade as he had vowed. Sir James Douglas, one of his companions from the start, promised to take his heart to the Holy Land (he was killed fighting Saracens in Spain and the heart was supposedly brought home to Melrose Abbey). Bruce died, possibly of leprosy, in 1329, and was buried at Dunfermline.

bleak. Driving can be slow, even on through-routes, as few of the roads are consistently straight.

Dumfries area The A710, fringing the coast to Dalbeattie (and beyond on the A711 to Kirkudbright), passes through lush country with good sea views. Explore **Rockcliffe** and **Kippford** and try the beach at Sandyhills Bay.

Galloway Forest Park The A712 is the main route through the extensive forest, with numerous stopping places with signed walks or wildlife trails. Blanket conifers dampen the landscape a little, but there are some wide open views.

Newton Stewart area From the A714, minor roads lead off into the hills and forests of **Glentrool**. An excess of trees spoils some of the views, but not all. **Loch Trool** is the starting point for many signed walks, including the ascent of Merrick – for which proper hill-walking gear isessential.

South of Newton Stewart, the **Machars** peninsula has a very different landscape. There are few trees in this rich dairy-farming country, and many coastal stopping points. **Whithorn** and the **Isle of Whithorn** (see page 89) are obvious destinations; the tiny village of **Garlieston** is also worth a look. The coastline north from Port Willam is lovely. **Wigtown** [⌒🖋 *www.wigtown-booktown.co.uk*] sells itself as Scotland's book town – and indeed there are numerous antiquarian and second-hand bookshops.

Stranraer area To explore the hammerheaded Rhins of Galloway, drive to the attractive **Portpatrick** (starting point of the Southern Upland Way) and then head south along minor roads towards **Logan Botanic Gardens**. In clear weather, head right down to the Mull of Galloway, as bleak a place as you could wish, for views of Ireland, not far distant. 🖋 *www.south-rhins.co.uk* will point you to good beaches.

For a taste of lonely moorland, head for **Glenluce** (visit the **Abbey** here) and then take the minor road to **New Luce** and then towards Barrhill. The landscape becomes wild and treeless, with expanses of heather in all directions. You may see hen harriers huntng beside the road.

WHERE TO STAY

£ – under £70 per room per night, incl. VAT

££ – £70 to £110 per room per night, incl. VAT

£££ – over £110 per room per night, incl. VAT

AYR
The Crescent
26 Bellevue Crescent, Ayr KA7 2DR
☎ (01292) 287329
📠 (01292) 286779
🖰 www.26crescent.freeserve.co.uk
'A gem of a guesthouse', run by a welcoming and thoughtful host. Bedrooms are spacious, bright and well-appointed. Dinner is not served; restaurants are within walking distance.
£ All year exc Christmas

BRODICK
Glencloy Farmhouse
Glencloy, Brodick, Isle of Arran KA27 8DA
☎ (01770) 302351
Wonderful views from spacious and attractive bedrooms in a Victorian sandstone farmhouse. Dinners use local produce.
£ Mar to mid-Nov

DALBEATTIE
Briardale House
17 Haugh Road, Dalbeattie DG5 4AR
☎/📠 (01556) 611468
Double-fronted house in large walled gardens, with roomy and comfortable bedrooms. Guests can relax in either the conservatory overlooking the garden, or in the quiet sitting room. Four-course dinner menus.
£ Mar to Oct

DARVEL
Scoretulloch House
Darvel KA17 0LR
☎ (01560) 323331
📠 (01560) 323441
🖰 www.scoretulloch.com
An isolated converted mill in high, green country, now a comfortable restaurant-with-rooms. Small but carefully designed rooms open on to the garden, and the clubby sitting room has bird books.
££ All year (See Where to Eat)

KIRKCUDBRIGHT
Gladstone House
48 High Street, Kirkcudbright DG6 4JX
☎/📠 (01557) 331734
A tall stone building offering bed and breakfast in the centre of Kirkcudbright (away from the noisy shopping area). The interior is bright and attractive, and the rooms agreeable. Hearty breakfasts.
£ All year

LARGS
South Whittlieburn Farm
Brisbane Glen, Largs KA30 8SN
☎ (01475) 675881
A warm welcome at a sheep farm in rolling countryside. Amenities include three bright and comfortable bedrooms, a lounge and breakfast room.
£ All year

LOCHRANZA
Apple Lodge

Lochranza, Isle of Arran KA27 8HJ
☎ /🖷 (01770) 830229

A large former manse, with four
bedrooms (all *en suite* and handsomely
furnished). Dinner is made from local
produce and herbs from the garden.
£ All year exc Christmas

NEWTON STEWART
Oakbank

Corsbie Road, Newton Stewart
DG8 6JB
☎ (01671) 402822
🖷 (01671) 403050

Bed and breakfast with good views
above town, in gardens which include a
croquet lawn. The three bedrooms are
spacious and comfortable. Dinner is
available with notice, and guests may
bring their own wine.
£ All year exc Christmas

OLD DAILLY
Hawkhill Farm

Old Dailly KA26 9RD
☎ (01465) 871232

Hospitality and comfort at a working
farm with three comfortable bedrooms,
originally a seventeenth-century
coaching inn. Good breakfasts are
served family-style in the dining-room.
£ Mar to Oct

PORTPATRICK
Carlton House

21 South Crescent, Portpatrick
DG9 8JR
☎ /🖷 (01776) 810253

Well-decorated bed and breakfast close
to the harbourfront. Some bedrooms

have sea views, as does the residents'
sitting room. No evening meals, but
packed lunches can be requested.
£ All year

Crown Hotel

9 North Crescent, Portpatrick DG9 8SX
☎ (01776) 810261
🖷 (01776) 810551

Popular and lively pub on the
harbourfront, offering a menu
dominated by seafood in a large and airy
split-level restaurant. Bedrooms are up a
steep staircase; one has a harbour view.
££ All year (See Where to Eat)

Knockinaam Lodge

Portpatrick, Stranraer DG9 9AD
☎ (01776) 810471
🖷 (01776) 810435

Dignified and peaceful house in a small
cove, with the sea almost reaching its
lawns and cliffs to either side. Bedrooms
are luxurious, and the imaginative menu
uses local fish and game.
£££ All year

SANNOX
Gowanlea

Sannox, Isle of Arran KA27 8JD
☎ (01770) 810253

Bed and breakfast on the seashore,
backed by mountains and glens. Three
simple bedrooms are available; guests
may bring their own wine to dinner. A
small supplement is charged for one-
night bookings.
£ All year

STRANRAER
Kildrochet House

Kildrochet, Stranraer DG9 9BB
☎ /🖷 (01776) 820216

Elegant family home built as a dower house in 1723, carefully restored and stylishly furnished. The three spacious bedrooms are *en suite*; a drawing room overlooks the terrace, and the pleasant garden has a croquet lawn.

£ *All year*

TROON
Lochgreen House
Monktonhill Road, Southwood, Troon KA10 7EN
☎ (01292) 313343
📠 (01292) 318661
🖥 www.costley-hotels.co.uk

Edwardian family hotel looking out over mature trees, neat lawns and flowerbeds, close to the golf course. Menus use fish, game and meat in exotic and traditional combinations. Bedrooms are spacious and well-equipped, and furnishings are in keeping with the era of the house.

£££ *All year (See Where to Eat)*

TURNBERRY
Turnberry Hotel
Turnberry, Ayrshire KA26 9LT
☎ (01655) 331000
📠 (01655) 331706
🖥 www.westin.com

Massive and impeccably run hotel, with sizeable and luxurious bedrooms overlooking the Firth of Clyde. Visitors can enjoy the health spa, sauna, solarium and heated indoor swimming pool in addition to golf and other outdoor pursuits.

£££ *Closed 18 to 27 Dec (See Where to Eat)*

WHITING BAY
Royal Hotel
Shore Road, Whiting Bay, Isle of Arran KA27 8PZ
☎ (01770) 700286

Large, detached sandstone hotel with wonderful views over the Firth of Clyde. Guests can use a comfortable sitting room and a garden seating area. Home-made evening meals are served in the spacious dining-room.

£ *Mar to Oct*

WHERE TO EAT

AYR
Fouters Bistro
2A Academy Street, Ayr KA7 1HS
☎ (01292) 261391
📠 (01292) 619323
🖥 www.fouters.co.uk

Bright cellar-bistro with Mediterranean décor, serving modern Scottish food. Lamb, beef, fish and game all appear in a varied repertoire of dishes. Desserts are more traditional, as are the 40 wines listed, starting with a house French at £12.95.

Mon–Sat 12–2 and 5.30–10; closed 25 and 26 Dec, 1 to 3 Jan

DALRY
Braidwoods
Drumastle Mill Cottage, Dalry KA24 4LN
☎ (01294) 833544
📠 (01294) 833553
🖥 www.braidwoods.co.uk

Restaurant in a pair of converted millers' cottages. Locally sourced ingredients play a key part in a contemporary and uncluttered menu. Despite limited choice, options are varied in fish, poultry and beef dishes and desserts are unusual.

Wed–Sun L 12–1.45, Tue–Sat D 7–9; closed first three weeks in Jan, 2 weeks in Sept/Oct

DARVEL
Scoretulloch House
Darvel KA17 0LR
☎ (01560) 323331
📠 (01560) 323441
🖥 www.scoretulloch.com

The quiet dining-room of this converted mill has plunging views to the valley below, and there is an airy conservatory brasserie. The four-course menus are unusual without being too exotic, and dishes are made from high-quality ingredients, including salmon smoked in the owner's smokehouse.

Open daily (See Where to Stay)

FAIRLIE
Fins
Fencefoot Farm, Fairlie KA29 0EG
☎ (01475) 568989
📠 (01475) 568921
🖥 www.fencebay.co.uk

A converted byre attached to a fish farm shop, this restaurant specialises in seafood – some landed from their own fishing boat, some smoked in-house. Lobsters are kept live on-site, as are rainbow trout. Scallops, oysters and tasty desserts also appear on the menu, and wine prices are reasonable.

Tue–Sun L 12–2.30, Tue–Sat D 6.45–9.30. Closed 25 and 26 Dec, 1 and 2 Jan

MINNIGAFF
Creebridge House Hotel
Minnigaff DG8 6NP
☎ (01671) 402121

Attractive stone building in three acres of gardens and woodland, once the residence of the Earls of Galloway. Bridges Brasserie is the pub part of the country hotel, and the Garden Restaurant offers attractive bar meals and lunchtime sandwiches. More expensive dishes cover fish, game, poultry, beef and particularly lamb; Sunday lunch is a carvery meal.

12–2.30 and 6–11.30; bar food 12–2 and 6–9 (10 Sat); restaurant Apr to Oct D only 7–9; closed 26 Dec

NEWTON STEWART
Kirroughtree Hotel
Newton Stewart DG8 6AN
☎ (01671) 402141
📠 (01671) 402425

Eighteenth-century house in landscaped gardens with a modern European menu including seafood, game and unusual desserts. A predominantly French wine list starts at £13.75, extending to three-figure clarets.

All week 12–1.30 and 7–9; closed 3 Jan to mid–Feb

PORTPATRICK
Crown Hotel
9 North Crescent, Portpatrick DG9 8SX
☎ (01776) 810261
📠 (01776) 810551

Handsome three-storey inn overlooking the harbour with a cool-toned bistro, non-smoking conservatory and cottagey bedrooms. The two bars offer a plain menu of sandwiches and basket snacks

such as scampi or scallops with chips.
The more expensive bistro menu has
high-quality fish, game, beef and salads.
*11–11.30, Sun 12–11.30; bar food
12–2.30, 6–10; snacks and afternoon tea
2.30–6; closed 25 Dec (See Where to Stay)*

TROON
Lochgreen House
Monktonhill Road, Southwood, Troon
KA10 7EN
☎ (01292) 313343
🖨 (01292) 318661
🖳 www.costley-hotels.co.uk
Eat in a relaxed and comfortable
atmosphere. Dishes are mostly
traditional with occasional flourishes;
seafood plays a large part, with a wide
range of game, poultry, beef and
desserts. A helpfully annotated wine list
includes six house wines, and 140 whisky
varieties.
*All week 12–2 and 7–9pm (See Where to
Stay)*

MacCallums' Oyster Bar
The Harbour, Troon KA10 6DH
☎ /🖨 (01292) 319339
The freshest seafood in an appropriate
location, with a view of the harbour and
its seals and fishing boats. A varied and
imaginative menu offers fish dishes
ranging from an upmarket battered cod
to European cuisine. Prices on the
primarily white wine list begin at £9.50.
*Tue–Sun L 12–2.45 (3.30 Sun), Tue–Sat D
7–9.45*

TURNBERRY
Turnberry Hotel
Turnberry, Ayrshire KA26 9LT
☎ (01655) 331000
🖨 (01655) 331706
🖳 www.westin.com
A range of eating options in this imposing
hotel. The Mediterranean-style Terrace
brasserie and the Clubhouse offer simple,
wholesome cooking. The expensive main
restaurant sees traditional French dishes
interspersed with modern Scottish food
using local produce.
Closed 18 to 27 Dec (See Where to Stay)

Edinburgh

Houses in Charlotte Square

- One of the most beautiful cities in Europe
- Splendid medieval and Georgian architecture
- Wealth of historic sights in a compact area
- Interesting hidden corners
- Increasingly vibrant atmosphere
- The Edinburgh Festival

EDINBURGH

At a glance

✓ Good for three- or five-day city breaks

✓ Excellent eating, sightseeing, shopping

✓ Uninhibited cultural blow-out during the Festival

✓ Increasingly good Hogmanay celebrations

✗ Steep hills, uncertain climate

✗ Deliberate policy of making life difficult for cars

Edinburgh rivals Prague or Stockholm in the natural beauty of its setting, and its architecture mostly lives up it. The packed medieval city huddled in the shelter of its volcanic crag expands into elegant Georgian crescents and terraces lining ridges and valleys, making a wonderful contrast between the Old Town and the New. It is a place of hills and sea, for the Castle on its crag in the centre and the bulky hump of Arthur's Seat are surrounded by lesser heights, while the estuary of the Forth girdles the city on two sides. So there is always a view, and usually a cold wind to go with it, for Edinburgh does not yield its pleasures lightly.

The capital of Scotland since early medieval times, and a fortress for centuries before that, Edinburgh has seen most of the moments of tragedy and brilliance which make up the history of Scotland. Its buildings are inhabited by many ghosts – Mary Queen of Scots witnessing the murder of her secretary, Montrose facing his executioners, Lord Cockburn scribbling his memoirs, and the sinister Burke and Hare selling the corpses of their victims to the surgeons.

There is much to see, for as well as all the historical sights, this is a city of gardens and galleries, and of curiosities half-hidden in out-of-the-way places. In early summer and again in autumn, the slanting northern light shows it at its best, and these times, when the city rests before and after its festival, are the best seasons to visit.

In the first edition of this Guide we wrote that Edinburgh was waiting, a capital without a nation, for something to happen to bring it centre-stage again. Now, something is indeed happening. Whether it is the rebirth of its Parliament and a consequent stirring of self-confidence, or simply a belated move to catch up with the renaissance of Glasgow, a sense of change is beginning to infect the old place. Buildings are springing up, led by the controversial new Scottish parliament. The city is growing faster than anywhere else in the United Kingdom; shops and restaurants are changing hands and styles; radical traffic-control policies are causing anguish and argument. Once again, with Silicon Glen to the west, and the Roslin Institute to the south, Edinburgh may be edging towards the forefront of medical and information technologies in a return to the heady days of the Enlightenment, when its scientific and publishing output led all Europe (see box on pages 112–13).

Key web sites

www.edinburgh.gov.uk The Edinburgh District Council site, with excellent guidance on events, the city-run museums and general information for visitors

www.ebs.hw.ac.uk/edweb A visitor's guide to Edinburgh compiled by the District Council and Heriot-Watt University. Very comprehensive on historical sights

www.edinburgh.org The tourist board site. Good on accommodation

www.camvista.com Contains several webcams in Edinburgh, including views of the castle and of Murrayfield

www.edinburgh-galleries.co.uk An excellent site listing current exhibitions at most of the art galleries in Edinburgh and the Lothians

www.edinburghpages.com An extensive directory of Edinburgh businesses, including shops and restaurants

www.electrum.co.uk Includes a useful guide to a few of Edinburgh's pubs

---

Getting around

Almost everything is accessible on foot, although the steepness of the hills may make it worthwhile to study the bus routes or to

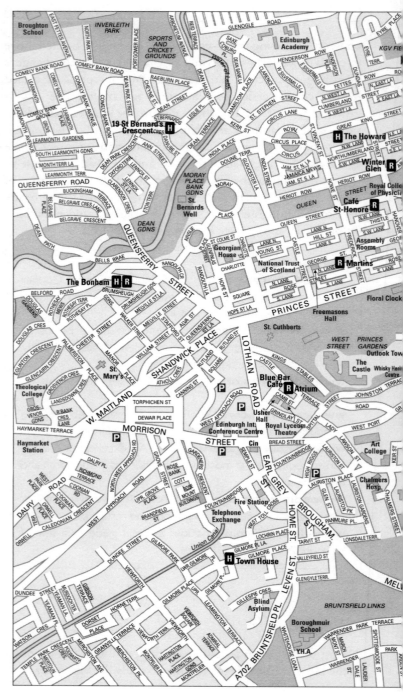

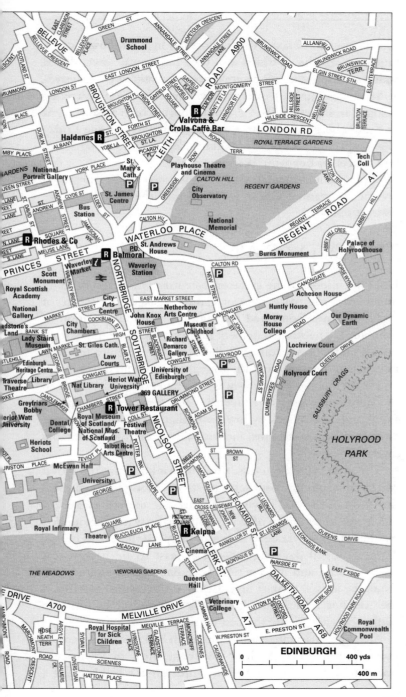

take the occasional taxi. Many visitors stay in guesthouse accommodation on the outskirts and take buses into town. Avoid taking a car into the city centre if possible: parking is expensive.

Several companies offer guided bus tours from Waverley Bridge, leaving every 10–15 minutes during high season (April to September) and less often at other times: try Guide Friday [☎ 0131-556 2244] or Scotline [☎ 0131-557 0162] to buy tickets for open-top bus tours of the city.

Historical and themed walks around the city are offered by several companies. Ghost walks around the Old Town are always popular.

THE OLD TOWN

Until the middle of the eighteenth century, the streets running down from the basalt plug of Castle Rock to the Palace of Holyroodhouse contained virtually the whole population of Edinburgh. The stone tenement houses which line the narrow wynds and closes leading off the High Street grew upwards rather than outwards, and their height was admired by foreign visitors in much the same way as skyscrapers are today. Here all the different classes of sixteenth- and seventeenth-century Edinburgh lived cheek by jowl, with dignitaries inhabiting the same buildings as artisans, and probably drinking in the same taverns or 'howffs'.

The main route from Castle to Palace is known as the Royal Mile, and is split into four separate streets. Along them you will find most of the Old Town's sights, historic and otherwise. On either side, the mouths of closes lead to courtyards surrounded by old houses, or via steep slopes and steps to the streets below. There is a full day's sightseeing at least to be had in this compact area, and if your time in Edinburgh is limited, you would be as well to start here. Begin at the castle, especially if the weather is clear, for the views of Edinburgh from the battlements are among the best there are.

After the smart citizens of Edinburgh had moved out to the more elegant streets of the New Town, the Old Town went downhill, and by the nineteenth century, much had become a slum. But restoration work has, on the whole, been a success, although some of the dingier areas of the Cowgate, which run parallel to the Royal Mile to the south, have still to be made attractive.

Top sights

Our Dynamic Earth

✓ *New high-tech attraction*
✓ *Good sight for children*

Looking like a smaller version of the ill-starred Millennium Dome at Greenwich, this purpose-built attraction is Edinburgh's millennial contribution to the twenty-first century. It lies in the shadow of Salisbury Crags – inspiration for geologists to this day – and in the same city where James Hutton first proposed erosion and uplift as the mechanisms responsible for the changing face of the Earth. So it is an appropriate sight for Edinburgh, and even if it is intellectually somewhat lightweight and relentlessly concerned with 'Experience', it is well conceived and great fun.

A 'time machine' – actually a lift – carries you through the 15 billion years since the Universe began, with suitable sound and light effects. Volcanoes spew steam, and there is an earth tremor (tamer than the average Edinburgh bus ride). The best part is a breathtaking 180-degree swoop over a glacier. A real iceberg, a cleverly mocked-up rainforest, plus some brilliant small-screen film of life in the oceans add to the enjoyment.

Children ought to love this sight, which makes a good break from the historic attractions in the area. However, unlike the National Museum of Scotland (see page 109) there is not much to draw the visitor back a second time. *[Easter to Oct, Mon–Sun 10–6 (last entry 5); Nov to Easter, Wed–Sun 10–5 (last entry 4), closed Mon and Tue; ☎ 0131-550 7800; ⬤ www.dynamicearth.co.uk]*

Edinburgh Castle

✓ *Old fortification, packed with history*
✓ *Cliff-top setting, wonderful views*

✓ *Increasingly good interpretation*
✓ *The Scottish crown jewels*

The age and the magnificence of the Castle's setting make a visit here compulsory *[HS; Apr to Oct, daily 9.30–5.15; Nov to Mar, 9.30–4.15;* ☎ *0131-225 9846;* 📞 *www.scottishculture. about.com].* The rock on which it stands dominates the city, and the views from its walls are superb. Inside, it is more like a small military town than a simple fortress, with a number of different things to see. Over the past decade, the interpretation for visitors has been getting better, although the extensive rebuilding over the centuries still makes it hard to puzzle out the historical sequence.

Touring the Castle is a matter of puffing up and down steep slopes or steps and pausing to look at the view. Guided tours are frequent in season, and Historic Scotland's custodians have a good store of anecdotes. There are also useful audio guides.

If you prefer to make your own way, the main points of interest are:

The Great Hall Built as a ceremonial room for James IV, at a time when the castle still doubled up as a royal residence, the Great Hall became a barracks in the eighteenth century and was restored in Victorian times in a gloomily medieval manner. However, the hammer-beam ceiling is outstanding. The Hall was the meeting place for the Scottish Parliament until 1639.

Mills Mount Battery Site of Edinburgh's 'one o'clock gun', originally fired as a time signal for shipping in the Forth. Even in the digital age, Edinburgh citizens still set their watches by the lunch-time explosion. The one o'clock gun now has its own association, and a museum in the castle. *[Daily, Apr to Sept 9.30–6; Oct to Mar, 9.30–5]*

Mons Meg A huge siege gun or bombard, manufactured in Flanders and given to James II in 1457. Useful interpretation explains how it was built, used and transported over Scotland's boggy roads. The gun spent some years in the Tower of London before being returned to Edinburgh in 1829, after a petition by Sir Walter Scott.

The National War Museum of Scotland Recently given an extensive makeover to render it more attractive to visitors, the museum now has numerous themed displays tracing aspects of Scotland's involvement in conflict. It is a fascinating place for military history buffs in particular [🖱 *www.nms.ac.uk*].

The Palace The nineteenth-century clock-tower makes this building look more like a town hall than a royal residence. Here, Mary Queen of Scots gave birth to James VI in a chamber not much larger than a cupboard. In 1830, the body of an infant wrapped in a cloth with the initial J was discovered behind a panel, giving rise to the legend that the real heir was stillborn, and that James was a last-minute substitute.

The crown jewels, or 'Honours' of Scotland are on display in a separate chamber, together with bronze models which you can handle to give you some idea of size and weight. The crown may once have been used by Robert the Bruce (though James V made it more imposing). It survived being melted down by Cromwell by being smuggled out of the besieged Dunottar Castle.

Here, too, is the Stone of Destiny (see box overleaf), which was restored to Scotland in 1996, 700 years after being looted from Scone Abbey by Edward I of England. If genuine, it is a remarkably plain and unadorned symbol of royalty.

St Margaret's Chapel A tiny twelfth-century chapel built in memory of Queen Margaret, who died in the castle in 1093. A pretty Norman chancel arch divides the miniature nave from the apse. You will need to slip in during a gap between two tour groups to have any chance of appreciating its peace.

The Scottish National War Memorial Sir Robert Lorimer transformed an old barrack block into a shrine to Scotland's war dead after the First World War. Opinions of his architecture vary from enthusiastic to scathing, but there is much that is sombre and moving about the place. Douglas Strachan's windows are mystical and beautiful.

The Stone of Scone

In 1996, with a good deal of pomp and ceremony, a medium-sized, undistinguished lump of sandstone was escorted over the Tweed at Coldstream on its way to a new home at Edinburgh Castle. The Stone of Destiny, or Stone of Scone, had been returned to Scotland after having lain in Westminster Abbey as a spoil of war for almost 700 years. It was not the first time it had been back to Scotland however. In 1950 four students succeeded in burgling the abbey and in smuggling the stone back home, creating a huge outcry amongst the English establishment. The 1996 restoration was widely seen by the Scots as a transparently political gesture on the part of the Conservative government; a gesture that in the event did it little good at the next elections.

Why so much fuss? The Stone of Destiny is surrounded by myths and legends going back to the dawn of recorded time. It is supposed to have been the stone on which Jacob pillowed his head, which after travels in Spain ended up in Scotland and became the coronation throne for Scottish kings. On his expedition to conquer Scotland in 1296, Edward I of England seized on the stone as a symbol of nationhood – and made clear his opinion of the place of Scotland in the wider scheme of things by removing it to London.

The likelihood that the stone now at Edinburgh Castle is the real Stone of Destiny is remote. There are rumours that King Edward was palmed off with a fake in the first place and that the real stone remains buried, its whereabouts known only to its hereditary keepers. You will also hear that during the stone's 'outing' in 1950, there was a roaring trade in copies, with no guarantee that the correct one went back to Westminster.

Whatever the case, the stone is one of those objects that carries a curious, symbolic charge. As such, it has its place in the history of Scotland.

Gladstone's Land (Lawnmarket)

✓ *Good historical recreation*
✓ *Ornate furnishings and fittings*

In the late seventeenth century, this house was owned by the prosperous merchant Thomas Gledstanes, and it has been kitted out by the National Trust to show what life at that time must have been like for Edinburgh's wealthy classes. Heavy oak furniture is ranged under a beautiful painted ceiling. Only the pig which might once have been kept under the front stairs is missing *[NTS; Apr to Oct, Mon–Sat, 10–5, Sun, 12–5;* ☎ *0131-226 5856;* ⚲ *via www.nts.org.uk].*

Museum of Childhood (High Street)

✓ *Excellent collection of childhood memorabilia*
✓ *Fun for families*

Founded in 1955 by Joseph Murray, a man who claimed that children were tolerable only after their baths and on their way to bed, this was the first museum of childhood in the world. The collection of toys, games, clothes, dolls' houses, teddy bears, toy soldiers and slot machines must be among the finest anywhere. Much of the material dates from the early years of last century, but there are older and newer toys as well. Many of the automata are still in working order, and the ancient house resounds with tinny music and other curious noises. It is a good place for both adults and children; the serious side is diluted by cryptic or amusing captions. The rooms are not that large, and the museum can be a bit of a squash at times. *[Mon–Sat 10–5, Sun (Jul, Aug and Sept) 12–5;* ☎ *0131-529 4142;* ⚲ *via www.edinburgh.org]*

National Museum of Scotland (Chambers Street)

✓ *Bright, modern museum*
✓ *Well-laid-out introduction to Scotland's past*
✓ *Good facilities*

Opened just in time for the new millennium, this is the long-awaited replacement for the fusty old historical and archaeological museum in Queen Street.

The building – light, airy and with intriguing design features throughout, is an undoubted success, especially in the way in which display areas have been interlinked, and the boldness with which works of art have been incorporated. The way in which the collections have been displayed makes the history instantly accessible too. Five themed areas split Scotland's past into manageable chunks, of which the sections entitled 'Early People' and 'The Kingdom of the Scots' have the most beautiful and precious objects. These include Celtic jewellery, the Monymusk reliquary, which may have held the bones of St Columba, some of the Lewis chessmen, and the silver of the Trapprain Treasure.

For a quick or not-so-quick introduction to Scotland's history, the museum is excellent, and a definite starting-point if you are travelling the rest of the country. The layout makes it more difficult to track down a particular object you may have heard about or seen reproductions of elsewhere – for this is very much a representative, not a comprehensive, display.

Information services are well up to standard, with many guided tours on different themes, audio headsets and a good information desk. A shop, café and classy rooftop restaurant round the place off. *[Mon–Sat 10–5, Tue 10–8, Sun 12–5;* ☎ *0131-247 4422/2429;* 🖰 *via www.nms.ac.uk]*

Outlook Tower (Castlehill)

✓ *Simple but effective visual show*
✓ *Exhibition of optical effects*

The camera obscura housed on the roof of this seventeenth-century house is one of Edinburgh's oldest tourist attractions, and still one of the best. A periscope and a sequence of mirrors project an image of the city outside on to a white table. This is the ancestor of today's webcam, with the difference that by stretching over the table, you can get buses to run up your arm. The building also houses displays of optical instruments – notably holographs, but the camera obscura is much the best part. *[Nov to Mar, daily 10–5; Apr to Oct, daily 9.30–6; July and Aug, daily 9.30–7 or 7.30 (10 weekends);* ☎ *0131-226 3709;* 🖰 *www.brightbytes.com/cosite/2edinb.html]*

Palace of Holyroodhouse

✓ *Rich historical background*
✓ *Recommended for Mary Queen of Scots fans*
✗ *Rather tedious staterooms*

Like Edinburgh Castle, the Queen's official Edinburgh residence is high on the list of 'necessary' sights for visitors. As palaces go, however, this one is a little disappointing, for the formal staterooms are hardly magnificent, despite the wonderful plaster ceilings, and there is an unlived-in feel to it – perhaps due to the fact that Holyrood was more or less neglected by British monarchs between James VI and Victoria. But its role in Scottish history and its links with Mary Queen of Scots still make a visit recommended.

The original palace gradually grew out of the lodging house at Holyrood Abbey, which the Scottish kings came to prefer to the draughty confines of the castle. Most of it was demolished when Holyrood was rebuilt for Charles II between 1671 and 1679, leaving one of the old towers intact, and this is the most interesting part of the visit. Here Mary Queen of Scots had her apartments, and here she witnessed the murder of her secretary, Rizzio, by a hostile group of nobles including her husband, Darnley. Examples of Mary's needlework are on display, as is the lovely Lennox jewel, and the painted ceiling of the outer chamber is magnificent.

Elsewhere in the palace, the Great Gallery contains Holyrood's greatest folly: the 89 portraits (originally 111) of Scottish kings painted by the Dutch painter, Jacob de Wet, in 1684. Each king possesses the prominent nose owned by Charles II – a quick way of proving the royal descent.

The high point of the seventeenth-century architecture is the central courtyard, where the harmonious proportions of the facades in Palladian style show the beginnings of the Classical idea in Scotland. *[Apr to Oct, Mon–Sat 9.30–5.15, Sun 9.30–4; Nov to Mar, daily 9.30–3.45; ☎ 0131-556 7371, recorded information ☎ 0131-556 1096; ⬤ via www.royalresidences.com]*

Royal Museum of Scotland

✓ *Vast and diverse collection*

The High Victorian architecture of this 1861 institution dovetails well with its new sister, the National Museum next door (there is an internal link between the two). The heavy grandeur of the exterior gives no hint of the bright glass-and-iron interior, built in imitation of the Crystal Palace. The collection is huge and eclectic, with sculpture from classical and Mesopotamian civilisations, costumes, jewellery, natural history and a totem pole. The best, and least conventional, part is the Power Room, which celebrates the Scottish engineering tradition, both through full-scale examples – such as the early steam engine – and through working models. A very much more traditional museum than the National Museum, this is nevertheless an excellent spot in which to while away a wet hour. *[All year, Mon–Sat 10–5, Sun 12–5;* ☎ *0131-225 7534;* 🖥 *via www.nms.ac.uk]*

The Scottish Enlightenment

Scots are capable of waxing fairly tedious about the disproportionate number of men of genius, especially inventors, that the nation has produced, but the period known as the Scottish Enlightenment, when Scotland led Europe in ideas, is widely recognised as extraordinary. What provoked the sudden upsurge in Scottish intellectual and artistic life between 1760 and 1790 is a matter for social historians, but the result was a gathering of minds in clubs, howffs and later at New Town dinner parties, where arguments could be thrashed out and discoveries communicated. The men of the Enlightenment were humane, moderate, curious, rational and above all enjoyed conversation and the society of others.

Chief among them was the philosopher David Hume, whose religious scepticism shocked many of his contemporaries, but whose ideas, particularly about causation, had, and have, enormous influence. Adam Smith, whose *Wealth of Nations* is the cornerstone of modern economics, was his friend. Then there was James Hutton, whose *Theory of the Earth* first proposed continuous erosion and uplift as the

The next best sights

Canongate Tolbooth

The lower end of the Royal Mile was once in the separate burgh of Canongate, and when the Edinburgh tolbooth was demolished, this one remained. The building, with its curious Germanic tower and turrets, dates from 1591; the clock, which looks as if it had just sprung from the front wall, like a cuckoo, is from 1884. Inside, the main attraction is an audio-visual exhibition called 'The People's Story'. It describes the everyday lives of Edinburgh people in the eighteenth and nineteenth centuries and, while a bit thin on exhibits and rather too worthily educational, it is a good counterbalance to the historical glamour of the Castle and Holyrood. *[Mon–Sat 10–5, Sun 2–5;* ☎ *0131-529 4057; via* 🖳 *www.edinburgh.gov.uk]*

mechanism by which the Earth's surface was under constant change, and Joseph Black, who discovered carbon dioxide. The interests of Lord Kames and Lord Monboddo extended beyond the law into linguistics, philosophy and history. The Adam family, the most famous architects of their age, Allan Ramsay and Henry Raeburn among the portrait painters and Robert Fergusson, whose vernacular poetry marked a new interest in Scots as a language, all lived during this period.

The 'second wave' of the Enlightenment came after the Napoleonic Wars, when, with figures such as Scott, Hogg, Cockburn and Jeffrey, and periodicals such as the *Edinburgh Review*, Edinburgh became a literary town par excellence. This pre-eminence was to last into the start of the Victorian period, when Edinburgh literary life went into a decline, with only Robert Louis Stevenson's affectionate and frustrated voice to give life to the city. Not until the 'Scottish Renaissance' of the 1930s, when writers such as Hugh MacDiarmid, Norman McCaig, Sidney Goodsir Smith and Robert Garioch started to reinject Edinburgh with political and literary life, was the Enlightenment to have any echo.

The Grassmarket

Immediately under the south face of the castle rock, the Grassmarket is most notorious as the site of Edinburgh's public executions until 1784. It used to be a haunt for Edinburgh's down-and-outs, as was the Cowgate, which runs darkly eastward, but most of the area has been smartened up, with some fashionable shops and pubs. One or two fascinating old shops inhabit West Bow, Victoria Street and Candlemaker Row which lead down to the Grassmarket. Look out for the one in Victoria Street selling every conceivable variety of brush.

The most notorious inhabitants of the Grassmarket were Burke and Hare, body-snatchers who turned to murder as a quick way of providing corpses for doctors to dissect. After Burke's execution, his skeleton was given to the Department of Anatomy at Edinburgh University, where it can still be seen. The duo feature in most of the city's 'ghost' tours – many of which depart from the High Street. [🖰 *via www. edinburgholdtown.org.uk]*

Greyfriars Churchyard

This was the setting for the signing of the National Covenant in 1638, when crowds gathered to sign for the right to worship in their own fashion. Memorials to many of Edinburgh's outstanding literary and scientific figures line the walls – sometimes rather neglected. This is also where Greyfriars' Bobby (see below) stood watch over his master's grave.

Huntly House (Canongate)

Edinburgh's local museum, a place full of curious relics from the city's past, is often ignored in favour of brasher attractions. Old-fashioned it may be, but it boasts Roman remains, some fine silverware, and the original Covenant of 1638 – a document which marked Scotland's determination not to have alien habits of worship imposed on the country by Charles I (see box on pages 156–7). *[Mon–Sat 10–5, Suns in Festival 2–5;* ☎ *0131-529 4143;* 🖰 *via www.edinburgh.gov.uk]*

John Knox House (High Street)

The oldest house on the Royal Mile (1490) looks suitably medieval as it juts out, slightly askew, into the High Street. The connection with Knox may be apocryphal, but it saved the house from demolition. The ground floor is a shop, but above it you will find a good painted ceiling and displays about the man who did more than anyone else to establish the Scottish Reformation. [*All year, Mon–Sat 10–5;* ☎ *0131-556 9579*]

Lady Stair's House (off Lawnmarket in Lady Stair's Close)

A literary museum to Robert Burns, Sir Walter Scott and Robert Louis Stevenson, and a useful place for anyone interested in those writers, with several curiosities on display. A trifle old-fashioned, and unlikely to interest children. [*via www.edinburgh.gov*]

Parliament House (High Street – Parliament Square)

Home of the Scottish Parliament from 1639 to 1707, this building is now the Court of Session – Edinburgh's legal heart. It is possible to visit the Parliament Hall, with its beautiful hammer-beam ceiling, during working hours. It is a sight which deserves to be better known. [*All year, Tue–Fri 10–4;* ☎ *0131-225 2595*]

St Cecilia's Hall (Cowgate)

An eighteenth-century music room, hidden away in the Cowgate and with restricted opening hours. It is not only a lovely room, but houses the Russell Collection of early keyboard instruments – comprehensive and fascinating. [*Wed 2–5, Sat 2–5;* ☎ *0131-650 2805;* *via www.music.ed.ac.uk/russell*]

St Giles' Cathedral (High Street)

The High Kirk of Edinburgh was only briefly a cathedral, but has kept the name. The church dates from the fifteenth century, but drastic restoration was found to be needed when

Edinburgh's old tolbooths and the small shops which surrounded the church were swept away in 1817. Unfortunately, the architect, William Burn, overdid things, leaving the bland exterior you see today. The tower, with its striking crown, is all that remains of the original beauty.

The interior is rather gloomy, though worth exploring to see the pre-Raphaelite stained glass and Sir Robert Lorimer's Chapel of the Thistle (1911), with an angel playing the bagpipes carved on the entrance arch. But the real interest of St Giles is historical. John Knox was minister here in the time of Mary Queen of Scots; here in 1637, Jenny Geddes flung her stool at the preacher in protest at the introduction of an anglicised prayer book – thus perhaps precipitating both the Scottish and English Civil Wars. Here, too, the scattered pieces of Montrose's body were buried after his rehabilitation at the Restoration. There is also a memorial to his enemy, the covenanting Marquess of Argyll, who lost his head at the same time. *[All year;* ☎ *0131-225 9442;* 🖱 *via www.scottishculture.about.com]*

Scotch Whisky Heritage Centre (Castlehill)

Only worth going to if you cannot visit a real distillery, the Centre nevertheless does a good, if superficial, job of introducing the history and techniques of whisky distilling in Scotland, mostly through a series of tableaux. The shop, with a very wide range of whiskies for sale, is worth seeing in its own right. *[Daily, 9.30–5.30;* ☎ *0131-220 0441;* 🖱 *www.whisky-heritage.co.uk]*

Talbot Rice Gallery

Inside the Adam-designed buildings of the Old College of Edinburgh University, this tiny and beautiful gallery, designed by William Henry Playfair, holds a superlative small collection of paintings and sculptures – many from the Low Countries of the seventeenth century. *[*☎ *0131-650 2211 for details of opening times;* 🖱 *www.trg.ed.ac.uk]*

Also in the area

Brodie's Close (Lawnmarket) This was the home of the infamous Deacon Brodie, respectable councillor by day and burglar by night, whose execution in 1788 was watched by huge crowds. His daytime trade as carpenter allowed him into the houses of his victims (and also to take wax impressions of their keys), while at night he and his contacts conducted their robberies. He took flight for Holland after trying to rob the Excise Office but foolishly wrote to his mistress on his journey, and this led to his capture. Brodie is supposed to have been the model for R. L. Stevenson's tale of Dr Jekyll and Mr Hyde. Opposite the close is a pub named after him.

Greyfriars' Bobby (George IV Bridge) A much-polished and photographed statue of a Skye Terrier commemorates the faithfulness of the dog who watched over his master's grave for 14 years. The memorial has become one of Edinburgh's most popular sights.

The Heart of Midlothian (High Street – Parliament Square) The heart-shaped pattern of cobbles in the street marks the position of Edinburgh's Old Tolbooth, which was built in 1466 and served as meeting chamber, law court and prison. It was demolished in 1817 (Walter Scott acquired the door for his home at Abbotsford). The opening of Scott's *The Heart of Midlothian* brings it back to life as it may have been.

Holyrood Sanctuary (Canongate) The circle of stones in the roadway at the foot of Canongate is where the Girth Cross once stood, marking the western boundary of the sanctuary of Holyrood Abbey. In a curious anachronism, this remained a sanctuary for debtors right up until 1880. Inside it they were safe from their creditors, and they were also allowed outside between Saturday and Sunday midnights. One of the most famous Abbey Lairds, as the debtors who sought shelter here were known, was Charles X of France, who abdicated in 1830, and was known in Edinburgh as Monsieur. The Edinburgh historian E.F. Catford relates how he used to go snipe-shooting on the slopes of Arthur's Seat, with the Edinburgh children pursuing him, crying, 'Frenchy, Frenchy, dinna shoot the spruggies' (sparrows).

James Court (Lawnmarket) Boswell and Dr Johnson stayed here before setting out on their famous tour to the Hebrides in 1773.

The Edinburgh Festival

For three weeks every August/September the character of Edinburgh changes radically as performers and audiences pour into the city. The first Edinburgh Festival was held in 1947. At a time when nearly every large city boasts an International Arts Festival, Edinburgh manages to hang on to its premier position as the world's largest.

The Edinburgh Festival is broadly divided in two. There are the 'official' events, with invited companies or performers, and the famous 'Fringe' where teeming hordes of amateur and professional performers compete frantically for audiences in about 180 different venues ranging from graveyards to galleries. In addition, separate film, television, book and jazz festivals also take place. A children's festival is held at Easter. Not to mention that perennial favourite, the Tattoo on the Castle Esplanade.

During the Festival, Edinburgh's normal respectability vanishes under a sea of leaflets. Weirdly be-costumed performers tout their events, grassy spaces fill with floodlights, student groups bed down in any spare space they can find. The Fringe has its own legends; the overnight discovery that is wafted like magic to London's West End is a less common phenomenon than the traditional performance to two old ladies and a tramp, but it has happened. Reviews in *The Scotsman* or the national papers are anxiously awaited, and there was fury when *The Scotsman* announced in 2000 that it was no longer going to review everything.

Mary King's Close (High Street – Parliament Square) In 1753, The Royal Exchange (now the city chambers) was built on top of one of Edinburgh's old closes. Mary King's Close had suffered severely in the plague of 1645 and was virtually deserted. You can go on a short but spooky tour [☎ *0131-557 6464]* of the underground remains. Look up 🐭 *via www.ebs.hw.ac.uk* for a detailed history and pictures.

For the first-time visitor, the Festival can be daunting. The best accommodation is booked months in advance, but if you arrive with no booking the Tourist Office can usually squeeze you in somewhere. Advance tickets for the big-name events of the official Festival, especially operas, sell out fast, and demand will be heavy for seats at any Fringe show that suddenly attracts attention. However, there is so much to choose from that it is unlikely you will be confined to an evening at home.

If you are an energetic Festival-goer you may visit exhibitions in the morning, take in one, or perhaps two, Fringe events in the afternoon, an official event in the evening, then as many more revues or late-night events as you have stamina for. A week at this pace and you will be suffering from severe culture shock, will have seen the inside of some very odd places and have sat through some very bizarre shows. You find out what is worth seeing and what is not by reading the reviews in *The Scotsman* or the London press, watching the round-ups and previews on television, and, best of all, by talking to people on buses, in pubs or in your hotel.

If you are serious about Festival-visiting, it is best if you order programmes around March/April from the Festival addresses which the Edinburgh Tourist Board (see page 16) can supply, and get your bookings (including accommodation) sent in plenty of time (postal bookings open from mid-April, telephone and counter bookings late in the month).

The Mercat Cross (High Street – Parliament Square) Edinburgh's Mercat Cross is a nineteenth-century recon- struction, with a few pieces of medieval stonework built in. The excuse for the demolition of the old cross in 1756 was that it held up the traffic, but there is a suspicion that it was destroyed because Bonnie Prince Charlie had his father proclaimed king here.

National Library of Scotland (George IV Bridge) One of the largest libraries in Britain is housed in an oppressive building just off the Royal Mile. The changing exhibitions of rare books and manuscripts should interest bibliophiles. *[All year, exhibi- tions summer only Mon–Sat 10–5, Sun 2–5;* ☎ *0131-226 4531;* ✆ *www.nls.ac.uk]*

The Scottish Parliament (Abbey Strand) At the time of writing, the site of the new Scottish Parliament building is still a hole in the ground, but it is already controversial, over- budget and running late. The design, by the Spanish architect Enric Miralles, promises to be striking. Once up and running, the Parliament is likely to be visitor-friendly, so may be worth a look. ✆ *www.scottish.parliament.gov.uk* has more about the building and what the parliament is up to.

Suggested excursion

Holyrood Park and Arthur's Seat Right behind the Palace of Holyrood, a remarkably wild stretch of country, culminating in the peak of Arthur's Seat, is a popular place for outdoor recre- ation. You can drive through the park, but walking is better. Climb Arthur's Seat from Dunsapie Loch for splendid, windy views, or walk through to Duddingston Village, an unspoiled enclave on the far side of the park, with a nature reserve and one of Edinburgh's oldest pubs. See ✆ *www.geowalks.demon.co.uk* for details of guided geological walks.

THE NEW TOWN

The New Town of Edinburgh was the brainchild of George Drummond. His vision was of a new residential town to replace the insanitary squalor of the old, rising on the fields beyond the Nor' Loch. An architectural competition was launched, and in 1767, a year after Drummond's death, the winning plan was chosen. It was by a virtually unknown architect, James Craig, and was simple but precise: two elegant squares linked by the three parallel streets now known as Princes Street, George Street and Queen Street.

At first, no one seems to have wanted to be the first to move out of the familiar clutter of the Old Town, but the new development rapidly became fashionable. The unity of design (which can still be seen beneath the Victorian and modern intrusions) was imposed by the City council, and reaches its climax in the perfection of Charlotte Square (1791) – Robert Adam's finest achievement. One of Edinburgh's best features, the open valley between Princes Street and the Old Town, was saved as open space, but only after an extensive lawsuit.

New development soon started on the hill sloping down to the Forth beyond Queen Street, where a second New Town, planned on the same lines as the first, but with more uniformity of frontage, sprang up between the grand enclosures of Royal Circus and Drummond Place. On the Moray Estate, immediately to the north of Charlotte Square, the grid-plan gave way to a series of linked circuses with some of the grandest architecture yet. Splendid terraces, designed for the wealthiest of Edinburgh's citizens, girdled the lower slopes of Calton Hill, while further building went on to the west of Charlotte Square – the area now known as the West End.

The result of this frenzied, often speculative, building is an expanse of Georgian architecture unrivalled in Britain. The New Town is a treasure trove for lovers of architectural detail, for within the streets, terraces and squares is an endless variation of design and ornament. It is a pleasure to walk around even if you have little knowledge of the period, for much of the New Town remains residential, much has been well

restored, and there are views, shops, pubs and constantly interesting corners to enjoy.

Top sights

The Georgian House (7 Charlotte Square)

✓ *Excellent historical recreation*
✓ *Ideal for Jane Austen lovers*

The National Trust for Scotland's figurehead property is a
recreation of gracious living sufficiently infectious to make
you long to have been born 200 years ago. The drawing room
stands ready for a formal evening, while in the comfortable
parlour you may catch an imagined whiff of snuff or hear
long-vanished voices debating the latest scathing piece from
the *Edinburgh Review*. The dining room is filled with gleaming
silver and heavy fabrics. It is the kitchen and adjacent china
cupboard and wine cellar, however, which are the most fascinating. Here you can sense the hectic activity around the open
range and imagine the huge numbers of copper utensils being
clattered from table top to scullery, while the bells in the
passage jangled a summons to attend on the drawing room.
There is a good scene-setting audiovisual programme to go
with the house, and the guides are very knowledgeable. *[NTS;
Apr to Oct, Mon–Sat 10–5, Sun 2–5;* ☎ *0131-226 3318;* ✒
via www.nts.org.uk]

National Gallery of Scotland (The Mound)

✓ *First-class collection of Old Masters*
✓ *Especially good Impressionists*
✓ *Imaginative layout*

The National Gallery has probably the finest collection of
paintings outside London, with few periods or styles left
unrepresented. The pictures in the main building are hung in a
series of octagonal rooms, and the claret-and-green colour
scheme is a copy of Playfair's original 1859 design. On the
upper floor is the excellent collection of French

Impressionists, and downstairs, in a modern extension, the collection of Scottish painting. Lighting is on the dim side throughout, and the hanging, designed to be like a garden of views, shapes and colours, is fascinating, but will not please everyone.

Of the early paintings, the *Madonna and Child* by Verrocchio is the undoubted star. Five Titians compete for attention, the erotic *Diana and Actaeon* prominent among them. El Greco's *The Saviour of the World* gazes, icon-like, from the wall. Goya's *El Medico* in his vermilion cloak warms his hands over a brazier. Rubens' *Feast of Herod* shows John the Baptist's head being uncovered in front of the nauseated Herod, while all the guests scramble for a look. Gainsborough's *The Hon. Mrs Graham* is a perceptive study of haughty beauty. Among the later works, Courbet's *Wave* is wonderful, Van Gogh is represented by twisted olive trees, Monet by frosted haystacks, and Cézanne by Mont St Victoire.

The Scottish collection is cramped in a room resembling a hotel foyer, but has some fine portraits. Many are by Henry Raeburn, including his well-known *Rev Robert Walker Skating on Duddingston Loch*, and by Allan Ramsay. William McTaggart's impressionistic landscapes form a radical contrast to the biscuit-tin fairy scene of Noel Paton's *The Quarrel of Oberon and Titania*. David Wilkie is represented by some of his highly coloured scenes of Scottish rural life. *[Mon–Sat 10–5, Sun 12–5;* ☎ *0131-624 6332;* ◗ *via www.natgalscot.ac.uk]*

The Royal Botanic Garden

✓ *Great for plant lovers and gardeners*
✓ *Good place to take a break from sightseeing*
✓ *Outlet for energetic children*

This is one of the best botanic gardens anywhere, and on a freezing day its sequence of bright, warm and modern plant houses, unfortunately dubbed 'The Glasshouse Experience' can be greatly appreciated. The collections of ericaceous plants from the tropics are particularly unusual, and the collections of rhododendrons and azaleas are renowned. In addition, a splendid peat garden, arboretum and newly-replanted rockery are fascinating. Above all, the garden's links with China are stressed, symbolised by the recent planting of an entire area with Chinese species. In no sense is this a formal garden. It is a big, wooded area, easy to lose yourself in, and ideal for a picnic, or as a space in which children can run unfettered. *[Winter 10–4; spring and autumn 10–6; summer (May to Aug) 10–8;* ☎ *0131-552 7171;* 🖱 *www.rbge.org.uk]*

The Scott Monument (Princes Street)

✓ *Great views of the city*

✓ *Suits adventurous children*

✗ *A head for heights is useful*

✗ *Steep, winding stairs. Can be a squeeze*

Few, if any, other writers have a memorial like this. A huge Gothic spire, pinnacled, buttressed and loaded with crockets, finials and statuettes, rises 200 feet and 6 inches above Princes Street Gardens, and acts as a canopy for a statue of Sir Walter Scott, seated with a book in his hand and his dog by his side. The monument, designed by a previously unknown draughtsman, George Kemp, and inaugurated in 1846, was funded by private subscription, most of it raised in Edinburgh.

The monument is said to draw much of its inspiration from Melrose Abbey, Scott's favourite Gothic building. Its niches are filled with statuettes of Scottish poets and characters from Scott's works. At the level of the first gallery there is a small museum. Climbing the 287 steps of the narrow spiral stair to the top is an exercise in persistence, rewarded by views of central Edinburgh which beat even those from the castle walls. Recent restoration of the stonework has left the monument looking curiously blotchy. *[Mon–Sat 9–8 (6 in May), Sun 10–6;* ☎ *0131-529 4068;* 🖱 *via www.scottishculture.about.com]*

Scottish National Gallery of Modern Art and Dean Gallery

✓ *Excellent representative collection*

✓ *Fine surrealist collection*

✓ *Good gallery shop*

Behind the neoclassical façade of John Watson's school is

housed the National Gallery's modern art collection. Displays frequently change, but most of the main periods of twentieth-century painting are represented. Although the collection was only begun in 1960, it boasts Picasso, Nash, a selection of Cubist paintings, and works by Hockney, Leger, Mondrian and others. The Scottish Colourists are well represented.

The Leith-born sculptor, Eduardo Paolozzi is featured in the lovely 1833 building of the Dean Gallery across the road. His giant *Vulcan* dominates the entrance, and a mock-up of his London studio (fascinating) is installed in one of the rooms behind. The Dean Gallery is also the place to come for the Surrealists, with Dali, Ernst and Man Ray among others. *[Mon–Sat 10–5, Sun 12–5;* ☎ *0131-624 6506;* 🖱 *via www.natgalscot.ac.uk]*

Scottish National Portrait Gallery

✓ *Recommended for everyone interested in Scottish history*
✓ *Lovely turn-of-the-century interior*
✓ *Good gallery shop and café*

With the departure of the archeological and historical collections, the Portrait Gallery has expanded and made itself more user-friendly. It is housed in a mock-Venetian palace at the Eastern end of Queen Street. Within the red-sandstone building, the stunning interior is packed with murals, including a Byzantine-style frieze of faces from Scotland's past. This is the place to come if you are at all interested in Scottish history, for the faces which scowl or beam from the walls include most of the main players from late medieval times onwards. A procession of mournful Stewart monarchs, nobles, churchmen and great thinkers and writers share the wall space. Here you will find Scott, Burns, Hogg, Boswell and Hume, along with Mary Queen of Scots, Montrose and Dundee. The collection moves well into the twentieth century, keeping up to date with the great and the good of Scottish life. An excellent shop and café add enjoyment. *[Mon–Sat 10–5, Sun 12–5;* ☎ *0131-624 6332;* 🖱 *via www.natgalscot.ac.uk]*

Exploring the New Town

Most of the New Town is built on the steep slope of the ridge which drops to the valley of the Water of Leith. The least painful way to explore it is to walk parallel to the slope where possible and use buses to get back up the hill. Visit the areas in the order in which they are listed as this way you visit the most important parts first and are saved too much of an uphill walk.

Princes Street Gardens, George Street, Charlotte Square

✓ *Fairly level walking*

✓ *Designer shops*

✓ *Charlotte Square architecture*

These streets form the heart of the original New Town. Princes Street retains little that is original and is full of chain stores. The open space of Princes Street Gardens is a more attractive route and boasts a floral clock, an outdoor theatre with summer concerts, plenty of benches and space for picnics.

George Street was designed to be the most important thoroughfare of the New Town. In spite of the parked cars it remains impressive, with end-to-end vistas, statues at road intersections, and enough unaltered buildings at least to feel Georgian. Smart shops are replacing the financial institutions as they move out to the new buildings of the West End, but some old ones remain, such as Aitken & Niven for tweeds, Hamilton and Inches for jewellery and Dickson and Macnaughton (in Frederick Street) for fishing tackle and outdoor wear.

At the west end of George Street, Charlotte Square is the New Town's *pièce de résistance*. It was designed by Robert Adam in 1791, and remains unspoiled. The old domed church, which is now West Register House, has changing displays of important documents from Scotland's past.

Heriot Row, Dundas Street, Great King Street

✓ *Architecture*

✓ *Art galleries, antique shops and eating places*

These streets and the smaller Northumberland and Cumberland Streets contain the best architecture of the so-called Second New Town. Heriot Row, fronted by gardens, has a wonderful unity of style. Great King Street is grander, but very harmonious. In Dundas Street and nearby Howe Street several galleries and antique shops offer a break from the architecture.

Around Moray Place

✓ *Outstanding architecture*

In 1822 Gillespie Graham drew up plans for the two circuses and crescent, which for many are the most impressive sections of the New Town. Every last detail, down to the railings, is part of the design; the overall harmony is remarkable, even if there is a hint of the bombastic. In the 12-sided Moray Place the buildings are at their grandest, with Tuscan porticos gazing on the central garden. The backs of many of the houses hang sheer above the Water of Leith. At the western end of this area, Queensferry Street leads down to the Dean Bridge and to further grand architecture of a later date in Belgrave Crescent and Eton Terrace.

Dean Village to Stockbridge

✓ *Waterside walk, mostly away from traffic*
✓ *Antique and craft shops in Stockbridge*

Telford's Dean Bridge carries traffic high above the Water of Leith where it runs through a gorge to the sea. Dean Village, at the bottom of this gorge, was once important for its mills, but is now a curious enclave of old (and much-restored) houses tucked away in the heart of the city. From Dean Village, it is possible to follow the river downstream, at the bottom of the gardens laid out to complement the dignified residences high above. This makes an attractive stroll, well away from the traffic. Detour to see the perfect architecture of Ann Street on the left bank. St Stephen Street on the right bank has long been the hang-out of antique and craft shops. The old village of Stockbridge has Raeburn Place as its centre – with a good mix of shops. Saxe-Coburg Place is another beautiful (though unfinished) late Georgian square. From this area, it is a relatively short walk to the Royal Botanic Garden. Numerous buses will take you back to the city centre.

Calton Hill

✓ *Views*

✓ *Curiosities*

✗ *Steep walk*

The hill which rises steeply above the east end of Princes Street is the place where Edinburgh's obsession with Athens is

---

The Union of the Parliaments, 1707

'I had not been Long There but I heard a Great Noise and looking Out Saw a Terrible Multitude Come up the High Street with a drum at the head of them shouting and swearing and Cryeing Out all Scotland would stand together, No Union, No Union, English Dogs and the like.' (Daniel Defoe 1660–1731)

It is ironic that the union of the Scottish and English parliaments came at a time when the two nations were closer to war than had been the case for almost half a century.

Under King William, in the period between 1689 and 1702, relations between Scotland and England had been uneasy, partly because of William's vendetta against France – Scotland's oldest ally – but mostly as a result of the Darien venture. Frustrated (by English interests) in setting up Scottish trading companies to the East Indies or to Africa, the Scots had turned their minds to establishing a colony of their own, on the Darien peninsula of Central America. It was an ill-starred scheme from the first, but active English hostility was held by many to be accountable for the failure of the colony. Scotland was bankrupt, for everyone with money to spare had invested in the scheme. A series of confrontational Acts of Parliament in England and Scotland over who should succeed to the British Crown worsened the situation, and in 1705 the Scots hanged a blatantly innocent English captain for alleged piracy.

---

most visible. The fragmentary Doric temple which you see from Princes Street is the National Monument, started in 1822 as a copy of the Parthenon in Athens, but never finished. A more successful classical monument is the little circular memorial to Dougald Stewart. The Nelson Monument (1807), a miniature battlemented tower, stands in stark contrast to the classical work around it. Calton Hill provides one of the best panoramas of Edinburgh, but after dark it becomes inhabited by some pretty strange types and is probably best avoided.

Yet, despite all this, active moves to create the Union were taking place. Under William's successor, Queen Anne, 31 commissioners from each country were appointed, and they managed to draft a treaty within nine weeks. In October 1706 the debate started in the Scottish Parliament to massive public hostility. There were riots in Glasgow and Dumfries, and the Lord High Commissioner's coach was stoned in Edinburgh. But the Scots had little choice: union offered freedom of trade and monetary compensation; independence meant probable bankruptcy and possible civil war. The treaty was approved by 110 votes to 69. The Scottish Parliament adjourned on 25 March 1707 and did not meet again for almost three centuries.

The Act of Union preserved the Scottish church, the law, the judicial system, the rights of the Scottish nobles and the privileges of the Scottish burghs. It approved the Hanoverian succession and gave the English the security they needed in facing the French. The Scots were to receive £400,000 'Equivalent' to reimburse the Darien investors and to provide a boost for industry. Whether it was a fair settlement, whether Scottish parliamentarians were bribed, whether the English have broken the terms of the treaty, and whether Scotland could have survived as an independent nation are still matters for (often heated) debate.

FURTHER AFIELD

If you are weary of the bustle of central Edinburgh, the following sights and outlying districts have much to offer.

The city has expanded over the years to take in several small settlements on its outskirts. The following three mostly retain an unspoiled core, and make good destinations for days out from the city centre.

Cramond

Cramond, at the mouth of the River Almond on the western outskirts of Edinburgh, is where the Romans based themselves on this bank of the Forth. In 1996 a Roman sculpture of a lioness was dredged out of the river (it is now in the Museum of Scotland). Cramond is a tranquil place, popular for weekend excursions from the city, with small yachts and motor boats lying off the river mouth. Walk up the River Almond to see the seventeenth-century bridge at the spot where James V was rescued from footpads by the local miller. If beachside walks are more to your taste than leafy riverbanks, go across the small ferry to a fine stretch of shoreline leading westwards towards Dalmeny.

Leith

Leith was and is Edinburgh's port, and has seen almost as much history as the city behind it. Mary Queen of Scots returned to her kingdom here on a melancholy day of mist, and later George IV landed to cheering crowds. Fiercely independent of Edinburgh for years, Leith was eventually forced to capitulate for administrative convenience in 1920. The port has been much polished up of late and many of its old buildings have been restored, though heavy lorries still make strolling through it something of a hazard. The area called the Shore, where the river makes its final curve to the sea, is the most pleasantly nautical part, and there are thriving lunchtime bars and bistros, many serving workers from the vast modern headquarters of the Scottish Office – a building worthy of a quick look.

Queensferry

There was a ferry over the Forth as long ago as 1129, but now the old village which grew up round it is completely over-shadowed by the two great Forth Bridges which sweep by it. However, the village, with its lovely old terraced houses and small museum, is still worth wandering round, while readers of Robert Louis Stevenson's *Kidnapped* will want to visit the Hawes Inn, from where David Balfour was lured aboard the brig *Covenant*.

Top sight

The Royal Yacht *Britannia* (Leith Docks)

✓ *Royal nostalgia*

Leith is the last resting-place of the former Royal Yacht, *Britannia* (launched on the Clyde in 1953), and she is now the chief reason why visitors venture down to Leith. A purpose-built exhibition centre, of which the Royal Launch is the centrepiece, provides the background to the life of the ship, with film footage of *Britannia* in various parts of the globe and touch-screens to fill in the factual details. The ship itself, with its 1950s interior design largely uneclipsed by later fashions, is toured with the aid of an audio-guide, which introduces you to the Royal apartments, the Queen's and the Duke's bedrooms, the dining room laid out for a state banquet, and the sparkling engine rooms. Along the way are intriguing titbits about royal life on board.

Space is limited, and groups of visitors depart at 20-minute intervals; on popular weekends you may have to wait some time. [*Daily, 10–4.30;* ☎ *0131-555 5566;* 🖱 *www.royalyachtbritannia.co.uk]*

The next best sights

Craigmillar Castle (Craigmillar, south of Duddingston)

Now almost surrounded by housing estates, this massive fortress is where the assassination of Mary Queen of Scots' husband, Darnley, was planned. Much of the old ruin remains; two successive curtain walls rise in front of a fourteenth-century tower house, with later ranges added to it. *[HS standard times;* ☎ *0131-661 4445;* ✆ *via www.historic-scotland.gov.uk]*

Dalmeny House (Dalmeny, west of Cramond)

Home of the Earl of Rosebery and one of a sequence of stately homes along the south bank of the Forth, this neo-Gothic house (1815) has splendid views over the Firth. The collection inside, including the library, owes much to the fifth Earl, who married the richest heiress in England, became Prime Minister in 1894 and had three Derby winners into the bargain. There is much fine eighteenth-century French furniture and some very unusual tapestries designed by Goya. The fifth Earl was an expert on Napoleon, and his collection of relics of the Emperor is also here. Dalmeny is very much a family home, and all these treasures are offered for admiration in a setting which could hardly be less like a stuffy museum. *[July and Aug, Sun, Mon and Tue 2–5;* ☎ *0131-331 1888;* ✆ *www.dalmeny.co.uk]*

Edinburgh Zoo (Corstorphine)

Edinburgh Zoo is built on the slope of Corstophine Hill to the west of the city centre. Its site is one of its best aspects, with good views over the city. The zoo has an especially endearing collection of penguins, and a well-designed pool to go with them. The Penguin Parade, when the birds exercise by shuffling off down the path, is always popular. *[Apr to Sept, 9–6; Mar and Oct, 9–5; Nov to Mar, 9–4.30;* ☎ *0131-334 9171;* ✆ *www.edinburghzoo.com]*

The Forth Bridges (Queensferry)

Queensferry is also the best spot from which to admire the Rail Bridge, which celebrated its centenary in 1990 and remains one of the finest cantilever structures in the world. The road suspension bridge, opened in 1964, complements it well. Try the pedestrian walkway over the Road Bridge for splendid views over the Forth, though the swaying sensation as lorries rumble past can be alarming. The bridge is increasingly congested, and there is talk of a third crossing being needed.

Lauriston Castle (Cramond Road South)

An old tower-house with a mansion added to it in 1827, this is a curious place, well worth seeking out among the quiet housing estates near Cramond. It was given to the city in 1926 by its last owners, the Reids, who came from families of cabinet-makers and sanitary engineers. The result is some fine panelling and remarkable plumbing, but Lauriston is especially interesting for the extraordinary collection of objects that the Reids assembled. They seem to have collected what they liked without regard for value or antiquity – huge numbers of commodes, masses of prints (some execrable), and a collection of wool mosaic pictures.

Part of the charm of Lauriston lies in the enthusiasm of the guides, who genuinely love the house and have time to spare. *[Apr to Oct, daily 11–5 (closed Fri and lunch hour); Nov to Mar, Sat and Sun, 2–4; Grounds: 9–dusk;* ☎ *0131-336 2060;* ✆ *via www.edinburgh.gov.uk]*

Suggested excursions

Inchcolm Abbey Boats run from Queensferry to the island of Inchcolm close to the Fife coast from Easter to the end of September *[*☎ *0131-331 4857 for details]*. The thirteenth-century abbey with its well-preserved monastic buildings is the goal of this trip, made all the better for its isolated setting among the busy shipping lanes of the Forth.

Water of Leith Walkway The steep valley where the river runs through the south-western suburbs of Edinburgh used to be populated by mills and other industry. With their demise, a walkway is becoming established along the valley. It makes a pleasing leafy stroll, with the old village of Colinton as a good starting point, and a visitor centre downstream to end up at. ✆ *www.waterofleith.edin.org* has further details.

Hogmanay

The idea of an Edinburgh festival to celebrate New Year (and bring in lots of visitors in the depths of winter) is a recent one. It seems to be going from strength to strength, helped on by the Millennium. A programme of events keeps visitors entertained for the days preceding Hogmanay, and fireworks, a funfair, street theatre and traditional celebrations at the Tron Kirk see in the New Year (street passes must be obtained in advance). New Year's Day, by contrast, can be a sobering and chilly experience, as many shops and businesses are shut. Some account is being taken of this, however, and there are usually further happenings, designed to ease you back into the real world. See pages 506–8 for more information about celebrations throughout Scotland.

WHERE TO STAY

£ – under £70 per room per night, incl. VAT

££ – £70 to £110 per room per night incl. VAT

£££ – over £110 per room per night incl. VAT

19 St Bernard's Crescent

19 St Bernard's Crescent, Edinburgh EH4 1NR

☎/📠 0131-332 6162

Magnificent bed and breakfast establishment, with a grand entrance and opulent rooms with eighteenth-century furnishings. The main bedroom has a William IV four-poster, another an old sleigh bed; both have thoughtful touches. Bathrooms are practical and well-equipped.

£ *Closed Nov to Mar*

Ashlyn Guest House

42 Inverleith Row, Edinburgh EH3 5PY

☎/📠 0131-552 2954

Fine Georgian house attractively decorated in period style, by the Botanical Gardens. 'Spotless and very comfortable' bedrooms and an elegant lounge. Breakfasts include Ayrshire bacon and freshly baked scones.

£ *All year exc Christmas*

The Bonham

35 Drumsheugh Gardens, Edinburgh EH3 7RN

☎ 0131-226 6050

📠 0131-226 6080

🖥 www.thebonham.com

Ultra-modern styling in a Victorian townhouse. Good-sized, well-thought-out bedrooms and powerful showers. The restaurant, two rooms knocked together, is contemporary and light, as is the food. Lunchtime and supper menus are health-conscious.

£££ *Closed 3–7 Jan (See Where to Eat)*

Bonnington Guest House

202 Ferry Road, Edinburgh EH6 4NW
☎ 0131-554 7610
Handsomely furnished listed Victorian guesthouse, offering a warm welcome and helpful advice on Edinburgh. The four bedrooms are comfortably furnished. Superb breakfasts are served and special diets can be catered for.

£ *All year exc Christmas*

Hopetoun Guest House

15 Mayfield Road, Edinburgh EH9 2NG
☎ 0131-667 7691
🖷 0131-466 1691
⌨ *members.aol.com/hopetoun*
Small terraced former manse near the university. Rooms are good-sized and comfortable; two look out over Arthur's Seat. Breakfasts are 'excellent, with a wide variety of choices', and the atmosphere is friendly and warm.

£ *All year exc Christmas*

The Howard

34 Great King Street, Edinburgh
EH3 6QH
☎ 0131-557 3500
🖷 0131-557 6515
⌨ *www.thehoward.com*
Discreet yet informal central hotel, comprising three Georgian townhouses. The interior is as elegant as the façade, and bedrooms are comfortable and refined. The contemporary '36'

restaurant next door is owned by the hotel.

£££ *Closed 22–27 Dec and 7 Jan*

Malmaison Edinburgh

1 Tower Place, Leith, Edinburgh EH6 7DB
☎ 0131-468 5000
🖷 0131-468 5002
Atmosphere and immaculate standards at this stylish hotel. Well-kept, comfortable bedrooms have imaginative touches. Visit the brasserie for straightforward and tasty meals, or the lively café-bar. Prices for dinner are reasonable, but the charge for breakfast is less so.

£££ *All year*

Sonas Guest House

3 East Mayfield, Edinburgh EH9 1SD
☎ 0131-667 2781
🖷 0131-667 0454
Pleasant Victorian townhouse a mile from Princes Street. The eight smallish bedrooms are light, bright and attractive. Traditional Scottish breakfasts with a vegetarian choice are served in the dining/sitting room. Evening meals are not offered but restaurants are nearby.

£ *All year exc Christmas*

Town House

65 Gilmore Place, Edinburgh EH3 9NU
☎ 0131-229 1985
⌨ *www.thetownhouse.com*
This Victorian manse has kept its period features while offering modern amenities. As well as a full Scottish breakfast, traditional porridge, kippers and smoked salmon fishcakes are available.

£ *All year exc Christmas*

Turret Guest House

8 Kilmaurs Terrace, Edinburgh
EH16 5DR

☎ 0131-667 6704

📠 0131-668 1368

🖥 www.turret.clara.net

The Turret is a listed building, a baronial stone terrace near the city centre. An impressive wooden staircase with minstrel's gallery sets the scene for attractive bedrooms. Hearty breakfasts include traditional full Scottish, salmon cakes, kippers and vegetarian options.

£ *All year exc Christmas*

WHERE TO EAT

Atrium

10 Cambridge Street, Edinburgh
EH1 2ED

☎ 0131-228 8882

📠 0131-228 8808

Smart and contemporary restaurant, rather dimly lit. Set-price menus offer a couple of choices per course, with a separate à la carte option.
Mediterranean-influenced dishes include fish and chicken, and are richly flavoured. Wines are well chosen but rather expensive.

Mon–Fri L 12–2, Mon–Sat D 6.30–10 (Mon–Sat 12–2.30 and 6.30–10.30 during Festival); closed D 24 Dec to 3 Jan

Balmoral, Number One

1 Princes Street, Edinburgh EH2 2EQ

☎ 0131-557 6727

📠 0131-557 8740

Spacious red-laquered and mirrored dining-room housed in the grand hotel by Waverley station. A pricey and largely traditional menu has contemporary touches. The three-course Market Menu is more affordable, featuring a roast and impressive desserts.

Mon–Fri L 12–2, all week D 7–10 (10.30 Fri and Sat)

Blue Bar Café

Cambridge Street, Edinburgh EH1 2ED

☎ 0131-221 1222

📠 0131-228 8808

Situated above the Atrium *(see above)*, with a more affordable menu. Ingredients are impeccable, with a range of unusual house specials. Main courses are robust, and contemporary nursery puddings complete the menu. Short but well-selected wine list.

Open Mon–Sat 12–3 and 6–11 (open Sun during Festival)

The Bonham

35 Drumsheugh Gardens, Edinburgh
EH3 7RN

☎ 0131-623 9319

📠 0131-226 6080

🖥 www.thebonham.com

Fashionable restaurant in a townhouse conversion, with polished wooden floors and gigantic mirrors. Diverse ingredients in bright combinations of flavour and texture characterise the dishes. A less expensive set-price menu is available, and the descriptive wine list is carefully chosen.

All week 12–2.30 and 6.30–10 (9.30 Sun); closed 3–7 Jan (See Where to Stay)

Café St-Honoré

34 NW Thistle Street Lane, Edinburgh
EH2 1EA
☎ 0131-226 2211
📠 0131-624 7905

Truly Gallic bistro hidden away down 'a
funny little lane', with distressed mirrors
and ornate lamps. A long menu covers
contemporary dishes and fish as well as
typical bistro fare. Service is relaxed, and
the lengthy wine list is reasonably priced.
Mon to Fri L 12–2.15, Mon–Sat D 5–10
(all week L and D during Festival); closed 1
week in Oct, 3 days Christmas, 3 days New
Year

Fishers

1 The Shore, Leith, Edinburgh EH6 6QW
☎ /📠 0131-554 5666

Former pub at one end of the
waterfront with a dark, bustling public
bar and lighter, calmer restaurant. Plenty
of well-cooked seafood on the menu, as
well as poultry, game and desserts.
International wine list.
All week 12–10.30; closed 25 and 26 Dec,
1 and 2 Jan

Haldanes

39A Albany Street, Edinburgh EH1 3QY
☎ 0131-556 8407
📠 0131-556 2662
🖳 www.haldanesrestaurant.com

Elegant place to dine, in the basement of
a Georgian hotel with opulent country-
house décor and a small walled garden.
Prime Scottish produce underlies the
set-price menus, with some enjoyable
puddings appearing. Some dishes attract
fairly high supplements.
Tue–Fri 12–1.30, all week D 6–9.30;
closed 25 and 26 Dec

Kalpna

2–3 St Patrick Square, Edinburgh
EH14 1AJ
☎ 0131-667 9890
📠 0131-443 9523

Hospitable and brightly decorated
restaurant offering a wide range of
Indian vegetarian cooking, with additional
specialities. The thali (one-plate meal) is
available in several versions, and lunch is
a particularly good-value buffet.
Mon to Sat L 12–2, all week D
5.30–10.30 (11 Fri and Sat May to Sept);
closed 25 and 26 Dec, 1 Jan, L Sat and D
Sun from Oct to April

Martins

70 Rose Street North Lane, Edinburgh
EH2 3DX
☎ 0131-225 3106

Welcome haven from the bustling city
centre, with bright, colourful interiors.
Organic vegetables and unpasteurised
cheeses play a large part on the
Mediterranean-influenced menu. Sticky
desserts and a cleverly chosen wine list
with tasting notes.
Tue to Fri L 12–2, Tue to Sat D 7–10
(6.30–11 during Festival); closed 1 week
Oct, 4 weeks from 24 Dec, 1 week
June/July

Restaurant Martin Wishart

54 The Shore, Leith, Edinburgh EH6 6RA
☎ 0131-553 3557
📠 0131-467 7091

An unassuming but effective open space
with discreet lighting and big tables is the
setting. Luxurious dishes are interspersed
with relatively humble ones, and include
fish, game, lamb, beef and seafood
accompanied by very good sauces. Well

chosen and affordable wine list.
*Tue to Fri L 12–2, Tue to Sat D 6.30–10
(10.30 Fri and Sat); closed 25 Dec, 1 Jan*

Rhodes & Co

3–15 Rose Street, Edinburgh EH2 2YJ
☎ 0131-220 9190
📠 0131-220 9199
Another entry in the Gary Rhodes empire. A ground-floor bar in glass, marble, leather and steel has an informal dining-room in wood and chrome above it. Comforting British cooking forms the basis, although straightforward dishes have a modern twist and rich and unusual sauces. The wine list is relatively reasonable.
All week L 12–2.30 (3 Sun), Mon–Sat D 6–10.30

Shore

3–4 The Shore, Leith, Edinburgh EH6 6QW
☎/📠 0131-553 5080
Handsome eighteenth-century stone building overlooking the Water of Leith. 'Consistently imaginative' cooking, with an emphasis on fish and shellfish, and simple puddings. The primarily white wine list offers plenty of choice and reasonable prices.
All week 12–2.30 (12.30–3 Sun), 6.30–10; closed 25 and 26 Dec, 1 and 2 Jan

Skippers

1A Dock Place, Leith, Edinburgh EH6 6LU
☎ 0131-554 1018
📠 0131-553 5988
🖳 www.skippers.co.uk
Converted pub, now an informal bistro

specialising in simply and sympathetically cooked fish. No-nonsense descriptions in the daily-changing menu, which includes some meat dishes. The helpfully annotated wine list is affordable.
All week L 12.30–2 (2.30 Sun), Mon–Sat D 7–10 (6.30–10 during Festival); closed 24 to 26 Dec, 31 Dec to 2 Jan, 1 week Feb/Mar, 1 week Sept

Tower Restaurant

Museum of Scotland, Chambers Street, Edinburgh EH1 1JF
☎ 0131-225 3003
📠 0131-247 4220
A long, thin dining-room above the Museum offers dramatic views. Seafood plays a large part in both traditional and contemporary dishes, but choices extend to beef, offal and vegetable options. Desserts cover both old and new styles.
All week 12–6 and 6–11; closed 25 and 26 Dec

Valvona & Crolla Caffè Bar

19 Elm Row, Edinburgh EH7 4AA
☎ 0131-556 6066
📠 0131-556 1668
🖳 www.valvonacrolla.co.uk
The family delicatessen, which imports ingredients twice weekly from Milan market, provides the basics. With their own bread and locally available items, the lunchtime dishes range from pizza to steak sandwiches or fish. Classic Italian desserts and innumerable Italian wines.
Mon–Sat L 12–3, D 6–9 2 evenings per month and Mon–Sat during Festival; closed 25 and 26 Dec, 1 and 2 Jan

Vintners Rooms

The Vaults, 87 Giles Street, Leith,
Edinburgh EH6 6BZ

☎ 0131-554 6767

📠 0131-467 7130

Atmospheric eighteenth-century
establishment complete with chandeliers
and cherubs, a large bar and small dining-
room. The French-inspired cooking is
gently modern, with plenty of seafood
and dramatic desserts. Wines are mostly
classical French and New World, with
some reasonably priced choices.
*Mon–Sat 12–2, 7–10; closed 2 weeks
Christmas to New Year*

Winter Glen

3A1 Dundas Street, Edinburgh
EH3 6QG

☎ 0131-477 7060

📠 0131-624 7087

Comfort, capacious chairs and well-
spaced tables in this stone-built
restaurant. Menus centre on traditional
ingredients, with fashionable add-ons.
Large portions of steak, venison, fish and
chicken are served on huge white plates.
About 30 wines appear on a largely
French list.
*Mon–Fri L 12–2, Mon–Sat D 6.30–'late';
closed 25 and 26 Dec, 1 Jan*

East Lothian and the Central Belt

Chatelherault

- Excellent coastline east of Edinburgh: sand, cliffs, seabirds
- Golf on the courses of Gullane
- Dramatic castles, stately homes and historical relics
- Wild moorland country in the Lammermuir and Pentland Hills

EAST LOTHIAN AND THE CENTRAL BELT

At a glance

✓ Good for short-break touring or seaside holidays

✓ Day excursions from Edinburgh or Glasgow

✓ Pleasant area for off-season trips

✗ Industrial dereliction in the Central Belt

✗ Main roads can be congested

Two revolutions have left their mark on this swathe of country – the Agrarian and the Industrial. The fertile strip of East Lothian between the Lammermuir Hills and the beaches of North Berwick and Gullane became the proving ground for the transformation of Scottish agriculture from a feudal system of strip-farming and common land into a productive and stable industry. The neat villages, the enclosed fields, the solid farmsteadings, the woods and the pastureland, which in many ways make East Lothian the most English of all the Scottish counties, are the products of this revolution. The model for the Agrarian Revolution was largely taken from south of the Border, but the Industrial Revolution really started in Scotland when James Watt turned the steam engine from an inefficient machine into an economical source of power, and the coal and iron resources of Lanarkshire and the Lothians fuelled the boom years of Scottish heavy engineering. Central Scotland was also where the petroleum age started, when paraffin and lubricating oils were commercially distilled from the shale deposits round Bathgate and Broxburn (see box on pages 146–7).

The Industrial Revolution has left terrible scars on the landscape between Edinburgh and Glasgow, and it will take decades before the environmental improvement programmes make a real difference to it. But if you can avert your eyes from the pink shale heaps and old coal tips, there is much of interest to be seen, for beneath the industrial debris lies a much older layer of Scotland. Everywhere in the region are memories of the past – Sir James Douglas setting fire to his castle, his food, his wine and his horses to deny them to the English; James IV being warned of his death at Flodden by an apparition in Linlithgow church; Mary Queen of Scots surrendering to her enemies at Carberry Hill and George IV supping turtle soup at Hopetoun.

This region, with neighbouring Dumfriesshire, was also the battleground for the final struggle of the Covenanters against the doctrinal impositions of the restored Stuart kings (see box, pages 156–7). For almost 30 years, in the face of every coercion, men and women deserted the churches where the law decreed they must worship and followed their outlawed ministers to the hills and bare moors to attend services. Isolated graves, a few memorials and a single museum are all that is left of them.

Key web sites

www.eastlothian.gov.uk Directory of East Lothian services put together by the council. Useful information on local sights and events

www.midlothian-online.com Round-up of sights and facilities

www.clyde-valley.com Town-based network with some good links

Good bases in East Lothian and the Central Belt

Accommodation can be a problem in Central Scotland, largely because Edinburgh and Glasgow are so close and tend to attract all the trade. In the country around both cities there are several plush hotels (often in venerable castles), and while these are used largely by business or sporting people and have correspondingly fat tariffs, you might find it worth ringing them at weekends or off-season to see if you can pick up a bargain. East Lothian has a number of old inns in its towns and villages, and

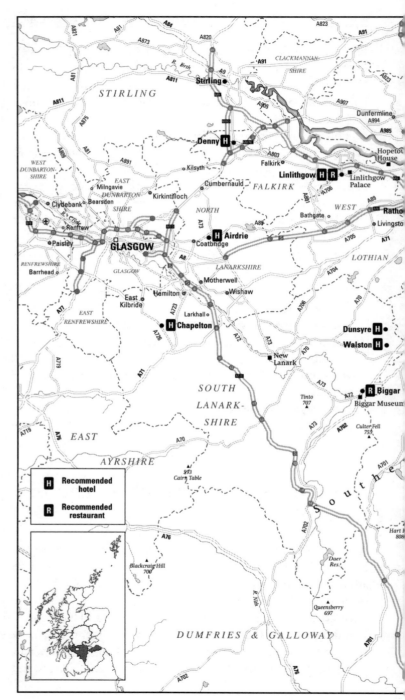

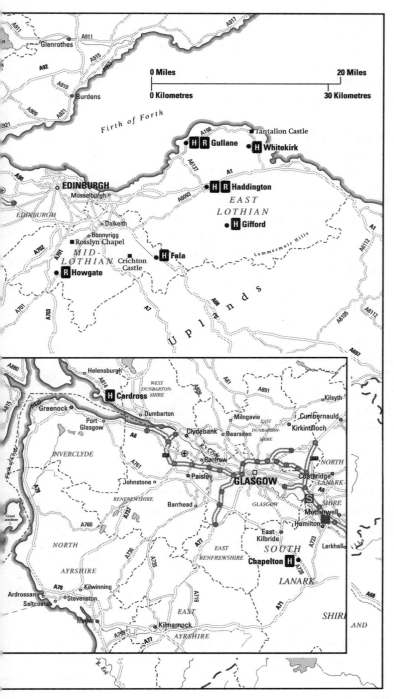

substantial numbers of seaside guesthouses and hotels in its coastal resorts. Elsewhere you are likely to find the scattered bed and breakfasts the best value – the biggest clutches are round Linlithgow and Lanark.

Haddington

✓ *Dignified market town*
✓ *Decent range of shops and accommodation*
✓ *Within easy reach of sea and hills*

This old burgh makes an ideal base for exploring East Lothian. It is a small but lively town, the centrepiece for the prosperous farming countryside. Streets lined with elegant eighteenth-century houses run from its old triangular marketplace down to the River Tyne.

Linlithgow

✓ *Good communications by road and rail*
✓ *Ancient burgh; interesting sights*
✗ *Town planners have made a mess of the old layout*

The ruins of the royal palace and the loch behind its High Street dominate this old town, the most attractive in West Lothian. It has managed to retain a little of its market-town tranquillity despite the coming of the canal, the railway and the

---

Birthplace of the petroleum industry

West Lothian is where the modern age began – at least that part of it which depends on oil. James Young, born in Glasgow in 1811, had the idea of distilling oil out of coal, and found an ideal, oil-rich coal at a mine near Bathgate. His first commercial success came with paraffin, which replaced whale and vegetable oils for lamps. Young soon turned to the shales which underlie much of West Lothian as an alternative raw material for his oil refining. A vast refinery sprang up at Addiewell, followed by one at Broxburn, and the characteristic pink slag heaps (bings) started to appear on the landscape.

M9 motorway. It is well placed for exploration of the southern coast of the Firth of Forth, and also for picking through the industrial archaeology of the area.

Stirling

The town makes a good base for the north–western part of the area and is described on pages 247–252.

EAST LOTHIAN

A mixture of sandy bays and rugged sandstone cliffs backed by rich farmland makes the coast east of Edinburgh a good destination as a day out from the capital. The Forth estuary itself suffers from pollution, but as the coastline turns south, the beaches become purer and wilder. Inland, the strip of fertile land between the sea and the Lammermuir Hills is a classically pastoral landscape of peaceful villages and rolling fields. The Lammermuirs are lonely, heatherclad hills, with good views from the northern slopes. The prettiest route runs from the tiny village of Garvald up past the Cistercian monastery at Nunraw, and on to the Whiteadder reservoir. This is a much prettier, if more time-consuming, way to reach Berwick-upon-Tweed than the A1.

Their colour comes from the high iron oxide content. The products of the refineries were at first paraffin, candles, lubricating and burning oils, but by 1910, 'motor spirit' was selling for one shilling a gallon for use in the new-fangled cars. The first diesel-powered ship built on the Clyde ran on Scottish diesel.

The Scottish oil industry was successful for about 100 years, but eventually became no match for oil found in liquid form. Gradually the mines and refineries closed. The bings (the most shapely are the 'Five Sisters' near West Calder) are all that is left.

Top sight

Tantallon Castle (east of North Berwick)

✓ *Dramatic situation*
✓ *Views*

The great red walls of Tantallon rise from red cliffs against which the sea lashes. A curtain wall with central keep/gate-house and two flanking towers cuts the neck of a peninsula, which drops sheer to the sea on the other three sides. It is a superb defensive position. Although time and the guns of Cromwell's general, Monk, have done their best to destroy it, Tantallon still overawes the visitor by its scale and setting. This was a Douglas stronghold, probably started in the late fourteenth century, and both a bargaining counter and a place of refuge for that powerful family when they were out of royal favour. [*HS; Apr to Sept, daily 9.30–6.30; Oct to Mar, Mon–Sat 9.30–4.30; Sun 2–4.30; closed Thur and Fri;* ☎ *(01620) 892727;* ⬛ *via www.scottishculture.about.com*]

The next best sights

Dirleton Castle

Dirleton Castle is colossal, older than Tantallon and almost as formidable. It stands in the centre of one of the most enchanting East Lothian villages. The gatehouse, where a modern wooden bridge replaces the old drawbridge, remains very imposing. As you walk up the long slope of the bridge, a round tower to your left is what remains of the thirteenth-century fortifications. The interior of this tower, with its domed Lord's Chamber, is the most impressive part of the ruin. Do not omit the beehive-shaped dovecote from your visit, and do not hurry through the garden either. [*HS; Apr to Sept, daily, 9.30–6.30; Oct to Mar, daily 9.30–4.30;* ☎ *(01620) 850330;* ⬛ *via www.scottishculture.about.com*]

Hailes Castle (near East Linton)

Hailes Castle neatly blocks the strategic route of the Tyne Valley. For a castle on the main invasion route from England a lot of it is still standing, some dating from before the Wars of Independence. The square donjon, the curtain walls and the remains of a sixteenth-century range are perhaps less memorable than the extremely unpleasant pit prisons and the peaceful setting on the banks of the river. *[HS; access from keyholder;* ☎ *0131-668 8800;* ✆ *via www.scottishculture.about.com]*

Lennoxlove House (near Haddington)

The seat of the Duke of Hamilton, the old, extended and revamped tower-house now contains much of the collection of portraits and chinaware which was removed from the huge Hamilton Palace before its demolition. The Hamiltons were the chief supporters of Mary Queen of Scots after her escape from Loch Leven. Mary's death mask is at Lennoxlove, as is the silver casket which once contained the series of letters purporting to prove Mary's obsession with Bothwell and her part in the conspiracy to murder Darnley. They are likely to have been forged (Mary herself was never allowed to see them) but served their purpose in helping to keep her exiled in England. For more on Mary Queen of Scots, see box on pages 254–5. *[Easter to Oct, Wed, Thur, Sat and Sun 2–4.30;* ☎ *(01620) 823720]*

Preston Mill (near East Linton)

This red-tiled seventeenth-century watermill with its conical-roofed kiln is surrounded by the sort of ducks-and-placid-water scenery which has made it the subject of countless paintings and photographs from the nineteenth century onwards. The working machinery inside is not, in this age of restored watermills, as rare a sight as it once was, but the age of the place and the excellent explanatory notices still make it essential visiting. *[NTS; Apr to Sept, Mon–Sat, 11–1 and 2–5, Sun 1–5; Oct, weekends only, 1.30–4;* ☎ *(01620) 860426;* ✆ *via www.nts.org]*

St Mary's Church (Haddington)

The fourteenth-century collegiate church was much battered by the English in the sixteenth century, and finally abandoned at the Reformation. A massive restoration programme has re-roofed it and given it back much of its old splendour. Concerts and other events are often held inside. *[Apr to Sept, Mon–Sat 11–4, Sun 9.30–4.30; ☜ via www.kylemore.btinternet.co.uk]*

Scottish Seabird Centre (North Berwick)

A bird observatory down by North Berwick Harbour, with powerful telescopes which allow you to focus on the seabirds mobbing the Bass Rock and the island of Fidra, offshore. Newly built at the time of writing and very smart. *[Daily 10–6; ☎ (01620) 890202; ☜ www.seabird.org.uk]*

Torness Power Station (south of Dunbar)

The bulk of Scotland's newest, and probably last, nuclear power station is a blot on the coastline, but offers free guided tours which are interesting and not too packed with propaganda. *[Mar to Sept, daily 9.30–4.30; Oct to Feb, Mon–Fri 9.30–11.30 and 1–4.30; weekends 1–4.30; ☎ (0800) 250255]*

Also in the area

Cove (signed off the A1, south of Torness Power Station) The remains of an improbably-sited fishing and smuggling harbour, reached on foot by a steep path and a tunnel through a cliff. Nothing much to see, but a bizarre place.

Museum of Flight (East Fortune, near Drem) The old RAF station here is now the home of the Museum of Flight, an outstation of the National Museums of Scotland. Its old hangar is crammed with aircraft ranging from the airship which made the first double crossing of the Atlantic to a Vulcan bomber. It is the largest collection of historic aircraft in Scotland. *[Daily 10.30–5; ☎ (01620) 880308; ☜ via www.nms.ac.uk]*

Myreton Motor Museum (Aberlady) A splendid collection of ancient vehicles, accessories and memorabilia. *[Easter to Oct, 10–6; Nov to Easter, 10–5; ☎ (01875) 870288]*

North Berwick Law and Traprain Law Two volcanic intrusions which dominate the flat land of East Lothian. North Berwick Law is conical, crowned with a whalebone and easily climbed from North Berwick. On Traprain Law a hoard of buried Roman silver was discovered in 1919 (now in the Museum of Scotland). It was the site of an ancient settlement many years before the Romans.

Phantassie Doocot (near East Linton) More than 500 nesting boxes line the walls of this old dovecot, witness to times when fresh meat was harder to come by than today and pigeons were bred for eating. Most Scottish dovecots are ruins at the edge of fields. This one has been lovingly preserved. *[Apr to Sept, Mon–Sat, 11–1 and 2–5, Sun 1–5; Oct, weekends only, 1.30–4;* ☎ *(01620) 860426]*

Towns and villages to explore

Dunbar

The town was once the site of one of the strongest castles on the coast, whose fragmentary remains dominate the lovely harbour (and provided most of the stone for it). The High Street has the typically broad layout of the old Scottish burgh and a particularly magnificent Town House. There is a fair selection of shops and some good strolls. The **John Muir House** marks the birthplace of the naturalist who pioneered America's National Parks *[Apr to Oct, Mon–Sat 11–1 and 2–5, Sun 2–5;* ☎ *(01368) 862585;* ✒ *www.muir-birthplace.org.uk].*

Haddington

East Lothian's county town, with much fine architecture from the eighteenth century and earlier, boasts an interesting range of shops. Leaflets are available to guide you round the streets. Pleasant walks by the River Tyne. For more information see ✒ *www.electrum.co.uk/cc*

Pencaitland and Gifford

Two attractive examples of villages that grew up in the wake of the agricultural reforms of the eighteenth century. Gifford is a good spot for lunch.

Stenton and Dirleton

Attractive, English-style villages, with proper greens and old houses. Stenton was once famous for its coven of witches.

Beaches and seashore

Barns Ness The rocks round here are interesting for geologists, with fossil coral beds and lumps of coal where a seam comes to the surface.

Bass Rock The Bass Rock is another volcanic lump, jutting up from the sea by North Berwick. Home to thousands of gannets in breeding season, it has also been used as a prison in its time. Boat trips leave from North Berwick regularly in summer and take about 90 minutes.

Gullane The sand on the coast around Gullane makes it ideal for golf courses, but there are plenty of sandy beaches too.

John Muir Country Park (Dunbar) A wild stretch of seashore round the mouth of the Tyne. Ideal for walking, not so good for sunning yourself.

North Berwick Traditional seaside resort for Edinburgh, with two beaches and a harbour to explore.

Seacliff A secluded beach just south of Tantallon Castle, with sand, rocks, and views of the Bass rock. Access is private (come prepared with change for the barrier).

SOUTH OF EDINBURGH

The old county of Midlothian rises from the suburbs of Edinburgh towards the Moorfoot Hills, cut by the valleys of the Esk and the Tyne. Old mining villages, now becoming commuter townlets, dot the landscape, but hide a number of ancient castles and other sights, well worth seeking out. The Pentland Hills, which end abruptly just where Edinburgh begins, provide fresh air and good walks for the capital's inhabitants.

Top sights

Crichton Castle (near Pathead)

✓ *Peaceful setting*
✓ *Unusual architecture*

This castle is a surprise. It is not until you arrive underneath its walls that you realise that not a trace of modern development is visible. The ruin sits on a sharp promontory above a haugh (flat piece of land beside a river) where the River Tyne meanders between trees – a landscape which inspired both Turner and Sir Walter Scott (in *Marmion*).

From the outside, the castle appears uncompromising and uncomfortable. However, once in the courtyard, you are confronted with a façade which seems to have come straight from the Italian Renaissance. An arcade is crowned by a wall studded with diamond facets, while at one end there was once a balcony, worthy of Romeo and Juliet, overhanging the courtyard. A proper Renaissance staircase, with treads, risers and the remains of carved embellishments, leads upwards to what were once grand rooms lit by large windows. This is the work of Francis Stuart, fifth Earl of Bothwell (nephew to Mary Queen of Scots' husband), who spent much of his life in Spain and Italy. Although he had his King to dinner in March 1586, he was too unstable a character to last long under the canny James VI. Eventually he fled abroad and never came back *[HS; Apr to Sept, daily 9.30–6;* ☎ *(01875) 320017;* ✆ *via www.scottishculture.about.com].*

A path runs between Crichton and Borthwick Castle, two miles distant. Borthwick is a very tall (eight floors) fifteenth-century tower, with twin keeps, and is one of the best-preserved medieval castles in Scotland. It was to Borthwick that Mary Queen of Scots and Bothwell came shortly after their marriage. Borthwick Castle is private (it is now an hotel), but the exterior is still well worth seeing.

Rosslyn Chapel

✓ *Weird and brilliant stone carving*
✓ *Increasingly fashionable New Age sight*

A massive restoration programme is rescuing Rosslyn Chapel from decay, and the air of neglect which it used to have is now gone. The chapel lies down a small track below the village of Roslin (best reached from the A703 or A701), and is an unassuming building from the outside. This impression is rapidly dispelled by the interior, for nowhere else in the country will you be confronted with such a superabundance of stone carving. Every surface which has lent itself to ornamentation has been covered in foliage, flowers, human figures and animals. Reactions vary, and many people find the chapel too over-decorated to be beautiful. The star piece of carving is the Apprentice Pillar, an even more elaborately encrusted piece of work than the rest, with its own (probably apocryphal) legend of the apprentice who carved it being murdered by the jealous master mason.

The chapel is fifteenth-century, though its style is early Gothic, and the aisle vaulting is very peculiar. It was the creation of William St Clair, who lived in Rosslyn Castle and felt that founding a luxurious collegiate church was a suitable spiritual compensation for his sumptuous baronial life. After his death the project fell into abeyance, with only the choir complete.

It is, however, the connection (via the ancient St Clair family) to the semi-secret worlds of the Templars, the Rosicrucians and the Masons, which forms Rosslyn's allure to New Agers. There are legends in abundance, from a sealed vault to rumours of the Holy Grail. The Trust which runs Rosslyn keeps an open mind, but concentrates on conservation. *[All year, Mon–Sat 10–5, Sun 12–4.45;* ☎ *0131-440 2159;* ✆ *www.rosslynchapel.org]*

The next best sights

Edinburgh Crystal Factory (Penecuik)

Home of the chunky cut glass found in most up-market department stores. Large visitor centre, shop, café, and the chance to see the glass being blown and cut and engraved. By booking in advance for a special tour, you can undertake some of the processes yourself. *[All year, Mon–Sat 9–5, Sun 11–5;* ☎ *(01968) 675128;* ✆ *www.edinburgh-crystal.co.uk]*

Scottish Mining Museum (Newtongrange)

The Lady Victoria Colliery, once the showpiece pit of the area, is now the Scottish Mining Museum. Only some of the colliery buildings are accessible, although there is a simulated coal face to see, and the museum contains probably the best steam-engine in Scotland – an enormous winding engine, gaily painted and still in full working order. The conditions of a miner's life are explored, using voice-overs and models in a well-put-together display. At the time of writing, the museum was threatened with closure, so check before going. *[Feb to Nov, daily 11–5; Dec and Jan by appointment;* ☎ *0131–663 7519;* ✆ *www.scottishminingmuseum.org]*

Suggested walks in the Pentlands

Cauld Stane Slap (reached from the A70) The old drove road across the hills from the Harperrig Reservoir passes between the East and West Cairn Hills, through the slap (break in hills) to West Linton. An excellent half-day's walk, though coordinating transport can be difficult because you need to have a car at each end, and buses are infrequent.

Glencorse Reservoir (reached from the A702) lies in a dog-legged valley under Turnhouse Hill, and the track up to it and

The Covenanters (1638–90)

The National Covenant, signed in Greyfriars churchyard in 1638, is the document which marks the beginning of a triumphant, terrible and bitter period in Scottish history. The Covenanting movement, which started as a proud, nationalistic and spiritual revolution, was to become an intolerant theocracy and eventually a pitiful remnant of stalwarts pursued and slaughtered by the forces of government. The events of these years are complicated, and intimately bound to the civil struggles going on in England, including the English Civil War.

1638 After riots in Edinburgh when King Charles I attempts to introduce an anglicised prayer book, the National Covenant is signed in Greyfriars. It makes no threats, merely rejects interference in the practice of the Reformed Kirk of Scotland. However, its appeal has to do with the symbolic nature of a covenant, drawn from the Old Testament; it is a bond between God and his chosen people. King Charles thinks it treason.

1638 In Glasgow, the Assembly of the Kirk becomes more radical. It abolishes bishops and disallows royal authority over the church. Charles attempts to raise an English army to curb this constitutional rebellion, but fails to invade. Subscription to the Covenant is made compulsory in Scotland.

1640 The Scots invade England to make Charles come to a settlement and force him, in 1641, to assent to the religious and constitutional changes. Splits now appear among the Covenanters, with some, Montrose in particular, unwilling to continue hostility to the King.

1643 Embroiled in a civil war they look like losing, the English Parliamentarians strike a deal whereby in return for Scottish military aid Presbyterianism will be established in England and Ireland. A Scottish army enters England.

1644–5 Montrose, now siding with the King, inflicts six defeats on the Covenanters in Scotland. Their confidence in their invincibility as God's chosen is severely dented.

1646–8 King Charles, defeated in war, surrenders himself to the Scottish Covenanting army, but refuses to sign the Covenant. The

Scots, unable to take an unregenerate King back to Scotland, are forced to hand him over to the English. The Covenanters split further, and eventually the extreme 'Kirk' party takes power, purging all those whose religious fervour does not measure up.

1649 Execution of Charles I. All the Scottish factions are horrified and Charles II is immediately proclaimed King in Scotland, while the English abolish the monarchy entirely. The rift between the two countries is complete.

1650 Oliver Cromwell invades Scotland and defeats the Covenanters at Dunbar.

1651 A Scottish invasion of England is defeated at Worcester. Charles II flees, leaving Cromwell to conquer Scotland and establish the Commonwealth. Scotland is under occupation for nine years.

1660 Charles II is restored. Over the next few years, the Covenants and all the acts passed by Covenanting parliaments in Scotland are repudiated. Bishops are reintroduced and kirk ministers from the previous regime must seek episcopal approval. Many ministers refuse to comply and become 'Outers'. Despite increasingly repressive measures, congregations follow them to 'Conventicles' in the hills rather than conform to the law.

1666 Covenanters from the west rebel and march on Edinburgh. They are defeated at Rullion Green. Executions follow.

1679 A further Covenanter rebellion is defeated at Bothwell Brig.

1680–88 Continued persecution of increasingly small, extreme, Covenanting minorities; the period known as the 'Killing Times'.

1685 The accession of Catholic James VII is such a threat to the established Scottish church that Presbyterianism becomes respectable again.

1688 James VII is deposed in an essentially English revolution.

1690 A mild version of Presbyterianism is re-established under William in a compromise between church and state. The Covenanting dream of establishing Christ's kingdom in Scotland is relegated to history.

up the Logan Burn is probably the most popular walk in the area. This part of the Pentlands has been designated a Regional Park, and there is a small visitor centre. It was on the southern slope of Turnhouse Hill that the battle of Rullion Green was fought in 1666. A pathetic army of fewer than a thousand Covenanters, mostly from the south-west, was defeated by General Tam Dalyell.

Threipmuir Reservoir (reached from the A70) An extensive stretch of water, with plenty of bird-life in its thick reed-beds. Up the hill behind, paths lead in towards the waterfalls at the head of Logan Burn

THE FORTH VALLEY

Along the south bank of the estuary, industry, ancient towns and stately homes form an incongruous mixture. It is tempting to rush between Edinburgh and Stirling on the M9, but the temptation should be avoided. Follow the A904 instead.

Top sights

Hopetoun House

✓ *Palatial stately house*
✓ *Lovely grounds to walk in*

This huge stately home is an amalgam of the work of Scotland's greatest architects. It was begun by William Bruce in 1699, extended and altered by William Adam in 1721, and finished off by his sons in 1767. Bruce's interior work remains intact in several rooms, and it is interesting to compare his warm, homely style with the magnificent formality of the Adam staterooms. The most striking feature of Hopetoun is the pine-panelled front staircase, with intricate carvings, modern mural paintings (though you would never guess) and the restored painted cupola where anxious cherubs support a cracked globe. Paintings abound, notably a specially commissioned series by Tideman, and there are portraits by Raeburn, Ramsay and Gainsborough.

Hopetoun's carefully landscaped grounds overlook the Forth Bridges, and are seen at their best from the rooftop viewing platform of the house. *[Easter to Sept, daily 10–5.30;* ☎ *0131-331 2451]*

Linlithgow Palace
✓ *Romantic ruin*
✓ *Great architecture*

Windowless, roofless and weathering, the palace is still an outstanding tour de force of Scottish architecture over 200 years. Started by James I around 1425 and finished by James VI in 1624, the building silently demonstrates the level of luxury and functional magnificence which the Scottish kings expected of their palaces.

Standing in the central courtyard, in front of the elaborate fountain – said to be a wedding present from James V to Marie of Guise – you have James VI's plain and harmonious Renaissance facade in front of you, with James I's massive medieval hall in the range to your right, the state apartments of James IV to your left, and the English-style gallery of James V behind you. The cascades of reddish stone which make up the four frontages are vigorous and harmonious. Everything else, even the Great Hall, or the vaulting at the head of the stair to the royal apartments, is something of an anti-climax after the courtyard.

The palace was burnt out in 1746, while being used by Hanoverian troops. Given Historic Scotland's achievements at Stirling Castle, it is to be hoped they will give some thought to restoring this great building too. *[HS; Apr to Sept, daily 9.30–6.30; Oct to Mar, Mon–Sat 9.30–4.30, Sun 2–4.30;* ☎ *(01506) 842896]*

The next best sights

Blackness Castle

From a distance Blackness looks just like a small ship stranded on the rocks. Its curious shape was determined by the rocky spit on which it was built in the fifteenth century. It guarded the harbour which served as Linlithgow's outlet to the sea, became a state prison, and ended as an ammunition store. A secret passage is said to have linked it to the House of the Binns.

Blackness is an example of a fortification where the response to the invention of siege artillery was simply to thicken the walls and to go on thickening them until in places they became a solid mass of stonework pierced by chambers for gunners. The transformation of Blackness into this bulwark took place between 1532 and 1567. The castle's fortifications proved no match for Cromwell, whose siege of 1650 did much damage (now repaired). *[HS; Apr to Sept, daily 9.30–6; Oct to Mar, Mon–Sat 9.30–4.30 (closed Thur and Fri pm), Sun 2–4.30;* ☎ *(01506) 834807;* ☝ *via www.scottishculture.about.com]*

House of the Binns

In contrast to its near neighbour, Hopetoun, this is a seventeenth-century Gothic stately home, notable mostly for the character of its most notorious owner, General Tam Dalyell. A dedicated royalist and enemy of the Covenanters and all their works, he fought for Charles II at Worcester, escaped from the Tower of London and helped defeat the Covenanters at Rullion Green (1666). The General's prowess against the godly was logically attributed to his alliance with satanic power, and in the entrance hall of the Binns you can see the magnificent table which the Devil hurled into a nearby pond after losing to Tam at cards. It remained there for 200 years. You leave the Binns with tales of flagellation parties and of Tam's waist-length beard (he refused to shave in protest at the execution of Charles I). He also raised that most famous of Scottish Cavalry regiments, the Scots Greys. *[NTS; May to Sept, daily 1.30–5.30 (exc Fri);* ☎ *(01506) 834255;* ☝ *via www.scottishculture.about.com]*

St Michael's Church (Linlithgow)

This fifteenth-century church boasts High Gothic window tracery as its most beautiful feature. The curious spire was lowered into position by helicopter in 1964. James IV saw an apparition in the south transept here, which warned him of his doom at Flodden. He went to war anyway and was killed, leaving his Queen to wait in vain for his return in the topmost room of Linlithgow Palace (still known as Queen Margaret's bower). *[June to Sept, daily 10–4; Oct to May, Mon–Fri 10–3.30;* ☎ *(01506) 842188]*

Torphichen Preceptory (near Linlithgow)

The tall grey building rising above the houses of the small village on the B792 a few miles south of Linlithgow was once the headquarters in Scotland of the great monastic-military order, the Knights Hospitallers of the Order of St John of Jerusalem. What remains are the tower and two transepts of their church. Parts of it date from the twelfth century, but most is fourteenth- or fifteenth-century. The vaulting of the crossing and transepts is monumental, and you can climb into the bell chamber above and look down on to the floor of the crossing. *[HS; Apr to Oct, Sat 11–5, Sun 2–5;* ☎ *0131-668 8800]*

Also in the area

The Antonine Wall (around Falkirk) The Romans built this turf barrier between Forth and Clyde around AD 140 when they decided to move their frontier defences north from Hadrian's Wall *[*☝ *www.tartans.com/article/antoninewall.html].* At **Rough Castle**, signposted from Bonnybridge, there are the earthworks of a large fort and the remains of a ditch and rampart. At Callander Park and Watling Lodge, both in Falkirk, the old defensive ditch can be seen. Bits and pieces of the wall can be found all the way along its line as far as Bearsden near Glasgow.

Cairnpapple Hill (Bathgate) A Bronze Age burial cairn crowns this low hill behind Linlithgow. There are spectacular views of much of Lowland Scotland and an ugly radio mast. *[HS; Apr to Sept, daily 9–6.30; Oct to Mar, daily 9–4.30;* ☎ *(01506) 634622;* ☝ *via www.stonepages.com]*

The Pineapple (north-west of Airth on the A905) An extraordinary folly in the shape of a 45ft-tall stone pineapple, with a little domed room right at the top under the leaves. It was built in 1761 by an unknown architect. If you fancy a holiday inside the fruit, contact the Landmark Trust *[☎ (01628) 825925]*, which leases the building from the National Trust for Scotland.

Suggested excursions

Bo'ness and Kinneil Railway Steam trains run over a three-mile stretch of track to visit **Birkhill Clay Mine** where clay for firebricks to line the furnaces of the Industrial Revolution was once dug. The railway holds open days of various kinds; you can even learn to drive a steam locomotive. Tours of the mine, where ancient fossils are embedded in the walls, are co-ordinated with train arrivals *[for timetable and fare details ☎ (01506) 822298; ☐ via www.srps.org.uk].*

The Millennium Link A massive project to restore the canals (Union and Forth & Clyde) which linked Edinburgh and Glasgow is under way. Excursions run from Linlithgow *[☎ (01506) 671215]* (where there is also a canal museum), and from Ratho. The most ambitious part of the project is the **Falkirk Wheel** *[☎ (01324) 671217; ☐ www.falkirk-wheel.com]*, which will link the two canals (under construction at the time of writing at the junction of the canals near Falkirk).

THE CLYDE VALLEY

The Clyde is probably the most celebrated of Scotland's rivers, though its popular image as a waterway surrounded by a hubbub of heavy industry is now long out of date. The Clyde in its lower reaches is becoming a recreational asset: walkways or country parks line its banks, and all is (nearly) tranquillity where once the night sky was lit by the glow of blast furnaces. In its upper reaches above Hamilton the Clyde is a beautiful river, well worth a leisurely day's journey through its various sights.

Top sights

Biggar Museums

✓ *Excellent collection of local museums*
✓ *Something for everyone*

Biggar's four museums and its puppet theatre may seem excessive for a small agricultural town with no great claim to fame, but they are places of considerable charm and interest, well worth visiting.

Gladstone Court, the oldest of the museums, is the result of its founder's inability to leave anything unsalvaged from a demolished building. Here you can find Biggar's old manual telephone exchange with rows of jack plugs on wires, and the nineteenth-century bank with its high wooden counter and air of Scottish financial integrity, together with the lovingly reconstructed interiors of many other shops and offices *[Easter to Oct, Mon to Sat 10–12.30 and 2–5, Sun 2–5;* ☎ *(01899) 221050]*.

Moat Park Heritage Centre, in an old church a few minutes away from Gladstone Court, is one of the best local museums in Scotland, with plenty of scale models and highly literate explanations. Poems by Hugh MacDiarmid introduce the geological section, while the Roman legionary in his glass case is covered in blood and carries the gory head of a vanquished tribesman *[Easter to Oct, Mon–Sat 10–5, Sun 2–5;* ☎ *(01899) 221050]*.

Greenhill, in a small dell below the town, is a rebuilt seventeenth-century farmhouse, turned into a Covenanting Museum. Relics are few, but the explanations of the conventicles and the persecutions of the 'Killing Time' are as good as is possible with such a confusing period. Among the furniture, there is a fine old press bed (a bed in a cupboard) *[Easter to Sept, daily 2–5;* ☎ *(01899) 221050]*.

Biggar Gas Works provide a completely contrasting piece of history, dating from the time when many small towns like

Biggar had their own local gas plant. Sheds contain various ovens and retorts, together with the machinery to ensure an adequate supply of light and heat to the town. All that is missing is the smell *[June to Sept, daily 2–5; ☎ (01899) 221050]*.

Purves Puppets Biggar's puppet theatre draws audiences of schoolchildren from the whole region. Even if there is no show on, you can usually look around the theatre and museum, but phone in advance *[☎ (01899) 220631]* to make sure.

Look up ✆ *www.biggar-net.co.uk/museums* for information about the museums.

New Lanark (near Lanark)

✓ *Attractive setting*
✓ *Fascinating industrial heritage*
✓ *Good combination of walks, shops, things to see*

On the banks of the Clyde at the bottom of a steep gorge behind Lanark lies Scotland's most important memorial to the Industrial Revolution. Now nominated a World Heritage Site, with more than 400,000 visitors a year, New Lanark was saved from the bulldozers in 1975.

New Lanark holds a unique place in social history, for it was here that Robert Owen, son-in-law of the founder of the cotton mills, David Dale, put into action the unfashionable principle that the welfare of an industrial workforce was of importance. Between 1814 and 1824 New Lanark became the scene of a pioneering social experiment. Education lay at the heart of this: no child under ten was allowed to work in the mills, while in the company's school both punishment and reward were banned, and singing and dancing were taught to all. A sick fund, a co-operative village shop and the introduction of adult education classes were also part of the experiment.

The three mills that remain were built between 1789 and 1826 and forcefully prove the point that industrial architecture does not have to be ugly. Around them cluster the other buildings of the community – the workers' housing, the Counting House, the Institute for the Formation of Character, and the School for Children. A 'ride' in one of the mills explores the history; there is a working spinning mule, a carding set (woollen yarn is on sale) and a large steam engine. Other exhibitions and restorations provide good historical insight, although this is far from being a slickly commercial sight.

Various craft enterprises fill the outbuildings of the old complex; there is plenty of space to sit, stroll or watch the river. Immediately above New Lanark, the **Falls of Clyde Nature Reserve** stretches along the bank. Half a mile's walk takes you to Corra Linn, the most famous and the best of the three falls where the Clyde plunges into its gorge. Guided walks through the reserve are available – enquire at New Lanark. *[All year, daily 11–5;* ☎ *(01555) 665262;* ☝ *www.newlanark.org]*

The next best sights

Bothwell Castle

This was once one of the most strategically important strongholds in Scotland, and a crucial point in the Wars of Independence. Its most notable feature is the ruined donjon, a great circular tower of enormous strength, which may have been almost all that existed of the castle in the thirteenth century. Held at first by the English then taken by the Scots in 1290, the castle became the object of Edward I of England's revenge in 1301. He commissioned an enormous siege tower as high as the parapet and this machine forced the surrender of the castle in less than a month. A small heap of round stones – precursors of cannon balls – salvaged during excavation, bear witness to the various sieges in the castle's history. *[HS; Apr to Sept, daily 9.30–4.30, Sun 2–4.30; Oct to Mar, Mon–Sat 9.30–4.30, closed Thur pm and Fri, Sun 2–4.30;* ☎ *(01698) 816894;* ☝ *via www.scottish-culture.about.com]*

Chatelherault Country Park (near Hamilton)

The French title of Duke of Chatelherault was given to James Hamilton, second Earl of Arran, in the middle of the sixteenth century. In a later century, the rich coal seams of this area brought huge prosperity to the Dukes of Hamilton, who built an enormous palace from the profits. All that now remains is the beautiful Hunting Lodge, which stands in the middle of the country park. Its restoration from total dereliction has been a remarkable success. Much of the plasterwork that adorns walls and ceilings has had to be re-created from photographs, while the urns and finials on the roof are also modern copies of the missing originals. A visitor centre built in the kennel yard, where the dukes' hounds once jostled, gives you some idea of how the lodge was built and how it was restored, and also has exhibitions on other aspects of the country park. *[Daily 10–5 (5.30 in summer); lodge closed Fri Oct to Mar;* ☎ *(01698) 426213; www.clyde-valley.com/hamilton]*

Craignethan Castle (off A72, north-west of Lanark)

This fifteenth-century castle is well preserved and under-visited. The approach road across a desolate, scrub-covered land suddenly reveals the ruins on their high spur above the Nethan. Enthusiasts of military architecture go to see its caponier – a dank, vaulted chamber built across the moat to help defend the place against artillery – but the ruins are worth a stop if you are at all fond of castles. *[HS; Mar to Oct, daily 9.30–6.30;* ☎ *(01555) 860364; www.clyde-valley.com/hamilton]*

Also in the area

David Livingstone Centre (Blantyre) The famous explorer came from Blantyre, and you can see the tenement where he was born, together with exhibitions about his life, and an imaginative interpretation of the Africa which he explored.

[Early Jan to Chr, Mon–Sat 10–5, Sun 12.30–5; ☎ *(01698) 823140;* ✆ *www.biggar-net.co.uk/livingstone]*

Paisley Museum & Art Galleries This excellent local museum is a little out of the way for most visitors. But the huge collection of Paisley shawls is fascinating *[Tue–Sat 10–5, Sun 2–5;* ☎ *0141–889 3151;* ✆ *via www.houston-menswear.co.uk/paisley]*. Combine the trip with a visit to **Paisley Abbey**, where rare medieval carvings are to be found in the beautifully restored church, and to the **Weaver's Cottage** at Kilbarchan, with relics of the cottage industry for which the area was once renowned *[Easter to Sept, daily 1.30–5.30; Oct, weekends only;* ☎ *(01236) 747712]*.

Summerlee Heritage Park (Coatbridge) An industrial museum exploring the engineering and mining heritage of the area. Combine a visit with swimming or skating at the nearby Time Capsule leisure centre if you have children with you. *[Apr to Oct, daily 10–5; Nov to Mar, 10–4;* ☎ *(01236) 431261]*

Suggested excursions

Clyde cruises The inlets and lochs of the Clyde estuary make for an interesting day afloat. Operators leave from Greenock, or you can catch one of the cruises on the *Waverley* – the last remaining ocean–going paddle-steamer in service *[*☎ *0141-221 8152;* ✆ *via www.paddlers31.freeserve.co.uk]*.

Tinto Hill is an isolated mini-mountain to the west of Biggar. Easily climbed by an obvious path, the views over much of central Scotland are magnificent.

WHERE TO STAY

£ – under £70 per room per night, incl. VAT

££ – £70 to £110 per room per night incl. VAT

£££ – over £110 per room per night incl. VAT

AIRDRIE
Easter Glentore Farm

Slamannan Road, Greengairs, Nr Airdrie ML6 7TJ

☎/📠 (01236) 830243

📶 www.glentore.vserve.co.uk

This single-storey working farmhouse, built in 1705, offers comfortable accommodation in unspoilt countryside. Breakfasts are hearty and supplemented by good home baking. A pleasant lounge with fine views is shared with the family.

£ All year exc Christmas

CARDROSS
Kirkton House

Darleith Road, Cardross G82 5EZ

☎ (01389) 841951

📠 (01389) 841868

📶 www.kirktonhouse.co.uk

Pleasant eighteenth-century small hotel, surrounded by fields and with views across the Firth of Clyde. Bedrooms are comfortable and well-equipped. Breakfasts and evening meals are served in the dining-room; two- or four-course suppers, table d'hôte, vegetarian or special diet meals are available.

£ Feb to Nov

CHAPELTON
Millwell Farm

Chapelton, Strathaven ML10 6SJ

☎ (01355) 243248

Farmhouse bed-and-breakfast accommodation. Three basic but comfortable and pristine bedrooms share a bathroom; all are on the ground floor and suitable for wheelchairs. A large, beamed lounge/dining-room is warmed by an open fire on cold days. Hearty breakfasts.

£ All year exc Christmas and New Year

DENNY
Lochend Farm

Carronbridge, Denny FK6 5JJ

☎ (01324) 822778

A working sheep farm with panoramic views. The traditional farmhouse and courtyard has two comfortable first-floor bedrooms, and the hearty breakfasts are made with ingredients from the farm.

£ Easter to Oct, or by arrangement

DUNSYRE
Dunsyre Mains Farmhouse

Dunsyre, Nr Carnwath ML11 8NQ

☎ (01899) 810251

A working beef and sheep farm set in unspoilt countryside. Guests are welcome to walk round and see the animals. Three good-sized bedrooms are available, and breakfast and evening meals are served in the dining-room.

£ All year

FALA
Fala Hall Farmhouse
Fala EH37 5SZ
☎ /📠 (01875) 833249
A warm welcome and two simple bedrooms are offered at this sixteenth-century farmhouse. There is no guests' lounge, but both bedrooms have TV; packed lunches are provided on request for those wishing to explore the area.
£ *All year exc Christmas*

GIFFORD
Eaglescairnie Mains
Gifford EH41 4HN
☎ /📠 (01620) 810491
Bed and breakfast on a working farm which has won an award for conservation work. The Georgian farmhouse has three large, attractive bedrooms, a spacious drawing room, conservatory, garden and hard tennis court. Scottish breakfasts are served and packed lunches are available.
£ *All year exc Christmas*

GULLANE
Golf Inn Hotel
Main Street, Gullane EH31 2AB
☎ (01620) 843259
📠 (01620) 842066
🖥 www.golfinngullane.com
This ancient coaching inn, with public bar and cocktail lounge, caters for the golfing fraternity. Bedrooms have been refurbished in yellow and blue, and the dining-room in orange; the residents' lounge is dignified and comfortable. Food is straightforward and tasty, with plenty of local seafood.
££ *All year*

Greywalls
Muirfield, Gullane EH31 2EG
☎ (01620) 842144
📠 (01620) 842241
🖥 www.greywalls.co.uk
Complete tranquillity in this Lutyens country-house hotel, overlooking the Firth of Forth. The bedrooms are comfortably furnished, with large, luxurious beds. Service and food are impeccable in the dining-room overlooking the golf course.
£££ *Closed Nov to Mar (See Where to Eat)*

HADDINGTON
Brown's Hotel
1 West Road, Haddington EH41 3RD
☎ /📠 (01620) 822254
🖥 www.browns-hotel.com
Excellent food and art offered with flair at this comfortable small hotel. Bedrooms are well-equipped and bathrooms handsome. The hotel is busiest in the evenings, when people arrive to sample the excellent food.
££ *All year*

LINLITHGOW
Thornton
Edinburgh Road, Linlithgow EH49 6AA
☎ (01506) 844693
📠 (01506) 844876
Welcoming and helpful owners in this large detached Victorian house. Guest accommodation in the more modern part has its own entrance and attractive bedrooms. A wide breakfast choice is offered in the dining-room; guests can use a lounge and the pretty garden.
£ *All year exc Christmas and New Year*

WALSTON
Walston Mansion Farmhouse
Walston, Carnwath ML11 8NF
☎ /✆ (01899) 810338
Family-friendly accommodation in
beautiful countryside. One double room
also has bunk-beds, another a four-
poster and single bed. Home-produced
organic meat and vegetables plus free-
range eggs are used at dinner (guests
may bring their own wine).
£ All year

WHITEKIRK
Whitekirk Mains Farmhouse
Whitekirk EH42 1XS
☎ (01620) 870245
✆ (01620) 870330
Bed-and-breakfast accommodation on a
working farm; traditional Scottish
breakfasts are served, and evening meals
are available at a restaurant on the edge
of the farm owned by the hosts.
£ Mar to Oct

WHERE TO EAT

BIGGAR
Culter Mill
Coulter Village, Biggar ML12 6PZ
☎ (01899) 220950
Ancient converted mill offering a varied
menu. A range of Mediterranean and
European dishes are served alongside
traditional game, fish and poultry dishes.
Desserts are likewise unusual.
Wed–Sun

GULLANE
Greywalls
Muirfield, Gullane EH31 2EG
☎ (01620) 842144
✆ (01620) 842241
🖰 www.greywalls.co.uk
Three-course lunches and four-course
dinners in this elegant Lutyens house
use regional ingredients (some organic),
and delicacies from the sea. Beef and
game are well-represented, and desserts
light. An impressive wine list covers all
price ranges.
All week, 12.30–1.45 and 7.30–9.15 (See
Where to Stay)

HADDINGTON
Garden Café
Lennoxlove House, By Haddington
EH41 4NZ
☎ (01620) 823720
Clarissa Dickson-Wright's simple
restaurant offers modestly priced dishes
in a range of traditional and
Mediterranean styles; exciting starters,
eastern dishes and appealing desserts
are also available on a wide-ranging
menu.
Tue–Sun L and Thur–Sat D

HOWGATE
The Howgate
Howgate EH26 8PY
☎ (01968) 670000
Bar, bistro and restaurant in a row of
refurbished farm cottages. All offer the
same traditional fare, mixed with some
nice modern touches. Beef, lamb, game,
poultry and seafood are served, and
desserts are individual variations on
popular favourites.

Tue–Sun 11–2.30 and 6–11; bar food and restaurant 12–2.30 and 6–10; closed 25 Dec, 1 Jan

LINLITHGOW
Champany Inn
Champany Corner, Linlithgow EH49 7LU
☎ (01506) 834532
📠 (01506) 834302
🖥 www.champany.com
Traditional, wooden-raftered round house specialising in Aberdeen Angus steak, served in very good cuts. Seafood and lamb vary the menu, with traditional desserts. The Chop and Ale House offers burgers using the same quality beef. Apart from the house wines, the extensive list is expensive.
Mon–Fri L 12.30–2, Mon–Sat D 7–10; closed 25 and 26 Dec, 1 and 2 Jan

RATHO
Bridge Inn
27 Baird Road, Ratho EH28 8RA
☎ 0131–333 1320
Farmhouse staging-post at the centre of the Edinburgh Canal Centre, overlooking the Union Canal. Snacks and fuller meals are served in the Pop Inn bar; dishes have an international flavour. There is a separate à la carte dining-room for more formal tastes.
Mon–Thur 12–11, Fri and Sat 11–midnight, Sun 12.30–11; bar food Mon–Sat 12–9, Sun 12.30–8; restaurant Mon–Sat 12–2, 6.30–9, Sun L 12.30–2; closed 25 Dec eve, 26 Dec, 1 Jan

Glasgow

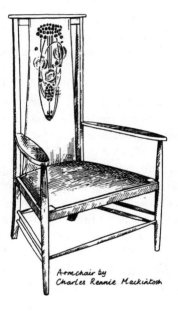

Armchair by
Charles Rennie Mackintosh

- Lively, vibrant, big-city atmosphere, good shopping, eating and nightlife
- Terrific galleries and museums
- The city of Charles Rennie Mackintosh – interesting architecture and design

GLASGOW

At a glance

✓ Good for three- or five-day city breaks

✓ Excellent all-weather, all-season destination

✓ Numerous festivals and cultural events

✓ A serious alternative to Edinburgh for a Scottish city holiday

✓ City-run sights (most museums) have free entry

✗ City-centre accommodation still a bit limited in range

✗ Cars not recommended in city centre

✗ Sights are scattered over a wide area. Be prepared to take public transport

It is now almost two decades since Glasgow began the metamorphosis from decaying, industrial dead-end, into the epitome of contemporary urban style and culture. Other British cities have followed in its wake, and even its old rival, Edinburgh, is beginning to look as if it is going places. But although it is no longer alone in reaching for a new image and a brighter future, Glasgow remains a uniquely interesting city. Its immense pride in its trading, manufacturing and political past seems to act as a spur to creativity rather than as a temptation to nostalgia. This is best exemplified in the transformation of an eighteenth-century bastion of wealth – the Royal Exchange – into one of the best galleries of modern art around.

The far-reaching changes of the last decades and the triumphant march of the bistro, the wine bar and the shopping mall do not, however, appear to have damaged the old Glasgow spirit. This may be because Glaswegians have a rare talent for dry self-mockery, combined with an infallible ability to puncture pretentiousness. You do not have to look far for the raucous, humorous, argumentative and slightly inebriated Glasgow made famous by its comics from Harry Lauder to Billy Connolly.

Glasgow's greatest attractions are its capacity to provide entertainment and its nineteenth-century architecture. The city is home to the Scottish Opera, the Scottish Ballet and the

Royal Scottish Orchestra, not to mention the renowned Citizens' Theatre, so opportunities for highbrow culture abound. Glasgow's long love affair with popular theatre is also far from dead – the Christmas pantomimes are a sell-out, and appearances by hypnotists, variety acts and comedians hugely popular. Try being among a Friday night audience for atmosphere. Even away from the theatres and concert halls, there is always something going on. The city bounces with energy – the reason why New Yorkers claim to feel more at home here than anywhere else in Britain.

As for the architecture, it is the work of Charles Rennie Mackintosh (1868–1928) that people most want to see; his most accessible buildings are the School of Art, the Willow Tea Rooms and nearby Hill House. But throughout the central streets, impressive, sometimes self-important, nineteenth-century warehouses and offices rear above the streets. Almost every style, from Palladian through Venetian to Egyptian, can be found, sometimes cleaned up and pristine, sometimes still covered in industrial grime.

Not everything about Glasgow is appealing. It is a sprawling, superficially ugly city, with great gaps torn in its centre by motorways and railways. It has suffered, especially in its outlying housing estates, from some of the worst planning mistakes of the 1960s, and is virtually split in half by expressways. The contrast with elegant, compact Edinburgh could hardly be greater. That contrast extends to the character of the two cities, and it is hardly surprising that each of them is subject to outrageous stereotyping – often propagated by the inhabitants of the other. Part of the enjoyment of visiting Glasgow and Edinburgh in sequence is to test whether their citizens really are warm-hearted, humorous, drunk and violent on the one hand or dignified, clean-living, stuck-up and offhand on the other.

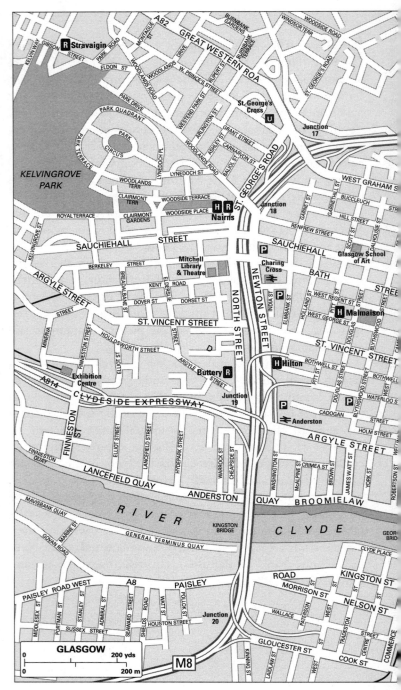

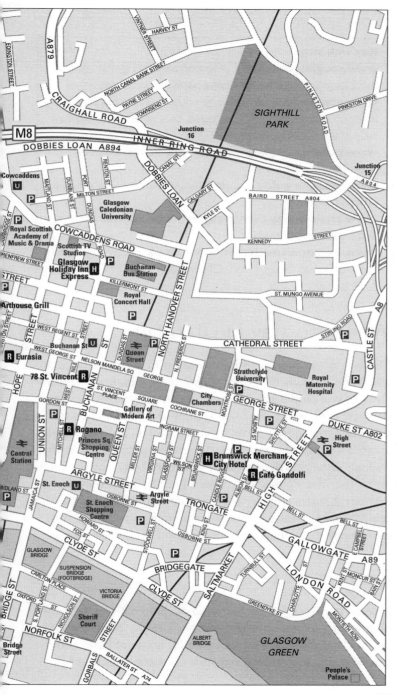

Key web sites

www.seeglasgow.com Comprehensive listing managed by the Glasgow Tourist Board. Useful background articles

www.glasgow.gov.uk The city council's site. Lots of information on transport and museums, plus an excellent virtual tour of the City Chambers

www.pure-dead-glasgow.com Idiosyncratic collection of interesting Glasgow links

www.glasgowguide.co.uk Comprehensive city guide, a little thin in places

www.clyde-valley.com/glasgow Good general listing of sights with virtual tours

www.personaltouch.freeserve.co.uk Nicely compiled introduction to Glasgow by a Glaswegian

Where to stay in Glasgow

The two obvious areas to base yourself in are the city centre with its numerous chain hotels (some of which offer short-break or weekend bargains) or the area round the University of Glasgow at Hillhead and Hyndland on the western side of the city. Here the hotels have more character and are supplemented by guesthouses, but the city centre is not within walking distance. Glasgow has been regrettably slow to catch on to the idea of the smart town guesthouse. Compared to Edinburgh, there are very few to be found anywhere near the centre. A wide choice of hotels is on offer, and although many are expensive, the number of budget options is growing.

Getting around

In some respects, Glasgow has yet to catch up with itself in terms of providing infrastructure for visitors. The city is too big to see on foot, and the routes of the colourful horde of buses and the extensive suburban railway network can seem baffling at first.

The circular subway – dubbed the Clockwork Orange because of the colour of its carriages – trundles round the periphery of the city centre, and is useful for sights on the western side of the city (but not the eastern). It takes 24 minutes to rattle around 15 stations. The most popular ticket is the Daytripper (£7.50 for one adult and up to two children) which is valid on all Strathclyde region transport systems for one day. A family daytripper ticket (£13 for two adults and up to four children) is also available. The Discovery ticket (adult £2.50) offers unlimited underground travel. The Roundabout Glasgow ticket (adult £3.50) offers unlimited travel on underground and mainline trains around Glasgow for one day; it comes with a free leaflet listing sights of interest.

City-centre parking is expensive and congestion is a problem; a car is not a good option and Glasgow has traditionally had low levels of car ownership. Travelling by taxi is certainly the quickest and liveliest way of getting around (Glaswegian taxi drivers are the chattiest, wittiest, kindest and perhaps the least comprehensible in Britain), but costs mount up.

If you need timetables or encounter travel problems, try the St Enoch Square Travel Centre [☎ 0141-226 4826]. The Travel Centre at Buchanan Street bus station can also provide help [☎ 0141-332 7133]. Much the best way of orientating yourself in Glasgow is to take a city bus tour; two companies run a mammoth and comprehensive round trip from George Square (running every weekday half-hour from April to October) [☎ 0141-248 7644 for details].

THE CITY CENTRE

Since medieval times, the centre of activity has moved westward from Glasgow's High Street. A neat grid-plan of streets, centred on George Square, contains the bulk of the city-centre shops and offices. The eastern side of this complex is known as the Merchant City. Here many of Glasgow's most dignified buildings are found, along with the most fashionable wine bars, designer outlets and lunch-time eateries.

Top sights

Gallery of Modern Art (Queen Street)

✓ *Splendid mixed-media collection by living artists*
✓ *Imaginative layout and interpretation*
✓ *Good for children*

Few modern art galleries have premises as magnificent as the old Glasgow Royal Exchange. The massive portico still suggests wealth and grandeur, while the interior is equally lavish, with gilded Corinthian pillars and high windows. The museum opened in 1996 and perfectly exemplifies the idea that art should be accessible and fun. The ground floor exhibition has the most impact. A superb kinetic sculpture, somewhere between a bicycle and a flying machine, draws groups of silent onlookers waiting for the performance to begin. This is echoed, at the far end of the room, by a grotesque collection of flying papier-mâché dragon devils. The dominant painting is Peter Howson's *Patriots*, one of the most disturbing portrayals of our times.

There are gentler works too: vivid photographs, strange anti-communist working contraptions, a clay floor, and a fibre-glass caricature of the Queen. The basement is full of interactive art and includes a kind of do-it-yourself mixing desk where you can play with sound and video clips.

It's an inspiring gallery for children, because there is so much that is unexpected, and quite a lot that is hands-on. Not all the art can stand the strain however, and some of the do-it-yourself gadgets are looking a bit worn. *[Mon–Thur and Sat 10–5, Fri and Sun 11–5;* ☎ *0141-229 1996]*

Glasgow Cathedral (Cathedral Square)

✓ *Terrific interior architecture*
✓ *One of the few surviving parts of medieval Glasgow*

One of the few relics of medieval Glasgow, this is also the only cathedral in Scotland to have survived the Reformation intact, and is a first-class, if rather gloomy, example of mid-thirteenth-century Gothic. As Scott's character Andrew Fairservice describes it, it has 'nane o' yere whigmaleeries and curliewurlies and opensteek hems about it' and indeed the exterior is very plain. The interior, though, is fascinating – especially in the choir, where the outgrowth of mouldings create a waterfall of stone pouring downwards from the clerestory to the forceful chutes of the aisle columns. The vaulted lower church, made necessary because of the fall of the land underneath the choir, is more forest-like, its massive piers sprouting springers in all directions. Here is to be found the tomb of St Kentigern. Other good parts of the cathedral are the Lady Chapel, with magnificent vaulting, and the unique rood screen. *[Apr to Sept, Mon–Sat 9–6.30, Sun 2–6.30; Oct to Mar, Mon–Sat 9–4.30, Sun 2–4.30;* ☎ *0141-552 6891;* 🖰 *via www.scottishculture.about.com]*

Glasgow School of Art (Renfrew Street)

✓ *All Mackintosh lovers*
✓ *Fascinating interior design*

This is the most famous of Charles Rennie Mackintosh's buildings, constructed between 1897 and 1909, and shows the architect at his most adventurous. Enthusiasts will be able to trace Mackintosh's influences, from Elizabethan mansion to Scottish baronial. The oriel windows, stretching over several floors, are the most eye-catching part of the exterior. The interior of the building is even more fantastical than the outside. The two-storey library has lamps like miniature ziggurats, and wood carved into endless fascinating shapes, while the top-floor gallery contains many splendid examples of Mackintosh furniture. The Glasgow School of Art has had, and still has, an inestimable influence on the success of generation upon generation of Glasgow painters. *[Tours of the interior: all year, Mon to Fri 11 and 2, Sat 10.30 and 11.30; additional tours in July and Aug: Sat and Sun 1pm;* ☎ *0141-353 4526;* 🖰 *www.gsa.ac.uk]*

The People's Palace (Glasgow Green)

✓ *Unique insight into Glasgow life*
✓ *Imaginative and quirky style*
✓ *Newly-restored Winter Gardens*

✓ *Good for children*
✗ *Not well signed; check directions in advance*

This wonderful museum started as a late-Victorian piece of cultural do-goodery for the deprived people of East Glasgow. Now it has become a splendid record of Glasgow life, and must be counted one of the most fascinating places in the city. The story of Glasgow unfolds on three floors, with themed areas carefully integrated into a coherent whole. The themes range from Glasgow's political idealism to the down-to-earth life of old Glasgow, with the 'Steamie', the 'Wally Close' and the 'Single End' featuring prominently. The combination of nostalgic appeal to the elderly and hands-on interest for the young, with imaginative use of sound dovetailed in, has been inventively and thoughtfully done. Sit on the bench from an Italian café, for example, and you are immediately aurally encased by a gossipy conversation which seems to be taking place at the next-door table. The section entitled 'The Patter' carries video clips from Stanley Baxter, Billy Connolly and Rab C Nesbit taking a dig at the Glasgow dialect and explaining for the ignorant what might be the meaning of 'Razza burdoora hairywullie?'

Do not leave without looking at the Winter Gardens at the rear, where the glass and ironwork has now been restored. (The tiles in the toilets depict scenes from Shakespeare and are worth a peek.) *[Mon–Thur and Sat 10–5, Fri and Sun 11–5;* ☎ *0141-554 0223;* 📖 *via www.clyde-valley.com/glasgow]*

The next best sights

City Chambers (George Square)

The lavishly ostentatious City Chambers were erected in 1888 in best Italian Renaissance style. No building says more about Glasgow's self-confidence in its Victorian heyday – take a tour of its magnificently (if sometimes excessively) decorated interior. Granite columns, marble capitals, mosaic upon mosaic, a massive staircase adorned with arches, more pillars and more purple and red marble culminate in a cupola of tinted glass. The council hall has carved mahogany in abundance, while the banqueting hall, with murals and arched ceilings, just stuns. *[Tours normally Mon–Fri, 10.30 and 2.30 (45 mins). It is advisable to call first:* ☎ *0141-287 2000;* ✆ *via www.glasgow.gov.uk]*

The Lighthouse (Mitchell Lane)

The old *Glasgow Herald* building was Charles Rennie Mackintosh's first public commission. Now it has been sensitively restored as Scotland's Centre for Architecture, Design and the City. There's an extremely good interpretation of what Mackintosh is all about, making it an ideal starting point for tracing the architect around the city. Temporary exhibitions and showcases for Glasgow designers fill the place out. *[Mon, Wed, Fri and Sat 10.30–5.30, Tue 11–5.30, Thur 10.30–7.30, Sun 12–5;* ☎ *0141-225 8414;* ✆ *www.thelighthouse.co.uk]*

Provand's Lordship

Opposite the Cathedral, across Castle Street, you will find Provand's Lordship , which is Glasgow's oldest house, dating from 1471. It was once the home of the Canon of Barlanark, and later became a sweet shop, a pub and a furniture-maker's workshop. It reopened in December 2000 after refurbishment. *[Mon–Thur and Sat 10–5, Fri and Sun 11–5;* ☎ *0141-553 2557]*

St Mungo Museum of Religious Life and Art (next to Cathedral)

St Mungo Museum of Religious Life and Art is housed in a modern building which fits in well with its medieval surroundings. The star exhibit here is Salvador Dali's *Christ of St John of the Cross*; nothing else in the building approaches the numinous power of this painting, and its presence alone should be sufficient reason for making your way to this museum. Other attractions are the concise history of religion in Scotland and an authentic Zen garden. *[Mon–Thur and Sat 10–5, Fri and Sun 11–5;* ☎ *0141-553 2557;* ✆ *via www.clyde-valley.com/glasgow]*

The Tenement House (Buccleuch Street)

The tenement is still Glasgow city centre's most typical form of housing, and this is your chance to see what life used to be like for the inhabitants. Miss Agnes Toward moved here in 1911 and died in 1975. Apparently unimpressed by modernity, she lived in a way almost unchanged from Edwardian times. You see her hall, parlour, bedroom, bathroom and kitchen with everything in place, from the box beds carefully tucked away in the walls to the great black kitchen range. Pots of jam stand in the cupboard, and the mangle and washboard remain by the sink. There's also an exhibition about tenement life. *[NTS; Mar to Oct, daily 2–5;* ☎ *0141-333 0183;* 🖥 *via www.nts.org.uk]*

Also in the area

The Barras (between Gallowgate and London Road) Glasgow's famous street market. You can buy everything from junk to fresh fruit, but it is not so much what is sold as the way it is sold that draws visitors. Lots of patter and earthy humour. Weekends are best. *[Mon–Fri 10–4, weekends 10–5]*

George Square An eclectic variety of statues populates Glasgow's central square. Sir Walter Scott is in the centre, on top of a Doric column. Queen Victoria, Robert Burns and James Watt are there, flanked by Glaswegians of varying degrees of fame. But George III, after whom the square is named, is not. The legend goes that his loss of the American colonies, and hence Glasgow's tobacco trade, saw to that.

Glasgow Green This large, open patch of greenery by the Clyde has long been the focus of all kinds of open-air activity, from football to political meetings. Freemen of Glasgow still have the right to graze a flock of sheep here. Nelson stands on a column at the western side, and a ceramic version of Queen Victoria is nearby. A boulder marks the site where James Watt had his brainwave about the steam engine.

Glasgow Necropolis is a magnificent graveyard on a hill behind the cathedral, covered with the elaborate tombs of rich industrialists and merchants. The figure of John Knox stands on top of a huge pillar, glowering down on them. Views of the city are very good.

Piping Centre (Cowcaddens) Dedicated to the bagpipe, the centre contains rehearsal rooms and a concert hall as well as a museum containing old and beautiful sets of pipes. A must for the enthusiast *[All year, daily 10–4;* ☎ *0141-353 0220;* ☜ *www.thepipingcentre.co.uk].*

Templeton Business Centre (opposite People's Palace) This one-time carpet factory is an extraordinary orange replica of the Doge's Palace in Venice. The story goes that the architect was asked to name his favourite building – this was the result.

Shopping

Glaswegians are well known for their shop-until-you-drop mentality, and one of the features of the New Glasgow is the extensive construction of shopping malls. Chief among these is **St Enoch's Shopping Centre** *[*☜ *www.stenoch.co.uk]*, which has the largest glass roof in Europe. The newest is the vast **Buchanan Galleries** behind Queen Street station, while the poshest is probably **Princes Square Shopping Centre**. The most fashionable is without doubt the **Italian Centre** (Ingram Street) with cafés and sculpture to go with the designer labels. The upsurge of malls has not harmed Glasgow's traditional shopping areas, notably Sauchiehall Street and Argyle Street and the streets in between.

Suggested walk

The Clyde Walkway The riverside promenade runs from the bottom of Saltmarket as far as the Scottish Exhibition Centre two miles away. It can be a windy walk, but an interesting one. Look out for the statue of 'La Passionaria' close to Glasgow

Bridge, set up to commemorate those Glaswegians who joined the International Brigade in the Spanish Civil War. The Finnieston Crane, once the largest in Europe, forms a distant landmark. It was used for loading locomotives on to ships. The miniature Sydney Opera House, known locally as The Armadillo, is the new Glasgow Auditorium. Beyond the soulless Exhibition Centre, the **Clyde Maritime Museum** (a.k.a. **The Tall Ship at Glasgow Harbour**) helps you to appreciate the city's long love-affair with the sea, and gives you the opportunity to board the *Glenlee* – the only Glasgow-built sailing ship still afloat *[Mon–Sat, 10–6]*. The newest sight in this

---

Interesting architecture in Glasgow

Blythswood Square A beautiful neoclassical square – the nearest Glasgow comes to the elegance of Edinburgh's Charlotte Square.

Ca'd'oro (Union Street) A cast-iron and glass building in lavish Venetian style, recently restored after a fire.

Gardner's Building (Jamaica Street) The first building in Europe to be constructed from cast-iron and glass, and a very elegant one.

Glasgow Royal Concert Hall (Buchanan Street) A squat, sandy modern building from the outside, the interior is worth seeing *[Tours usually run Mon–Fri at 2pm;* ☎ *0141-353 8000;* ⫍ *www.grch.com]*

Hutchesons' Hall (Ingram Street) This was the site of a hospital founded in the seventeenth century. The statues of its founders, made in 1649, now occupy niches in the pretty early nineteenth-century building, with its neat white clock tower and spire. The hall on the first floor is open, and well worth seeing for its rich decoration *[Mon–Sat 10–5;* ☎ *0141-552 8391;* ⫍ *www.nts.org.uk]*.

Merchant's House (West George Street) A further lavish memorial to Glasgow's trade. Amazons support the windows,

---

area is the **Glasgow Science Centre**, due to open in 2001 and promising much [☎ *0141-420 5000;* ● *www. gsc.org.uk*].

THE UNIVERSITY AND THE WEST END

At one time the Great Western Road was going to be remodelled in favour of the car. Luckily, motorway developments came to a halt, but the change of plan has left central Glasgow linked to the West End of the city by only the most tenuous of threads

and a sailing ship tops the dome. The banqueting hall is amazing [☎ *0141-221 8272 for access times*].

The McLellan Galleries (Sauchiehall Street) The Galleries now contain the largest temporary exhibition space in Britain outside London, hosting half a dozen major exhibitions a year.

St Vincent Church (St Vincent Street) An extraordinary building by Alexander 'Greek' Thomson – a mixture of styles harking back to ancient Egypt and ancient Greece with smatterings of India. Now a hotel.

Trades Hall (Glassford Street) A Robert Adam building from 1794, still fulfilling its original function as a home for Glasgow's 14 guilds. Go in to see the banqueting hall and the saloon.

Virginia Galleries (Virginia Street) Glasgow merchants once haggled over cargoes of tobacco or sugar here. Now Glasgow shoppers bargain for antiques.

Willow Tea Rooms (Sauchiehall Street) A reconstruction of Charles Rennie Mackintosh's best-known interior. It is one of four tea rooms he was commissioned to design, and is above a jeweller's shop. Typical Mackintosh high-backed chairs pierced with little squares are grouped round the tables; mirrors and painted glass decorate the walls [*Mon–Sat 9.30–4.30, Sun 12–4.30;* ☎ *0141-332 0521;* ● *www.willowtearooms.co.uk*].

Glasgow festivals

Because of its size, Glasgow is the best Scottish city to visit for its ceaseless round of cultural events. It has taken festivals of one kind or another very much to its heart. Whereas Edinburgh is best known for its International Arts Festival, Glasgow's events offer greater diversity. As well as mounting its own Hogmanay Celebrations, Glasgow sees the Scottish Curling Championship (February), the Lord Provost's Procession (June), a renowned International Jazz festival (July) and the World Pipe Band Championhips (August). These staples are supplemented by a different series of exhibitions or themed events, usually including architecture and food somewhere along the line. Full details of all events are at
◝ *www.seeglasgow.com*

across the gulf of the motorway. The easiest way for the visitor to reach the University area is by the 'Clockwork Orange' subway.

Top sights

Glasgow Art Gallery and Museum (Kelvingrove)

✓ *Good collection of paintings*
✓ *Imaginative ideas on display*

This is the largest and among the oldest of the Glasgow museums and galleries. The huge red building at the foot of the hill below Glasgow University was purpose-built to house the city's collections, and was opened in 1901. By today's tastes it is vastly impractical as a museum, with a cathedral-sized, echoing, central hall, miles of colonnaded stone galleries and lofty exhibition rooms.

Both the museum section and the art gallery have collections of terrific range and quality. The museum is particularly strong in arms and armour, archaeology and natural history. The art gallery is notable for its British and French paintings of the nineteenth century, but has fine Italian and Flemish works from earlier periods too. Much is being done here to make the objects and the pictures as exciting and relevant to the general visitor as they possibly can be. For example, an Imperial Trooper straight from the set of a *Star Wars* film is displayed alongside a suit of late-medieval armour, with the similarities carefully pointed out. Even the serried rows of butterflies in glass cases are made interesting by explanations of why such research collections are needed and how they are used.

At the time of writing, it was rumoured that money may be made available to refurbish the museum, in which case it may close for a period. *[Mon–Thur and Sat, 10–5, Fri and Sun 11–5;* ☎ *0141-287 2700;* ⛵ *via www.clyde-valley.com/glasgow]*

The University of Glasgow

✓ *Very good museum*
✓ *Excellent art gallery, with extensive Whistler collection*
✓ *Reproduction of Mackintosh's house*

Founded in 1451, the university moved to this site in 1870, away from its old position on the High Street. It now forms a complex of buildings around its Victorian Gothic centrepiece *[⛵ www.gla.ac.uk]*. Once through the 1951 memorial gates, you will find the visitor centre. If you do not have time to tour everything, try to see the splendidly Gothic Bute Hall and the Hunterian Museum with its geological, numismatic and archaeological collections *[Mon–Sat, 9.30–5;* ☎ *0141-330 4221]*. On no account miss the Hunterian Art Gallery. The doors, by Eduardo Paolozzi, are the first indication of the gallery's style. Inside, the paintings are hung to splendid effect. The collection is small but surprisingly comprehensive, and, for followers of J.M. Whistler, unrivalled outside Washington DC. The gallery also boasts further examples of Glasgow painters and a superb collection of prints, including some by Hockney, Picasso and Dürer.

At one end of the gallery is a reconstruction of the home of Charles Rennie Mackintosh. There are three floors' worth of his fascinating furniture, and plenty of ideas for budding cabinet-makers and interior designers alike. *[Mon–Sat, 9.30–5; Mackintosh House closed at lunch hour]*

The next best sight

Museum of Transport

The huge collection of vehicles of all kinds forms a comprehensive record of Glasgow's history in the manufacture of cars, locomotives and ships. Trams, steam engines and ranks of cars fill the cavernous space of Kelvin Hall, and models of Clyde-built ships populate an upper gallery. Efforts are made at bringing the interpretation up to date, but, for the non–enthusiast, the presentation can be a little barren. *[Mon–Thur and Sat 10–5, Fri and Sun 11–5;* ☎ *0141-287 2700;* 🖰 *via www.scottishculture.about.com]*

Suggested walks

Botanic Gardens The gardens are rather put in the shade by the huge glasshouse of Kibble Palace, brought here on a boat from Loch Long in the late nineteenth century and now filled with ferns. But the surrounding gardens make for a pleasing stroll, with a rock garden, a herb garden and plenty of space to sit. *[7–dusk; Kibble Palace 10–4.45;* ☎ *0141-334 2422;* 🖰 *via www.clyde-valley.com/glasgow]*

Kelvingrove Park The park, between the Kelvingrove Art Gallery and Museum and the University, is the most pleasant open space in the city. The massive fountain standing in the park commemorates the Lord Provost under whom the waters of Loch Katrine were piped into Glasgow to form the water supply, helping to reduce the awful statistics of death from cholera and typhus in Glasgow's Victorian slums. A walkway runs up beside the River Kelvin towards the Forth and Clyde canal, where the Kelvin Aqueduct (1790) and the Maryhill Locks are the things to see.

Park Conservation Area This cloistered little enclave of houses and towers, reached from the centre via Woodlands Road, has been likened to an Italian hilltop town. It forms a neat piece of early nineteenth-century town-planning – a series of quiet streets lined by dignified houses. It's worth finding for the views of Kelvingrove Park and of the city.

Entertainment and nightlife

Glaswegians love to be entertained, and you'll have no difficulty in finding something different for each night of your stay. Check the listings in the *Evening Times* or in the fortnightly publication *The List*. For most Glasgow venues, credit card bookings can be made [☎ 0141-287 4000/5511 *or by calling in at the Ticket Centre in Candleriggs*]. Most nights you'll find either challenging modern drama or provocatively staged classical drama at the Citizens Theatre in the Gorbals [☎ 0141-429 5561]; touring productions and local amateur dramatics at the King's Theatre [☎ 0141-287 5006]; variety at the Pavilion [☎ 0141-332 1846]; fringe theatre at the Tron [☎ 0141-552 4267] and Cottier Theatre [☎ 0141-357 3868]; and a mixed programme from touring companies at the Mitchell [☎ 0141-287 4529]. Epic modern productions find a home at the Tramway [☎ 0141-287 3900].

Glasgow is also the home of Scottish Opera, which operates from the Theatre Royal [☎ 0141-332 9000]. The Royal Scottish National Orchestra plays summer proms and a winter season at the Glasgow Royal Concert Hall [☎ 0141-332 6633].

For folk music and jazz try various pubs, including Babbity Bowster [☎ 0141-552 5055], Blackfriars [☎ 0141-552 5924] and Rab Ha's [☎ 0141-553 1545], the popular pasta/pizza bar Di Maggio's [☎ 0141-334 8560], and the Brewery Tap [☎ 0141-339 8866]. A new generation of Glaswegians has discovered the joy of the ceilidh; to join them in a Gay Gordons or Strip the Willow, visit the Riverside Club on Clyde Street [☎ 0141-248 3144].

Football is Glasgow's secular religion. Celtic play at the remodelled Celtic Park in the East End [☎ 0141-551 8653]; Rangers in their exemplary Ibrox Stadium [☎ 0141-427 8800]. 'Old Firm' matches, when the two meet, remain a clash of the titans.

SOUTH OF THE CLYDE

To explore down here you will need a car, or else to have grown accustomed to the buses, for the sights are scattered and few are within walking distance of the city centre.

Top sights

The Burrell Collection

✓ *Brilliant collection of art and antiquities*
✓ *Fascinating modern building in semi-rural setting*
✓ *Good café and restaurant*

The Burrell Collection is the result of one wealthy man's lifetime passion for art. Sir William Burrell was a steamship owner, who spent his money on amassing one of the most interesting collections to be seen in Britain. He donated it to Glasgow in 1944, on condition that the collection should be exhibited in a purpose-built gallery in a rural setting away from Glasgow's polluted atmosphere. It was 1983 before the new brick and glass gallery in Pollok Country Park was opened to the public.

The building and its surroundings form a wonderful setting for the collection. Architectural features from old houses and castles are built into its interior walls, and the artefacts and sculptures from the Ancient World are exhibited against a background of foliage.

The collection ranges from Ancient Egypt and China through furniture, glassware, silverware, tapestries and stained glass, to the paintings and drawings which are its backbone. There is no single work of art that you would travel miles to see, but the variety and quality of the collection as a whole is outstanding. It is in the fields of medieval furniture, glass and woodcarving, and nineteenth-century French painting that the collection has its major strength.

The gallery has been conceived and laid out to enable the beauty of the objects to make their own impact. A very good restaurant, with medieval stained glass in its windows, provides material refreshment. *[Mon–Thur and Sat 10–5, Fri and Sun 11–5;* ☎ *0141-287 2550]*

Pollok Country Park and House

✓ *Homely, classical house with great paintings*
✓ *Excellent complement to the nearby Burrell*
✓ *Extensive parkland – good for walks*

The estate of Pollok was held by the Maxwell family from 1269 to 1966, when it was donated to Glasgow. It has now been turned into a country park in the middle of the city, and a most tranquil place it is, with a herd of Highland cattle mournfully surveying the strollers and the golfers.

Pollok House lies at the centre. Inside the neoclassical house a superb collection of Spanish, Dutch and British paintings is set out in the airy rooms. In particular, there are fine works by William Blake, Hogarth, Goya, El Greco and Murillo. It is foolish to traipse hotfoot to the Burrell and neglect Pollok, though all too many do. Apart from anything else, the formal gardens round the house are beautiful.

Possible routes for walkers are signed on information panels, but the park also offers large areas of open space in which to relax on a fine day. *[Apr to Oct, daily 10–5; Nov to Mar, 11–4;* ☎ *0141-616 6410;* 🖱 *via www.nts.org.uk]*

The next best sights

House for an Art Lover (Bellahouston Park)

Another example of Glasgow's willingness to use its past constructively, this is a design by Mackintosh which was not turned into reality until the 1990s. Originally, the house was an entry for a German architectural competition in 1901, but was finally built in Glasgow as a centre for Glasgow School of Art postgraduates. A number of rooms are open to the public, however, including the music room and more formal dining room. A video presentation recalls how the house was researched and constructed according to Mackintosh's plans. *[Apr to Sept, daily 10–4 (closed Fri); Oct to Mar, weekends 10–4, weekdays by arrangement;* ☎ *0141-353 4449;* 🖱 *www.houseforanartlover.co.uk]*

Scotland Street School

Built to Mackintosh's design in 1906, the old school has been turned into a Museum of Education, complete with relics from Victorian times onward, plus a suitably formidable atmosphere. Installation of a new lift has recently led to the discovery of some original tiles, and the museum is closed at the time of writing, while they are evaluated and conserved. *[Mon–Thur and Sat 10–5; Fri and Sun 11–5;* ☎ *0141-287 0500]*

Also in the area

The Gorbals This is the one district of Glasgow that everyone has heard of. Its notoriety came largely from Alexander MacArthur's novel No Mean City which luridly described its slums and its razor-wielding gangs. In the 1960s, the Gorbals was bulldozed and replaced with tower blocks, which have vanished in their turn. Now it is a district with low-density housing schemes. These days you go through the Gorbals to visit the Citizens' Theatre or the Tramway Theatre, with its huge space for epic productions, or to admire the lines of the modern Glasgow Central Mosque. The local web site is ✒ *www.gorbalslive.org.uk*

WHERE TO STAY

£ – under £70 per room per night, incl. VAT

££ – £70 to £110 per room per night, incl. VAT

£££ – over £110 per room per night, incl. VAT

Brunswick Merchant City Hotel

106–108 Brunswick Street, Glasgow
G1 1TF
☎ 0141-552 0001
📠 0141-552 1551
Large hotel for those on a budget, east of the city centre. The food is unremarkable, but the hotel remains good value.
£ *All year*

Devonshire Hotel

5 Devonshire Gardens, Glasgow
G12 0UX
☎ 0141-339 7878
📠 0141-339 3980
Well-run luxury hotel with one or two huge rooms and a tiny restaurant area. Handsome public rooms and

comfortable, well-appointed bedrooms.
£££ *All year*

Glasgow Guest House

56 Dumbreck Road, Glasgow G41 5NP
☎ /📠 0141-427 0129
A warm welcome and good service on
the outskirts of Glasgow. Two of the
seven bedrooms are equipped for
disabled access. The glass-roofed
courtyard makes a sunny breakfast
room, and there is a refrigerator for
guests' use.
£ *All year*

Glasgow Hilton Hotel

Camerons, 1 William Street, Glasgow
G3 8HT
☎ 0141-204 5555
📠 0141-204 5004
Lavish, well-run international hotel with
comfortable bedrooms and public
rooms. Not for those on a budget.
£££ *All year*

Glasgow Holiday Inn Express

165 West Nile Street, Glasgow G1 2RL
☎ 0141-331 6800
📠 0141-331 6828
No-frills budget hotel situated next to
the Royal Concert Hall offering fresh,
bright and spacious bedrooms.
Altogether better value than other
central Glasgow hotels.
£ *All year*

Kirklee Hotel

11 Kensington Gate, Glasgow
G12 9LG
☎ 0141-334 5555
📠 0141-339 3828
📠 www.kirkleehotel.co.uk

Fine Edwardian sandstone terrace with
an impressive hallway and many
original features. The *en suite* bedrooms
are well-equipped, and the handsome
lounge overlooks the garden. Breakfast
is served in the bedrooms.
£ *All year exc Christmas*

Malmaison Glasgow

278 West George Street, Glasgow
G2 4LL
☎ 0141-572 1000
📠 0141-572 1002
📠 www.malmaison.com
Stylish Gallic hotel with elegant
bedrooms in a converted church, the
Grecian exterior giving way to pilastered
chic. Visit the stylish café or in-house
gym. Tasty meals are served in the
undercroft, with a quirky wine list.
£££ *All year*

Nairns

13 Woodside Crescent, Glasgow G3 7UL
☎ 0141-353 0707
📠 0141-331 1684
📠 www.nairns.co.uk
Beautifully designed restaurant-with-
rooms. Four large, comfortable
bedrooms; the upper two imaginative
and feminine; the lower two
contemporary and striking. Two
restaurants are themed in austere
charcoal and white, and menus change
weekly.
£££ *Closed Christmas and New Year (See
Where to Eat)*

One Devonshire Gardens

1 Devonshire Gardens, Glasgow
G12 0UX

☎ 0141-339 2001

📠 0141-337 1663

📀 www.one-devonshire-gardens.co.uk

Much of this luxury townhouse hotel has
been refurbished in a light and modern
style. The drawing room is still traditional
and luxurious, as are the well-appointed
bedrooms.

£££ All year (See Where to Eat)

Town House

4 Hughenden Terrace, Glasgow G12 9XR

☎ 0141-357 0862

📠 0141-339 9605

📀 www.thetownhouseglasgow.com

Relaxed, spacious guesthouse in a fine
old Victorian house. Bedrooms retain
their individuality. The large sitting room
has squashy sofas, a real fire and well-
stocked bookshelves. Soup and
sandwiches are available in the evenings.

££ All year

WHERE TO EAT

78 St Vincent

78 St Vincent Street, Glasgow G2 5UB

☎ 0141-248 7878

📠 0141-248 4663

📀 www.78stvincent.com

The nineteenth-century French
brasserie evoked by this central
Glasgow restaurant is belied by the
contemporary menu. Seafood and beef
dishes generally please; wines are well
chosen and affordable.

12–3 and 5–10.30 (10.45 Fri and Sat, 10
Sun); closed 25 Dec

Arthouse Hotel, Arthouse Grill

129 Bath Street, Glasgow G2 2SY

☎ 0141-221 6789

📠 0141-221 6777

📀 www.arthousehotel.com

Former Glasgow School Board offices
converted into a handsome hotel and
restaurant. The Arthouse Grill downstairs
has a Guinness and oyster bar, as well as a
Japanese teppanyaki grill. Well-cooked
modern European dishes include fish,
pork and lamb as well as unusual desserts.

All week 12–11, teppanyaki Mon–Sat
12–3 and 6–10

Buttery

652 Argyle Street, Glasgow G3 8UF

☎ 0141-221 8188

📠 0141-204 4639

Handsome restaurant with mirrored bar,
impressive paintings and dark oak
panelling. A wide range of European-
influenced food appears on the
ambitious and inventive menu, which
uses fresh ingredients in poultry, lamb
and seafood dishes.

Mon–Fri L 12–2.30, Mon–Sat D 7–10.30;
closed 25 Dec, 1 Jan

Café Gandolfi

64 Albion Street, Glasgow G1 1NY

☎ 0141-552 6813

📠 0141-552 8911

The variety and quality of food available
raise the Café above the ordinary sort.
A quarterly-changing menu is
experimental and unusual, with an
international flavour. Fine home-made

wholemeal bread is sold with lunchtime salad, and the puddings range from traditional Scottish to European.
Mon–Sat 9–11.30, Sun noon–11.30

Eurasia

150 St Vincent Street, Glasgow G2 5NE
☎ 0141-204 1150
📠 0141-204 1140
A Scottish and Oriental fusion menu is available in a stylish wood and glass restaurant with an open-to-view kitchen. Scottish produce underlies the menu, and unusual and tasty desserts follow Chinese and Thai dishes. The wine list is mostly French.
Mon–Fri L 12–2.30, Mon–Sat D 7–11; closed bank hols

Nairns

13 Woodside Crescent, Glasgow G3 7UL
☎ 0141-353 0707
📠 0141-331 1684
📱 www.nairns.co.uk
This stylish monochrome restaurant run by Nick Nairn offers well-cooked local ingredients in a traditional menu. Poultry, beef, seafood and rich desserts all make an appearance in a wide repertoire of dishes.
Mon–Sat 12–2, 6–9.30; closed 25 and 26 Dec, 1 and 2 Jan (See Where to Stay)

Number Sixteen

16 Byres Road, Glasgow G11 5JY
☎ 0141-339 2544
📠 0141-576 1505
Small, split-level restaurant offering a sensible menu that incorporates variety without being too ambitious. Fish and vegetable main courses predominate,

although chicken and steak also appear. Desserts are unusual, and the short wine list is reasonably priced.
Mon–Sat 12–2.30 and 5.30–10; closed Christmas, first two weeks in Jan

One Devonshire Gardens

1 Devonshire Gardens, Glasgow G12 0UX
☎ 0141-339 2001
📠 0141-337 1663
📱 www.one-devonshire-gardens.co.uk
Luxurious and traditional townhouse hotel, offering a classic European menu. Food is understated and well-balanced; portions can be large, but dishes are rarely heavy. A somewhat expensive French wine list predominates.
Sun–Fri L 12.15–2, all week D 7.15–10 (See Where to Stay)

La Parmigiana

447 Great Western Road, Glasgow G12 8HH
☎ 0141-334 0686
📠 0141-332 3533
An Italian's Italian restaurant, with a 'happy atmosphere' and assured modern cooking. Set lunches and pre-theatre menus are excellent value, as are generous fish and shellfish stews. Pasta dishes and superb desserts are also notable. The wine list is Italian and reasonably priced.
Mon–Sat 12–2.30 and 6–11; closed 25 and 26 Dec, 1 and 2 Jan, Easter Mon

Puppet Theatre

11 Ruthven Lane, Glasgow G12 9BG
☎ 0141-339 8444
📠 0141-339 7666
Snug Edwardian interiors and an oddly-shaped conservatory give this restaurant

an offbeat yet romantic air. Cooking is as contemporary as the décor is quaint; Oriental influences can be seen in main courses, and traditional desserts have a modern twist.

Tue–Fri and Sun L 12–2.30, Tue to Sun D 7–10.30; closed 26 Dec, 1 and 2 Jan

Rogano

11 Exchange Place, Glasgow G1 3AN
☎ 0141-248 4055
📠 0141-248 2606
🖥 www.rogano.co.uk

Fine art-deco styling in a restaurant fitted out in 1935. Fish and seafood predominate on the menu, although beef and lamb do appear. Both traditional and unusual desserts complete the meal options. The wine list is somewhat expensive.

All week 12–2.30 and 6.30–10.30; closed 25 Dec, 1 Jan

Stravaigin

26 Gibson Street, Hillhead, Glasgow G12 8NX
☎ 0141-334 2665
📠 0141-334 4099
🖥 www.stravaigin.com

Bright, modern basement restaurant with an international menu, using ideas from various cuisines with fine Scottish ingredients. Seafood, game, offal and chicken appear in both rustic and elegant dishes; desserts are wide-ranging. The annotated wine list is reasonably priced.

Fri and Sat L 12–2.30, Tue to Sun D 5–11.30; closed 25 and 26 Dec, 1 and 2 Jan

Ubiquitous Chip

12 Ashton Lane, Glasgow G12 8SJ
☎ 0141-334 5007
📠 0141-337 1302
🖥 www.ubiquitouschip.co.uk

Set down a cobbled mews, this restaurant offers carefully sourced produce in simple yet imaginative dishes using a wide range of game, beef, pork, seafood and fish. Different menus in the brasserie-style Upstairs and the more traditional dining-room.

All week 12–2.30 and 5.30–11; closed 25 Dec, 1 Jan

Argyll and around

Iona Abbey

- Huge, thinly populated land of rugged peninsulas and long sea lochs
- Best coastal scenery in Scotland
- Islands to suit all tastes
- The birthplace of the Scottish nation and of its religious heritage
- Excellent area for sailing, gardens and wildlife

ARGYLL AND AROUND

At a glance

✓ Good for self-catering and cottage holidays

✓ Island holidays and island-hopping

✓ Ideal area for families

✓ Some of the best gardens in Scotland

✗ Can be very wet; terrible midges

✗ Difficult communications. A car is essential

Its deeply indented coastline and a web of offshore islands make Argyll at once distinct and enticing. The view across sea lochs and firths is almost always decorated by close or distant land masses of overlapping hills and mountains, misty or sharp contours, and shapes that are forever changing as you drive along. Reflections of mountains, castles or sheep-dotted slopes are true and sharp in this land of narrow and mirror-smooth bands of water.

Most sights in Argyll are minor, but there is a fair variety. Popular spots include Inveraray, home to one of Scotland's most famous castles, and Oban, busy fishing port and tourist centre. Closer to Glasgow is Charles Rennie Mackintosh's unmissable Hill House. The hill fort of Dunadd, the capital of the ancient kingdom of Dalriada, gets its fair share of visitors; it is surrounded by one of the highest concentrations of prehistoric monuments anywhere in Scotland. Amongst the castles, many of which are in advanced stages of ruin, are Kilchurn on Loch Awe, and Castle Stalker – both with atmospheric settings. Early Christian chapels, hermits' cells and weathered crosses dot the landscape, spreading out from Iona, the sacred heart of old Scotland and still a centre of popular pilgrimage.

The Inner Hebridean islands included in the chapter – Mull, Colonsay, Islay, Jura, Coll and Tiree among them – vary from very small to very large, and from flat and fertile to mountainous and desolate. In many cases the smaller they are, the more interesting: consider the religious importance of Iona, the freakish geology of Staffa, or the lush and untrampled

Colonsay. But if you are after total seclusion, look further north. Above all, be warned that the loch-pierced mainland and erratic ferry schedules are not designed for time-conscious travellers; do not assume that you can slip in a quick island tour to top up your Scottish experience. Yet you should not exclude the islands from your itinerary if you do have time; each is fascinating and distinct.

Key web sites

www.argyll.online.co.uk Brilliant general guide to the region; comprehensive and informative

www.scottish. heartlands.org The Area Tourist Board's site; sentimental but colourful

www.isle-of-bute.com Excellent guide to Rothesay and the rest of Bute

www.oban.org Directory for the Oban area

www.loch-awe.com Directory for Loch Awe area

www.isle.of.mull.com All you need to know about Mull and Iona

www.colonsay.org.uk Community web site from this tiny island

www.islaywhisky.com Vital starting point for anyone interested in Islay's distinctive product

---

Good bases in Argyll

Arrochar

✓ *Well located for exploring Loch Lomond and Loch Fyne*
✓ *Handy base for hill-walkers*
✗ *Not many facilities*

A small village stretching along a mile of shore, with many B&Bs looking out across Loch Long to uninhabited mountains. It occupies a fine boating and walking area and is central for the high moorland and mountains to the north and the Cowal Peninsula to the south.

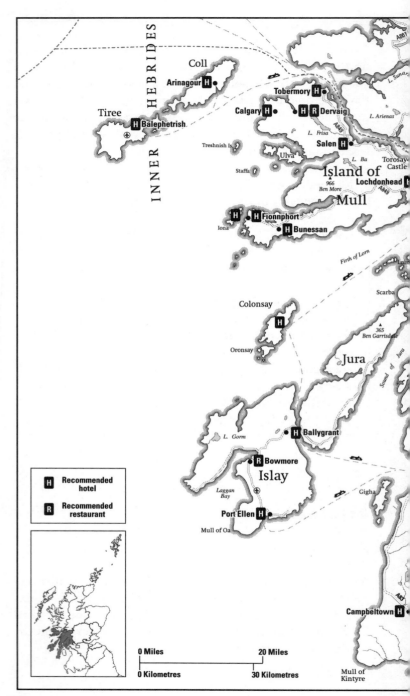

INNER HEBRIDES

Coll

Arinagour H ●

Tiree

H **Balephetrish**

L. Sunar

A861

Tobermory H ●

Calgary H ● ● H R **Dervaig**

L. Arienas

L. Frisa

Salen H ●

Treshnish Is.

Ulva

Torosay
Castle

Staffa

Island of

966
Ben More

Lochdonhead H

A849

Mull

H ● H **Fionnphort**

● H **Bunessan**

Iona

Firth of Lorn

Luin

Scarba

Colonsay

H

365
Ben Garrisdate

Oronsay

Jura

Sound of Jura

H **Ballygrant**

L. Gorm

R **Bowmore**

Islay

Laggan
Bay

Gigha

Port Ellen H

Mull of Oa

H **Recommended hotel**

R **Recommended restaurant**

0 Miles   20 Miles

0 Kilometres   30 Kilometres

Campbeltown H

Mull of
Kintyre

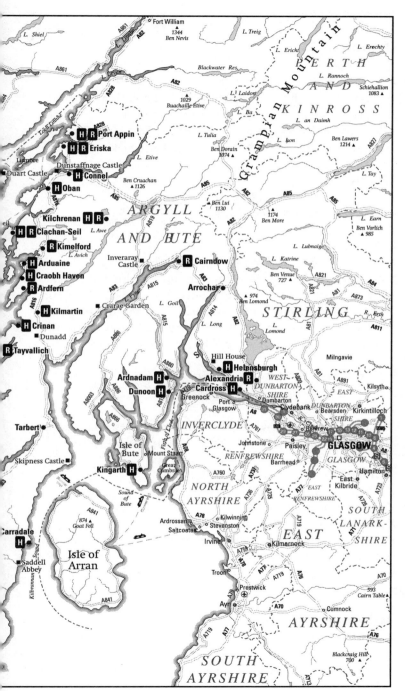

203

Dunoon

✓ *Good base for Cowal and Bute*
✓ *Ample accommodation, decent facilities*

This is a good town for strolling in, with four miles of promenade and a large harbourside park complete with castle ruin. You are unlikely to find accommodation on the last Friday and Saturday in August, when the Cowal Highland Gathering takes place.

Oban

✓ *Wide choice of activities in the area*
✓ *Good ferry connections in all directions*
✓ *Rail connections*
✗ *Not a lot to do in town*
✗ *A very wide choice of accommodation, but not all of it is good*

Oban is perfectly placed for day trips up and down the coast, and is the port that links the mainland with Mull, Coll and Tiree. Smaller ferries to many of the little islands in and around its harbour leave from landings just outside town. It has the best selection of restaurants and shops for miles around.

Port Charlotte

✓ *Very pretty large village in good setting*
✓ *Nearby attractions*

Much the nicest of Islay's small towns and villages, with a good hotel, a local museum, and a street of whitewashed cottages.

Tarbert

✓ *Well-positioned for taking day trips to the islands*
✓ *Attractive, small loch-side town*
✗ *Long journey to reach it*

A small place, with no real sights to speak of, but pleasant and not often inundated by tourists. The main part of town, facing west, curves round a very deep harbour. The range of restaurants and accommodation is average.

Tobermory

✓ *Pretty small town, with a fair range of accommodation and shops*
✓ *Good base for exploring Mull*

Mull's capital, near the north-east tip, can be reached via

ferry from Oban. The town consists of one great swoop of harbour street, with some houses raked up the hill behind; colourful and unassuming guesthouses are scattered around outside the town, and there are a few mid-range hotels on the harbour.

LOCH LOMOND, COWAL AND BUTE

This area of country closest to Glasgow naturally sees the most visitors, and where the famous Loch Lomond is concerned, real dangers of overcrowding are present, especially on the busy western bank. Dumbarton and Helensburgh are used by commuters, while Dunoon and Rothesay are long-established resorts for holidaying Glaswegians. But away from these places, especially in the remote folds of Cowal, or the peaceful farmlands of Bute, you will encounter few people and some fine landscape.

Top sights

Hill House (Helensburgh)

✓ *One of the best Mackintosh buildings*
✓ *Wonderful setting*

Charles Rennie Mackintosh built this house for the publisher Walter Blackie in 1902. Outside the gates are six large street lamps, constructed from recently discovered Mackintosh sketches; inside the house, bold, angular shapes are mixed with jubilant, decorative patterns of sinuous, swirling lines. The colour scheme of black, pinks and purples is equally self-confident. Restrained by cost and by Blackie's taste, Mackintosh had to forgo designing every bit of furniture and decoration, but you have to look hard to find a single hinge or nail at odds with his grand scheme. The dining-room shows how clever he was at integrating Blackie's old furniture with Art Nouveau. The house is essential visiting for Mackintosh fans, and nearly everyone will find pleasure in the harmonious design. You can stock up on Mackintosh motif tea towels, mugs and books at the gift shop, and there is now a tea-room. Hill House has been suffering from excessive numbers of visitors; if you turn up at peak times you may be asked to wait before being allowed in. *[NTS; Apr to Oct, daily 1.30–5.30;* ☎ *(01436) 673900; via www.GreatBuildings.com]*

Mount Stuart (Isle of Bute)

✓ *Lavish Victorian Gothic mansion*
✓ *Unique interior, unrivalled outside Cardiff Castle*
✓ *Extensive grounds with good walks*
✓ *Well-run sight with plenty to see and do*

Only recently opened to visitors, Mount Stuart is one of the most extraordinary houses in Britain. The scale of expenditure needed to create its marbled, gilded and colonnaded interior is mind-boggling, but then the 3rd Marquess of Bute, who started it in 1877, was one of the richest men in Europe. The end result is a place that stuns; a mixture of cathedral, fantasy castle and palace. But it could never be called a cosy home. Tours lead visitors through the echoing entrance hall, up the marble stairway, around the gallery, panelled with stained glass, and through various bedrooms and libraries, each more luxurious than the last. The visit culminates in the chapel, whose scale alone is closer to a parish church. Mount Stuart is very different from the usual run of stately homes, and really ought to be seen, even at the cost of travelling specially to Bute for the purpose.

The acres of grounds, with gardens, seashore and woodland walks and a children's play area, extend Mount Stuart's attraction, and make it easily possible to spend a whole day here. Shops, a tea-room and audio-visual are on tap. *[Mid-Apr to end Sept, daily exc Tue and Thur; house: 11–3.30, grounds: 10–5;* ☎ *(01700) 503877; www.mountstuart.com]*

The next best sights

Dumbarton Castle

The castle sits on a high, steep-sided rock near where the River Leven flows into the Clyde. It was once the most important fortress in western Scotland, but there is little of it left, apart from a magazine, some ramparts and a few gun batteries. It is worth climbing to the top for the sake of the views over the Firth of Clyde. *[HS; Apr to Sept, Mon–Sat 9.30–6.30, Sun 2–6.30; Oct to Mar, Mon–Sat 9.30–6.30, Sun 2–4.30;* ☎ *(01389) 732167;* 🖰 *via www.scottishculture. about.com]*

Rothesay Castle

Rothesay Castle was probably first built in the late twelfth century, though the earliest confirmed is date is 1230, when Norsemen stormed it. There are no other circular core castles in Britain, and Rothesay's round silhouette is startling. Its solid, ivy-covered walls are more than 130 feet in diameter. Of the four great drum towers, one is still standing. Cottages once filled the middle, as demonstrated by a small but illuminating model in the Great Hall. A reconstructed wooden ceiling hung with Gothic-style wheel lamps shows how the principal chamber might once have looked. *[Apr to Sept, daily 9.30–6; Oct to Mar, Mon–Sat 9.30–4.30, Sun 2–4.30, closed Thur pm and Fri;* ☎ *(01700) 502691;* 🖰 *via www.scottishculture.about.com]*

Younger Botanic Garden (north of Dunoon on A815)

These wonderful gardens were planted in 1870 and 1880, so their star sight, the avenue of Giant Redwoods, is now well into its second century. This is a woodland garden, with superb rhododendrons, a formal conifer garden and a network of trails, few of which are steep. Useful booklets from the visitor centre explain the garden's background and importance. *[Mar to Oct, daily 9.30–6;* ☎ *(01369) 706261;* 🖰 *via www.rgbe.org.uk]*

Also in the area

Ardkinglas Woodland Garden (by the Head of Loch Fyne) A big woodland garden with magnificent trees, in the process of being restored back to its 1875 glory at the time of writing. It is very well placed near the junction of the A83 and A815, an ideal spot for a break in the journey. [☎ *(01499) 600263]*

St Blane's Church (Kingarth, South Bute) St Blane was born on Bute in the sixth century and a monastery dedicated to him was built here. The narrow, roofless chapel is twelfth-century, and worth seeing for the delicately carved Romanesque arch of the chancel. [*Access at all times;* ☎ *0131–668 8800;* 🖱 *via www.isle-of-bute.com]*

Victorian toilets (Rothesay) Restored to its full glory, this pier-head public convenience is a place of sumptuous tiling, copper pipework and gurgling cisterns. Men have a free run of the place; women must wait until no males are around before being shown in. Unfortunately, when we inspected, the toilets were less than clean. [🖱 *via www.isle-of-bute.com]*

Towns and villages to explore

Dunoon

The largest town on the Cowal Peninsula, with many fine houses remaining from Victorian and Edwardian days when wealthy Glaswegians came on holiday. The four miles of prom-enade are as popular for evening strolls now as they were then. Castle Hill, a spacious green park above the pier, rises steeply to the few remaining fragments of a thirteenth-century castle from where you can see many miles of shore and sea. A statue of Highland Mary, whom Robert Burns almost married, stands just below. The place really buzzes on the last Friday and Saturday in August, when the Cowal Highland Gathering overtakes the town. Ferry connections run from Gourock. [🖱 *www.cowal-dunoon.com]*

Rothesay

The old resort has an endearingly buoyant air during the summer months, and has recently had a face-lift; the cast–iron Winter Garden Pavilion has been returned to its former exuberant glory and yachts, sea birds, bathers, and even porpoises populate the wide harbour. Ferry connections run from Wemyss Bay. [⌢☗ *via www.isle-of-bute.com]*

Scenery and touring routes

The Arrochar Alps This is the name given to the group of mountains clustered around the head of Loch Long. They include Ben Arthur, also known as 'The Cobbler', with its rocky peak, and the shapely crest of Ben Ime. Views from the 'Rest and be Thankful' pass at the top of Glen Croe (on A83) are good. [⌢☗ *via www.duncolm.freeserve.co.uk]*

Kyles of Bute The narrow arms of the sea which make Bute into an island are often filled with yachts. Seen from high on the A8003 north of Tighnabruich on a fine day, the Kyles look blue and peaceful.

Loch Lomond [⌢☗ *www.loch-lomond-info.co.uk]* Apart from the busy weekends when the bonny banks are almost hidden by traffic, Loch Lomond's beauty is undiminished. Studded with islands, and with the shapely peak of Ben Lomond reflected in the water, it is hardly surprising that this is such a popular spot. Much of the west bank is geared up for tourists, with marinas, golf and picnic places, but the east bank, with no through road beyond Rowardennan, remains much more peaceful. The long–distance walking route, the West Highland Way, starts near here. To go with Loch Lomond's status as Scotland's first National Park, a new visitor centre is opening in 2001. Cruises on Loch Lomond mostly leave from Balloch. A number of operators offer different routes or island landings.

West Bute Almost anywhere along the island's pastoral south-west coast gives magnificent views of the distant mountains of Arran.

Ferry routes in South Argyll If cost is no object, head towards the west via the Wemyss Bay– Rothesay crossing. Tour Bute, then cross to the mainland by the ferry from North Bute to Colintrave. Drive through Tignabruich to Portavadie, then cross Loch Fyne to Tarbert. This route avoids the long journey down Loch Fyne and gives you a chance to see Bute. If the weather is good, the ferry crossings give excellent views.

NORTHERN ARGYLL

The old districts of Lorn, Benderloch and Appin contain the most rugged country and the highest mountains in Argyll. The coastal scenery is better further south. Loch Awe, the longest freshwater loch in Scotland, and Loch Fyne, an even longer finger of the sea, split the area up, making east–west communication hard, while the uninhabited hills around Loch Etive barricade Argyll from the North. So this is still secret country, with only the old resort and ferry port of Oban to give it a taste of urban life. Facilities for tourists are relatively good however, for this part of the world is much relished by those who know it, and the area draws plenty of visitors, many of them on their way to Iona.

Top sights

Crarae Garden (on A83 south of Furnace)
✓ *Wonderful setting in a steep glen*
✓ *Magnificent azaleas and maples*
✗ *Some steep walking*

For our money, this is the most spectacular of the Scottish West Coast gardens, often described as the closest Scotland comes to a Himalayan gorge. Azaleas and rhododendrons grow from niches in the rocks which fringe a steep torrent, and drop flame-coloured petals into the peaty water. Huge specimen conifers tower above the rapids and there are groves of acer and eucalyptus. Three colour-coded walks, lasting from half an hour to two hours, criss-cross their way up the glen, leading you through a landscape which intrigues in its combination of inspired planting and natural grandeur.

At the time of writing, Crarae has fallen on hard times, and might have to close if rescue plans do not come to fruition. This would be a terrible loss. *[All year, daily; summer 9–6; winter, daylight hours;* ☎ *(01546) 886388;* ✓🍴 *www.crarae-gardens.org.uk]*

Dunadd and Kilmartin Sights (near Kilmartin)

✓ *Unique complex of prehistoric and later sights*
✓ *Scotland's first capital*
✓ *Strange, uncharacteristic landscape*

Amongst all the rocky outcrops of mid Argyll, the flat, boggy land to the north of the Crinan canal comes as surprise. The Iron Age fort of Dunadd, which crowns a single craggy spur in the middle of the fields, was once the stronghold of the Kingdom of Dalriada. This was founded by an Irish tribe – the Scots – whose influence spread outwards until it dominated the whole mainland. There is not much left to see on the hill, apart from a footprint carved in the rock and tumbled stone walls. Yet this was the place where modern Scotland began, so it is worth the climb, as are the views *[*✓🍴 *via www.kilmartin.org]*.

From Dunadd, you can just see the village of Kilmartin, where the **Museum of Ancient Culture** *[daily 10–5]* is an excellent introduction to the prehistoric cairns and burial chambers which litter the area. Many of them are laid out in a straight line, for reasons unknown. Exploring the substantial remains of the **Nether Largie Cairns** and of the **Templewood Stone Circle** *[*☎ *0131-668 8800;* ✓🍴 *via www.stonepages.com]* reveals strange carvings and markings on the stones, adding to the mystery. Finally, **Kilmartin Church** has a imposing collection of richly carved medieval crosses and gravestones, including what may be the earliest figure of Christ to be found in Britain *[Access at all times;* ☎ *0131-668 8800]*.

Dunstaffnage Castle (north of Oban)

✓ *Imposing remains of medieval fortress*
✓ *Beautiful setting*

Certainly the best of Argyll's many ruined castles to visit if time or enthusiasm is limited, this old stronghold dates back to 1275, and commands the sea at the point where Loch Etive drains into Loch Linnie. Robert the Bruce took the castle from the MacDougalls in 1309, and by the late fifteenth century it was in Campbell hands. Flora Macdonald was briefly imprisoned here in 1746 on her way to confinement in London. A seventeenth-century tower-house and three earlier towers are linked by massive curtain walls on a solid rock foundation. Views out to sea and over to the island of Lismore are terrific. *[HS; Apr to Sept, Mon–Sat 9.30–6.30, Sun 2–6.30; Oct to Mar, 9.30–4.30, closed Thur pm, Fri and Sun am;* ☎ *(01631) 562465;* 📞 *via www.scottish.culture.about.com]*

Inveraray Castle

✓ *Big baronial stately home*
✓ *Of special interest to all Campbells*

From the outside, the seat of the Duke of Argyll, head of Clan Campbell, is one of the uglier creations of eighteenth-century Gothic Revival. The interior, however, is very much more elegant: elaborately gilded in French style, with fine plasterwork, ceramics, and above all a massive collection of arms and armour to look at. The state dining-room is a French *tour de force*, with delicate flower garlands painted within panels defined by gilt mouldings. Much of the fine period furniture is also French. The spectacular arms room and large, stone-floored kitchen are other highlights. It is a relaxed place to visit too: you have a pleasant sense of feeling welcome, even if your name is not Campbell.

The castle was planned in 1745 by the third Duke. It was to be built on the elevated site then occupied by the town of Inveraray, so the town was simply re-located to its present position, an ample demonstration of the power and wealth of the Dukes, who had played a central, if not always admirable, role in Scottish history for generations. Their portraits hang throughout the building, and their lives are documented in exhaustive detail. *[Apr, June, Sept and Oct Mon–Thur and Sat, 10–1 and 2–5.45, Sun 1–5.45; July and Aug, Mon–Sat 10–5.45, Sun 1–5.45;* ☎ *(01499) 302203; ⁀ via www.scottish.culture.about.com]*

The next best sights

Arduaine Garden (on A816, south of Oban)

This seafront garden is acknowledged to hold one of the most outstanding rhododendron collections in the country. Its setting is not quite so good as Crarae, but there are fine views to the sea, and a network of relatively gentle paths through stands of trees and colourful shrubs. *[NTS; daily 9.30–sunset;* ☎ *(01852) 200366; ⁀ via www.nts.org.uk]*

Auchindrain Township Open Air Musuem (on A83, south of Inveraray)

The township was a working farm until the middle of the twentieth century, and the last to be run on communal-tenancy terms. Twelve tenants paid a single rent to the Duke of Argyll and worked plots of land, annually reallocated (by lot) to give every farmer a turn at the best. Houses and barns, a few thatched but most with red corrugated roofs, are spread out beside a narrow burn. A few are ruined shells, but most are furnished in period style, with fascinating insights into the daily life of the township, and how the inhabitants kept it going. A good sight for children. *[HS; Apr to Sept, daily 10–5;* ☎ *(01499) 500235; ⁀ via www.historic-scotland.gov.uk]*

Bonawe Iron Furnace (Taynuilt)

A fascinating relic of early industry, this is an almost complete charcoal–fuelled iron smelting plant, set up in 1753. Its position on the shores of Loch Etive was chosen for the easy sea transport and for the extensive oak forests, which were coppiced to produce the charcoal. Cannonballs for the Napoleonic Wars were one of the main products. Lucid displays explain the process of manufacture, and it has been suggested that this ancient factory is merely mothballed, awaiting demand. *[Apr to Sept, Mon–Sat 9.30–6.30, Sun 2–6.30; ☎ (01866) 822432; ✆ via www.historic-scotland.gov.uk]*

Inveraray Jail

This is a cleverly conceived recreation of Scottish prison life and rural justice in the eighteenth and nineteenth centuries, using the buildings of the old prison. Try out the hammocks (or the bare wood floor) and crank the hard labour machine as you listen to grim tales of prisoners' fates. The courtroom (1820) is always in session, and you can sit amongst the grey-clad models and listen to the trial of a farmer accused of an insurance fraud. The Crime and Punishment exhibition, relating cases of benighted suspects and evil criminals, rounds out the visit. A good sight for older children. *[Apr to Oct, daily 9.30–5; Nov to Mar, daily 10–4; ☎ (01499) 302381]*

Oban Rare Breeds Farm Park (on unclassified back road, east of Oban)

Rare breeds farms are ever more common is Scotland, but this is one of the best and longest-established. Uncommon varieties of cattle, sheep, pigs, poultry and goats roam small enclosures – many are very friendly. The hilltop setting and the views are good too. Great fun for smaller children. *[Late Mar to Oct, daily 10–5.30; ☎ (01631) 770608/770604; ✆ www.oban-rarebreeds.com]*

Also in the area

Ardchattan Gardens (north shore of Loch Etive) Very pretty gardens surround the ruins of an old priory chapel, with medieval tombstones. Carvings of skeletons, skulls and cross-bones abound. *[Apr to Oct, daily 9–6; ☎ (01796) 481355]*

Carnasserie Castle (north of Kilmartin) A ruin for enthusiasts only, since there are no facilities and few explanations, but a good example of a sixteenth-century mix of fortress and home. Access is by a short, steepish track. *[Open at all times;* ☎ *0131-668 8800;* ⓘ *via www.kilmartin.org]*

Castle Stalker (near Appin, north of Oban) One of the most romantically placed castles in Scotland, Castle Stalker is built on a tiny islet at the mouth of a bay, and can be seen from the A828. It is not usually accessible to the public, but played a prominent part in the closing scenes of *Monty Python and the Holy Grail.*

Cruachan Power Station (near Dalmally) Right inside the shapely mountain of Ben Cruachan at the head of Loch Awe there is a power station, running off water stored high on the mountainside. From a visitor centre by the road, tours depart into the heart of the hill to see the massive turbines. *[Easter to Nov, daily 9.30–5 (6 Jul and Aug);* ☎ *(01866) 822518]*

Falls of Lora (Connel, north of Oban) Where Loch Etive drains into the sea, the tide rushes over an underwater ridge, creating a spectacular tide race. You can glimpse it from the Connel Bridge as you drive on the A828, but it is safer to stop in Connel and poke around the back lanes for a good view.

Kilchurn Castle (Head of Loch Awe) A massive ruin, built by the Campbells in 1550. The setting is very photogenic. Access is by a muddy track from the A85, or more comfortably by steamboat sailings from Lochawe pier *[Ferry company* ☎ *(01838) 200400].*

Oban Seal and Marine Centre (Barcaldine, on south shore of Loch Creran) Good for a rainy day, the centre displays many marine creatures, including seals, in different environments. *[Daily 10–6; July and Aug 9–7;* ☎ *(01631) 720386]*

St Conan's Kirk (Lochawe) A bizarre and wonderful church, built in 1907, and incorporating almost every architectural style imaginable. The result is (surprisingly) a success *[* ⓘ *via www.loch-awe.com].*

Towns and villages to explore

Inveraray

A very pretty large village on the banks of Loch Fyne, almost in the shadow of Inveraray Castle. The Georgian cottage architecture is extremely attractive. A major stopping point for tour coaches, Inveraray has a surprising number of shops, most selling Scottish goods. As well as Inveraray Jail, it is worth seeing round the *Arctic Penguin*, a 1911 iron ship tied up by the quay. All sorts of marine memorabilia are to be found inside. *[Daily 10–6]*

Oban

The tourist centre and ferry port of Oban *[✆ www.oban.org.uk]* is the only sizeable place in the region, and attracts visitors because of the number of activities available in the immediate area, especially day visits to Mull and Iona, or walks on the offshore islands of Kerrara and Lismore. The town itself is not wildly exciting, but has a fair smattering of rainy day activities, including the **Oban Distillery** *[All year Mon–Fri 9.30–5 (8.30 July to Sept), plus Sats from Easter to Oct; ☎ (01631) 572004]*. Its chief curiosity is **McCaig's Folly**, a nineteenth-century coliseum crowning Oban's hillside. The view of town, harbour and islands from up here is superb, even if the folly itself falls short of expectations. McCaig was a local banker, but his attempt to immortalise himself while providing employment for hard-up townsfolk bankrupted him.

Scenery and touring routes

Appin Peninsula A brief detour from the A828 brings you down to the pretty hamlet of Port Appin. You can wander along the coastal road, with good views, or cross on the ferry to Lismore for an island walk.

Ardfern Peninsula Turn west off the A816 south of Kilmelford to Ardfern (an attractive centre for yachting and riding). The island-studded Loch Craignish is extremely pretty, while there are sea and island views from Aird, and the ancient Craignish Castle to look at.

Back route to Oban Turn south at Taynuilt on the unclassified route up Glen Lonan. This breaks out into rough, open country, with splendid views of Cruachan. Stop to see **Angus's Garden** and the **Oban Rare Breeds Farm Park** (see page 214).

Loch Awe round trip The longest stretch of fresh water in Britain has a road running along each bank – neither especially crowded. On the west bank, forests often spoil the view, but offer numerous stopping places and forest walks. In early summer, detour to Ardanaiseig from the B845 to see the rhododendron gardens. The southern end of the loch is the most attractive scenically, but the trip north is made interesting by views of the shapely Ben Cruachan mountain at the head.

Suggested excursions

Lismore and Kerrera There's a car ferry from Oban to **Lismore**, but most visitors take the foot crossing from Port Appin and walk. The flat island is ideal for gentle walks or bicycle rides, with fine views both east and west, a single unfrequented road, ruined castles to explore, and an island shop for refreshments. **Kerrera** is a steeper, wilder island, with no roads to speak of, but a sandy beach on the west coast, a ruined castle, and again, wonderful views. You will never see any crowds. The passenger ferry leaves from the road to Gallanach, south of Oban [☎ *(01631) 563665]*.

Loch Etive Cruise The only way of penetrating the fastness of the hills to the back of Glencoe is by water. Half day cruises leave from **Taynuilt** and travel up the loch, with items of interest being pointed out. There's a good chance of seeing deer and other wildlife. Cruises leave at 10.30am and 2pm in the summer months [☎ *(01866) 822430;* ◔ *via www.oban.org.uk]*.

Seil, Easdale and Luing A trip to these islands makes a great day out from Oban. **Seil** is not actually an island; it is linked to the mainland by the famous hump-backed 'bridge over the Atlantic'. It is a quiet place, full of small cottages, until you reach Ellenabeich, where numerous craft shops bear witness to the popularity of a visit to the tiny island of **Easdale** [⌂ www.easdale.co.uk], just offshore. Once it thrived on slate mining – indeed, the island is almost quarried away. Now, a tiny village of white cottages (no cars) is the only sign of life. A visit to the excellent Folk Museum is essential. The ferry trip takes five minutes. The journey to **Luing** is just as short. This island, also once a centre for slate, is bleaker than Seil, but gives wonderful sea views, especially of the Garvellach islands offshore. Stop at Cullipool to retrieve a souvenir slate from the thousands lying by the sea's edge.

KNAPDALE AND KINTYRE

South of the Crinan Canal, built to save boats the arduous journey round the Mull of Kintyre, Argyll narrows to the long trailing peninsula of Kintyre, almost cut in two at one point by the Tarbert isthmus. Knapdale is the district north of Tarbert, where all the interest lies in the heavily indented western coastline, with wonderful views out to Islay and Jura. Below Tarbert, the Kintyre Peninsula becomes ever more isolated, culminating in the cliff landscape of the Mull itself. If you tour the length of the peninsula, note that the west coast road is fast but unexciting, while the east coast road is very slow, but has great views to Arran.

Local sights

Saddell Abbey (south of Carradale)

The remains of this old Cistercian abbey are fairly scanty, since it has been ruined since the sixteenth century, but it is worth seeing for the collection of carved grave slabs, dating back to medieval times, which have nearly life-sized figures of knights and warriors engraved on them. The setting is very peaceful and sheltered. *[Open at all reasonable times]*

Skipness Castle (near Claonaig)

Claonaig is the departure point for the small Arran ferry. Just to the north, the massive reddish ruins of Skipness Castle are well worth seeing, although you can only explore round the outside. It is a thirteenth-century fortress, built to dominate the Kilbrannan Sound, and there is a lot of it left. The peaceful setting and the views add to the enjoyment *[☎ 0131-668 8800]*.

Towns and villages to explore

Campbeltown

A surprisingly big place, for such an isolated position, Campbeltown was once a centre for whisky distilling and for fisheries. There is little left of the prosperity, and the place can be bleak. It does, however, have a fine early medieval cross isolated on a roundabout, a dignified Victorian museum full of curiosities and a strange sight on the tidal island of Davaar, where a man named Archibald Mackinnon painted a vivid picture of the crucifixion on the wall of a cave (an easy walk, but check the tide times first).

Crinan

This is little more than a hamlet at the end of the canal which bears its name. It is, however, a very picturesque spot, with a flight of locks leading down a basin full of moored boats, and excellent views out to sea. Walking along the towpath of the Crinan canal makes a good and peaceful walk.

Tarbert

Another nicely laid-out small town on a bay of Loch Fyne, with a fair choice of places to stay and eat in. Ferries leave for Kintyre from here, and from Kennacraig, a few miles down the west coast, for Islay, Colonsay and Oban. There is an extremely ruinous castle above the town, and the **An Tairbeart Heritage Centre**, which has a useful tea-room, a display on local history and a woodland park. *[Easter to Oct, daily 10–6;* ☎ *(01880) 820190]*

Tayvallich

One of the prettiest places in Argyll, this small village curves round the edge of an inlet of Loch Sween. Yachts fill the water in front of the cottages, and there is a sandy bay facing the sea over the hill to the back of the village. There's also an excellent place to eat at the Tayvallich Inn.

Scenery and touring routes

Kilberry The B8024 runs round the western side of Knapdale, with the turn off south of Lochgilphead. It is a very slow way of reaching Tarbert, but passes through typical Kintyre scenery – small clusters of cottages, farms, bracken and trees. There are lovely views out to sea all the way. Kilberry makes a good stopping point, with an excellent inn in which to eat.

Loch Sween Both sides of this lovely sea loch are worth driving down. At its head, the water is so sheltered, it is seldom other than glassy smooth. On the western shore, the road runs past a narrow sea inlet to Tayvallich, and then on to Keillmore at the tip of a peninsula, with fine views to the mountains of Jura and a very early Christian chapel to see. The road on the eastern shore runs through uninspiring forestry to start with, but soon breaks into open country, passing Castle Sween, one of the oldest fortresses in Scotland (ruined by a caravan site). Kilmory Knap chapel, at the end of the road, is another well-preserved early Christian monument.

Southend and the Mull of Kintyre At its very end, Kintyre bulges into a series of hills, which meet the sea as towering cliffs. Head south from Campbeltown towards Southend, where there is a shingly beach. You will need to walk to reach the lighthouse on the Mull, and it is a fairly steep haul back.

Beaches and seashore

Carradale Sands This is a sheltered beach of fine sand on the east coast, which is popular on sunny days.

Machrihanish A wonderful wild stretch of sand to the west of Campbeltown. Not a beach for sunbathing, unless you are lucky, but great for long, windblown walks.

THE ISLANDS

The group of islands off the coast of Argyll are part of the Inner Hebrides. Between them they offer much diversity in terms of their size, their landscape, and their popularity with visitors. Mull is by far the largest, and can absorb its many visitors with ease. The smaller islands are harder to reach and less visited, but more beautiful. From the relatively well-populated Islay and the barren wilderness of Jura to the tiny island of Gigha, there is something for all tastes.

Mull

✓ *Relatively easy access*
✓ *Excellent for wildlife enthusiasts*
✓ *Good walks*
✓ *Day trips from Oban*
✗ *Touring the island involves long drives on slow roads*
✗ *The long road through South Mull to Iona is single-track and infested by tour coaches*

Mull is a big, bleak island, with only a few outbreaks of fertility to set against the forests and moorland. The draw for most visitors is Mull's wild coast, much of it accessible only on foot. Walking is the way to get the most out of the island; the next best activity is to explore by sea, taking boat trips to Iona and Staffa and anything else on offer. Touring the island by car takes time; the reward is some spectacular views, especially from the west coast. Sights on Mull are generally small in scale, but very diverse.

Access is easy. Car ferries run from Oban to Craignure and Tobermory, from Lochaline to Fishnish and, in season, from Kilchoan on Ardnamurchan to Tobermory.

Top sights

Duart Castle

✓ *Restored medieval fortress in great setting*
✓ *Of particular interest to McLeans*

The bulky Duart Castle is perched at the end of a promontory overlooking Loch Linnhe and the Sound of Mull, making for wonderful views from the battlements. Seat of the Maclean chiefs for centuries, but confiscated after the 1745 Jacobite rising, the castle was bought back and restored by Fitzroy Maclean in 1912. The welcome is friendly, and there is much McLean memorabilia to see, as well as some the original features of the 1912 restoration. *[May to Oct, daily 10.30–6;* ☎ *(01680) 812309;* 🖥 *via www.mull.zynet.co.uk]*

Torosay Castle (near Craignure)

✓ *Friendly stately home with fine gardens*
✓ *Arrive by miniature railway*

Its closeness to the ferry terminal at Craignure makes Torosay popular, particularly since the narrow-gauge Mull Rail provides an unusual and charming means of access *[Runs Easter to mid-Oct;* ☎ *(01680) 812494].*

Torosay is a Victorian residence, run with an approachable friendliness that is refreshing. The history of the house is available through scrapbooks, game records and photographs, while a sequence of fine paintings and solid Edwardian furniture give the house a lived-in atmosphere. The formal terraced gardens are lovely, and there is a good shop and tea-room. *[Easter to Oct, daily 10.30–5; Nov to*

Easter, garden only, 10.30–sunset; ☎ *(01680) 812421;* 🖱 *via www.holidaymull.org]*

Town to explore

Tobermory

Mull's little capital is a very attractive fishing port, with colourful painted houses lining a sheltered bay *[*🖱 *via www.isle.of.mull.com].* It has a surprising variety of shops, pubs and eating places along the sea front, and makes an excellent refuge during a wet spell. The tiny but comprehensive **Mull Museum** *[Easter to Oct, Mon–Fri 10–4; Sat 10–1]* is worth exploring, while the **Hebridean Whale and Dolphin Trust** *[*☎ *(01688) 302620;* 🖱 *via www.gn.apc.org]* is engaging and educational. The big event in Tobermory's past was the sinking of one of the galleons from the Spanish Armada close to the harbour. The lure of salvaging underwater treasure has drawn the hopeful ever since, but nothing of real worth has ever been found.

Suggested walks

Mull is something of a walker's paradise, and detailed booklets of routes of different lengths and difficulty can be obtained in most island shops and tourist offices. The following are some of the best-known – none should be undertaken casually. Proper equipment and information on tides (for coastal walks) are a necessity. Further information about walks on Mull can be found via 🖱 *www.holidaymull.org*

Carsaig Arches (South Mull) A long, rough coastal walk west of Carsaig brings you to these spectacular eroded caves, passing the 'Nun's Cave' on the way.

Mackinnon's Cave (West Mull) On the northern side of the roadless and rugged Ardmeanach Peninsula, this is a huge sea cave, only accessible at low tide. The track to Balmeanach Farm takes you to a path leading to a magnificent clifftop and then steeply down to a beach of large boulders.

MacCulloch's Tree (West Mull) On the extreme west of the Ardmeanach Peninsula the silhouette of a 50 million-year-old tree is exposed on the cliff face. The theory runs that it was engulfed by volcanic debris, then fossilised. The tree has suffered more damage since its discovery in 1819 than during the previous 50 million years, but it is now protected. It is a ten-mile round trip to reach it, and you must plan to get there on a falling tide.

Scenery and touring route

The West Coast The slow and tortuous road up the western coast of Mull (B8035 and B8073) provides some spectacular views. The best section is the southern shore of Loch na Keal, with views out to the strangely shaped Treshnish Islands in the distance, and to the island of Inch Kenneth in the foreground. Towering cliffs flank the road. From the high ground at the top of the Ardmeanach Peninsula further good views can be obtained. You can get back to the main road at Salen, or drive on north, looking over to Ulva and ending up at the sands of Calgary.

Beaches and seashore

Ardalanish Bay (south Mull) A couple of miles south of the road to Iona (turn off at Bunessan), this is an attractive, little-known bay with shingly sand.

Calgary (north-west Mull) The best sand beach on Mull is popular, yet rarely crowded. The Canadian city takes its name from the tiny village here.

Suggested excursions

The island-studded waters around Mull provide plenty of opportunities for boat trips. Information on the many different operators can be found in Oban, Tobermory, Dervaig, Ulva Ferry, Fionnphort and on Iona. Seasickness pills may be necessary as the journeys can be very bouncy.

Ardnamurchan By taking advantage of the ferry from Tobermory to Kilchoan, you can cut out the long drive which is otherwise needed to get to the most westerly point of the Scottish mainland. Sandy beaches, seals, a lighthouse and terrific views are the reward (see page 405).

Staffa The one boat trip no one should miss. The island, with its weird basalt columns and the famous Fingal's Cave, really is an extraordinary place. No postcard view can do justice to the echoing grandeur of the cave which inspired Mendelssohn's overture. There is usually time to walk over the island, where you are likely to see puffins.

Treshnish Isles *[via www.hebrideantrust.org and www.mullbirds.com]* A popular excursion for bird lovers, since these volcanic outcrops teem with guillemots and puffins. Choose a calm day for preference. You will also see seals and most trips allow for a landing on Lunga.

Ulva A very popular island with walkers, close to the West Coast. A short crossing from Ulva Ferry takes passengers over. The population is now tiny, and the wildlife seldom disturbed.

Whale and dolphin watching Boat trips run from Tobermory to look for marine mammals (and any other wildlife) *[☎ (01688) 400223]*.

Iona

✓ *Beautiful and peaceful island*
✓ *Central to Scotland's religious history; early crosses and monuments; birthplace of the Celtic church*
✓ *Gentle walks through good coastal scenery*
✗ *Sights can be very crowded*
✗ *No cars allowed*

It is well worth the long slow drive through Mull and the short ferry journey to reach Iona, even on a day trip. 'The morning star of Scotland's faith' is small (three by one-and-a-half miles) and mostly flat and windswept, but its importance to Christianity is great, and the peacefulness of the place, much touted in brochures, really exists. St Columba, turning his back on his native Ireland, came to Iona in 1563 with 12 companions and founded the monastery which became famous throughout the Christian world. The Celtic church spread from here all across northern Scotland. Iona was eventually ravaged by Viking raiders and the remaining monks were moved to Dunkeld. What was left of the monastery was ransacked during the Reformation. The restoration began in 1938, and Iona is now the setting for a long-established Christian Community [🖰 *www.iona.org.uk*]. The Iona Cathedral Trust now owns the sacred precincts; the rest of the island belongs mostly to the National Trust for Scotland. Find more information via 🖰 *www.isle.of.mull.com*

Local sights

The Abbey Complex

Built near the site of Columba's original foundation, the abbey buildings appear stark and severe against the expanse of green and blue which lies beyond. The Abbey church has, of course, been massively restored, but the north transept and arcade of the north wall of the choir, along with some elaborate carvings, are original. The Abbey Museum has a rich collection of cross-marked gravestones, and there is an excellent bookshop. The eighth-century St Martin's Cross is remarkably complete, with serpent-and-boss ornament on the east face and holy figures on the other. The restored twelfth-century St Oran's Chapel nearby is the island's oldest building, and arguably the most handsome. Of pinky-grey stone, it is unadorned save for its one splendid Norman doorway with bold chevron and beak-head decoration on three round arches. To take in the abbey, cross, chapel and graveyard, with the sea and Mull beyond, stand on the small knoll directly opposite the entrance. This is Torr an Aba, where Columba's cell is said to have been. *[Open all year; ☎ (01681) 700404]*

Iona Heritage Centre

A homely place, less crowded than the religious monuments, and with some interesting displays about Iona's secular life and history. *[Apr to Oct, Mon–Sat 10.30–6.30; ☎ (01681) 700576]*

The Nunnery

In the centre of Iona's little township (Baile Mor), the pink granite ruins have been transformed by colourful flowerbeds planted out around the old walls. It was founded in 1203, at the same time as the Benedictine monastery. Now it forms a most peaceful spot for a sunny day.

St Martin's Cross

Some distance away from the other old crosses around the abbey, this is by far the most impressive and one of the oldest (it is eighth-century). Carved biblical scenes decorate one side, with typical Celtic patterning around.

Suggested walks

Despite throngs of day-trippers in and around the main sights, finding tranquil spots is easy. **The Bay at the Back of the Ocean** on the western coast is a place of coloured pebbles, including the green 'Tiree marble' and lumps of white limestone washed ashore from a wreck. A stroll north from here takes you past numerous rocky coves. There are further sandy beaches in the north of the island – usually deserted.

Coll and Tiree

✓ *Isolated island holidays*
✓ *Beaches, surfing, windsurfing (Tiree)*
✗ *Very windy and exposed*

✗ *Nothing to do in wet weather*
✗ *Very limited facilities*

Coll and Tiree are both quiet, gentle islands, whose attractions for visitors are undisturbed peace, birdlife, views, coastal scenery and gentle walking. They lie to the west of Mull and can be reached by ferry from Oban, or, in the case of Tiree, by plane from Glasgow.

Both islands are flat, but where Tiree is fertile and sprinkled with crofts, Coll is more conventionally Highland, with hard rock and peat hags, and has a much smaller population. Both islands have magnificent, deserted beaches – those on Tiree are likely to be populated by surfers and windsurfers, for the island's waves are excellent and the wind is constant. Sunshine is common out here away from the rain–attracting hills, but so too are strong Atlantic gales.

There is little point in using a car – hiring a bicycle is cheaper and a more sensible way of getting around. There are a number of small sights – prehistoric remains and a ruined castle or two. Guesthouses and self-catering accommodation are available on both islands. You should be able to buy enough for picnics locally, but do not expect anything sophisticated in the islands' shops.

Information on the Internet is available via 🐭 *www.scotland-inverness.co.uk* or 🐭 *www.hebrideantrust.org*

Islay

✓ *Relatively populous, varied island, not on the usual tourist routes*
✓ *Very friendly inhabitants*
✓ *Recommended for birdwatchers, golfers and whisky-lovers*
✓ *Good touring and walking*

Islay is among the most populous and fertile of the Hebrides. It owes much of its stability and its good roads to its distilling industry, for the island produces a unique variety of dark, smoky malt whisky. It is not conventionally beautiful, with no great mountains or outstanding scenery, but it has excellent beaches, rich birdlife and lots of intriguing corners to explore. *[🐭 via www.scotland-inverness.co.uk or 🐭 www.ileach.com (the Islay newspaper's web site)]*

Local sights

The Islay Woollen Mill (on A846)

Visit the well-stocked gift and clothing shop here. The mill was established in 1883 on the site of an earlier seventeenth-century enterprise. You are free to walk around the antiquated and dusty workshop and inspect the rare Spinning Jenny and Slubbing Billy. *[Apr to Dec, Mon–Sat 10–5; Jan to Mar, Mon–Fri 10–5, Sat 1–5;* ☎ *(01496) 810563;* 📱 *via www.isle-of-islay.com]*

Kildalton Cross (East coast)

The island's most highly prized artefact stands in a small churchyard towards the end of a narrow, isolated road. The Kildalton Cross was carved (probably by a sculptor from Iona) 1,200 years ago. It is impressively large and neatly decorated with Celtic motifs and favourite scenes of David and the lion, Cain and Abel, and the Virgin and child. It is weathered of course, but the figures are still clear.

Museum of Islay Life (Port Charlotte)

A small museum simply crammed with objects from Islay's past and present. It is an excellent place to learn about the island's heritage. *[Apr to Oct, Mon–Sat 10–5, Sun 2–5;* ☎ *(01496) 850358;* 📱 *www.islaymuseum.freeserve.co.uk]*

Also in the area

The American Monument (Mull of Oa) A bulbous, rocket-shaped monument commemorates the American troops lost when the *Tuscania* was torpedoed off Islay in 1918. The monument is a popular goal for walks over this wild corner of Islay.

Distilleries Packed into a relatively small area, six distilleries offer tours. The process is much the same in all, but the end product is not. **Ardbeg** *[*☎ *(01496) 302236]*, **Laphroaig** *[*☎ *(01496) 302418]* and **Lagavulin** *[*☎ *(01496) 302730]* are all near Port Ellen. **Bowmore** *[☎ (01496) 810441]* is in Bowmore village while **Caol Ila** *[☎ (01496) 840207]* and **Bunnahabhain** *[☎ (01496) 840646]* are near Port Askaig. Phone for information on visiting.

Finlaggan (near Port Askaig) An island in the loch here was once the headquarters of the Lordship of the Isles, the federation of clans which dominated the western seaboard of Scotland. Descendants of the Norse settlers, their galleys provided swift communication between the islands, and they were a constant menace to land-bound Scottish kings. The Lord of the Isles was usually a member of Clan Donald. There is not much to see at Finlaggan, but a visitor centre explains how archaeologists are slowly unearthing the remains of the ancient council hall.

Towns and villages to explore

Bowmore
The island's biggest settlement. Noted for its curious round church, its good pub (Harbour Inn) and its swimming pool.

Port Charlotte
A very attractive little township of white cottages in a lovely setting. The Museum of Islay Life, the Islay Cheese Company and the Wildlife Information Centre are all here.

Port Ellen
The main ferry port. Not the most beautiful of villages, but close to three distilleries.

Portnahaven
Another attractive fishing village, with houses scattered around the steep slopes leading to the harbour.

Beaches and seashore

Laggan Bay A long and relatively sheltered stretch of sand, backed by dunes and a golf course.

Loch Gruinart A somewhat muddy estuary, now a nature reserve. Come here during the winter months to see Islay's huge population of barnacle geese. The visitor centre has telescopes.

Machir Bay Out on the wild Rhinns of Islay, this lovely deserted sandy beach is great for a windy walk. Swimming is dangerous.

Saligo Bay Smaller than Machir Bay, this beach is just as beautiful and just as dangerous.

Suggested excursion

The Islay–Oban ferry On a fine, calm day, the trip from Islay to Oban (or vice versa) is one of the most spectacular sea journeys in the world. The uninhabited west coast of Jura, the island of Colonsay and all the scattered islands of the Firth of Lorn are on view. It is an unforgettable experience, although if the weather is rough it may be unforgettable for different reasons, so take seasickness precautions. The trip will need planning – consult ferry timetables [*www.calmac.co.uk*]. You will probably have to spend at least one night at the far end before returning, if you do not take a car.

Jura

✓ *Day trip from Islay*
✓ *Very isolated, rough walks*
✓ *Cycling on the single, almost empty road*
✓ *Recommended for wildlife*

Jura's cone-shaped peaks, the Paps of Jura, have been landmarks for passing ships down the ages. They are best seen from a distance; close to, they turn out to be scree-covered lumps. Wildlife, remote moor and timeless seascapes are Jura's assets. Red deer graze nonchalantly beside Highland cattle. Wild goats are commonplace, and you have a better chance of spotting an eagle than in most places. Views out to sea from the island's one road are especially rewarding because of the height from which you look over the water.

Craighouse is the only real settlement, and it would almost fit into the shadow of its distillery. Otherwise, crofts and cottages are the only sign of habitation. [🖱 *www.juradevelopment.co.uk*]

In the area

Corrievreckan A path winds north from the end of the road towards the Gulf of Corrievreckan, which divides Jura from Scarba. Arrive one hour after low tide to see and hear the most dangerous tide race in Scotland. It is named after the legendary Breacan who anchored his boat here by a rope of maidens' hair. One maiden had been untrue; the rope parted and Breacan was drowned. Walking the whole distance is tough going. If you ask at the Jura Hotel in Craighouse, there may be occasional four-wheel drive trips up here, although walking will still be necessary.

Isle of Jura Distillery (Craighouse) The whisky from Jura is different again from that of Islay. The island's only distillery runs tours by appointment. [☎ *(01496) 820240*]

Jura House Garden Between the ferry pier and Craighouse, the grounds of Jura House provide one of the few patches of fertile greenery on the island. There are marked paths to explore and a lovely walled garden. The house itself is not open but a tea tent is usually open for business. [*Daily 9–5;* ☎ *(01496) 820315*]

George Orwell's House Right in the north of the island, the isolated farmhouse of Barnhill is where Orwell wrote *1984*. You need to walk to get to it and you can't go inside, so it is a sight for enthusiasts only.

Colonsay and Oronsay

✓ *Perfect for a tranquil, isolated island holiday*
✓ *Richly varied small islands; good garden, wonderful beach*

Colonsay [*www.colonsay.org.uk*] lies 25 miles from the mainland and, with Oronsay, is only ten miles long from tip to toe. It has several historical and archaeological sites, but you will probably remember it best for its tranquillity. Quiet, undemanding and with only three ferries per week, it is the perfect retreat, though in danger of becoming an island with more holiday homes than permanent residents. Apart from one hotel and a couple of bed and breakfasts, all accommodation is self-catering.

Colonsay is an island of green pastures, fine beaches, cliffs, rocky coves, woodlands, moors and lochans (small lochs) covered in water-lilies. Five hundred varieties of local flora and 150 species of birds have been recorded.

In the area

Colonsay House Garden A lush woodland garden packed with rhododendrons, slowly being rescued from decades of neglect. The wilderness is half the fun – pushing through the exotic shrubs is like exploring a jungle. Choose a fine day. *[Easter to Sept, Wed 12–5 and Fri 3–5.30;* ☎ *(01951) 200211]*

Kiloran Bay The best beach in the Hebrides, a magnificent half-mile-long, semicircular bay of honey-gold sand, with rarely more than a few people on it.

Oronsay Priory The island of Oronsay is separated from Colonsay by a tidal strand. It is an easy walk across at low tide (driving is possible, but not recommended) to see the remains of the fourteenth-century Priory which was supposedly founded on the spot where St Columba first landed. He left Oronsay for Iona because he could still see his native Ireland. Now there is a small museum of ancient carved gravestones within the old Prior's House and the beautiful medieval Oronsay Cross.

Standing stones Prehistoric remains litter the island. 'Fingal's Limpet Hammers' at Kilchattan are the most imposing of many standing stones.

Gigha

✓ *One or two days' island stopover*
✓ *Tiny, charming island, with garden and beaches*

Gigha, connected by ferry from Tayinloan, lies just three miles off the west coast of Kintyre [⌁ *www.isle-of-gigha.co.uk*]. It is a tiny island, criss-crossed with dry-stone dykes and with everything in miniature, from the trout loch to the golf course. Gigha has only one road, so a bicycle is the best transport. Head for the lush **Achamore Gardens** *[dawn to dusk; ☎ (01583) 505254]*. Created by Sir James Horlick (of hot drink fame), who owned the island, they make the most of Gigha's mild climate and acid soil. Azaleas, rhododendrons, camellias, palms and palm lilies all thrive in the almost frost-free conditions. The best beaches are in the north of the island: look out for scallop shells to collect and beware jellyfish.

WHERE TO STAY

£ – under £70 per room per night, incl. VAT
££ – £70 to £110 per room per night, incl. VAT
£££ – over £110 per room per night, incl. VAT

ARDNADAM
Lochside
Fir Brae, Ardnadam, Sandbank PA23 8QD
☎ (01369) 706327
Near Holy Loch, with splendid views to Strone and Blairmore, this whitewashed, attractive Edwardian house offers three immaculate bedrooms. Breakfast is served family-style in the dining-room.
£ *Mar to Nov*

ARDUAINE
Loch Melfort Hotel
Arduaine, Oban PA34 4XG
☎ (01852) 200233
📠 (01852) 200214
⌁ www.loch-melfort.co.uk
Relaxed, traditional hotel in a lovely lochside setting, with views along the Sound of Jura. Bedrooms are simple and fresh in the new wing, and pleasantly old-fashioned in the main house; all but one have a loch view. Seafood dominates the menu in the Skerry Bistro and main dining-room.
££ *Closed Jan to mid-Feb*

ARINAGOUR
Garden House
Arinagour, Isle of Coll PA78 6TB
☎ /🖷 (01879) 230374
Remote working farm, surrounded by an
RSPB reserve. Informal surroundings
include two comfortable bedrooms, a
walled garden and a cosy sitting room.
Dinner and packed lunches can be
provided.
£ *All year*

BALEPHETRISH
Sandy Cove
26 Balephetrish, Isle of Tiree PA77 6UY
☎ (01879) 220334
A friendly and welcoming white-painted
house overlooking the bay to the
Outer Hebrides. The one letting
bedroom has a private bathroom, and
guests are welcome in the comfortable
lounge.
£ *All year exc Christmas*

BALLYGRANT
Kilmeny Country Guest House
Ballygrant, Isle of Islay PA45 7QW
☎ /🖷 (01496) 840668
Comfortable *en suite* bed and breakfast
offering peace and quiet and good food.
Two of the three spacious bedrooms are
on the ground floor. Imaginative five-
course evening meals are optional, and
guests can bring their own wine.
£ *All year exc Christmas and New Year*

BUNESSAN
Assapol House
Bunessan, Isle of Mull PA67 6DW
☎ (01369) 860279
🖷 (01681) 700445
⌇🖥 www.assapolhouse.demon.co.uk

Smart but friendly family hotel, with a
peaceful atmosphere. Bedrooms are
well-equipped and the sitting room has
loch views. Enjoyable menus offer a
choice at each course.
£££ *Closed Nov to Mar*

CALGARY
Calgary Farmhouse Hotel
Calgary, Tobermory, Isle of Mull
PA75 6QW
☎ /🖷 (01688) 400256
⌇🖥 www.calgary.co.uk
Modern facilities in comfortable
accommodation by one of Mull's most
beautiful beaches. Three bedrooms are
on the ground floor; some enjoy the bay
view, as does the terraced lounge.
Licensed restaurant.
£ *Easter to Oct*

CAMPBELTOWN
Balegreggan Country House
Balegreggan Road, Campbeltown
PA28 6NN
☎ /🖷 (01586) 552062
Peace and quiet in a rural setting with
lovely views over Campbeltown Loch.
The three bedrooms are all *en suite*.
Substantial breakfasts include traditional
Scottish choices with free-range eggs
and venison sausages.
£ *All year*

CARDROSS
Kirkton House
Darleith Road, Cardross G82 5EZ
☎ (01389) 841951
🖷 (01389) 841868
⌇🖥 www.kirktonhouse.co.uk
Pleasant eighteenth-century small hotel,
surrounded by fields and with views

across the Firth of Clyde. Bedrooms are comfortable and well-equipped. Breakfasts and evening meals are served in the dining-room; two- or four-course suppers, table d'hôte, vegetarian or special diet meals are available.
£ *Feb to Nov*

CARRADALE
Dunvalanree
Port Righ Bay, Carradale PA28 6SE
☎ (01583) 431226
📠 (01583) 431339
🖥 *www.milstead.demon.co.uk*
Guesthouse with refurbished bedrooms. The à la carte menu offers locally sourced ingredients and a selection for vegetarians. Plenty of outdoor activities nearby.
£ *All year*

CLACHAN-SEIL
Willowburn Hotel
Clachan-Seil, Isle of Seil, Oban PA34 4TJ
☎ (01852) 300276
📠 (01852) 300597
🖥 *www.willowburn.co.uk*
Friendly small hotel with first-class food in a tranquil spot. Indoor activities for rainy days include games, books, musical instruments and binoculars for bird-watching.
£££ *Closed Jan and Feb (See Where to Eat)*

CONNEL
Dunfuinary
Connel PA37 1PG
☎ (01631) 710300
Good-value accommodation in a beautiful setting, with a colourful garden. Breakfasts are 'excellent', rooms are spacious and well-appointed.
£ *Easter to late Oct*

CRAOBH HAVEN
Buidhe Lodge
Craobh Haven PA31 8UA
☎ (01852) 500291
Modern timber building on the shore of this small island reached by a safe causeway. Bedrooms are cosy, simple and on ground level. One large lounge/dining-room, and a balcony with sea views. Dinner served by arrangement.
£ *All year exc Christmas*

CRINAN
Crinan Hotel
Crinan, Lochgilphead PA31 8SR
☎ (01546) 830261
📠 (01546) 830292
🖥 *www.crinanhotel.com*
Relaxed hotel with comfortable bedrooms, where the Crinan canal meets the sea. The sea theme continues in the furnishings and the three bars. The top-floor seafood restaurant serves the catch of the day – when there is none it does not open. A table d'hôte menu is served in the split-level dining-room.
£££ *Closed Christmas*

DERVAIG
Druimard Country House
Dervaig, Isle of Mull PA75 6QW
☎/📠 (01688) 400345
Welcoming and comfortable country house with ambitious food and views over Glen Bellart. Mull's Little Theatre stages productions in the grounds, and the theatrical theme continues in the sunny conservatory, the bar and the smart dining-room.
£££ *Closed Nov to Mar (See Where to Eat)*

Balmacara

Kilmore, Dervaig, Isle of Mull
PA75 6QN
☎/📠 (01688) 400363
Modern bed and breakfast
accommodation. Breakfasts and home-
cooked evening meals are served in a
conservatory with wonderful views.
Advance bookings must be more than
one night.
£ *All year exc Christmas*

DUNOON
Abbot's Brae Hotel

West Bay, Dunoon PA23 7QJ
☎ (01369) 705021
📠 (01369) 701191
🖥 www.abbotsbrae.co.uk
Fine Victorian hotel in an enviable
wooded location with spectacular views
over the Firth of Clyde. Spacious
bedrooms are restful and tastefully
furnished. Excellent meals.
£ *All year*

Enmore Hotel

Marine Parade, Dunoon PA23 8HH
☎ (01369) 702230
📠 (01369) 702148
🖥 www.enmorehotel.co.uk
Peace and comfort are evident at this
well-run hotel. The double Jacuzzi in .
Room 2 is the highlight of the bright
bedrooms here. Imaginative food.
££ *Closed Chr; restricted service Dec to Feb*

ERISKA
Isle of Eriska

Eriska, Ledaig, Oban PA37 1SD
☎ (01631) 720371
📠 (01631) 720531
🖥 www.eriska-hotel.co.uk
First-rate comfort in a superb country-
house hotel on a private island. The
interior of this Scottish baronial
mansion is all antiques, tapestries,
panelling and plaster friezes.
Accomplished six-course dinners and
luxurious bedrooms.
£££ *Closed Jan (See Where to Eat)*

FIONNPHORT
Dungrianach

Fionnphort, Isle of Mull PA66 6BL
☎ (01681) 700417
Isolated cottage with spectacular views
to Iona, just above a pretty beach. The
two bedrooms are *en suite*, and
breakfast is served in the family lounge's
dining area.
£ *Mar to Nov*

HELENSBURGH
Greenpark

Charlotte Street, Helensburgh
G84 7SE
☎/📠 (01436) 671545
'Wonderful' Art Deco house with
parquet floors and a walnut staircase.
Plenty of modern comforts in the
bedrooms, and a guest sitting room.
Breakfast choices range from traditional
Scottish to waffles.
£ *Apr to Oct*

IONA
Argyll Hotel

Isle of Iona PA76 6SJ
☎ (01681) 700334
📠 (01681) 700510
🖥 www.argyllhoteliona.co.uk
Modest but pleasing hotel on the Mull-
facing waterfront. Simple furnishings in
the bedroom and plant-filled lounges.

Food is traditional and tasty, with a main-course vegetarian option.
£ *Closed 30 Oct to 1 Apr*

ISLE OF COLONSAY
Seaview
Isle of Colonsay PA61 7YR
☎/📠 (01951) 200315
Crofter's house with a splendid view over fields to the sea. Three bedrooms and a self-catering cottage are available; meals are served in the conservatory.
£ *Apr to Oct*

KILCHRENAN
Taychreggan
Kilchrenan, Taynuilt PA35 1HQ
☎ (01866) 833211/833366
📠 (01866) 833244
🖥 www.taychregganhotel.co.uk
Former drovers' inn, stylishly renovated, with views over Loch Awe. Modern art adds colour to the formal interior. Superior bedrooms in the main house; loch views in the restaurant.
£££ *All year (See Where to Eat)*

KILMARTIN
Tibertich
Kilmartin PA31 8RQ
☎ (01546) 810281
Working farm with spectacular views in a peaceful location. Three tasteful bedrooms and two self-catering cottages; an enclosed garden provides a safe play area.
£ *Mar to Nov*

KINGARTH
New Farm
Mount Stuart, Kingarth, Isle of Bute PA20 9NA
☎/📠 (01700) 831646

Attractive restaurant-with-rooms on a large sheep and dairy farm. Breakfast, lunch and imaginative dinners are served communally and made with home-grown or local ingredients.
£ *All year*

LOCHDONHEAD
Old Mill Cottage
Lochdonhead, Isle of Mull PA64 6AP
☎/📠 (01680) 812442
Guesthouse and self-catering in the Old Mill. Breakfast is served in the adjacent licensed restaurant which also serves expertly cooked à la carte meals.
£ *All year*

OBAN
Dungrianach
Pulpit Hill, Oban PA34 4LU
☎/📠 (01631) 562840
Victorian house set in four acres of woodland with beautiful views across the sea to the islands and an informal, personal approach. The two attractive bedrooms are *en suite*, and much effort has been put into the garden.
£ *Easter to Sept*

Kilchrenan House
Corran Esplanade, Oban PA34 5AQ
☎/📠 (01631) 562663
A cut above the average Oban bed and breakfast, this handsome Victorian turreted house has been lovingly restored. A comfortable and stylish sitting room and the breakfast room overlook the harbour. Victorian period character is also evident in the comfortable bedrooms.
£ *Closed Nov to April*

Manor House

Gallanach Road, Oban PA34 4LS

☎ (01631) 562087

📠 (01631) 563053

Stylish late-Georgian dower house hotel with friendly service and good food, on the headland overlooking Oban's seafront. The menu relies heavily on local ingredients – fish from the Western Isles, game, lamb and beef from the hotel's estate. Bedrooms are confidently traditional.

£££ *Closed Sun eve to Tue eve, Nov to Feb*

PORT APPIN
Airds Hotel

Port Appin, Appin PA38 4DF

☎ (01631) 730236

📠 (01631) 730535

🌐 www.airds-hotel.co.uk

A superb and sophisticated former ferry inn, in a lovely setting. The two lounges have period features and loch views; bedrooms are sumptuous. Dinners are based on fresh native ingredients.

£££ *Closed 6 to 26 Jan, 20 to 27 Dec (See Where to Eat)*

PORT ELLEN
Glenmachrie

Port Ellen, Isle of Islay PA42 7AW

☎/📠 (01496) 302560

The helpful hostess in this farm guesthouse offers maps, guidebooks and local knowledge to make the most of your time on the island. Meals are excellent, with substantial breakfasts.

££ *All year*

SALEN
Killiechronan House

Salen, Isle of Mull PA72 6JU

☎ (01680) 300403

📠 (01680) 300463

Peacefully located in a lovely glade at the head of Loch na Keal. Elegant and atmospheric lounges set the scene for the richly decorated dining-room, with a European menu. Spacious and well-furnished bedrooms are full of extras.

£££ *Closed 1 Nov to mid-Mar*

TOBERMORY
Broomhill

Breadalbane Street, Tobermory, Isle of Mull PA75 6PX

☎ (01688) 302349

Old manse with wonderful views across the water to the hills, enjoyed by all the comfortable bedrooms. Breakfast is served in the sun room, with its own fridge for guests' use and hot and cold drinks.

£ *May to Oct*

WHERE TO EAT

ALEXANDRIA
Cameron House, Georgian Room
Loch Lomond, Alexandria G83 8QZ
☎ (01389) 755565
📠 (01389) 759522
🖰 www.cameronhouse.co.uk
Victorian portraits decorate a baronial
house with beautiful views over Loch
Lomond. The rather expensive menu is
contemporary European, combining
local ingredients and luxuries in
confident dishes. Richness is interspersed
with humbler materials, and the pricey
wine list is global.
*Tue to Fri L 12–1.45, Tue to Sun D 7–9.45;
closed 26 Dec, bank hols*

ARDFERN
Galley of Lorne
Ardfern PA31 8QN
☎ (01852) 500284
The Galley Bar's blackboard offerings
are staple bar food, but dishes are
supplemented by locally sourced
seafood. Light lunches are also
available, and children have their own
menu.
*Summer 11am–midnight, Sun noon–
midnight, winter 11–11, Sun 12–11; bar
food 12–2 and 6–9 (8 in winter);
restaurant Easter to Nov 12–2 and 6–9;
closed 25 Dec*

BOWMORE
Harbour Inn
The Square, Bowmore PA43 7JR
☎ (01496) 810330
📠 (01496) 810990
🖰 www.harbour-inn.com

Small, well-run inn with a friendly
atmosphere. Lunch or dinner menus
offer robust dishes including game and
fish; there is an extensive whisky list, and
the imaginative wine choices are
reasonably priced.
*All week 12–2.30 and 6–9; closed Sun Oct
to Easter*

CAIRNDOW
Loch Fyne Oyster Bar
Clachan, Cairndow PA26 8BL
☎ (01499) 600236
📠 (01499) 600234
This converted cow byre at the head of
the loch specialises in seafood. A take-
away shop sells a wide range of items,
and the dining-room and conservatory
offer simply cooked fish, shellfish and
seafood.
*All week 9–9 (9–6 Mon to Fri Nov to
Mar); closed 25 and 26 Dec, 1 and 2 Jan*

CLACHAN-SEIL
Tigh an Truish
Clachan-Seil, Isle of Seil PA34 4QZ
☎ (01852) 300242
Simple, home-made pub food served in
a leisurely atmosphere at this
eighteenth-century stone inn. Plenty of
fish, seafood, beef and rich puddings are
on the blackboard menu. Wine prices
are modest.
*Summer 11–11.30 (Sun 12.30–11.30);
winter 11–2.30 (Sun 12–2.30) and
5–11.30; bar food and restaurant 12–2.15
(Sun 12.30–2.15) and 6–8.30; closed 25
Dec and 1 Jan*

Willowburn Hotel

Clachan-Seil, Isle of Seil PA34 4TJ

☎ (01852) 300276

📠 (01852) 300597

🖳 www.willowburn.co.uk

Above-average, keenly-priced food is offered in this small, friendly hotel. Four-course meals plus coffee offer gourmet treatment of seafood, beef and lamb. Vegetables come from local market gardeners, and desserts are a high point.

All week D only 7–8; closed Jan and Feb (See Where to Stay)

DERVAIG
Druimard Country House

Dervaig, Isle of Mull PA75 6QW

☎ /📠 (01688) 400345

The fine five-course dinners in this Victorian manse are cooked in homely Euro-Scottish style, and include Mull produce supplemented by the kitchen's own herbs and salad items in season. The only choice is at the dessert course, and the meal is completed with cheese. Fairly priced wine list.

All week D only 7–8.30 (6.30–8.30 when theatre playing) (See Where to Stay)

ERISKA
Isle of Eriska

Eriska, Ledaig, Oban PA37 1SD

☎ (01631) 720371

📠 (01631) 720531

🖳 www.eriska-hotel.co.uk

This 'peculiarly enchanting' hotel offers a six-course menu where seafood features prominently. Native ingredients, with a few cosmopolitan additions, are beautifully cooked. Desserts can be a

high point, and wines are favourably priced.

All week D only 8–9 (See Where to Stay)

KILCHRENAN
Taychreggan

Kilchrenan, Taynuilt PA35 1HQ

☎ (01866) 833211/833366

📠 (01866) 833244

🖳 www.taychregganhotel.co.uk

Old stone house in a romantic and peaceful setting beside Loch Awe. The four-course dinners have an option at each stage, and the classical menu is skilfully cooked. Vegetarian dishes fascinate, and desserts are rich. The largely French wine list is reasonably priced.

All week, D only 7.30–8.45 (See Where to Stay)

KILMELFORD
Cuilfail Hotel

Kilmelford PA34 4XA

☎ (01852) 200274

Creeper-covered stone building tucked in a hollow of the Argyll hills, with excellent food and a discreet, cheery bar. In summer the restaurant offers a separate menu, with some items available in the bar.

Summer 11–11, winter 12–2.30 and 6–11; bar food and restaurant 12–2.30 and 6.30–9.30

PORT APPIN
Airds Hotel

Port Appin, Appin PA38 4DF

☎ (01631) 730236

📠 (01631) 730535

🖳 www.airds-hotel.co.uk

This neat and well-kept house in an idyllic setting is comfortable rather than luxurious. Flawless ingredients are cooked expertly in the four-course menu, and seafood is well-represented. Confident desserts, fine breads and appetisers; breakfasts are worth staying for.

All week D only 7.30–8.30 (See Where to Stay)

Pierhouse
Port Appin PA38 4DE
☎ (01631) 730302
🖷 (01631) 730400
Beside Loch Linnhe, with views across to Lismore and beyond to Mull, this no-nonsense restaurant offers very fresh, plainly presented seafood. Fillet or sirloin steak is also served, as are vegetarian options. The 50-plus wine list is fairly priced.

All week 12.30–2.30, 6.30–9.30; closed 25 and 26 Dec

TAYVALLICH
Tayvallich Inn
Tayvallich PA31 8PL
☎ (01546) 870282
Quality food in one of Argyll's prettiest villages, overlooking Loch Sween. The bar menu makes the most of local produce, especially fish and shellfish from the loch. More ambitious dishes using the same good local ingredients are served in the restaurant.

Summer 11–midnight (1am Fri and Sat), winter 12–2.30 and 6–11; bar food and restaurant 12–2 and 6–9; closed 25 Dec, 1 Jan

Stirling and Perth

Caledonian pine

- Boundary country between Lowlands and Highlands, with landscapes from raspberry fields to wild moorland
- Outstandingly beautiful rivers, two historic towns
- Heather, castles, skiing, Mary Queen of Scots
- The shapely mountains of Schiehallion and Ben Lawers, and the lovely Glen Lyon

STIRLING AND PERTH

At a glance

✓ The area offers easy touring holidays: no really lengthy drives

✓ Short breaks based in Stirling or Perth

✓ Good for dipping in and out of the Highlands

This large area of central Scotland has enough variety for several holidays. The geological boundary separating the Lowlands from the Highlands runs diagonally across it, so wherever you go you are in easy reach of both mountain scenery and the attractions of the Lowland valleys. Historically, it is one of the most intriguing parts of the country. The Picts and the Romans left traces here, while many of the most critical moments in Scotland's history were witnessed by the old towns and castles of the area.

Although the cities of Edinburgh and Glasgow have moved Scotland's centre of gravity south of the River Forth, it was the

---

Highlands and Lowlands

Like many another vanishing tribal society, the Highlanders of Scotland started to become the subjects of romantic legend the moment they ceased to be a threat. Two centuries' worth of tartanry, bagpipes and clan gatherings have totally obscured the apprehension with which the Highlands were once regarded. As late as 1773, Dr Johnson provided himself with a pair of pistols before venturing into the mountains, though Boswell persuaded him to leave them behind.

Before 1746, the Highlands posed a threat to the government of Lowland Scotland. The area and the people were feared because the allegiances, the language and the way of life of the Highland clans bore little relationship to those of their Lowland compatriots – or indeed to those south of the border. It is hardly surprising that when a Highland army erupted into England, reaching Derby and causing George II to make plans to flee the country, its final defeat at Culloden should have been followed by savage suppression of the

---

fertile lands beyond that natural river barrier which were the strategic heartland of the kingdom in medieval times. Many battles, including Stirling Bridge (1297) and Bannockburn (1314) were fought here, while it was to the quiet priory of Inchmahome that Mary Queen of Scots was taken to keep her out of English clutches.

The Forth may have formed a barrier to invaders from the south, but trouble has not always come from that direction. The royalist forces of Montrose emerged from the northern mountains to inflict two terrible defeats on the Covenanters at Tippermuir (1644) and Kilsyth (1645), and it was from the same direction that Dundee led his Highlanders to the Jacobite victory at Killiecrankie in 1689. Half a century later, the troops of Prince Charles Edward Stuart descended from the mountains to take Perth at the start of the last of the Jacobite uprisings – that of 1745.

Highland way of life. Highland dress was banned, the carrying of weapons forbidden, and the jurisdiction of the chiefs removed.

The breaking up of Highland society, begun in 1746, continued throughout the eighteenth and nineteenth centuries. Poverty, emigration, famine and eviction were to smash the clan system and depopulate the land. When you enjoy the emptiness and solitude of a Highland glen, remember that it was not always so.

Today, information technology, the slow influx of settlers and the deliberate fostering of the Gaelic language may be offering a new future to the Highlands. Long-distance working now enables a crofter to work part-time dealing with data for an employer many miles away. More people seem to be fleeing the cities for a less stressful life in the country. Whether all this will provide a long-term answer to the long-term decline of the Highlands, or whether it is just another kind of exploitation, has yet to be seen.

So there is an ambiguity about the fertile countryside round Perth and Stirling, with its magnificent, spate-heavy rivers, its sunny fields and its chains of low hills: it is at once the centre of old Scotland and its vulnerable edge.

Key web sites

www.perthshire.co.uk Web site of the Perthshire tourist board. Useful travel links and events listing

www.heartlander.scotland.net A network of sites covering the Highland area of Perthshire

www.aberfoyle.co.uk Useful site for the Trossachs area

www.rannoch.net Comprehensive community site for the Rannoch area, with plenty of information

www.strathearn.com Another good community web site, this time for the area west of Perth

---

Good bases in the area

Aberfeldy

✓ *Small and quiet*
✓ *Within reach of inspiring mountain country*
✗ *Not many facilities*

Aberfeldy is an attractive town where it is possible to feel part of the local life even in high season. While it lacks a huge choice of places to stay, it is well situated on the banks of the Tay, right in the centre of the best mountain country in the region.

Perth

✓ *Ideal location on the edge of the Highlands*
✓ *Good shops and a range of accommodation*

Perth is large, bustling and not at all touristy. It does not have much left by way of old buildings, but there are a few curiosities and some fine green spaces. Getting there by road or rail is easy, and the town makes an excellent touring base for Strathearn, the Angus glens and the Highlands.

Pitlochry

✔ *Good walking base close to attractive country*
✔ *Wide choice of accommodation*
✘ *Gets crowded; can be bleak in bad weather*

The town retains some of the atmosphere of a Victorian holiday spot. It is extremely busy in season but manages to remain unspoilt. There is a superabundance of places to stay. Pitlochry is also a good place from which to explore the valleys of the Tay and the Tummel.

Stirling

✔ *Historic town dominated by old castle*
✔ *Interesting old town centre*
✔ *Good communications in all directions*
✘ *Immediate surroundings not attractive*
✘ *Some steep streets*

A constant round of live performances and street activities keeps Stirling buzzing in summer. You will find much to see in the town itself, its castle alone being worth the better part of a day's exploration. Finding somewhere to stay presents little difficulty, and the town is in the best possible position for exploring the Trossachs and the Ochils.

STIRLING AND AROUND

Stirling, strategically situated between Highlands and Lowlands, was an important fortress and a favourite haunt of the Scottish renaissance court. Since those days, industrial development on the Forth estuary has somewhat spoiled its outlook, but not so much that it should be ignored. Fine countryside in the Ochil hills or the Campsie fells is close by, and less than an hour's journey takes you to the Trossachs, often billed as the Highlands in miniature and blessed with fine scenery – if rather too many visitors.

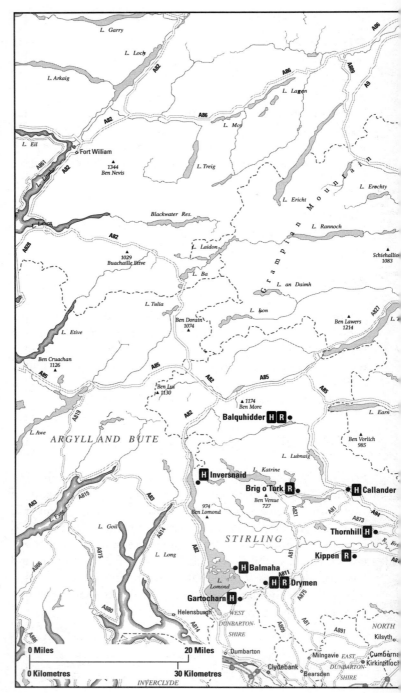

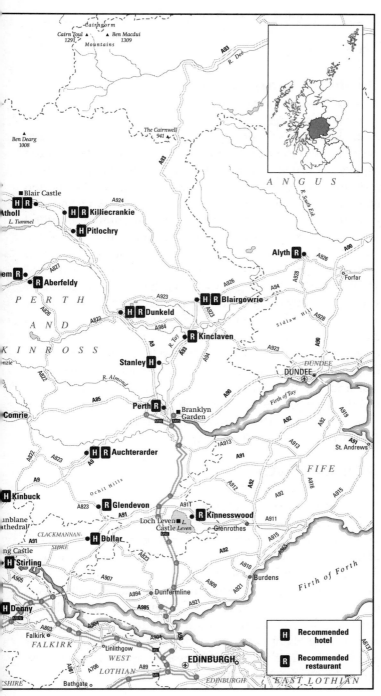

249

Top sights

Dunblane Cathedral

✓ *Wonderful restoration of a venerable church*
✓ *Superb wood-carving*

After 300 years of ruin, the interior was lavishly re-crafted under a restoration programme started in 1889. This period happily coincided with the revival of craftsmanship in stained glass and wood, so the result is an ancient, weather-beaten building containing some of the finest wood-carving and glass work in the country. The windows, featuring austere, beautiful faces subtly worked in lilac and palest blue, shine behind the eroded pillars of the nave, with contributions by the artists Kempe, Strachan, Davis (the lovely Nunc Dimittis windows) and Webster. The carving of the pews, the screen and the choir stalls was mostly designed by Sir Robert Lorimer, and repays close scrutiny by revealing a Noah's Ark-full of animals crouching in the choir stalls, while every pew in the nave is carved with a different flower. The modern work fits well into the simple Gothic fabric of the building, which is seen at its best from the outside, especially if you look at the west front and the south side, where a pinkish Norman bell-tower seems grafted on to the thirteenth-century walls behind. *[www.dunblanecathedral.org.uk]*

Stirling Castle

✓ *Dramatically situated castle and palace*
✓ *Brilliant restoration of Renaissance Hall*
✓ *Terrific views*

Like Edinburgh Castle, Stirling Castle is built on a volcanic plug, with the town clumped beneath. Inside the massive outer defences the chief thing to see is the newly rebuilt Great Hall, the focal point for court ceremonies in the sixteenth century. A massive restoration project, using authentic materials and involving the construction of a new hammer-beam roof, has returned the Hall to the way it would have looked when new in 1500. The huge fireplaces still heat the room, but now with hot air blown down the chimneys.

The palace, next door, is the next target for restoration. It has one of the earliest classical façades in Britain, with French-inspired statues, gargoyles, string courses and pediments. Inside, the royal apartments are currently used to display the Stirling Heads, a series of beautifully carved wooden bosses which once adorned the ceilings.

The chapel is the third building worth seeing. It now has a distinctively modern interior, with a wooden vaulted ceiling and new oak floor. But the frieze painted for the visit of Charles I in 1633 still remains.

Apart from these three great buildings, there is much else of interest. Some of it – the wall walks, the batteries of cannon, and the various defensive walls – is military in origin, but much, such as the sunny bowling green or the nicely restored kitchens, belong to Stirling's time as a palace. Within one of the old buildings is the Regimental Museum of the Argyll and Sutherland Highlanders, very well laid-out, and with its own stories to relate [🖰 www.argylls.co.uk]. This part of the castle is also where James I murdered the Earl of Douglas and is reputed to have thrown his corpse from the window.

In various nooks and crannies of the castle, Historic Scotland has laid on displays, illustrating, for example, the lifestyle of various artisans in the sixteenth century using models and sound effects. The castle is well run, and guides are expert and approachable. [Apr to Sept, daily 9.30–6; Oct to Mar, daily 9.30–5; ☎ (01786) 450.000; 🖰 via www.scottishculture.about.com]

The next best sights

Bannockburn Heritage Centre (south of Stirling, signed from M9)

Robert the Bruce's victory over the English at Bannockburn carries a huge burden of symbolism in Scotland, but the battle-field has changed enormously since 1314 and is now mostly built over. The Heritage Centre tells the story of the battle as well as possible, and provides audio-guides for exploration of what remains of the battlefield. Despite the massive modern memorial and the stone where Bruce grounded his standard, it is all a little like a public park. *[Daily, Mar and Nov to Xmas, 11–4.30; Apr to Oct 10–5.30;* ☎ *(01786) 812664;* ☞ *via www.nts.org.uk]*

Battle of Bannockburn

The eight-year campaign fought by Robert the Bruce to drive the English from Scotland and to be recognised as king inside his own country reached its climax at Bannockburn in June 1314. For a leader who understood the virtues of guerrilla warfare, the prospect of fighting the enormous force brought to Scotland by Edward II must have been a dreadful one. He was forced into it by the rash bargain made between his brother, Edward, and the English garrison of Stirling Castle: if the castle were not relieved by mid-summer it would surrender. The English rose to the challenge, and Bruce had to confront them to retain any credibility.

The dispositions made by Bruce, including skilful choice of ground and the digging of pits, would probably not have saved the Scots, but a terrible tactical mistake by the English played into their hands. Before the battle, the English appear to have withdrawn for the night into boggy ground near the bank of the Forth, the worst possible terrain for the English heavy cavalry.

On seeing this the next day, Bruce went over to the attack, using his few cavalry to neutralise the opposing archers and his infantry to confine the English within a constricted and marshy space. The sheer size of the English army and its inability to manoeuvre caused chaos. The battle, hard fought for most of the day, seems to have reached a turning point with the appearance of Scottish reinforcements – traditionally thought to be the camp-followers – who appeared over the skyline at a moment critical for English morale. The battle turned to rout. Edward II fled, first to Stirling and then, hotly pursued, to Dunbar and Berwick.

Castle Campbell and Dollar Glen

From the car park up in the hills behind Dollar, a path descends into Dollar Glen (NTS, open all year). If you are not fit enough for this steep route, use the more straightforward road leading on from the car park. At the bottom of Dollar Glen, the Burn of Care and the Burn of Sorrow meet in a tangle of rock faces and tumbled slabs, with cleverly engineered walkways leading through the narrow gaps. Eventually, steep steps lead you from the depths of the Burn of Care and you see the walls of Castle Campbell above you. In keeping with all the Care and the Sorrow, it used to be called Castle Gloom, but never really merited this name, for it is a sunny spot, with splendid views across the Forth Valley to the Pentland Hills. The grim fifteenth-century tower at the castle's centre is virtually intact, its four rooms on four floors linked by a wheel stair. Around it, the remains of later buildings are less overtly designed for defence, and there is even a tiny two-arched loggia tucked into a sunny corner of the courtyard. *[HS; Apr to Sept, daily 9.30–6.30; Oct to Mar, Mon–Sat 9.30–4.30, Sun 2–4.30, closed Thur pm and Fri;* ☎ *(01259) 742408;* 🖰 *via www.scottishculture.about.com]*

Doune Castle

This fortress above the River Teith was built by one of the most powerful and unscrupulous men in medieval Scotland, Robert Stewart, first Duke of Albany. He is widely suspected of having had the heir to the throne murdered and his younger brother, James, kidnapped by English pirates. When James eventually returned to Scotland as king, one of his first acts was to eradicate the Albany family for high treason. Four of them were beheaded at Stirling, and Doune castle was forfeited to the crown. Meanwhile, the original Duke had died in his bed, in his eighties.

Doune Castle was designed to be both strong and imposing and it is an awe-inspiring place, with severe curtain walls and a massive gate-tower. In its three halls and extensive kitchens enormous fireplaces remove some of the chill from the air. Thorough restoration in 1883 led to some rather peculiar refurbishing of the biggest rooms (banners, heavy dark wood and flagstoned floors). *[HS; Apr to Sept, daily 9.30–6.30; Oct to Mar, Mon–Sat 9.30–4.30, Sun 2–4.30, closed Thur pm and Fri;* ☎ *(01786) 841742;* 🖱 *via www.scottishculture.about.com]*

Mary Queen of Scots

It is hardly surprising that tragedians have found inspiration in the reign of Scotland's most famous queen: her life seems to belong more to the stage than to the pages of history. After her husband François II of France died, she returned to Scotland in 1561 at a time when the country was poised between France and England, and between the forces of Roman Catholicism and Protestantism.

Her very existence posed threats or offered opportunities to half of Europe. She was, in the eyes of many Catholics, already the legitimate Queen of England, and certainly had a strong claim to the succession should Queen Elizabeth die childless. Within Scotland, the Protestant lords and ministers regarded her with deep suspicion, while the Catholics expected her to reinstate the old Church. The young queen found no substitute among the self-interested Scottish nobility for the steady counsel she had become used to from her Guise relatives in France.

Mary's tolerance and humanity in the midst of this political mire have greatly appealed to nineteenth- and twentieth-century sensibilities. Yet they were inappropriate qualities in a sixteenth-century ruler. Mary's far more devious cousin, Elizabeth of England, was a less likeable person but a more successful Queen.

The beginning of Mary's reign in Scotland was a success. It was her marriage to the feather-brained Lord Darnley in 1565 that sealed her fate. An immediate rebellion against the couple was put down, but as Mary herself became disillusioned with Darnley the opportunities for those who desired to destabilise her rule increased. The murder of her secretary, Rizzio, with Darnley at the head of the killers, is one of the most distasteful episodes.

Inchmahome Priory

The ruins of the old priory stand a short distance south of the A873 on an island in the middle of the Lake of Menteith, one of the few expanses of water in Scotland that is not called a loch. A five–minute crossing on Historic Scotland's ferry will

The murder of Darnley in Edinburgh in 1567, when the house in which he was sleeping was blown up (though Darnley himself was found strangled in the garden), cast a taint of suspicion on the Queen from which she never recovered. Her marriage to the Earl of Bothwell, who was closely involved in the plot to kill Darnley, took place a bare three months later – a scandalous union.

Many of the nobles who immediately took up arms against Bothwell and the Queen had given Bothwell their secret approval only a month before. This may have helped him to persuade the Queen into marriage, but it did him no good now. At Carberry Hill near Edinburgh the rebellious nobles outfaced the smaller army of Bothwell and the Queen. Mary submitted herself to the safe conduct of the nobles, who included many of the conspirators in the murder of Rizzio.

Safe conduct turned out to mean imprisonment at Loch Leven and an enforced abdication in favour of the infant James. When the Queen escaped, the speed with which she gathered an army showed her support still to be strong. Her defeat at Langside was followed by the rash decision to seek shelter in England. Mary seems always to have hoped for Elizabeth's friendship, but the latter perceived her as a threat and so held the Scottish Queen in detention, refusing to meet her.

The threat posed by Mary as a centrepiece of Catholic plotting eventually became too great for the English government to bear. In 1586 she was secretly tried on the charge of conspiring to assassinate Elizabeth. The evidence against her seems largely to have been fabricated. Her inevitable execution – at Fotheringhay Castle in Northamptonshire – followed, despite Elizabeth's long reluctance to sign the death warrant.

take you to the island.

It was to Inchmahome that the young Mary Queen of Scots came in 1547 to keep her from the English, who had just defeated the Scots at the Battle of Pinkie. The following year she set sail for France and marriage to the Dauphin. She was not to return for 12 years.

The priory ruins are well preserved, especially the east window of the church with its five lancets. In the grounds Mary's Bower, Mary's Garden and Mary's Tree remain as memories of the island's most famous visitor. [*HS; Apr to Sept, daily 9.30–6.30;* ☎ *(01877) 385294;* ◔ *via www.aberfoyle.co.uk*]

The National Wallace Monument
(north-east of Stirling)

In the wake of the film *Braveheart* [◔ *www.macbraveheart.co.uk*], visitor numbers to this Victorian folly, which sticks up from Abbey Craig to the north of Stirling, have rocketed. The view from the top is not as good as from Stirling Castle, but you have the compensation of standing where Wallace once stood watching the English army winding its way over the Forth before the battle of Stirling Brig in 1297. Inside the tower, audio-visual presentations introduce you to the background behind Wallace's revolt and the First Wars of Independence, and you can see the sword which was supposed to have been his. [*Daily: Jan, Feb, Nov and Dec, 10.30–4; Mar, May and Oct, 10–5; June and Sept, 10–6; July and Aug, 9.30–6.30;* ☎ *(01786) 472140;* ◔ *via www.scottishculture.about.com*]

Also in the area

Clach of Mannan (Clackmannan) A detour to the small town of Clackmannan reveals the remains of a sixteenth-century tolbooth and a fourteenth-century tower on the outskirts. But the chief curiosity here is the Clach of Mannan, by the tolbooth. This is a large stone on a modern plinth, which may or may not be sacred to a pre-Christian sea-god, and may or may not be very old indeed. It sits contentedly with lorries rumbling past, and may well outlast everything round about it.

William Wallace

By the end of 1296 Edward I of England had thoroughly conquered Scotland, deposing John Balliol (known as 'Toom Tabard' – empty coat) and turning the country into an occupied province. Yet, by the very next year, Scotland was stirring with revolt against English rule. This movement was largely inspired by the small landowners, among whom was William Wallace, the son of a Renfrewshire knight.

Wallace, the recent *Braveheart* film notwithstanding, is a shadowy figure. His achievement in crystallising the resistance to English occupation was extraordinary. The nobles, including Robert the Bruce, were fickle or timorous by turns, and more inclined to respect rank than ability. Nevertheless, Wallace conducted successful guerrilla warfare against the English and, together with Andrew de Moray, inflicted a major defeat on their army at Stirling Brig in 1297. After this, he was knighted and elected Guardian of Scotland in the name of the exiled King John.

However, guerrilla tactics did not save the Scots at Falkirk in 1298, when Edward appeared on the scene with another army. The Scottish pikes were no match for the English archers, and the battle became a rout. Wallace was forced to flee and shortly after resigned the Guardianship. He was eventually captured – perhaps betrayed – in 1305, and executed in London with the barbarity reserved for traitors, on the command of a king whose sovereignty he never acknowledged.

Towns and villages to explore

Stirling

Stirling stands on about the only piece of firm ground in the marshy flatlands round the tidal River Forth. For hundreds of years it was the lowest point at which the Forth could be bridged, so the town commanded all routes northwards. That it overlooks seven battlefields is hardly surprising.

Like Edinburgh, which it uncannily resembles in miniature, Stirling has a grey castle on a crag and a warren of old buildings ranging down the steep slope to its east. It is a friendly, carefree town, less dignified than Edinburgh, but ready to remind you that its place in Scotland's history is just as important.

Stirling was a favourite royal residence, and some fine buildings remain, especially the Guildhall (1634), the Church of the Holy Rude (1415) and the eroded façade of Mar's Wark, a Renaissance-style demonstration of wealth. Best of all is the low, multi-arched Old Bridge (1400) across the Forth, still in use as a footbridge.

Things to see in town include the **Old Town Jail** *[Apr to late Sept, daily 9.30–6; late Sept to Oct, daily 9.30–5; Oct to Mar daily 9.30–4;* ☎ *(01786) 450050]*, where live performance in summer helps create a suitably penal atmosphere, and **Argyll's Lodging**, a dignified seventeenth-century house, whose various incarnations are outlined in the exhibitions held inside *[HS; Apr to Sept, daily 9.30–6.30; Oct to Mar, Mon–Sat 9.30–6.30, Sun 2–4.30;* ☎ *(01786) 450000]*. Despite the steepness of the streets, the town is good to wander through, for it has a pleasantly relaxed atmosphere, and numerous cafés and pubs in the streets leading up to the castle. *Whistlebinkies* in St Mary's Wynd is one of the most atmospheric.

Stirling's forte, so far as the visitor is concerned, is live performance. In summer, the town is alive with actors, dancers and fiddlers, and set-piece events are staged too. For more information about the town, see ☜▮ *www.stirling.co.uk*

Scenery

The Campsie Fells To the south-west of Stirling, the Campsie Fells conveniently separate the industrial unpleasantness of the western Central Belt from the upper Forth Valley. Unless you climb to the top of the range, you may not suspect that the suburbs of Glasgow lie on the far side. The hills provide a breath of fresh air and some rural peace and quiet for many people, and the A818 road, which runs beside the River Carron through the pretty village of Fintry and on to the equally attractive Drymen, is unspoilt and makes a gentle outing.

East Loch Lomond The road running along the eastern shore of Loch Lomond ends at Rowardennan and only campers, caravanners, picnickers and walkers use it. From near Balmaha you can look out over the wooded islands which stud the southern half of the loch and watch the pleasure boats pottering round them. Numerous coves, walks and picnic places exist, and energetic souls set out here to walk the long-distance West Highland Way [*www.west-highland-way.co.uk*] which runs up Loch Lomond to finish at Fort William. Ben Lomond, which rises over 3,000 feet above the loch on this shore, is best climbed from Rowardennan.

A slow but attractive way of reaching the loch is to take the B829 from Aberfoyle, passing Loch Ard, Loch Chon and Loch Arklet to end at the minuscule hamlet of Inversnaid.

Loch Voil From the A84 north of the Trossachs proper, an unclassified dead-end road strikes west. Many visitors go to see Rob Roy's grave at Balquhidder; not so many persevere on the twisty lochside road which flanks Loch Voil and Loch Doine. It is a beautiful road, winding beneath ancient trees, and with the mountains at the head of the glen gradually closing in.

The Ochil hills These rounded, grassy half-mountains run north-eastward from Stirling to Newburgh on the Tay, diminishing gradually in size as they go, with fine views north and south to reward those few visitors who climb to explore their tops. The small mill towns of Menstrie, Blairlogie, Alva and Tilliecoultry (collectively called the Hillfoots) were built to take advantage of the water rushing down the steep glens on their southern side. Apart from the odd mill shop, little of the textile industry is left today. If touring by car, take the A823 up Glen Devon and into Glen Eagles for a taste of the scenery.

Rumbling Bridge Gorge The gorge at Rumbling Bridge is one of the most magnificent in Scotland, though you might never guess it was there, since the road (A823) leaps it without a dip. Keep a sharp look-out for the signposted car park just to the north of the bridge, and walk to the edge of the chasm which the River Devon has carved from a fault in the rock. Walkways run around the edge. The Deil's Mill, where a horrible rumble rises out of the depths, is especially worth stopping at. The nineteenth-century bridge which now carries the road over the gorge was built directly above its predecessor, which remains slung underneath it, creating a peculiar effect. The old bridge had no parapet, and must have taken steely nerves to cross on horseback.

The Trossachs This is the name usually given to the rugged country lying between Callander and Loch Lomond. A favourite spot for tourists to the Highlands since Victorian times, it is still heavily populated by tour coaches today, for the combination of lochs and mountains is both photogenic and easily accessible. Many of the hills are now swathed in conifers, however, and the area is really better explored on foot or by bicycle than by car. **Loch Katrine** is by reputation the most beautiful loch in the area, although you need to walk to see the best parts, or take a trip on the *SS Sir Walter Scott* from the pier at the end of the loch. The **Queen Elizabeth Forest Park** (visitor centre on A821 near Aberfoyle) offers numerous routes for walkers, and a forest drive [☛ *via www.aberfoyle.co.uk*]. Hillwalkers aim for the relatively easy summits of Ben Venue or Ben Ledi. Another popular and easy walk is to the Bracklinn Falls [☛ *www.b-mercer.demon.co.uk*] close to Callander, while a cycle route runs up the western shore of Loch Lubnaig.

The centre of activity is the nondescript town of **Callander**, with the smaller, less overtly touristy **Aberfoyle** [☛ *www.aberfoyle.co.uk*] as a satellite base and refreshment stop. Both places are well provided with a range of cafés, souvenir shops and places to stay at, although both become very crowded on summer weekends.

The only wet-weather attraction in the area is the **Rob Roy and Trossachs Visitor Centre** (Callander) *[Jan to Feb, weekends only 10–5; Mar to May and Oct to Dec, daily 10–5; June to Sept, daily 9.30–6;* ☎ *(01877) 330342]*, whose multi-media exhibits focus on the region's most famous figure, Rob Roy McGregor. Heavily romanticised by Sir Walter Scott (and later by the 1995 film *Rob Roy*), the cattle-rustler, outlaw and part-time patriot is in reality one of the less memorable of Scotland's historical figures. The Trossachs tourist industry will do its best to convince you otherwise.

PERTH AND AROUND

Like Stirling, Perth is situated on the border between Highlands and Lowlands. Set between the beautiful river valleys of the Tay and the Earn, with the estuary of the former stretching eastwards towards Dundee, the city is centrally located in a large swathe of agricultural countryside. Northwards, the hills begin, gradually dominating the land-scape, until you have passed out of central Scotland and have reached the very different landscape of the Highlands proper.

Top sights

Loch Leven Castle (Kinross)

✓ *Romantic island setting*
✓ *Essential sight for Mary Queen of Scots fans*

This ancient ruin on an island in Loch Leven had a long history even before its most famous prisoner arrived. The island may have been fortified during the English occupation under Edward I and captured by Wallace and/or Robert the Bruce, later resisting renewed attempts by the English to take it. By 1567 the victorious nobles who had captured Mary Queen of Scots at the Battle of Carberry reckoned it to be an ideal place in which to isolate their prisoner and enforce her abdication.

In those days, the loch was larger, the island smaller, and the castle primitive by sixteenth-century standards. Mary's jailers seem to have been coldly hostile.

The Queen's escape has all the elements of a good thriller – the loyalty of the orphan Willie Douglas, whom she persuaded to help her, the careful stealing of the keys, the holing of all the boats except the one needed, and finally the moment of highest drama as the Queen crossed the courtyard in disguise, fearing last-minute discovery.

There was no happy ending. In spite of the fact that supporters flocked to her, Mary's army was fatally beaten at Langside 11 days after her escape in May 1568. She fled south and decided to cross the Solway and seek help in England. Instead, she found further imprisonment and eventual execution, 19 years later.

In contrast to its cruel history, Loch Leven Castle is a peaceful place today. Little remains of the old ruin, but the atmosphere lingers and the setting is superb. Come on a day without much wind (boats do not run if it is rough), and preferably with some sun, for there is nowhere to shelter. *[HS; Apr–Sept daily 9.30–6.30 (Regular ferry from Kinross);* ☎ *(0378) 040483;* 🖱 *via www.scottishculture.about.com]*

Branklyn Garden (Perth)

✓ *Town garden, packed with flowers and shrubs*
✓ *Best in spring (azaleas) and late summer (gentians)*
✓ *Easy walking*

In contrast to Scotland's many wild or woodland gardens, this is a neat town garden behind a large villa on the south-eastern fringe of Perth. Few keen gardeners will leave without being inspired, if not by the splendour of the peat-loving plants, then by the design, which makes the garden feel much larger than it is. Within the garden, which covers barely two acres, there is room for a rockery, a pond and banks of rhododendron, azalea, primula, gentian and meconopsis. There is also a small alpine house with its own rarities. It is worth coming to the garden soon after it opens, as it can become crowded. *[NTS; Mar to Oct, daily 9.30–sunset;* ☎ *(01738) 625535;* 🖱 *via www.nts.org.uk]*

The next best sights

Glenturret Distillery (west of Crieff)

This is the oldest distillery in Scotland and one of the most relaxed to visit. It has a low-key feel about it despite the efficiency of the tours and the extensive shop. The surroundings are pretty, and it is possible to walk from the distillery into the wooded grounds on the far side of the River Turret. *[Feb to Dec, Mon–Sat 9.30–6, Sun 12–6; Jan, Mon–Fri 11.30–4;* ☎ *(01764) 656565;* ☝ *www.glenturret.com]*

Huntingtower Castle (west of Perth)

The castle may have an uninspiring setting on the very edge of the A85, but it is worth stopping to see some of the earliest painted ceilings to be found in Scotland. It used to be owned by the Ruthven family, notorious and unpleasant conspirators. They were at the forefront of the plot to murder Rizzio, Mary Queen of Scots' secretary, helped imprison Mary on Loch Leven, and kidnapped the young James VI in 1582, after which they held him for ten months. The castle does have one romantic legend: the 'maiden's leap' between the two towers refers to the first Earl's daughter, who, forced to leave her lover's bed in a hurry on hearing her mother's approach, made this perilous jump. *[HS; Apr to Sept, daily 9.30–6.30; Oct to Mar, Mon–Sat 9.30–4.30, Sun 2–4.30, closed Thur and Fri;* ☎ *(01738) 627231;* ☝ *via www.scottishculture.about.com]*

Kinross House Gardens (Kinross)

The house was built by the architect Sir William Bruce in 1686 for himself. It is not open but you can admire the grey classical frontages, which are perfectly complemented by the garden. At its centre, a formal design directs the eye towards Loch Leven Castle seeming to float on the loch beyond, while the scents and colours of the herbaceous border and shrubbery fill the air under the enclosing walls. *[Apr to Oct, daily 10–7;* ☎ *(01577) 862900]*

Meigle Museum (north-east of Coupar Angus)

This small museum with its collection of Pictish stones (see page 304) should not be missed by anyone with an interest in the distant past. *[*☝ *via www.darkisle.com]*

Scone Palace (north-east of Perth)

This huge mansion has ample space for tour coaches. Its extensive grounds include a maze and adventure playground and it is popular for family days out. The house itself is old, but its exterior has suffered from nineteenth-century neo-Gothic excess. The interior is notable for a very fine collection of porcelain and French furniture. The site of Scone Abbey, where so many Scottish kings were crowned, can be seen in the grounds although it was entirely destroyed at the Reformation. *[Easter to Oct, daily 9.30–4.45;* ☎ *(01738) 552300;* 🖰 *www.scone-palace.co.uk]*

Also in the area

Abernethy Tower (M90, Junction 9) The small village was once the hub of a Pictish kingdom and an important centre for the Celtic church. An eleventh-century round tower by the churchyard is the only evidence that remains.

Black Watch Regimental Museum (Perth) The history and honours of the famous regiment are housed in an old tower house. It is a friendly and welcoming place, especially to those with regimental connections. *[May to Sept, Mon–Sat 10–4.30; Oct to Apr, Mon–Fri 10–3.30;* ☎ *0131–310 8530]*

Drummond Castle Gardens (south of Crieff) A formal Italianate seventeenth-century garden, with a huge ornate sundial.

Earthquake House (Comrie, west of Perth) Comrie lies right on the Highland fault, and is known as the 'shaky toun', for it experiences more earth tremors than anywhere else in the country. The world's first seismometer was set up here. Earthquake House has explanatory panels and a model of this early instrument. *[*🖰 *via www.strathearn.com]*

Fowlis Wester, St Bean's Church (west of Perth on A85) The church in this tiny village has a handsome Pictish stone and a piece of MacBean tartan which went to the moon. [🖱 *via www.strathearn.com]*

Innerpeffray Library (south of Crieff on B8062) The oldest library in Scotland, it houses a collection of rare books which is the more astonishing for being in such a tiny place. *[Apr to end Sept, Mon to Sat 10–12.45, 2–4.45; Oct to Mar, 2–4, closed Thur;* ☎ *(01764) 652819;* 🖱 *via www.strathearn.com]*

Meikleour Beech Hedge (north-east of Perth on A93) The roadside hedge was planted in 1746 and is now 110 feet high. It is trimmed every ten years. [🖱 *via www.scottishscenery.org.uk]*

Roman Forts (west of Perth) The Romans established a series of outposts in the broad valley of Strathearn. The chief of these was Ardoch Roman Camp, just outside Braco, which guarded the road south. Its extensive earthworks remain. The Roman remains in the area are under intensive archaeological investigation – the Roman Gask project. [🖱 *via www.morgue.demon.co.uk]*

Tulliebardine Chapel (north-west of Auchterarder) An isolated barn-like building on a minor road, which is actually a fifteenth-century collegiate chapel with an interior almost unaltered.

Vane Farm (east shore of Loch Leven) is an RSPB reserve. In winter, thousands of geese and duck come to the loch. There are telescopes in the visitor centre and trails leading to hides overlooking the loch. *[Apr to Dec, daily 10–5; Jan to Mar, daily 10–4;* ☎ *(01577) 862355;* 🖱 *via www.rspb.org.uk]*

Towns and villages to explore

Crieff

Situated where the Lowlands and Highlands meet, Crieff used to hold one of the biggest trysts (cattle fairs) in Scotland. Today it is an easy-going market town, taking advantage of its position to gather tourists into its shops and its tiny museum. Crieff Visitor Centre [☞ *www.crieff.co.uk*] to the south of town has numerous outlets for locally made products, including pottery and paperweights. A number of hotels date from Crieff's days as a nineteenth-century resort, among them the massive Crieff Hydro. Numerous guesthouses are also to be found if you want to stay for a night or two.

Kinross

This is an attractive small town on the banks of Loch Leven, very much the centre for the fishermen and birdwatchers (see Vane Farm, above) who visit the loch. The wild, pink-fleshed Loch Leven trout are famous for their number and their flavour. *[Anglers can call* ☎ *(01577) 863407 to book a place in one of the boats on the loch]*

Perth

St John's town of Perth was supposedly founded by the Romans and has not looked back since. It gained from being close to Scone Abbey, the traditional coronation spot of Scottish kings, and had several religious houses of its own until John Knox's fiery sermons of 1559 inflamed the mob to pillage them all. In one of the monasteries, Blackfriars, James I came to a grisly end at the hand of an assassin in 1437.

A pleasant place, with a pedestrianised high street and a good range of shops and eating places, Perth has all the hallmarks of a prosperous country town. Its **museum** *[Mon–Sat 10–5;* ☎ *(01738) 474170]* reflects this in its fine collection, notably of local silver. Other places to visit in town include the working watermill at **Lower City Mill** *[Easter and Apr to Nov, Mon–Sat 10–5; shop open all year;* ☎ *(01738) 627 958]* where you can watch oatmeal being ground and the **Church of St John**, which has been remodelled down the centuries since Edward I worshipped in it during his 1296 campaign of conquest, most notably by Sir Robert Lorimer in 1926. Art lovers should go to the **Fergusson Gallery** to see the country's best collection of works by John Duncan Fergusson, a leading Scottish Colourist *[Mon–Sat 10–5;* ☎ *(01738) 441944]*. Perth's green spaces of

North and South Inch beside the Tay are ideal for a stroll and for watching Perth's citizens taking the air. A sculpture trail combines art and fresh air. Look up Perth via ⚲ *www.scottish-towns.co.uk*

St Fillans

The small, attractive village at the eastern end of Loch Earn is named after a sixth-century missionary from Ireland, whose relics were carried into battle at Bannockburn. St Fillans is a centre for watersports, and has some good short walks on the hillsides near the village, particularly around Glen Tarken (get hold of a leaflet about it from Crieff Tourist Information Office). [⚲ *via www.strathearn.com*]

Scenery and touring routes

Glenalmond From just west of Perth, you can follow the River Almond westward towards its source. Stop at Buchanty to visit the waterfall, where you may see salmon leaping, and traverse the narrow confines of the Sma' Glen. You can walk further up the river where it parts company with the road, heading higher into the hills.

Glen Artney Another dead-end road into the hills, especially beautiful when the heather is out.

Glen Lednock An attractive short drive up into the hills above Comrie, with the impressive 'Deil's Cauldron' in the River Lednock to admire.

Strathmore The long lowland valley stretching north-east of Perth is Scotland's raspberry country. If you are there in July or early August, numerous farms offer pick-your-own opportunities.

NORTH FROM PERTH

Three routes lead northwards into the Highlands. The A9 is the main one, bedevilled by traffic and bad road design, but with several things to see en route. To the east, the A93 leads up into the bleak hills around Glenshee, traversing the Cairnwell pass before heading for Braemar and Deeside. The third route, to the west, runs up from Crieff to Aberfeldy. It is a slow but attractive road, taking you towards the splendid scenery around Loch Rannoch and Loch Tay.

Top sight

Blair Castle (Blair Atholl)

✓ *Well-run stately home in pleasant grounds*
✓ *Intriguing collections of Victoriana*

This rambling, white baronial castle on the southern fringes of the Highlands is a most pleasing stately home. It is smartly run, has extensive grounds, and is full of family clutter (and some nobler items) dating back at least four centuries. It does not take itself too seriously – just sets out to give its visitors a memorable day, and this is one of the chief factors in its success.

Thirty-two rooms are on the self-guided tour – enough for the keenest of castle-visitors to feel satiated. Some of the rooms in the old service wing have display cases full of intriguing objects – Victorian umbrellas and reticules, fine china, Jacobite relics and much more. Even the nursery display is composed of objects 'discovered at different times throughout the castle' – and it is easy to imagine, even today, an Edwardian doll being found beneath a cushion somewhere and added in.

The wall decorations in the entrance hall are composed entirely of pistols, muskets and pikes. The Georgian section is where Blair Castle goes suddenly elegant, boasting fine plasterwork and elegant furniture. The Atholl Highlanders' room commemorates the Duke's own private army (the only one sanctioned in Britain), and the huge ballroom, redolent of a Gothic tithe barn, is lined with stags' antlers. *[Easter and Apr to Oct, daily 10–6 (last entry 5);* ☎ *(01796) 481207;* ☞ *www.blair-castle.co.uk]*

The next best sights

Castle Menzies (near Aberfeldy)

This creepy-looking pile across the Tay from Aberfeldy and beyond the tiny village of Weem was derelict for years. Clan Menzies got hold of it in the nick of time and it has now been restored as a Clan Centre. It is also a splendid example of a 'Z-plan' fortification (a castle with a tower on diagonally opposite sides of the main wing). There is not much to see inside, apart from a few intriguing objects found behind the old walls, including a single green satin eighteenth-century lady's shoe. *[Apr to Oct, Mon–Sat 10.30–5, Sun 2–5;* ☎ *(01887) 820982; ◔ via www.scottishculture.about.com]*

Dunkeld Cathedral

When the Vikings drove St Columba's monks from Iona in about 729, it was to Dunkeld that they came. Its religious importance was further established by the cathedral, which dates from the twelfth century. Today it is a quiet ruin – the nave roofless, the choir still serving as parish church, but notable for the quality of the window tracery. At the back of the building, the huge scraggy larch tree is the 'parent larch', possibly the first grown in Scotland. It was planted in 1737. *[Apr to Sept, Mon–Sat 9–6.30, Sun 2–6.30; Oct to Mar, Mon–Sat 9.30–4, Sun 2–4.30;* ☎ *0131-668 8800]*

Edradour Distillery (east of Pitlochry)

This is the smallest distillery in Scotland, worth visiting for its friendly lack of formality and the fact that, for the moment, it is free from the money-grubbing practices now found in many larger, more famous establishments. *[Mar to Oct, Mon–Sat 9.30–5, Sun 12–5;* ☎ *(01796) 472095; ◔ via www.scotch-whisky.org.uk]*

Killiecrankie (north of Pitlochry)

The steep, wooded gorge was the scene of a dramatic battle in the Jacobite uprising of 1689, when a charge of Highland clans under 'Bonnie' Dundee put a lowland army to flight. Dundee was fatally wounded in the battle however, and without his leadership the uprising fizzled out. The visitor centre has a full explanation of the battle and its background. Most visitors come for the beauty of the wooded gorge here, and to see the 'soldier's leap' where a fleeing Englishman jumped for his life over the River Garry. The National Trust has installed a network of paths and signed walks along the gorge, well worth strolling along. *[NTS; grounds: all year; visitor centre: Apr to Oct, 10.30–5.30; ☎ (01796) 473233; via www.heartlander.scotland.net]*

Scottish Crannog Centre (Kenmore, near Aberfeldy)

A crannog was an Iron-Age lake dwelling, created by building a house on a foundation of piles in shallow water. Remains have been found in Loch Tay, and this is a complete reconstruction, built as nearly as possible by ancient methods. You can walk out along the causeway to the crannog and see a reconstructed home, with tools and utensils based on Iron-Age technology. *[Apr to Oct, daily 10–5.30; ☎ (01887) 830583; www.crannog.co.uk]*

Also in the area

Fortingall Yew (west of Aberfeldy) This tiny village contains the oldest living thing in Europe, a yew tree which is possibly 3,000 years old. You can begin to appreciate the timescale when you read that all the fragments of wood were once one huge trunk, whose circumference in 1776 was 65 feet. The tree has suffered much from souvenir hunters, bow-makers and festival bonfires, but it still lives on. *[via www.rannoch.net]*

The Hermitage (near Dunkeld, signed from A9) This is a folly on the banks of the River Braan, built in 1758 and called Ossian's Hall or the Hermitage. A mile's walk through woodland leads you there. Beyond lies Ossian's Cave – another piece of artifice. The whole walk, with its waterfall, gorge and little bridge, reflects the late eighteenth-century taste for the picturesque. It is still utterly charming, with only a faint hint of the ridiculous. [⌂ *via www.nts.org.uk*]

Loch of Lowes (east of Dunkeld) This is one of a series of glacial lochs east of Dunkeld which run in a chain towards Blairgowrie and are known as the Stormont lochs after the district they lie in. Loch of Lowes is the largest, and is a nature reserve. From a hide you may be able to watch the ospreys which spend part of the year here. Even if there is none, the visitor centre will have information on what other kinds of bird you are likely to see. [⌂ *via www.swt.org.uk*]

Pitlochry Salmon Ladder Beneath the massive dam and power station at the outlet of Loch Faskally, thick glass windows allow you to peer into the swirling waters of the Fish Pass, a series of ascending pools by the side of the dam allowing salmon upstream to spawn. Although you can often see nothing but an empty tank, a random visit will occasionally find a salmon or sea trout poised inside the glass. An electronic recorder counts the fish passing up the ladder.

The 'Pot-bound larch' (Dunkeld) From Dunkeld, drive up the east bank of the Tay to Dunkeld House and persuade someone at the hotel to show you the pot-grown larch in the grounds. This huge specimen started life in an eighteenth-century greenhouse before being planted out, and its enormous roots still faithfully reproduce the shape of the pot in which it was grown.

St Mary's Church (Grandtully, north-east of Aberfeldy off A827) This church, dating back at least to 1533, looks like a barn attached to the neighbouring farm. Inside, however, the ceiling is richly decorated with medallions and heraldic crests, probably done around 1636. It is the pleasure of finding a small hidden treasure which makes a visit here rewarding. [*Always open*]

Towns and villages to explore

Aberfeldy

Aberfeldy is little more than a large village with an attractive square and a few shops. If you do not want to stay in the bustle of Pitlochry, Aberfeldy is unrushed and well situated for touring [✆ via *www.heartlander.scotland.net*]. Aberfeldy is distinguished by General Wade's bridge across the Tay, widely seen as his *tour de force* (see box). Note the Aberfeldy swimming pool – useful for bored children on wet days [☎ *(01887) 820*]. The local beauty spot, the **Birks** (birches) **o' Aberfeldy**, owes its fame to a poem by Burns, and the walk up the miniature glen behind the town to the Falls of Moness is pretty.

General Wade

Sent to Scotland in 1724 in the aftermath of the 1715 Jacobite uprising, General Wade was the man who built the roads and bridges through the Highlands which still largely determine what you can see from your car and what you cannot. These roads, a network of military communication where none had previously existed, were built to keep the Highlands pacified. Ironically, they were put to use by Charles Edward Stuart during his campaign in 1746. Now they are mostly hidden beneath tarmac, though many of his bridges remain, notably at Aberfeldy. Some stretches are left where modern road-makers have chosen a different route, notably at the Corrieyarrick pass (built 1735), which runs between Laggan and Fort Augustus. 'If you had seen these roads before they were made, you would get down on your knees and bless General Wade' runs the old saying.

Blair Atholl

This is a modest village in the shadow of Blair Castle, and looks appropriately ducal. It is a good base from which to tackle some of the long walks that thread through the lumpy mountains of the district of Atholl to the east. [✆ via *www.heartlander.scotland.net*]

Dunkeld

After the battle of Killiecrankie in 1689, Dunkeld was the scene of a further battle, in which the Highland forces were defeated. In the process, medieval Dunkeld was torched. It was rebuilt in best eighteenth-century style, and many of the houses have been restored by the National Trust for Scotland, making it a very pretty place to stop on the road north. [*via www.scottish-towns.co.uk]*

Killin

A popular village at the head of Loch Tay, blessed with the scenic **Falls of Dochart**, which can be viewed from the road. It has a number of gift and craft shops, a few small eating places, and **The Breadalbane Folklore Centre** *[Mar to May and Oct, daily 10–5; June and Sept, daily 10–6; July and Aug, daily 9–6; Feb, weekends only, 10–4;* ☎ *(01567) 820254]*, chiefly worth visiting to learn the story of St Fillan and to see his healing stones, which have been kept in the area since the Dark Ages. [*www.killin.co.uk]*

Pitlochry

After the coming of the railway in 1863, Pitlochry became a favoured mountain resort for visitors to the Highlands [*via www.heartlander.scotland.net]*. It is dominated by hotels, and is neither beautiful nor historic, but it has managed to retain a pleasing leisurely atmosphere. This may be because it is a good place for gentle walks, especially along the banks of the man-made **Loch Faskally**. You can walk as far as the pass of Killiecrankie or take one of numerous shorter round-trips. Boats can also be hired. The old village of Moulin on the outskirts of Pitlochry makes another interesting stroll, with a pleasant pub at its end, while a stiffer walk beyond the golf course up the hill of Craigower (NTS) rewards you with fine views. The **Festival Theatre** is known for performing eight different plays in six days, in season. The tent-like foyer recalls the marquee in which the theatre started.

Scenery and touring routes

Ben Lawers Rising above Loch Tay, this shapely mountain has been a National Nature Reserve since 1975. The best view is from a distance, from the road on the south bank of Loch Tay. For a closer look, take the road which runs over the mountain's shoulder to Glen Lyon. Here you will find a visitor centre *[Apr to Sept, daily 10–5;* ☎ *(01567) 820397;* ◥ *via www.nts.org.uk]*, with information on the unique habitat of the hill. Various walks are suggested, but your chances of spotting the rare alpines for which Ben Lawers is famous are remote unless you know exactly what you are looking for. Ben Lawers is a friendly sort of mountain for a hill walk, and correspondingly popular. If you want mountain solitude, go somewhere else.

Drumochter Pass After Blair Atholl the A9 leaves the southward–flowing river valleys and heads up Glen Garry to this bleak pass at the top of a great barrier of peat bog and dour hillside which separates the districts of Atholl and Badenoch. It is one of the bleakest places in Scotland. On one side lies the mountainous hump of the Sow of Atholl, mirrored by the Boar of Badenoch on the other. It always seems to be raining on Drumochter.

Glen Lyon This is the longest glen in Scotland, and one of the loveliest. Glen Lyon was populous Campbell territory for many years; now it is almost deserted, apart from the odd farm. The outlawed Macgregors were here too, persecuted by the Campbells of Glenorchy and Lawers (who bred a bloodhound suckled by a Macgregor woman, so that the dog would know the smell of its enemy).

The entrance to the glen beyond Fortingall is half–hidden and dramatically steep. Then the scenery relaxes, the river broadens and becomes good for picnics and the glen opens up into an attractive valley between the steep slopes of Ben Lawers on the left and Carn Gorm on the right. You can escape via the road over the shoulder of Ben Lawers, or continue to the wild end of the glen.

Glenshee The hills on either side of the A93 are unshapely great mounds which become higher and more barren as you penetrate deeper into them, with scree streaking the upper slopes of Creag Leacach and the Cairnwell at the head of the pass. This road used to be notorious for the Devil's Elbow – a steep hairpin which was the bane of buses and was frequently blocked by snow. Now the road is straight, graded and anonymous, though the disintegrating remains of the old hazard lie just beyond the fence.

Loch Rannoch round trip Starting and finishing at Kinloch Rannoch, this is an excellent drive round the prettiest loch in the area [⌂ *via www.rannoch.net*]. On the northern shore, birch forest comes down to the water's edge, dusty gold in autumn, silver-green in spring, with the aquamarine or slate grey of the water seen through the trunks. There are numerous places at which you could stop. On the southern shore, and worth all the drive to see, is the **Black Wood of Rannoch**. This pine forest contains some of the few gnarled survivors of the great Caledonian forest, and a beautiful place of light and air it is, with great lumps of moss and heather as its floor, and pines of all ages, alder and birch growing in profusion. Various paths snake through its depths.

Schiehallion The triangular peak of this mountain dominates Loch Tummel, and can be seen from miles away. The best view of it is probably from the eastern end of Loch Tummel, at the spot known as the Queen's View. The usual route for climbing starts from the unclassified road running west from the B846. Schiehallion is precipitous in places, and not for the unprepared. [⌂ *via www.rannoch.net*]

WHERE TO STAY

£ – under £70 per room per night, incl.
VAT
££ – £70 to £110 per room per night,
incl. VAT
£££ – over £110 per room per night,
incl. VAT

AUCHTERARDER
Gleneagles
Auchterarder PH3 1NF
☎ (01764) 662231
📠 (01764) 662134
🖥 www.gleneagles.com
Impressive edifice built in the roaring
twenties, retaining much of its glamour,
especially to golfers. State-of-the-art
sporting and pampering facilities; roomy,
stylish bedrooms. The grandiose
restaurant offers a traditional Scottish
table d'hôte menu.
£££ *All year*

BALMAHA
Oak Tree Inn
Balmaha, Loch Lomond G63 0JQ
☎ (01360) 870357
📠 (01360) 870350
Built in 1997 from a nearby dismantled
country house, this inn with wonderful
views of Loch Lomond offers seven
simple bedrooms. A public bar and
restaurant provide good à la carte
meals.
£ *All year*

BALQUHIDDER
Calea Sona
Balquhidder FK19 8NY
☎ /📠 (01877) 384260

Charming house in a small, peaceful
village with fine views and two simple
but attractive rooms. Breakfast is served
in the high-ceilinged lounge.
£ *All year exc Christmas*

Monachyle Mhor Hotel
Balquhidder, Lochearnhead FK19 8PQ
☎ (01877) 384622
📠 (01877) 384305
🖥 www.monachylemhor.com
A remote, romantic converted
farmhouse where Lochs Voil and
Doine meet, with superb mountain
views. Bedrooms are comfortable;
courtyard rooms have rustic exposed
beams.
££ *All year (See Where to Eat)*

BLAIR ATHOLL
Woodlands
St Andrews Crescent, Blair Atholl
PH18 5SX
☎ /📠 (01796) 481403
Calm and relaxing bed and breakfast
with fresh-baked bread and vegetarian
choices; guests may bring wine to dinner.
Telephone in advance as closure periods
are irregular.
£ *Variable opening times depending on
owner's commitments*

BLAIRGOWRIE
Glenshieling House
Hatton Road, Blairgowrie PH10 7HZ
☎ (01250) 874605
Bed and breakfast with six bedrooms –
one adapted for wheelchair users – plus
a self-catering lodge. The residents' bar is

well stocked and packed lunches can be provided.

£ *All year*

Kinloch House

By Blairgowrie PH10 6SG
☎ (01250) 884237
📠 (01250) 884333
🖳 *www.kinlochhouse.com*

A formal country-house hotel in a peaceful location with views of Loch Marlee and the Sidlaw Hills. A cosily traditional lounge extends from the oak-panelled hall and gallery into the cocktail bar, then to the conservatory. Spacious bedrooms have good-sized bathrooms.
£££ *Closed 18 to 29 Dec (See Where to Eat)*

CALLANDER
Leny House

Leny Estate, Callander FK17 8HA
☎ (01877) 331078
📠 (01877) 331335
🖳 *www.lenyestate.com*

Luxury accommodation in grand Victorian style at this mansion house. Bedrooms have superior fittings; breakfast is served in the main house and guests can have evening meals in a nearby inn.
££ *Mar to Oct*

DENNY
Lochend Farm

Carronbridge, Denny FK6 5JJ
☎ (01324) 822778

A working sheep farm with panoramic views over moorland and Loch Coulter. Part of a courtyard of buildings, with two comfortable bedrooms. Hearty breakfasts feature farm ingredients.
£ *Open Easter to Oct, or by arrangement*

DOLLAR
Castle Campbell Hotel

11 Bridge Street, Dollar FK14 7DE
☎ / 📠 (01259) 742519

Neat and friendly hotel in a Georgian coaching inn. Bedrooms have modern showers and the dignified sitting room offers leather sofas. Seafood predominates in the bright, modern dining-room; the cosy bar offers a light lunch menu.
££ *Closed 1 Jan*

DRYMEN
Dunleen

Milton of Buchanan, Drymen G63 0JE
☎ (01360) 870274

Simple but comfortable and spotless bed and breakfast surrounded by large, colourful gardens. Breakfast is served in the spacious lounge to make the most of the views. Packed lunches can be provided.
£ *May to Oct*

DUNKELD
Kinnaird

Kinnaird Estate, Dunkeld PH8 0LB
☎ (01796) 482440
📠 (01796) 482289
🖳 *www.kinnairdestate.com*

An outstanding eighteenth-century country-house hotel offering luxury and taste. The dining-room, with views down to the Tay Valley, provides gourmet food using prime ingredients. Bedrooms are high-ceilinged and splendid, with modern touches.
£££ *Closed Mon to Wed during Jan and Feb (See Where to Eat)*

GARTOCHARN
Ardoch Cottage
Main Street, Gartocharn G83 8NE
☎ /📠 (01389) 830452
📧 *freespace.virgin.net/ardoch.cottage/ index.htm*
Whitewashed cottage overlooking rolling countryside towards Ben Lomond. Three peaceful bedrooms. The owner uses fresh local produce for memorable meals.
£ *All year*

INVERSNAID
Inversnaid Lodge
Inversnaid, Aberfoyle, Stirling FK8 3TU
☎ (01877) 386254
📧 *www.inversnaidphoto.com*
A peaceful former shooting-lodge on the inaccessible east bank of Loch Lomond. Darkrooms, studios and photography books are for the courses run here. The atmosphere is relaxed, and bedrooms simple. Guests share a large table for homely food.
£ *Closed Nov to Apr*

KILLIECRANKIE
Killiecrankie Hotel
Killiecrankie, Pitlochry PH16 5LG
☎ (01796) 473220
📠 (01796) 472451
📧 *www.killiecrankiehotel.co.uk*
Smart and friendly country-house hotel offering peace and quiet in a wonderful Highland setting. The simple, bright interior is informal; the cosy sitting room opens on to the garden. Crisp, cottagey bedrooms.
£££ *Closed Jan, Mon & Tue in Dec, Feb and March (See Where to Eat)*

KINBUCK
Cromlix House
Kinbuck, Dunblane FK15 9JT
☎ (01786) 822125
📠 (01986) 825450
A stern exterior belies the warm and intimate décor of this country hotel. Guests can use a quarry-tiled conservatory, a mint-green drawing room, a cosy library and three dining-rooms (where each course has two choices with plenty of game). Large, quirky bedrooms.
£££ *Closed 2 to 20 Jan*

PITLOCHRY
Craigatin House
165 Atholl Road, Pitlochry PH16 5QL
☎ /📠 (01796) 472478
A 'wonderful' large detached house in an acre of grounds. Fourteen bedrooms, one suitable for wheelchair users, one with a kitchen. Traditional Scottish breakfasts are served in the dining-room or the conservatory.
£ *All year*

STANLEY
Newmill Farm
Stanley PH1 4QD
☎ /📠 (01738) 828281
Mixed arable farm six miles north of Perth. The sixteenth-century farmhouse has four letting bedrooms, and guests can use the lounge with its log fire. A varied breakfast menu caters for hearty appetites, and there are plenty of good restaurants nearby.
£ *All year exc Christmas*

STIRLING
Castlecroft
Ballengeich Road, Stirling FK8 1TN
☎ (01786) 474933
📠 (01786) 466716
Beneath the rocky outcrop of Stirling Castle, this modern house has lovely views and a very pretty garden. Views are best from the lounge, with panoramic windows and a telescope. Six comfortable bedrooms (two suitable for wheelchair users).
£ *All year exc Christmas and New Year*

Forth Guest House
23 Forth Place, Riverside, Stirling FK8 1UD
☎ (01786) 471020
📠 (01786) 447220
A Georgian terrace guesthouse, hung with pretty hanging baskets and close to the town centre. Six cosy bedrooms are all *en suite*. Breakfast is served at separate tables in the attractive dining-room.
£ *All year*

THORNHILL
Cairnsaigh
Doig Street, Thornhill FK8 3PZ
☎/📠 (01786) 850413
☎ (0800) 980 4809
🖰 *www.cairnsaigh.freeserve.co.uk*
Large, modern bungalow with panoramic hill views. Traditional Scottish dishes are on the menu; guests may bring wine. All three comfortable rooms are on the ground floor; access is easy but entrances are not wheelchair-approved.
£ *All year*

WHERE TO EAT

ABERFELDY
Farleyer House
Aberfeldy PH15 2JE
☎ (01887) 820332
📠 (01887) 829430
🖰 *www.farleyer.com*
Native produce plays a large part in the food served in both the relaxed bistro and the more formal dining-room. Local beef and lamb, Tay salmon, venison and even ptarmigan are given a modern treatment; enjoyable desserts. Wines are wide-ranging and reasonable.
All week 12–2.30 and 6–9.30

ALYTH
Drumnacree House
St Ninians Road, Alyth PH11 8AP

☎/📠 (01828) 632194/633355
A formal hotel dining-room with a set-price dinner for residents, and a cheerful, child-friendly bistro with hearty food. An open-to-view wood-fired chargrill produces anything from ribeye Aberdeen Angus steaks to a whole suckling pig for parties of eight or more. Tasty, varied and unpretentious food.
Tue–Sun 12–1.45 and 6.30–9

AUCHTERARDER
Auchterarder House
Auchterarder PH3 1DZ
☎ (01764) 663646
📠 (01764) 662939
🖰 *www.wrensgroup.com*

Baronial mansion set in 17 acres, with a refined approach to cooking. Lamb, venison and fish main courses predominate, with successful desserts on traditional gourmet dinner and lighter lunch menus. An extensive international wine list.

All week 12–2 and 7–9.30

BALQUHIDDER
Monachyle Mhor Hotel

Balquhidder, Lochearnhead
FK19 8PQ
☎ (01877) 384622
📠 (01877) 384305
🖥 www.monachylemhor.com

Stunning scenery surrounds this country-house hotel. The walled garden provides the kitchen with vegetables and herbs, and game is locally shot. Fish, game and 'disgracefully decadent' desserts are included in the expert repertoire. A classically inclined wine list is mostly French.

All week 12–2 and 7–8.45 (See Where to Stay)

BLAIR ATHOLL
Loft

Blair Atholl, By Pitlochry PH18 5TE
☎ (01796) 481377
📠 (01796) 481511

Hotel and spa complex occupying a nineteeth-century loft. Food is offered in a variety of locations – snacks and light lunches in the conservatory and on the roof terrace overlooking the swimming pool, or full meals in the dining-room. Food and décor have a Mediterranean flavour, though traditional roasts are also served.

All week 12–2 and 6–9; closed Mon–Thur Jan to March

BLAIRGOWRIE
Kinloch House

Blairgowrie PH10 6SG
☎ (01250) 884237
📠 (01250) 884333
🖥 www.kinlochhouse.com

Locally sourced beef, free-range poultry and vegetables from the walled garden. Dishes on the four-course set-price menu can be exchanged for items on the Scottish menu, or supplemented by seafood or steak; plenty of game appears in winter. The accessible wine list is predominantly French.

Sun L 12.30–2, bar L all week, D all week 7–9.15 (See Where to Stay)

BRIG O'TURK
Byre Inn

Brig o'Turk FK17 8HT
☎ (01877) 376292

Tiny Victorian inn converted from a cow byre. The beamed main bar has a log fire, old pews and comfortable chairs. Bar menu main courses are adventurous, as are the elaborate evening dishes. Traditional desserts.

Summer: Wed–Mon and winter Fri–Sun 12 (12.30 Sun) to 12 (11 in winter); bar food L 12–2.30, D (not on Sat) 6.30–9

COMRIE
Deil's Cauldron

27 Dundas Street, Comrie PH6 2LN
☎ (01764) 670352

Small, low-ceilinged listed building at the entrance to Glen Lednock, with its beautiful walks. A tiny bar, comfortable

seating area and small restaurant. Printed menus offer solidly traditional Scottish food. The short evening menu offers some more exotic choices; the wine list is surprisingly long.
Wed–Sat 12–2.30 and 6–11, Sun 12.30–2.30 and 7–11; closed Christmas and New Year; bar food 12–2.30 and 7–9 (but check in winter)

DRYMEN
Clachan Inn
2 Main Street, Drymen G63 0BP
☎ (01360) 660824
One of the oldest pubs in Scotland, kept as a traditional hostelry. Bar food is equally traditional and hearty, but with vegetarian choices; a separate restaurant operates under the same roof; desserts include a daily steamed pudding.
11–midnight, Sun 12.30–11.30; bar food and restaurant 12–4 (Sun 12.30–4) and 6–10; closed 25 Dec and 1 Jan

DUNKELD
Kinnaird
Kinnaird Estate, Dunkeld PH8 0LB
☎ (01796) 482440
📠 (01796) 482289
🖥 www.kinnairdestate.com
A stunning vista from the dining-room of this lavishly proportioned mansion. Attractive frescoes give a light and intimate feel, and the expertly classical menu is European. Small local producers supply lamb and beef, and the estate provides vegetables, fish and game. The expensive wine list is well-chosen.
All week 12.30–1.45 and 7.15–9.30; closed Mon to Wed in Jan and Feb (See Where to Stay)

GLENDEVON
Tormaukin Hotel
Glendevon FK14 7JY
☎ (01259) 781252
Eighteenth-century drovers' inn, set in the Ochil Hills. The bar menu has all the usual meals with additional modern dishes and exotic treatments of traditional ingredients. A range of vegetarian dishes is available, and a separate children's menu has appealing desserts. A more expensive evening menu is à la carte.
11–11, Sun 12–11; bar food 12–2 and 5.30–9.30, Sun 12–9.30; restaurant 6.30–9.30; closed 10 days in Jan

KILLIECRANKIE
Killiecrankie Hotel
Killiecrankie PH16 5LG
☎ (01796) 473220
📠 (01796) 472451
🖥 www.killiecrankiehotel.co.uk
Cooking here is founded on local ingredients – Aberdeen Angus beef, native game, fish and shellfish. The flavours are international however, and the unusual mingles with traditional European dishes. Good-value wine list.
All week D 7–8.30; closed Jan, Mon and Tue Dec to March (See Where to Stay)

KINCLAVEN
Ballathie House
Kinclaven, By Stanle PH1 4QN
☎ (01250) 883268
📠 (01250) 883396
🖥 www.ballathiehousehotel.com
Baronial hotel beside the River Tay. The kitchen blends traditional with modern cooking in a menu that includes

salmon, beef, lamb and unusual desserts. The extensive wine list is reasonably priced.

All week L 12.30–2, D 7–9

KINNESSWOOD
Lomond Country Inn

Kinnesswood KY13 9HN

☎ (01592) 840253

Relaxed Victorian inn on the slopes of the Lomond Hills, with views over Loch Leven. The lunch bar menu offers a range of unusual salads, omelettes, pasta and curries. The set-price Scottish menu is good value.

All week 11–11; bar food and restaurant Mon–Fri

KIPPEN
Cross Keys

Main Street, Kippen FK8 3DN

☎ (01786) 870293

Welcoming country inn built in 1703, offering bar food and a more formal Vine Restaurant. The same reasonably priced menu is offered at lunch and dinner, and includes some unexpected and international dishes. Puddings are traditional and home-made. Smaller portions for children and OAPs.

Mon to Fri 12–2.30 and 5.30–11 (5.30–12 Fri), Sat 12–2.30 and 5.15–12, Sun 12.30–11; bar food 12–2 and 5.30–9.30, Sun 12.30–2, 5.15–9.30;

restaurant all week D only 7–8.45; closed 25 Dec eve, 1 Jan

PERTH
Let's Eat/Let's Eat Again

77 Kinnoull Street, Perth PH1 5EZ

☎ (01738) 643377

📠 (01738) 621464

33 George Street, Perth PH1 5LA

☎ (01738) 633771

This smart but casual pair of restaurants, with their warm atmosphere, offer 'unrivalled value for money locally'. Plenty of variety on the menus, which change regularly; a sensible approach embraces quality ingredients. Short, reasonably priced wine list.

Tue–Sat 12–2 and 6–9.30; closed 2 weeks Jan, 2 weeks July (Let's Eat); 2 weeks Feb, 2 weeks July (Let's Eat Again)

WEEM
Ailean Chraggan

Weem PH15 2LD

☎ (01887) 820346

This small hotel overlooks the Tay, with two terraces and a garden for summer eating. The same menu is served throughout, with the emphasis on local ingredients. Snacks are always available, and there is a separate 'Waggon' children's menu.

11–11, Sun 12.30–11; bar food and restaurant 12–2 and 6–9.30 (8.30 winter); closed 25 and 26 Dec, 1 and 2 Jan

Fife and Angus

St. Andrews Cathedral

- Gentle, fertile landscapes with the great glens of Angus to the north
- Many historic sights
- Varied coastline with ancient fishing towns
- St Andrews – home of golf

FIFE AND ANGUS

At a glance

✓ Good for three-night stays, based in St Andrews
✓ Well-placed for outings from Edinburgh or Perth
✓ Golfing expeditions
✓ Seaside jaunts
✓ Pictish remains

The peninsula of Fife lies between the twin firths of Forth and Tay. North of the Tay, the Grampian mountains rise above the fertile countryside of Strathmore, bounding the district of Angus. Fife and Angus are rich farming country for the most part, and the inland scenery, except where the Angus glens penetrate the Grampian massif, is unspectacular, though wherever you find a hill you will usually find first-class views to go with it. It is the coast which draws most visitors – either to see the ancient trading ports and fishing villages along the coast of Fife, or else to play the renowned golf courses. St Andrews is not only the home of golf; it was once the religious and academic centre of Scotland.

Dundee, on the north bank of the Tay, is the fourth largest city in Scotland. Famous for the three Js of jute, jam and journalism, it also has a long history as a trading, ship-building and whaling port.

Key web sites

www.standrews.com The Fife tourist board's web site, a good starting point

www.angusanddundee.co.uk A decent general guide to Angus; individual entries can be a bit scanty

www.angus.gov.uk The district council's site. Excellent for information on the Angus towns and their sights

---

Good bases in Fife and Angus

Dundee

✓ *Lively town*

✓ *Good base for exploration of Angus*

✗ *Not a pretty place*

Scotland's fourth largest town may seem like just another industrial city fallen on hard times, but it has a humour and accent all its own, good facilities and some very interesting things to see.

Earlsferry and Elie

✓ *Peaceful seaside towns*

✓ *Within easy reach of Edinburgh and of all Fife*

These two burghs form the most attractive resort on the north Forth coast. They are blessed with a long seafront with rocks, golf and caravans at one end and sand and a lighthouse at the other. The towns are old, and there are attractive houses to see.

St Andrews

✓ *Old university town, full of history*

✓ *Wide range of accommodation*

✓ *Good beaches nearby*

St Andrews has few rivals in the region. The ruins of its cathedral and its castle mark its previous importance, while the Royal and Ancient Golf Club on the sandy links is the symbol of its modern claim to fame. It has the oldest university in Scotland to lend life to the streets, a wide choice of hotels and guesthouses to stay in, and some magnificent beaches within easy striking distance.

FIFE

The ports of Fife once provided Scotland's trading link with Europe. Long before Glasgow became important, merchants here were busy importing and exporting to the Baltic, the Hanseatic ports and the Low Countries. Timber, cloth, fish and

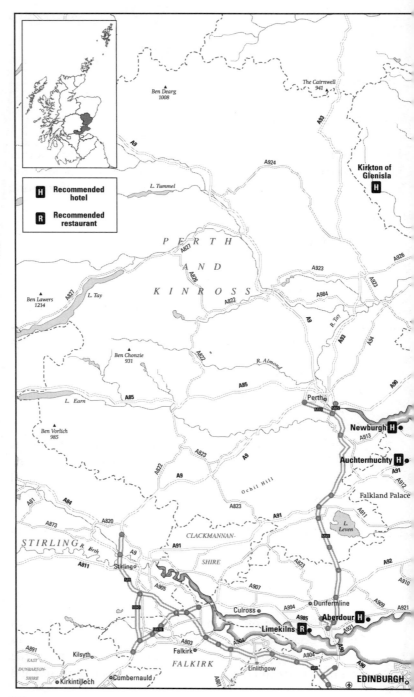

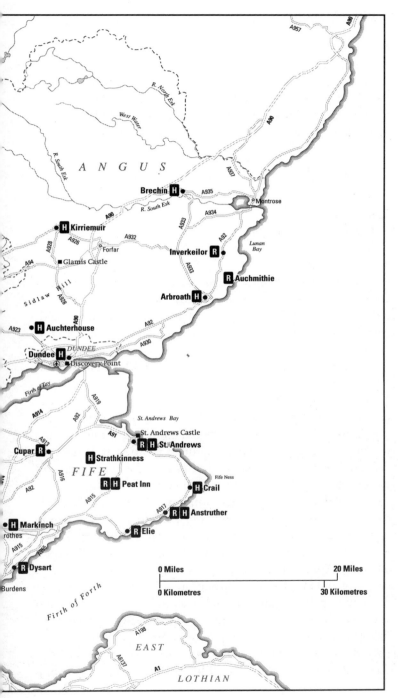

wool were the staples of this trade, and the long history of weaving in the small towns of Angus is linked to it. You can find echoes in the Baltic timber that lines the rooms of old houses, and in the domestic architecture of places like Culross, Pittenweem or Crail, with its hints of Holland or Lübeck. Now these old towns are backwaters, but are fascinating to explore.

Top sights

Culross

✓ *Well-preserved ancient trading burgh*
✓ *Architecture*
✗ *Can get crowded*

Lost in an industrial landscape, the sixteenth-century burgh of Culross survives intact, rescued and restored over a 50-year period. Four or five steep cobbled streets are lined with pantiled and harled cottages; a small square has a replica mercat cross and a seventeenth-century tolbooth which now acts as the visitor centre (web site information about the town is at ☛ *www.culross.org*).

At the top of the steep hill behind the village are the remains of **Culross Abbey** *[Daily, summer 10–dusk; winter 10–4;* ☎ *0131-668 8800]*. The old choir and tower are now the site of the parish church, and there is little left of the rest. Nevertheless, it is worth the climb for the peaceful surroundings and the views over the Forth.

The Palace is the grandest house in Culross, and the place to see how prosperous merchants used to live. Sir George Bruce made his money from coal and salt panning and used Baltic timber and Dutch tiles to decorate his grand house. There are spiral stairs and corner rooms, old fireplaces and a fireproof and burglar-proof strongroom. The panelling and the decorative painting are the high points. The house has been suitably filled with sixteenth- and seventeenth-century furniture and the garden reflects the horticulture of the same period *[NTS; Apr to May and Sept, daily 1.30–5, Jul and Aug 11–5;* ☎ *(01383) 880359]*. **The Study** with its panelling and painted ceiling is well worth looking at, if open *[NTS; Apr to Sept, daily 1.30–4.30;* ☎ *(01383) 880359].*

Falkland Palace

✓ *Beautiful architecture in a lovely setting*
✓ *Colourful garden*
✓ *Real tennis court*

Falkland was once the favourite hunting lodge of the Stewart kings. James IV and James V were responsible for most of what you see today, which is a Renaissance chateau, owing much to the French. The frontages are decorated with pillar buttresses, medallions and ornate dormer windows, and some crafty work has been done on the south range to give an impression of a symmetry which does not in fact exist.

The interior of the south range was restored by the hereditary keepers of the palace after 1887, and the rooms are close to the style of the seventeenth century, with exact reproductions of furniture and painted ceilings. Among many ancient pieces, look out for the ornate James VI bed and the magnificent tapestries. Two rooms in the east range have also been restored as bedchambers, one as the 'King's Room' containing the seventeenth-century Golden Bed of Brahan, made in the East Indies.

Outside, the Tennis court (royal or 'real' tennis) is the oldest in Britain. A local club plays on summer weekends if you want to see a game.

The Garden was laid out after the Second World War to complement the frontage of the palace rising behind it. It is a mass of herbaceous colour from May onwards, while its subtle design only gradually reveals itself as you walk round. Do not leave Falkland without wandering round the old burgh, where there are some well-preserved and photogenic old houses. *[Apr to May and Sept to Oct, Mon–Sat 11–5.30, Sun 1.30–5.30; June to Aug, Mon–Sat 10–5.30, Sun 1.30–5.30;* ☎ *(01337) 857397;* ✆ *via www.nts.org.uk]*

St Andrews Castle

✓ *Spooky dungeon and underground tunnel*

Poised strikingly on the sea's edge, the castle was actually the bishop's palace – and a notable prison for reformers. Here, Cardinal Beaton, one of the most prominent figures in the Catholic Church's fight against the Reformation, watched the reformer Wishart being burnt beneath the walls, and here, his own murdered body was displayed to the crowd. Not much is left of the building, but two fascinating features remain. One is the bottle dungeon, carved 24 feet down into the rock and narrowing towards the trapdoor at the top, through which prisoners were dropped. The other is the mine and counter-mine. When the reformers (disguised as masons) broke into the castle and murdered Beaton in 1546, they held the place for a year against all efforts to take them. One such effort was a mine – a tunnel from outside the walls – against which the chosen defence was an opposing tunnel – the counter-mine – driven to meet it. You stumble down the narrow counter-mine to the spot where besieged and besiegers met in an underground clash, pedes-

---

The Picts

The picti, or painted ones, was the name given by the Romans to the inhabitants of the land beyond Hadrian's Wall. In the third century AD, most of what is now Scotland was under Pictish rule, but 700 years later, after the unification of Picts and Scots under Kenneth MacAlpine in AD 843, they appear to have been either absorbed or subjugated.

For a race which left behind it such graphic monuments in stone and silver, frustratingly little is known about the Picts. Although Pictish kings began to be converted to Christianity as early as the sixth century, during St Columba's lifetime, we have no identifiable manuscripts from Pictish monasteries to rank with those from Anglo-Saxon England (though the famous Book of Kells may be a Pictish manuscript). We have no knowledge of what language the Picts

trians scurrying along the pavement above your head. A joint entry ticket to the castle and cathedral is available. *[HS; Apr to Sept, daily 9.30–6.30; Oct to Mar, Mon–Sat 9.30–4.30, Sun 2–4.30;* ☎ *(01334) 476452;* 🖱 *via www.saint-andrews.co.uk]*

St Andrews Cathedral

✓ *Evocative ruin of Scotland's greatest cathedral*
✓ *Fine setting*

Not much remains of what was once the greatest church in Scotland, but luckily what the Reformation mob and the stone-quarriers left behind is striking. The great east front stands alone and unsupported by prop or buttress. At the opposite end of what was once the nave, the single remaining spike of the west front hangs above the small houses of Market Street like a spiritual lightning conductor. Round these, the foundations, sections of arcaded wall, a few thirteenth-century windows and the stumps of great pillars are all that remain of a building which was started in 1160 and consecrated in 1318 in the presence of Robert the Bruce.

spoke – where we find the Ogam script carved on stones it is unintelligible – while Latin records are confined to a list of Pictish kings and a few inscriptions. Nor, apart from what we can see on their carved monuments or interpret from the remains of their houses, do we know much about what they looked like (at one time they were thought to have been pigmies but evidence from burials shows otherwise), how they lived, or how their society worked, although the historian Bede claimed that they practised matrilineal succession.

What we do have are the symbol stones which once must have existed in hundreds or even thousands over the land. These enigmatic and elaborately beautiful works of art show us glimpses of a culture of which it would be a joy to know more.

Nearby, the twelfth-century **Church of St Regulus** has re-emerged into the light with the cathedral's ruin. A single square tower, over 100 feet high, rises from a forest of gravestones, with a small Saxon choir at its base. This was the predecessor of the cathedral. Climbing the tower in the constrictions of the tiny spiral stair can be claustrophobic and dizzying, but the view of the town from the top is worth the effort. From here you can see how all the cathedral precinct was enclosed by a strong wall. Outside the wall lie the foundations of the even earlier Celtic church, St Mary of the Rock, whose clergy were gradually displaced in favour of Augustinian canons.

Do not leave the cathedral without looking at the **museum**, where among the collection of early Christian sculptured stones is a sarcophagus, a blend of Pictish and Anglian work, with David killing a lion. *[HS; Apr to Sept, daily 9.30–6.30; Oct to Mar, Mon–Sat 9.30–4.30, Sun 2–4.30;* ☎ *(01334) 472563;* ⬛ *www.saint-andrews.co.uk]*

The next best sights

British Golf Museum (St Andrews)

Golfing memorabilia and high-tech gadgetry provide endless fun for aficionados. Touch-screen computers allow you to test your knowledge of the game or to watch the winning shot of the 1974 Open. There are curiosities for the non-initiates too, such as the history of golf-ball making, from the days of the leather-and-feather ball onwards, or the fact that James II banned the game – it was keeping people from archery practice. *[Easter to Oct, daily 9.30–5; Nov to Mar, 11–3 (closed Tue & Wed);* ☎ *(01334) 460046;* ⬛ *www.britishgolfmuseum.co.uk]*

Deep Sea World (North Queensferry)

A local quarry was flooded to create Deep Sea World. A moving walkway crosses the 'ocean floor' with fish of all descriptions swimming above and alongside. There are also handling tanks and other displays. A great sight for children, and good for a wet day. *[Mar to Oct, daily 10–6; July and Aug,*

10–6.30; Nov to Mar, Mon–Fri 11–5, weekends 10–6;
☎ *(0930) 100300 (50p per minute);* 🖰 *www.deepseaworld.com]*

Fife Folk Museum (Ceres)

A strong sense of community permeates this museum, demonstrated by the book of donations – some items even come from
Canadian emigrants. This manages to give life and unity to the
collection of domestic utensils, scales, milk churns and relics of
the weaving industry. *[Easter and May to Oct, daily 2–5;*
☎ *(01334) 828180;* 🖰 *via.www.standrews.com]*

Hill of Tarvit (near Cupar)

Built by Sir Robert Lorimer in 1906, Hill of Tarvit house was
designed as a showcase for the collection of paintings, furniture
and porcelain amassed by the Dundee jute manufacturer
Frederick Sharp.

The public rooms provide 'correct' settings for the collections they were designed to hold: the entrance hall looks
baronial enough to show off the Flemish tapestries which hang
there, while the drawing-room is pure eighteenth-century
France. The magnificence of the Palladian-style dining-room
sets off the Georgian furniture which fills it.

The Dutch paintings, silverwork and Chinese porcelain are
all good. Do not ignore the more modern side of the house
with its Wizard vacuum cleaner with continuous suction and
the shower with its ascending spray. Do not miss the gardens
either – another Lorimer design. *[Apr, May, Sept and Oct,
weekends 1.30–5.30; June to Aug, 11–5.30; Garden: Apr to Sept,
9.30–9; Oct to Mar, 9.30–4.30;* ☎ *(01334) 653127;* 🖰 *via
www.nts.org]*

Kellie Castle (near Pittenweem)

This castle is well worth the short diversion from the coast, even
if you only have time to look at the exterior. Two fifteenth-
century towers are linked by a later sixteenth-century building,
and the result is a curious T shape. A walk round the outside
reveals contrasting architecture, from the four-square simplicity

of the eastern tower, to the corbelling and crow-step gables of the south-west one. Kellie was restored by the Lorimer family, including the architect, Robert. The interior is adorned by their work and governed by their taste. The ancient painted panelling and the fine seventeenth-century plaster ceilings are complemented by paintings, fabrics and furniture which are often Lorimer in inspiration or design. *[NTS; Apr to Sept, daily 1.30–5.30; Oct, weekends 1.30–5.30; Gardens: all year, 9.30–sunset;* ☎ *(01333) 720271;* 🖳 *via www.nts.org]*

Scotland's Secret Bunker (south of St Andrews)

This amazing Cold War command centre only came off the top secret list in 1993. Deep underground beneath a fake farmhouse, and sheltered against nuclear attack, a huge concrete labyrinth was built to act as the seat of government and military command in the event of the unthinkable. Authentic down to the last detail, bleak and uncomfortable, and with all the 1950s technology intact, this is a sobering and fascinating place to visit. *[Easter to Oct, daily, 10–5;* ☎ *(01333) 310301;* 🖳 *www.secretbunker.co.uk]*

Scottish Deer Centre (west of Cupar on A91)

Once you have seen the excellent audio-visual and taken a tour round the fields to look at the nine species of deer, you come away both well informed and well satisfied. A good sight for children. *[Apr to Oct, 10–6; Nov to Mar, 10–5;* ☎ *(01337) 810391;* 🖳 *via www.standrews.com]*

Scottish Fisheries Museum (Anstruther)

An extensive collection in a friendly museum includes creels, models and old photographs, the reconstructed sitting-room of a fisherman's house, and genuine fishing boats under cover. *[Apr to Oct, Mon–Sat 10–5.30, Sun 11–5; Nov to Mar, Mon–Sat 10–4.30, Sun 2–4.30;* ☎ *(01333) 310628;* 🖳 *www.scottish-fisheries-museum.org]*

Also in the area

Monument to Alexander III (Kinghorn) This marks the spot where Alexander III, the last of Scotland's Celtic kings, was thrown off a cliff by his horse in 1286. He was apparently hurrying, heedless of advice to the contrary, to rejoin his second bride, the sensuous Yolande of Dreux. His death marked the end of Scotland's golden age and ushered in the conflict with England.

'Robinson Crusoe' Statue (Lower Largo) Alexander Selkirk, whose adventures inspired Daniel Defoe to write *Robinson Crusoe,* was born in this small seaport in 1676. A statue by the harbour commemorates him.

Towns and villages to explore

Dunfermline

Dunfermline [🖱 *via www.dunfermlineonline.net]* was the seat of kings when Edinburgh was just a windy fortress. The old ballad, *Sir Patrick Spens,* starts with the King sitting 'in Dunfermline toun, drinking the bluid-red wine', before despatching the hero on an ill-fated voyage to Norway. The **Abbey** *[Apr to Sept, daily 9.30–6.30, Sun 2–6.30; Oct to Mar, Mon–Sat 9.30–6.30, Sun 2–4.30, closed Thur pm and Fri;* ☎ *(01383) 739026]* is the chief thing to see. When Scotland's saintly Queen Margaret, fleeing from the Norman Conquest of England, married Malcolm Canmore in 1067, she proceeded to establish a priory on the site of an old Celtic church, which eventually became the abbey. Her shrine in the old Lady Chapel became a place of pilgrimage. The twelfth-century nave of the abbey, the walls of the huge refectory and a wall of the palace are what remain.

In 1818, while the foundations for the parish church were being dug, the remains of Robert the Bruce were unearthed. A plaster cast was taken of his skull, and he was left to lie in peace. The words 'King Robert the Bruce' are woven in stone on the balustrade of the tower of the church. The adjacent **Abbot House** *[daily 10–5;* ☎ *(01383) 733266]* has exhibitions to put flesh on the bones of the history.

Dunfermline was the also the birthplace of Andrew Carnegie, the American millionaire philanthropist. The cottage where he was born is now a museum about his life *[Apr to Oct, Mon–Sat 11–5, Sun 2–5; June to Aug, Mon–Sat 10–5; Nov to Mar, daily 2–4;* ☎ *(01383) 724302]*, but his most eloquent memorial is the beautiful park of Pittencrief Glen, which he bought and gave to the town.

St Andrews

St Andrews was medieval Scotland's spiritual heart. The men who ruled here as bishop or archbishop – Lamberton, Beaton, Sharp – were often as powerful as Scotland's kings. St Andrews owed its pre-eminence to the tradition that the Greek monk Regulus landed here with relics of the apostle Andrew in the year 345. St Andrew became patron saint of Scotland, and his relics remained here until they were lost during the Reformation.

St Andrews has the third oldest university in the United Kingdom, founded in 1411. The reflector telescope was invented here, and Mary Queen of Scots planted a thorn tree in the grounds. Its students wear red gowns – legend has it that they could be more easily recognised entering brothels if thus clad. The best way of seeing the university's ancient buildings is to take one of the organised tours, which usually run twice daily from June to August *[*☎ *(01334) 476161 for information]*.

Most foreign visitors come to St Andrews because of golf, for the Royal and Ancient Golf Club is now recognised as the ruling body of the sport, and St Andrews with its many courses draws enthusiasts from all over the world. Almost all the golfing activity takes place at the north-western corner of the town, where the Royal and Ancient Club House stands. Here are the big (and pricey) golfing hotels, and the museum of golf.

If your interests lie elsewhere, there is still much to enjoy. The untouched medieval street pattern fans out from the cathedral, and there has been little architectural vandalism. The **St Andrews Preservation Trust Museum** in North Street has relics of old St Andrews, mostly from Victorian times *[Easter and May to Sept, daily 2–5;* ☎ *(01334) 477629]*. The **West Port**, at the head of South Street, is a rare example of an old burgh gateway, still holding up the traffic. If you come to the town during Lammas Fair (the second Monday and Tuesday in August), you will find the centre packed with stalls and amusements.

In College Street, spare a thought for one of Scotland's more romantic lovers, Pierre de Châtelard. This French gallant seems to have conceived a passionate obsession for Mary Queen of Scots, to the extent of twice intruding into her bed-chamber. The second occasion was once too many – the cross in the street marks the spot of his execution. His last words were 'Adieu the most beautiful and most cruel princess of the world'.

For web site information about the town, see ⌐ *www.saint-andrews.co.uk*

Fishing towns of the East Neuk of Fife

Exploring the old fishing ports and harbours along the south-east coast of Fife makes a good day's outing. Each has its own atmosphere and its own links to the past. Look up more detail on the area via ⌐ *www.eastneukwide.co.uk*

Anstruther This is the biggest and the most touristy of the East Neuk towns. It has a long harbour and a small sandy beach. Boats leave for the Isle of May (see below) or will take you out on fishing trips.

Crail The most compact and the prettiest of the East Neuk towns has a winning combination of a broad High Street, a delicate golden-brown harbour with steep wynds running down to it, a crescent of sand backed by cliffs and a strong smell of fish to prove authenticity. There is a tiny town museum *[Easter and June to Sept, Mon–Sat 10–1, 2–5, Sun 2–5;* ☎ *(01333) 450869]*. A short walk along the coastal path will afford you clear views of the Bass Rock and North Berwick Law on the far side of the Forth.

Pittenweem Pittenweem was once the twelfth richest town in Scotland, and the substantial seventeenth-century houses are a mark of that prosperity. The harbour is attractive, with piles of orange or green nets drying in the sun, and seagulls wheel above the fishing boats.

St Monans From the west, St Monans' T-shaped fourteenth-century church seems to be standing on its own. However, steep wynds leading down to the cottage-lined harbour lie beyond it and there is more modern housing on top of the hill. Inside the church, a model ship hanging from the roof emphasises the community's reliance on the sea, and you can even hear the waves on the rocks outside.

Beaches and seashore

The beaches of the small towns on the north coast of the Forth have been popular since the coming of the railway. Further east and north, the coast becomes wilder.

Aberdour *[⌂▮ www.bigwave.demon.co.uk]* The sandy beach to the east of the old town is a long-time family favourite. In Aberdour itself, the **castle** *[HS; Apr to Sept, daily 9.30–6.30; Oct to Mar, Mon–Sat 9.30–4.30 (closed Thur pm and Fri), Sun 2–4.30;* ☎ *(01383) 860519]* is in ruins, but has lovely gardens.

Elie and Earlsferry *[⌂▮ www.elie.co.uk]* Strung out around a bay between a rocky headland and a sandy one, these two burghs have gradually merged into one large seafront village. Elie, at the eastern end of the bay, is where the sand is and where the harbour lies tucked under the lighthouse. Earlsferry has a rocky headland and some prosperous and substantial houses.

St Andrews West Beach Backed by the renowned golf courses, the West Beach is a long, exposed, dune-backed stretch of sand pounded by the breakers of the North Sea. The further you venture along the more you will have it to yourself.

Tentsmuir North of St Andrews, this great stretch of beach, dunes and pine forest extends from the northern bank of the Eden estuary almost as far as Tayport at the mouth of the Tay. The area offers two nature reserves, as well as networks of coastal or inland walks and picnic sites. Although a popular spot for fine weekends, Tentsmuir is too big to become crowded, and is recommendable for a day by the sea (though swimming may be hazardous because of currents).

Suggested excursion

Boat trip to the Isle of May Anstruther is the starting point for trips to the Isle of May, which lies some five (often choppy) miles out into the Forth. Birds are the draw here, especially the puffins. Boats run between May and September, and depend on the tide; the trip takes four to five hours including time on the island. Warm clothes and a picnic are essential [☎ *(01333) 310103 for information]*.

ANGUS

The city of Dundee lies at the heart of the old district of Angus, and absorbs much of its energies. Outside the town, fertile, rolling countryside leads gradually upwards into the foothills of the Grampian mountains, here pierced by long, beautiful glens. Angus has been a centre of civilisation since prehistoric times, and there are numerous remains. The enigmatic Pictish stones here are among the best in the country.

Top sights

Discovery Point (Dundee)

✓ *The ship in which Captain Scott first sailed to the Antarctic*
✓ *Imaginative multi-media displays*
✓ *Good sight for children*
✗ *Some steep stairs on board the ship*

The Royal Research Ship *Discovery* was the vessel in which Captain Scott first voyaged to Antarctica in 1901, some years before his ill-fated expedition to reach the South Pole. Commissioned from a Dundee shipyard, she eventually returned to her home port, and is now berthed on the banks of the Tay, close to the town centre.

With the ship itself as the central focus, a multi-media exhibition in an adjacent modern building takes visitors through the story of the voyage, from its planning in the heyday of Antarctic exploration to the reality of spending two long winters locked in the pack ice. This is followed by exploration of the ship itself, which has been restored to the condition she was in when she set sail. Finally, Polarama, a hands-on, interactive exhibition, allows children (and adults) to test out their ideas of the Antarctic climate and landscape through a series of cunningly devised experiments. *[All year, daily;* ☎ *(01382) 201245;* 🖱 *www.rrs-discovery.co.uk]*

Glamis Castle (north of Dundee)

✓ *Exceptionally well-run stately home*
✓ *Connections with the Queen Mother and Macbeth*

Among the rollings hills of lowland Angus, twelve miles from Dundee, this ancient mix of palace and tower house rises over its sheltering woodland like a curious pink sugar sculpture. The history of Glamis goes back to the fourteenth century, and throughout the tour you find yourself shifting from medieval halls to vast Edwardian drawing and dining rooms, from suits of armour to billiard tables. The high spots are the drawing room, its furniture arranged exactly as shown in a tinted sepia photograph and a portrait of the 3ʳᵈ Earl of Strathmore wearing curious 'transparent' armour, the chapel with its painted ceiling panels, and the various rooms where the Queen Mother grew up. At the final stop, in the shadow of a large stuffed bear, the guide cites the Macbeth connection, but strongly plays it down. The visitor is left with the impression that the reality of Glamis' story is far more interesting than anything Shakespeare came up with.

A huge baroque sundial and a charming Italian garden are some of the features of the extensive garden and grounds. A nature trail and picnic area are also there. [*Apr to Oct, 10.30–5.30; July and Aug, 10–5.30; Nov, 10.30–4;* ☎ *(01307) 840393;* 🖱 *via www.great-houses-scotland.co.uk*]

The next best sights

Angus Folk Museum (Glamis)

This museum is housed in a number of old cottages in the village of Glamis and stuffed with artefacts from the everyday life of the nineteenth and early twentieth centuries. It makes an excellent counterpoint to the splendours of the castle. The cottages are themed so that you move from a laundry to a weaving room, kitchen, schoolroom and nursery. A well-put-together and well-laid-out place. [*NTS; Apr to Sept, daily 11–5; Oct, weekends;* ☎ *(01307) 840288;* 🖱 *via www.nts.org*]

Arbroath Abbey

A satisfactory amount is left of the great red thirteenth-century abbey church in Arbroath, certainly enough to see that it must once have been a splendid place, lit by the huge round window in the western gable and the remarkable lancets in the transepts. There is plenty here for architecture enthusiasts, while the fifteenth-century sacristy and abbot's house are sufficiently complete to give a good impression of the monastic life. The gatehouse which once led into the walled precinct of the monastery remains intact. [*HS; Apr to Sept, Mon–Sat 9.30–6.30, Sun 2–6.30; Oct to Mar, Mon–Sat 9.30–4.30;* ☎ *(01241) 878756;* 🖱 *via www.angus.gov.uk*]

Edzell Castle (near Brechin)

This ruined red castle was built by the Lindsays in the sixteenth century. Its unique, and most charming, feature is the pleasance, a tiny walled garden, created in 1604 in that short period between the union of the crowns and the outbreak of the civil and religious wars when it seemed that Scotland had time at last for a few luxuries. It is beautifully maintained and planted – an entrancing spot. *[HS; Apr to Sept, daily 9.30–6.30; Oct to Mar, Mon–Sat 9.30–4.30, closed Thur pm and Fri, Sun 2–4.30;* ☎ *(01356) 648631;* ✆ *via www.angus.gov.uk (choose Brechin)]*

House of Dun (east of Brechin)

This William Adam mansion is primarily for lovers of elaborate plasterwork; the huge trophies and emblems which decorate the public rooms are extraordinary. They are held to contain cryptic Jacobite symbolism. The chief character to have influ-

---

Pictish stones

The majority of carved Pictish stones are concentrated in eastern Scotland, especially around Strathmore in Tayside, the fertile areas of Moray, Banff and Aberdeenshire, and the Tain and Dornoch peninsulas. A couple of hundred have survived, and many more may lie buried or built into houses. These stones seem to have been carved between the sixth and ninth centuries, and vary from unshaped slabs of stone with designs incised into them, to elaborate monuments or Christian cross-slabs with intricate patterns and figures carved in relief. The stones are remarkable enough for the scale and beauty of their carving, but what must intrigue even the most casual onlooker is the meaning of the symbols with which many of them are embellished. Mirror and comb, double disc, Z-rod, serpent, crescent and the curious beast known as the 'swimming elephant' are the most common, and they appear alike on their own, as part of a secular scene, or on a Christian cross-slab. Furthermore, they are common to all of Pictland,

enced the house was Lady Augusta, an illegitimate daughter of King William IV. She was responsible for most of the fine needlework in the house and did a lot of work in the gardens, collecting plants from the surrounding countryside on outings in her yellow carriage. *[NTS; Apr, May, Sept and Oct, weekends 1.30–5.30; June to Aug, daily 11–5.30; Gardens: all year, 9.30–sunset;* ☎ *(01674) 810264;* ✆ *via www.nts.org]*

McManus Art Gallery and Museum (Dundee)

Built as a memorial to Prince Albert, this museum is a wonderful shrine to Victoriana. A high-ceilinged gallery contains collections of the over-elaborate china, glass and silver gilt which once graced Victorian dinner tables, while the Victorian gallery is expertly hung and displays ranks of sentimental paintings with titles such as 'Funeral of the First Born'. There are also good displays on Dundee's history and

---

their use cutting across boundaries between tribes or kingdoms.

What these symbols meant to the people who used them (and they were not just carved on stones but on humbler objects too) is unknown. One theory is that the stones are memorials to people or events denoted by the symbols. Another is that they are property markers, with the symbols representing different genealogies. Neither of these interpretations seems entirely satisfactory when you are confronted by the detail of the carved symbols themselves.

Pictish stones were mostly free-standing uprights. Many remain in their original positions in open countryside, and it can be quite a job to track them down. Others are to be found in churchyards to which they have been moved. The best indoor collections are at Meigle in Tayside, St Vigeans in Angus, St Andrews in Fife, Dunrobin Castle in Sutherland and in the Museum of Scotland in Edinburgh.

its industries. Great fun. *[Mon–Sat 10–5, Tue 10–7, Sun 12.30–4; ☎ (01382) 432084]*

Meigle Museum (north-west of Dundee)

Just in Perthshire, but an obvious sight for visitors to Angus, this small museum has the best collection of carved Pictish stones in the country, dating from the seventh to the tenth centuries. The room is dominated by three great stone cross-slabs, almost entirely covered in intricate carving. One shows Daniel in the lions' den, the lions pawing at him like over-grown cats while Daniel pats their heads. Beautiful interlaced patterns shroud the edges of another slab, and on the rear are examples of most of the enigmatic symbols – disc, Z-rod, swimming elephant, and mirror and comb – which appear on many Pictish stones, and whose meanings are lost to us (see box on pages 302–3). *[Apr to Sept, daily 9.30–6.30; ☎ (01828) 640612; ⓦ via www.darkisle.com]*

Verdant Works (Dundee)

An excellent industrial museum, this restored jute works takes visitors through the history of the industry on which Dundee built its nineteenth-century prosperity. Working machinery weaves jute into cloth, for which there is little demand today, especially since the Post Office gave up using jute for its mailbags. *[All year, daily; ☎ (01382) 225282; ⓦ via www.rrs-discovery.co.uk]*

Also in the area

Aberlemno Pictish Stones (north-east of Forfar) Four wonderful stones are to be found here. The best, with its entwined beasts and its battle scene, is in the churchyard.

Claypotts Castle (Dundee – Broughty Ferry) For castle-lovers, an extreme example of the Scottish habit of corbelling out the tops of towers to create extra rooms, to bizarre effect in this case. *[Irregular times; ☎ (01382) 731640 for information; ⓦ via www.scottishculture.about.com]*

Finavon Hill (north-east of Forfar) is crowned by the remains of one of the most accessible vitrified forts in the country. There are still wrangles over whether the fused stonework of these Iron Age defences was created by deliberate burning of fires round them, or whether it was the result of enemy assault.

Iron Age forts at Caterthun (north-west of Brechin) Two very well-preserved Iron Age forts are found together on low hills thrusting out from the Grampians. A good walk, with a worthwhile goal.

St Vigeans Pictish Stones This tiny village on the northern outskirts of Arbroath was named after a seventh-century Irish saint. In one of the cottages you can see the collection of Pictish stones found nearby. Although not quite so inspiring as the collection at Meigle they are more than worth the brief excursion. *[Open at all times;* ☎ *0131-668 8800]*

Towns and villages to explore

Arbroath

Arbroath *[* 🖰 *via www.angus.gov.uk]* is known for its 'smokies' (smoked haddock), its abbey, and for the declaration of Scotland's freedom from English overlordship which was signed here in 1320 (see box below). The ruins of the abbey stand squarely at the centre of this solid red sandstone town. Down by the harbour, every second house has a sign offering fresh smokies. Boat trips run from the harbour to visit local caves and cliffs or to go sea fishing. The Signal Tower Museum *[all year, Mon–Sat 10–5, plus Sun 2–5 in July and Aug;* ☎ *(01241) 875598]* gives an insight into the local fishing and jute industries, with careful explanations of how smokies are produced.

Brechin

Most people pause in this steep little town *[* 🖰 *via www.angus.gov.uk]* to look at the round tower *[access at all times]*, which dates from the tenth century and is similar to those found in Ireland. It stands beside the little cathedral, much of which was either restored or rebuilt at the beginning of the century, although parts are thirteenth-century. The other attraction is the Caledonian Steam Railway *[Easter, May to Sept and Dec, Sun only;* ☎ *(01561) 377760].*

Dundee

Dundee was the city of the three Js: Jute, Jam and Journalism. It was jute that turned it into a flourishing industrial town, while the jam and the journalism have had more influence on the rest of the country. Dundee is where marmalade, using Seville oranges, was first invented, and it is the home of the *Beano* and other publications from the D.C. Thomson stable.

Dundee is not a pretty place, but equally it is a city without artifice, with plenty of humour and plenty of life. It suffered from constant sackings during Scotland's many wars, and little survives from before the nineteenth century. Sculptures and murals brighten up the modern architecture, and the success of the **Dundee Contemporary Arts** centre has put the city on the map as a cultural stop-off point *[Galleries and shop: Tue–Sun 10.30–5.30; Centre and café 10.30–12;* ☎ *(01382) 432000;* ⌁ *www.dca.org.uk].*

The best view is from the top of **Dundee Law**, a volcanic plug sticking out of the city centre. Beneath you, the Tay road bridge runs apparently diagonally across the estuary. The rail bridge lies a little further upstream, and you may be able to pick out the stumps of its predecessor beside it – a reminder of the disaster of 1879 when it collapsed as a train was crossing it. The famous elegist of the disaster, William McGonagall, lived in Dundee for much of his life (information about him can be found on the internet at ⌁ *www.dundee22.freeserve.co.uk*). Widely hailed as the worst poet in Scotland if not the world, McGonagall is something of a cult figure:

So the train mov'd slowly along the Bridge of Tay
Until it was about midway,

Then the central girders with a crash gave way
And down went the train and passengers into the Tay
The Storm Fiend did loudly bray
Because ninety lives had been taken away
On the last Sabbath day of 1879,
Which will be remembered for a very long time.

Forfar

The old weaving town, its High Street lined with solid nine-teenth-century buildings, lies six miles south-east of Kirriemuir. Go to see the museum, called the **Meffan** *[Mon–Sat 10–5;* ☎ *(01307) 464123;* 📖 *via www.angus.gov.uk]*, which takes you back to Forfar's past, with old shops and re-created sounds and smells, and presents some fairly disturbing scenes of the witch-burning which was once a favourite activity here.

Kirriemuir

J.M. Barrie, creator of Peter Pan, was born in Kirriemuir. His **Birthplace** at 9 Brechin Road is easily missed if you are not keeping a close watch. Exhibits in this small museum include Barrie's writing desk, accounts of theatrical performances, photographs and newspaper cuttings. For our salacious era, the cuttings suggesting that Barrie was more than just a friend to the Llewellyn boys he eventually adopted make intriguing reading. *[NTS; Apr to Sept, Mon–Sat 11–5.30, Sun 1.30–5.30; Oct, Sat 11–5.30, Sun 1.30–5.30;* ☎ *(01575) 572646;* 📖 *via www.nts.org]*

Montrose

With its tidal basin behind it and the sea in front, Montrose looks like a town from a Dutch painting as you approach it from the south. It has played a remarkably small part in history, and remains a peaceful, rather sleepy place, with a broad High Street. The **museum** *[Mon–Sat, 10–5;* ☎ *(01674) 673232;* 📖 *via www.angus.gov.uk]*, which was purpose-built in 1842, has prints, paintings, boxes of shells and stones and curious pieces of historical flotsam, such as a bicorn hat, said to be

Napoleon's. There is also an evocative message found in a bottle: ' No water on board, provisions all gone. Ate the dog yesterday, 3 men left alive …'

The Declaration of Arbroath

The Declaration of Arbroath, which was signed on 6 April 1320, confirmed the Scottish nobility's support for the kingship of Robert the Bruce, and was taken to the Pope at Avignon. It was an important step in Scotland's intense diplomatic effort after Bannockburn to gain international recognition for the independence won on the battlefield. The declaration was probably drafted by the abbot of the time, Bernard de Linton. If so, he had a good line in rhetoric, as the ringing phrases of the document's most famous passage (in translation from the Latin) prove: 'For, so long as one hundred remain alive, we will never in any degree be subject to the dominion of the English. Since not for glory, riches or honours do we fight, but for freedom alone, which no good man loses but with his life …'

Scenery and touring routes

The Angus Glens *[⌂ via www.angus.gov.uk]* The glens running into the Grampians make an attractive contrast to the lowlands of Angus. The hills surrounding them are high, rounded lumps, often heather-covered, which merge into the high plateaux which separate Strathmore from Deeside. A network of old tracks and drove roads radiates from the head of the Angus glens, notably from Glen Clova and Glen Doll, making excellent medium-distance walks. For exploring by car, both Glen Clova and Glen Prosen, with roads on either side, allow round trips, while you can travel furthest into the mountains up Glen Esk. **Glen Clova** is where Scott planned his expedition to the Antarctic. A memorial stands by the foot of the glen. This is probably the most popular of the Angus glens. **Glen Esk**, north of Edzell, is a long haul through rolling scenery. Loch Lee, at the head of the glen, is a good spot for walking if you like a watery backdrop. The Glenesk Folk

Museum makes a good stopping point *[Easter to May, weekends and Mons, 12–6; June to Oct, daily 12–6;* ☎ *(01356) 670254]*. **Glen Prosen** is open, with attractive woodlands.

Reekie Linn Waterfall Follow the B954 north from near Alyth to Bridge of Craigisla for Reekie Linn, one of Scotland's best waterfalls: the river Isla plunges suddenly into a deep gorge. From the car park there is little warning of what is to come, but a very short walk brings you to the top of this 'smoking fall'. Wild broom clouds the whole place yellow in early summer. The urgent warnings to take care are justified – there is little protection.

Beaches and seashore

Lunan Bay The cliffs north of Arbroath are suddenly broken by the sweep of this classically beautiful beach, found on many a postcard but often deserted for all that *[☖ via www.good-beachguide.co.uk]*. Above the sand there is the gaunt ruin of a red sandstone castle, while at either end of the bay rocky headlands jut into the sea.

Montrose Basin *[☖ via www.angus.gov.uk]* is almost land-locked, and becomes a great pool of mud at low tide. Attractive it is not, but for naturalists it is one of the best places to see ducks and waders in huge numbers. There's a wildlife centre equipped with CCTV, telescopes and binoculars. *[Apr to Oct, daily 10.30–5; Nov to Mar, daily 10.30–4;* ☎ *(01674) 676336]*

WHERE TO STAY

£ – under £70 per room per night, incl. VAT
££ – £70 to £110 per room per night, incl. VAT
£££ – over £110 per room per night, incl. VAT

ABERDOUR
Hawkcraig House
☎ (01383) 860335
Guesthouse on cliffside with sweeping views of Edinburgh and the Forth rail bridge, offering two peaceful bedrooms. A sunny conservatory and two lounges are available. Dinner menus are varied and well-cooked.
£ Closed Nov to Mar

ANSTRUTHER
The Hermitage
Ladywalk, Anstruther KY10 3EX
☎ (01333) 310909
📠 (01333) 311505
Beautifully maintained bed and breakfast close to the harbour of a picturesque fishing village. The letting rooms are arranged in two suites, each with two bedrooms; all look either over the harbour or the walled garden.
£ All year exc Christmas

ARBROATH
Farmhouse Kitchen
Grange of Conon Farm, Arbroath DD11 3SD
☎ (01241) 860202
📠 (01241) 860424
Large farmhouse in a landscaped garden, surrounded by picturesque countryside.

An 'excellent' traditional Scottish breakfast offers a wide choice, including Arbroath smokie. Well-equipped bedrooms include refrigerators, fresh fruit, dressing robes and trouser-presses.
£ All year

AUCHTERHOUSE
Old Mansion House
Auchterhouse, Dundee DD3 0QN
☎ (01382) 320366
📠 (01382) 320400
This atmospheric Jacobean manor house offers sumptuous rooms and ambitious dinners. The distinctly Scottish menu varies from three to five courses. Charming bedrooms have refurbished bathrooms and period features.
££ All year

AUCHTERMUCHTY
Ardchoille Farm
Dunshelt, Nr Auchtermuchty KY14 7EY
☎ /📠 (01337) 828414
Home comforts and notable cooking in a rural setting. The three small but comfortable bedrooms look towards the Lomond Hills. Meal ingredients are organic where possible, and preserves and bread are home-made. Memorable communal dinners (bring your own wine).
£ All year exc Christmas and New Year

BRECHIN
Doniford
26 Airlie Street, Brechin DD9 6JX
☎ (01356) 622361
Large Victorian house offering warm and comfortable accommodation in a quiet

residential part of this market town. Breakfasts are served in the kitchen dining area; guests can use the large patio, TV lounge and garden.

£ *All year*

CRAIL
Selcraig House

47 Nethergate, Crail KY10 3TX

☎ (01333) 450697

📠 (01333) 451113

Attractive eighteenth-century stone house, with Victorian/Edwardian décor but modern facilities. The former lounge is now a four-poster suite, one first-floor twin room has its own sitting area, and the conservatory acts as a guest lounge.

£ *All year*

DUNDEE
Aberlaw

230 Broughty Ferry Road, Dundee DD4 7JP

☎/📠 (01382) 456929

Late-Victorian villa set back from the road in a neat garden, offering spacious and comfortable accommodation. Bedrooms are tasteful. 'Delicious' breakfasts are served in a sunny room with a hardwood floor.

£ *All year exc Christmas and New Year*

KIRKTON OF GLENISLA
Glenmarkie Farmhouse

Kirkton of Glenisla PH11 8QB

☎ (01575) 582356

Farmhouse and riding-centre complex at the end of a picturesque forest track. Compact, simply furnished bedrooms and a comfortable lounge. Packed

lunches can be provided; dinner is by arrangement.

£ *Apr to Nov*

KIRRIEMUIR
Purgavie Farm

Lintrathen, by Kirriemuir DD8 5HZ

☎/📠 (01575) 560213

Working farm emphasising guests' comfort, with spacious *en suite* rooms. Optional evening meals made with seasonal produce; vegetarian meals and packed lunches are all available on request.

£ *All year*

MARKINCH
Balbirnie House

Balbirnie Park, Markinch, Glenrothes KY7 6NE

☎ (01592) 610066

📠 (01592) 610529

🖥 www.balbirnie.co.uk

Handsome Georgian mansion in peaceful parkland – grandeur without pomp. From the inviting Long Gallery, gilt mirrors and sumptuous furnishings create an aura of understated elegance throughout. The Orangery restaurant offers a rich traditional European gourmet menu.

£££ *All year*

NEWBURGH
Ninewells Farmhouse

Woodriffe Road, Newburgh KY14 6EY

☎/📠 (01337) 840307

Attractive old farmhouse offering simple and comfortable accommodation. One bedroom is a 'triple' for three adults, and all have bathrooms. Breakfast is served at one large table, and guests can use a pleasant lounge.

£ *Apr to Oct*

PEAT INN
Peat Inn

Peat Inn, Cupar KY15 5LH

☎ (01334) 840206

📠 (01334) 840530

Excellent accommodation and extraordinarily good food in a former coaching inn. The bedrooms of this restaurant-with-rooms are in a separate annexe; eight spacious split-level suites are tasteful and luxurious, with Italian marble bathrooms.

£££ *Closed 25 Dec and 1 Jan (See Where to Eat)*

ST ANDREWS
Glenderran Guest House

9 Murray Park, St andrews KY16 9AW

☎ (01334) 477951

📠 (01334) 477908

Small Victorian house close to the Old Course and the historic town centre. The five attractive bedrooms and 'luxury mini-suite' are all *en suite* and full of thoughtful touches. Guests can use the lounge/dining area and honesty bar; vegetarian options are available at breakfast.

£ *All year*

Old Course Hotel

Old Station Road, St Andrews KY16 9SP

☎ (01334) 474371

📠 (01334) 477668

🖥 *www.oldcoursehotel.co.uk*

Luxury hotel overlooking the world-famous golf course. The interiors are a lavish mix of modern and traditional styles. Up-market shops, a spa complex and two restaurants tempt guests; the Sands Bistro serves pasta and chargrills, and the Road Hole Grill is a clubby restaurant serving traditional European dishes.

£££ *Closed Christmas*

STRATHKINNESS
Fossil House and Cottage

12–14 Main Street, Strathkinness, St Andrews KY16 9RU

☎/📠 (01334) 850639

🖥 *www.fossil-guest-house.co.uk*

Two Victorian stone buildings in lovely gardens with a pond, croquet lawn and barbecue. The lounge has satellite TV and videos, the conservatory games and interesting oddments. Bedrooms are smallish but full of thoughtful extras. Varied and substantial breakfasts.

£ *All year*

Rufflets

Strathkinness Low Road, St Andrews KY16 9TX

☎ (01334) 472594

📠 (01334) 478703

🖥 *www.rufflets.co.uk*

Rambling, turreted mansion with a delightful parterre garden and very good food. Bold colours are everywhere, especially the Garden Restaurant. The Music Room brasserie doubles as a bar. Generous-sized bedrooms have handsome bathrooms; two share a terrace with garden views.

£££ *Closed first two weeks in Jan*

WHERE TO EAT

ANSTRUTHER
Cellar

East Green, Anstruther KY10 3AA
☎ (01333) 310378
📠 (01333) 312544

The generally old-fashioned air of this restaurant is reinforced by the traditional cooking; plenty of fish and shellfish, fresh and simply cooked. Tables are converted sewing machines, and the handwritten wine list is worldwide but slightly pricey.
Wed–Sat L 12.30–1.30, Mon–Sat D 7–9.30; closed Mon D Nov to Mar

AUCHMITHIE
But 'n' Ben

Auchmithie DD11 5SQ
☎ (01241) 877223
📠 (01241) 430901

The waves crashing on the craggy shore can be enjoyed from the dining-room of this homely restaurant. Traditional Scottish cooking with the emphasis on seasonality – locally sourced fish, shellfish and Aberdeen Angus beef. Coffee comes with rum and coconut truffles.
Wed–Mon L 12–2.30, Wed–Sat and Mon D 7–10

CUPAR
Ostlers Close

25 Bonnygate, Cupar KY15 4BU
☎ (01334) 655574
🖱 www.ostlersclose.co.uk

The food in this small cottage is founded on well-sourced materials. Organic vegetables, free-range duck, dived scallops, unusual potatoes, local game, fresh fish, well-hung beef and rare-breed lamb underlie the well-cooked dishes.
Tue, Fri and Sat L 12.15–2, Tue–Sat D 7–9.30; closed first 3 weeks Jan, 2 weeks Sept/Oct

DYSART
Old Rectory

West Quality Street, Dysart KY1 2TE
☎ (01592) 651211

'Clean, warm, efficient, friendly with real quality food at staggeringly low prices'; this inn retains its Georgian splendour and interesting features. The lunch menu is capped at a low price and centres round a buffet; there is a separate bar menu as well as à la carte in the evenings.
Tue–Sat 12–3, 7–12, Sun 12.30–4; bar food and restaurant 12–2 (3 Sun), 7–9.30; closed 1 week mid–Jan, 2 weeks mid–Oct

ELIE
Ship Inn

The Toft, Elie KY9 1DT
☎ (01333) 330246

Well-oiled and busy pub, with fine views of the beach, bay and pier. From the garden, patrons can watch the cricket and rugby matches played on the beach at low tide. The menu includes plenty of fish and seafood, and traditional sticky desserts.
Mon–Thur 11am–midnight, Fri and Sat 11–1am, Sun 12.30–midnight; bar food and restaurant Mon–Sat 12–2 and 6–9 (9.30 Fri and Sat), Sun 12.30–2.30 and 6–9; closed 25 Dec

INVERKEILOR
Gordon's

32 Main Street, Inverkeilor DD11 5RN

☎ /🍽 (01241) 830364

This small restaurant with its stone-slabbed floor and beamed ceiling offers assured cooking of fine ingredients, served in large portions. Unexpected combinations are brought off successfully with all courses. Wines are reasonable, but not as imaginative as the food.

Tue–Fri and Sun L 12–1.45, Tue–Sat D 7–9; closed last 3 weeks Jan, 2 weeks Oct to Nov

LIMEKILNS
Ship Inn

Halketts Hall, Limekilns KY11 3HJ

☎ (01383) 872247

Genuine welcome, service and value in this fisherman's pub with views over the Firth of Forth to the bridges downstream. The very reasonably priced menu offers traditional pub fare beside more classic dishes.

11–11 (12 Thur–Sun); bar food L only Mon–Fri 12–2, Sat and Sun 12.30–2.30

PEAT INN
Peat Inn

Peat Inn, Cupar KY15 5LH

☎ (01334) 840206

🍽 (01334) 840530

White-painted former coaching house at a crossroads, as traditional in its cooking as its décor. Lightly cooked dinners are made with first-rate ingredients; presentation is precise. Helpful, unpretentious wine list.

Tue–Sat 12.30–1 and 7–9.30; closed 25 Dec, 1 Jan (See Where to Stay)

ST ANDREWS
West Port

170–172 South Street, St Andrews KY16 9EG

☎ (01334) 473186

🍽 (01334) 479732

Thoroughly up-to-date multi-faceted operation, with café-bar, walled beer garden and large restaurant. The global food ranges from sushi roll to confit leg of pigeon. Impressive presentation and and an enterprising, fairly priced wine list.

Tue–Sun 12–2 (2.30 Sat and Sun) and 6.30–9.45

The North-East

Whisky Distillery

- A country of contrasts – flat lowlands, rocky coastline and desolate mountains
- An excellent area for castles, gardens and rivers
- The ancient seaside city of Aberdeen
- Balmoral and 'Royal' Deeside
- Big concentration of whisky distilleries to visit

THE NORTH-EAST

At a glance
- ✓ Good for touring holidays of five to ten days
- ✓ Enjoyable three- to five-day tours of the Moray Coast
- ✓ Tough walking holidays
- ✓ Excellent area for families with older children

The Grampian mountains, rising to their highest and most desolate in the Cairngorm range, form a largely impassable massif in the centre of Scotland. Round them on three sides run the lowlands of Kincardine, Aberdeenshire, Buchan, Banff and Moray. Three things draw visitors to this area: the whisky distillery country of lower Speyside, the scenery and the romance of 'Royal Deeside', and the great castles of Aberdeenshire. However, there is more to enjoy than these, including high mountains, two coastlines and several secret corners, such as the valleys of the River Findhorn and the River Don.

The North–East has a superabundance of castles and fine country houses. There are ruins of great fortresses (Kildrummy, Huntly) and Georgian mansions (Haddo, Duff), but the area is renowned above all for its beautiful tower–houses, a style of architecture which developed out of the old castles by growing upwards and outwards

For a family seaside holiday, head for the beaches of Nairn or Lossiemouth; for Highland scenery and tough walking, Braemar and Deeside are the best areas. For gentler but still strenuous walking, try the area round Tomintoul. For fishing, unless you can afford to pursue salmon on the Dee or the Spey, start your researches with the Avon, the Don or the Ythan. For touring, head for the valley of the Don, although the coastal trail along the Moray Firth would be a good alternative. For castles, the area north and west of Aberdeen is the place to start. Golfing is excellent all along the north coast; naturalists should head for the east coast. If you want to bury yourself in local life, go to the farmlands of the Mearns or of Buchan. Spend at least a day in Aberdeen. A taste of all of these would probably provide the most satisfactory holiday of the lot.

Key web sites

www.moray.org Very useful directory for Speyside, put together by Moray Council

www.agtb.org The Aberdeen and Grampian tourist board's site

www.thisisnorthscotland.co.uk The web site of the regional newspaper, the *Press and Journal*. Lots of local goings-on and fascinating archive material

www.ift.net/webit A reasonable general guide to Aberdeenshire, with some useful material

www.abdn.ac.uk Aberdeen University's site. It takes persistence to find your way past course details, etc., but there is some useful stuff for the visitor here

Good bases in the North-East

Aberdeen

✓ *Thriving city life*
✓ *Good eating and nightlife*
✗ *Accommodation is expensive*
✗ *Takes time to get in and out of*

Scotland's third-largest city is lively and interesting. The oil industry has brought high standards to restaurants and has provided some nightlife, but high prices have come in its wake too.

Banchory

✓ *The nicest small town on Deeside*
✓ *Within easy reach of Aberdeen*

Of the small towns on the River Dee, Banchory is best placed for castle-visiting. It is a smart place, with enough business trade from Aberdeen to push accommodation prices up a little, and it is also a popular stopping place on tours of the Dee Valley.

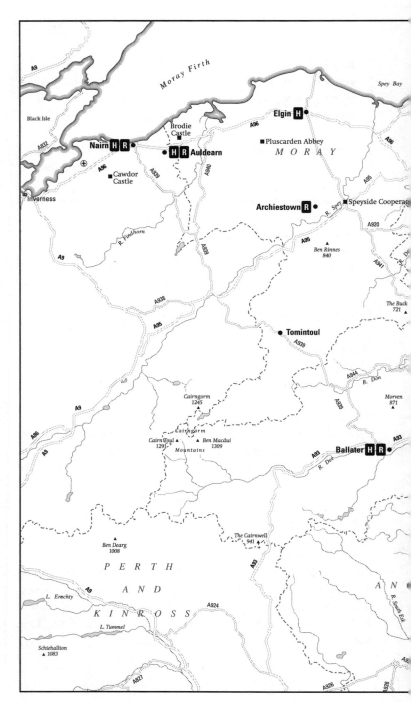

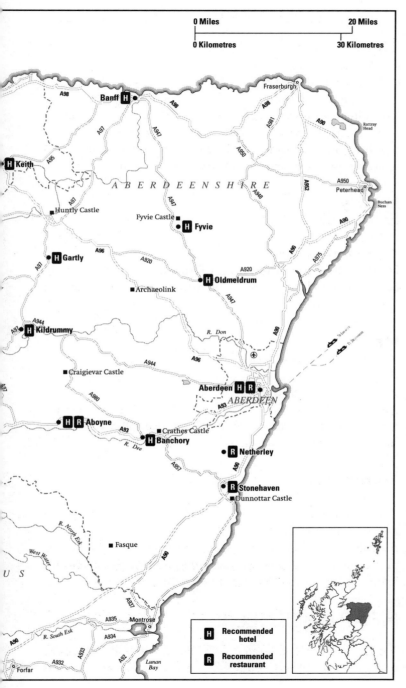

0 Miles | 20 Miles
0 Kilometres | 30 Kilometres

Fraserburgh

Banff **H**

Rattray Head

H Keith

A B E R D E E N S H I R E

A950

Peterhead

Buchan Ness

■ Huntly Castle

Fyvie Castle ■ **H** Fyvie

H Gartly

H Oldmeldrum

■ Archaeolink

R. Don

H Kildrummy

A944

A96

■ Craigievar Castle

H R Aberdeen

A B E R D E E N

H R Aboyne

■ Crathes Castle

H Banchory

R. Dee

R Netherley

R Stonehaven

■ Dunnottar Castle

R. North Esk

West Water

■ Fasque

R U S

R. South Esk

Montrose

Lunan Bay

Forfar

H Recommended hotel

R Recommended restaurant

Elgin

✓ *Well-positioned, historic town*

✓ *Fair range of accommodation*

✓ *Not far from seaside*

This old town grew up around its medieval cathedral and is now the shopping centre for the rich countryside around. The beach at Lossiemouth is close, as are the distilleries of Speyside, and there are a number of historic sights nearby.

Huntly

✓ *Elegant, attractive town*

✓ *Fishing*

✗ *Too quiet for some tastes*

Huntly Castle dominates this small town. Not much goes on, but it is a good place from which to explore the north-east corner of the region.

Nairn

✓ *Wide range of accommodation*

✓ *Seaside*

✓ *Good roads east and west*

A friendly, quiet seaside town on the Moray Firth, with sandy seashore close by and the wooded Findhorn Valley to explore. Inverness is within easy reach.

Tomintoul

✓ *walks and tour of high country*

✓ *small community*

✗ *isolated, not many facilities*

A small village high on the edge of the Grampians, very well placed for walking in the hills, for dropping down to visit the Speyside distilleries or for touring the valley of the Don.

NEAR ABERDEEN

A wide semicircle, centred on Aberdeen, will lead you from a rocky, inhospitable coast, through the lovely valleys of the Dee,

Don and Ythan, into the foothills of the high Cairngorm mountains. Much of the land is fertile and wooded, and here stand the great castles and houses for which the area is famous. It is an ideal part of the world to tour, following the rivers or cutting through the countryside. North of Aberdeen, the land flattens and becomes almost treeless, an area which can be both bleak and beautiful.

Top Sights

Archaeolink Prehistory Park (near Inverurie)

✓ *Outdoor reconstructions of Iron Age life*
✓ *Very useful resource centre for local exploration*
✓ *Good family sight*

In an area rich in prehistoric remains, this is a very useful sight. It consists of an outdoor area, where a reconstruction of an Iron Age Farm, complete with livestock and farmers, forms the centrepiece, and an indoor area, which has several interpretative exhibitions as well as a good library, bookshop and resource centre. The outdoor elements of the sight are still being added to, but it is already interesting and fun.

Come here to put together a collection of leaflets to guide you round the nearby Pictish, Stone Age and Iron Age sights. These range from stone circles to hill forts; most will involve walking. In particular, seek out the Pictish Maiden Stone near Chapel of Garioch. It shows Jonah and two whales along with a Z-rod symbol and the swimming elephant. For more on Pictish stones, see the box on pages 302–3. [*Apr to Oct, daily 10–5;* ☎ *(01464) 851500;* 🖥 *www.archaeolink.co.uk*]

Craigievar Castle (west of Aberdeen)

✓ *Great architecture*
✓ *Over-the-top interior*

Craigievar is widely held to be the most perfect tower-house in Scotland. Unfortunately, it was not built for the convenient shepherding of bus-loads of visitors, and the National Trust has been keen to discourage mass tourism, so you won't find many references to it in tourist literature. But the castle is worth finding, for the architecture is fascinating. The solid L-shaped trunk of the house blossoms effortlessly into a whole village-worth of gables and balustrades.

Internally, Craigievar is very odd. Its builder, William Forbes of Menie, who 'made a goodly pile merchandising at Danzig', was obviously keen to impress. It is difficult to admire Danzig Willie's medieval-style hall, complete with vaulted ceiling, musi-cians' gallery and massive coat of arms, without suffering the temptation to giggle. But the quality of the work is excellent. There is scarcely a room without a superb moulded plaster ceiling. At the very top of the house, the Long Room runs the entire width of the castle and is plain and beautiful with its small alcoves. [NTS; May to Sept, daily 1.30–5.30; ☎ (01555) 860364; 👆 via www.caledoniancastles.btinternet.co.uk]

Crathes Castle (south-west of Aberdeen)

✓ Beautiful old tower-house, full of things to see
✓ Superb gardens
✓ Great sight for everyone

This is the very best of the Aberdeenshire sights, combining a sixteenth-century tower-house with a twentieth-century garden which is enthralling to keen gardeners. The heart of the main house is an L-shaped building with narrow slits for windows. At about third-floor level the house starts growing outwards, with towers, turrets and rooms bulging out of the walls. It is rather like a huge beech tree.

Crathes is famous for its painted ceilings, which are among the best in Scotland. Three remain, with a whole gallery of characters, emblems, mottoes, grotesques and patterns taking up every cranny of the awkward spaces around the beams. Unfortunately, little of the decoration in the vaulted High Hall has survived, though there is enough to show how pretty it must have been. The finest room in the castle is the Long Gallery right at the top, which has a beautiful oak-panelled ceiling and views over the gardens below.

The gardens at Crathes are the work of the thirteenth baronet and his wife, Sybil. In the walled garden and among the old yew hedges in front of the castle, they planted a series of colour gardens starting around 1926. The most unusual border is the Colour Garden, where yellow, red and bronze combine superbly. There is a further wild garden among the trees beyond the old wall. The plant sales area is good evidence of the skill and interest of the gardening staff. *[NTS; House: Apr to Oct, daily 10.30–5.30 (timed ticket system); Garden: All year, daily 9–sunset;* ☎ *(01330) 844525;* ☛ *www.nts.org.uk]*

Dunnottar Castle (south of Aberdeen)

✓ *Spectacular clifftop setting*

In about 1382 Sir William Keith, Great Marischal of Scotland, came into possession of a massive crag, almost split from the mainland, perfectly suited to a castle. He quickly demolished the church which stood on the crag, getting himself excommunicated in the process, but in exchange built himself a virtually impregnable fortress.

A litter of buildings from different periods now covers the crag, dominated by the fifteenth-century keep. When living conditions there became too primitive, a large, comfortable mansion was built. The restored drawing-room here allows superbly contrasting views of angry sea and peaceful courtyard.

Dunnottar was important in the period of the Scottish civil and religious wars in the 1640s. Here the seventh Earl Marischal watched his land being burnt by Montrose (see box, pages 332–3), while one of the Covenanting ministers to whom he had given refuge, told him 'Trouble not, for the reek will be a sweet-smelling incense in the nostrils of the Lord'. It was here too that the Scottish crown jewels were sent for safety during Cromwell's invasion of 1650, to be smuggled out again during the eight months' siege in 1651. There was a final sorry chapter of persecution after the restoration of Charles II, when 167 Covenanters were crammed into a tidal dungeon (the Whig's Vault). *[HS; Apr to Sept, Mon–Sat 9–6, Sun 2–5; Nov to Easter, Mon–Fri 9–sunset;* ☎ *(01569) 762173;* ☛ *via www.scottishculture.about.com]*

Fasque (on B974 north-west of Montrose)

✓ *Edwardian house, lost in a time warp*
✓ *Atmospheric interior*

Fasque is not one of the main features of the usual Aberdeenshire tourist trail, but we consider it to be unmissable. It is a neglected, damp-ridden, rotting white elephant of a house, seemingly abandoned around 1914, and left undisturbed ever since. In the servants' hall, ranks of chairs stand covered in dust, waiting for domestic staff who will never return. Cupboards open on heaps of rust-covered candlesticks and boot-trees. A double staircase of wonderful proportions leads you up from the quiet hallway to the drawing-room above, where again, everything – portraits, furniture, china – waits suspended in its slow decay. The only moving things are the deer cropping the grass beyond the windows. This was Prime Minister Gladstone's family home, and one small room holds mementos – a collection of cuttings, small gifts from constituencies and addresses from admirers.

Despite the damp and the weak light-bulbs, this is a house which recalls a bygone way of life more potently than any of the burnished stately homes elsewhere. *[May to Sept, daily 11–5; ☎ (01561) 320569]*

Fyvie Castle (north-west of Aberdeen)

✓ *Grand, rather odd tower-house*
✓ *Eccentric taste in the interior*
✓ *Paintings*

No one can accuse Fyvie of lacking character, though whether you love it or hate it depends on your taste. It is a Z-shaped mix of palace and castle, which straggles across its surrounding lawns like a snake which has swallowed a carpenter's rule.

Internally, the castle bears the stamp of Lord Leith, who had the luck to marry an American heiress and make a fortune in the Illinois Steel Company. In 1889 he bought Fyvie, and proceeded to refurbish and extend it in his own inimitable style. This is seen to best effect in the astonishing Gallery, a room in the 'modern antique' mode, where a giant self-playing organ contrasts with seventeenth-century tapestries and the massive French Renaissance fireplace. Several magnificent plaster ceilings remain from earlier periods, as does Fyvie's most beautiful feature, the great pinkish wheel stair, which rises for four floors.

Lord Leith knew what he was doing when it came to painting. The portraits at Fyvie are renowned. Batoni's portrait of William Gordon, a Byronic figure poised with drawn sword against a classical background, was in the castle before Lord Leith came, but he is responsible for assembling the Raeburn portraits – he was especially fond of tracking down portraits of his Aberdeenshire connections. The portraits of Mrs Gregory and of John Stirling of Kippendavie and his daughter are worth the whole journey to Fyvie to see.

Fyvie has mysteries too – notably the secret vault below the Charter Room, which has never been opened because of an unpleasant curse. Attempts to gain entry are supposed to result in the death of the laird and the blindness of his wife – and this has twice occurred. [NTS; late Apr to May and Sept, daily 1.30–5.30; June to Aug, daily 11–5.30; Oct, weekends only 1.30–5.30; ☎ (01651) 891266; ᠂ www.nts.org.uk]

The next best sights

Aden Country Park and Aberdeenshire Farming Museum (west of Peterhead)

The park is extensive and has masses of walks and nature trails as well as an adventure play area. Ranger-led walks and other activities take place – a family day out will be rewarding. The farming museum at the park's centre offers a good introduction to the old Aberdeenshire farming life, which had its own distinctive customs. [Park: Apr to Oct, daily 7–8; Nov to Mar, 7–7; ☎ (01771) 622857; Museum: May to Sept, daily 11–4.30; ☎ (01771) 622906; ᠂ via www.buchan.org.uk]

Balmoral Castle (on A93 east of Braemar)

Queen Victoria, a passionate convert to the delights of the Highlands, bought Balmoral in 1852 to use as a holiday home.

The old house was virtually gutted and rebuilt, and the grounds laid out largely according to Prince Albert's taste – which was gloomily Germanic.

The grounds and a couple of rooms of Balmoral are open to the public in early summer (before the royal family goes on holiday), drawing huge crowds of curious visitors. For Windsor family enthusiasts, there are plenty of interesting pieces of royal history, and the grounds are beautifully kept and an excellent place for a walk. *[Apr to July 10–5;* ☎ *(01339) 742334;* ✆ *www.balmoral-castle.co.uk]*

Castle Fraser (west of Aberdeen)

The appearance of the castle at the end of its avenue is distinctly French. Most of the furnishings are nineteenth-century and on the scanty side, though they give an excellent idea of how such a castle was lived in at that time. The grounds (best appreciated from the roof) have more antiquity about them – they bear the stamp of eighteenth-century land-scaping. The walled garden is sheltered and colourful. *[NTS; Easter to May and Sept, daily 1.30–5.30; June to Aug, daily 11–5.30; Oct, weekends only 1.30–5.30;* ☎ *(01330) 833463;* ✆ *via www.nts.org.uk]*

Corgaff Castle (on A939 at Cockbridge)

This is a miniature sixteenth-century white tower surrounded by a curious star-shaped wall, on the edge of the wild hills. After a long history, it became a Hanoverian guard-post after Culloden, and this period produced the exterior fortification. The interior restoration represents life as it was lived for the garrison: five or six double beds fill the small rooms. Corgaff lingered on as a military post until 1831, although by then the soldiers were watching for illicit stills rather than Jacobites. *[HS; Apr to Sept, daily 9.30–6.30;* ☎ *(01975) 651460;* ✆ *via caledoniancastles.btinternet.co.uk]*

Drum Castle (south-west of Aberdeen)

This is a castle where a mansion house has been tacked on to a square thirteenth-century keep. The storeroom, the upper hall and the battlements demonstrate what an impregnable (if uncomfortable) fortress the old tower used to be. Views from the battlements are worth the steep climb. The interior of the mansion house has been heavily Victorianised, but a few of the older features remain. There are good portraits of the Irvine family, who held Drum from the time of Robert the Bruce. A small arboretum in the grounds provides a pleasant short walk. *[NTS; Easter to May and Sept, daily 1.30–5.30; June to Aug, daily 11–5.30; Oct, weekends only 1.30–5.30;* ☎ *(01330) 811204; ✆ via www.scottishculture.about.com]*

Glenbuchat Castle (on A97 west of Alford)

This ruined, unfrequented, sixteenth-century Z-plan castle above the River Don is worth a stop. Enough of it remains to give a good impression of what it was like to live here – rather comfortable by the look of things. The last laird is one of the tragic figures of the Jacobite years. He joined the 1745 rising at the age of 68, and was with Prince Charles Edward at Culloden. Thereafter, with a price on his head, he was forced to spend months dodging the Redcoats before escaping to France, where he died in poverty. *[HS; open at all times;* ☎ *0131-668 8800; ✆ via www.scottishculture.about.com]*

Haddo House (north-west of Aberdeen)

This Adam mansion makes a good contrast to the turrets and pinnacles of other Aberdeenshire castles. Much of the interior is Adam revival from 1880 rather than the real thing (such as the papier-mâché ceiling mouldings and Adam-style fireplaces, for example), but the effect is still splendid. Haddo is furnished as a family home, with comfortable clutter rather than suits of armour. There is a chapel, with some Burne-Jones designs, and a Queen's Bedroom, where hangs a portrait of Queen Victoria aged four, looking just like a large plum. Numerous operas, choral concerts and plays take place at Haddo, as well as other activities throughout the season (call the Arts Trust Office ☎ (01651) 851770 for information). *[NTS; Easter to Sept, daily 1.30–5.30; Oct, weekends only 1.30–5.30;* ☎ *(01651) 851440; ✆ via www.nts.org.uk]*

Kildrummy Castle (on A97 west of Alford)

Kildrummy was once a huge medieval fortress, the seat of the Earls of Mar and symbol of that family's power and status. Edward I of England may have supervised the building of the four towers and imposing gatehouse. He no doubt regretted this, for Kildrummy became a Bruce stronghold and held out against the English until the garrison was betrayed when a treacherous blacksmith set fire to the grain store in return for as much gold as he could carry. His payment was in the form of molten metal poured down his throat. *[HS; Apr to Sept, daily 9.30–6.30;* ☎ *(01975) 571331;* 🖰 *via www.caledoniancastles.btinternet.co.uk]*

Kildrummy Castle Gardens

Colonel Ogston bought Kildrummy Castle in 1898 and built a new castle near the ruins. Needing a garden to go with it, he commissioned a Japanese firm to make a water garden in the ravine which once provided the defensive cover for the back of the old castle. Since the colonel's time the gardens have gone through periods of neglect, but are now well re-established. The primary appeal of the planting is the blending of acers and rhododendrons among the rocks. *[Apr to Oct, daily 10–5;* ☎ *(01975) 571277]*

Leith Hall (north-west of Inverurie)

Leith Hall started life as a simple laird's house, its oldest section dating from 1650, and was gradually extended over the following centuries. The Leith-Hay family lived here before giving it to the National Trust for Scotland, and the history of the house is really the history of the family. There are fine Georgian rooms, with lots of family portraits and one or two good pieces of furniture. The gardens are a high point, with extensive and colourful herbaceous borders. *[NTS; Easter to May and Sept, daily 1.30–5.30; June to Aug, daily 11–5.30; Oct, weekends only 1.30–5.30;* ☎ *(01464) 831216;* 🖰 *via www.nts.org.uk]*

Peterhead Maritime Heritage Museum

A slick modern museum in this somewhat grim fishing town outlines the long struggle to prize fish from northern waters.

There are sections on whaling, and on the oil industry. It's a useful place to learn from, and a visit to Peterhead harbour, usually with plenty of fishing boats, will enhance the experience. *[Apr to Oct, Mon–Sat 10–5, Sun 12–5; Nov to Mar, telephone for information;* ☎ *(01779) 473000]*

Pitmedden Garden (north-west of Aberdeen)

This intricate seventeenth-century formal garden was created by Sir Alexander Seton around 1675, but had to be re-created from scratch in the 1950s – it had become a kitchen garden. The restoration is a success, with the planting of four great parterres. Three of them follow the seventeenth-century designs for the gardens at Holyrood in Edinburgh. The garden is sunk beneath the level of the ground, for it is essential to see the patterns from above. From the terrace you gaze down to the maze of box hedges and 40,000 colourful annuals, from which the designs and lettering are created. *[NTS; May to Sept, daily 10–5.30;* ☎ *(01651) 842352;* 🖰 *via www.nts.org.uk]*

Also in the area

Bullers of Buchan (south of Peterhead) The Bullers (boiler) is a collapsed sea cave, with a chasm over 200 feet deep. A narrow arch of rock separates it from the sea. A legend goes that a local laird, when drunk, won a bet by galloping around the chasm on horseback, but contemplation of this feat, once he had sobered up, was enough to make him die of shock. Dr Johnson insisted on exploring the place by boat.

Grampian Transport Museum (Alford) The museum has a large, if antiseptically displayed, collection of ancient vehicles. Children are allowed to climb on some. A narrow-gauge steam railway is part of the set-up. *[🖰 www.gtm.org.uk]*

Grassic Gibbon Centre (Arbuthnot, south of Stonehaven) A small museum set up in the village where Lewis Grassic

Gibbon spent much of his life, with the background on the author and his life. *[Apr to Oct, daily 10–4.30;* ☎ *(01561) 361668;* ✆ *www.stonehaven.org.uk/grassic]*

New Slains Castle (south of Peterhead) A short, puddle-strewn walk from the A975 takes you these dramatically situated cliff-edge ruins. The castle dates from 1598 and was turned into a large mansion before being abandoned. Dr Johnson was impressed by it in 1773, and the tangle of stone in its airy situation is still worth seeing. *[✆ via www.scottishculture.about.com]*

Towns and villages to explore

Stonehaven

Despite the fact that its beach is more shingle than sand, the old fishing town of Stonehaven remains a popular resort. The oldest part is by the harbour, with the newer, predominantly Victorian town stretching up the hill behind. It is a gentle, old-fashioned sort of place – relaxed rather than raucous, and more suited to brisk strolls around the harbour than to getting a suntan on the beach. It has a sea-girdled **golf course** and a wonderful open-air **art deco pool**. The place comes to life on Hogmanay, with a fire festival all of its own. The old **Tolbooth** on the harbour's edge is Stonehaven's most venerable building, now a small museum and tea-room. *[✆ www.stonehaven.org.uk]*

Braemar

This small town lies on the edge of the Grampian Mountains at the bottom of the road from the Cairnwell pass. It is a centre for walkers, climbers and skiers, though at 1,100 feet above sea level it is scarcely a balmy resort. The **Braemar Gathering**, held in September, has the highest snob-value of all Highland Games, since the royal family usually puts in an appearance. The Gathering is also one of the largest and best, noted for the piping. Braemar is a popular stop on the Deeside tour, so you will find shops, cafés and places to stay. *[✆ via www.royal-deeside.org.uk]*

Banchory

Banchory is sufficiently close to Aberdeen to be within commuting distance, as well as making an excellent place for entertaining business clients, for the fishing on the Dee is renowned. Banchory's shops and tea-rooms are worth strolling around. An exploration of the valley of the River Feugh, which joins the Dee here, takes you into peaceful woodland, where in autumn the crimson rowan, russet bracken and pale yellow birch are as well coordinated as if an interior designer had arranged them. [*via www.royal-deeside.org.uk*]

Suggested excursions

Deeside (Braemar to Banchory) One of the most popular tours in Scotland follows the River Dee past the gates of Balmoral and on eastwards. The scenery is a glowing combination of heather, water and pine woods. There is, however, something slightly packaged about it, as if Nature had deliberately produced an assemblage designed to appeal to postcard manufacturers.

Glen Muick (Ballater) Loch Muick, at the top of this glen, was Queen Victoria's favourite beauty spot. A lot of visitors come in the queen's footsteps, and there is a car park and information centre at the end of the road. From here, several good walks are on offer along the shore of the loch. You can also set out to climb Lochnagar.

The Lecht Road (A939), running between Tomintoul and Strath Don, is a splendid piece of eighteenth-century engineering, built by the military after the 1745 rising. It is one of the first roads in Scotland to be blocked by blizzards, for expanses of windswept moorland stretch in all directions, a blaze of purple when the heather is in bloom. The climb up to the pass from Tomintoul is relatively gentle but the road rushes in sweeps down the other side until, in a suddenly green valley just beyond the few scattered houses of Cock Bridge, you reach the River Don and Corgaff Castle. This is much the prettiest way to cross from Speyside to Aberdeen.

Linn of Dee (Braemar) This waterfall lies as far up the river as you can get by road, and makes a pleasing drive or walk from Braemar. Beyond, the estate of Mar Lodge (owned by the National Trust for Scotland) offers endless opportunites for walks in wild country. Linn of Dee is also the starting point for a series of tough walks through the heart of the Grampians. The best-known of these runs through the mountain trench of the Lairig Ghru to Rothiemurchus and the Spey Valley. Another route runs southwards to Glen Tilt with a branch to Glen Feshie.

James Graham, Marquess of Montrose (1612–1650)

In the confused tangle of the Scottish civil wars of the seventeenth century, the figure of Montrose stands out as the single personality whom it has been possible to cast in a romantic light, thanks to his loyalty to his king, Charles I, his abilities as a leader of men in the tradition of Wallace or Bruce, and his death at the hands of his Covenanting enemies.

Montrose was among the first to sign the 1638 Covenant, and for the first years of the confrontation between King Charles and the Scots was firmly on the Covenanting side. However, as the Covenanters increasingly began to demand the subordination of king to kirk and parliament, Montrose, who perceived only anarchy in this course of events, became increasingly alienated. It was the signing of the Solemn League and Covenant in 1643, by which the Scots agreed to join the English armed rebellion against King Charles, which seems to have made up Montrose's mind for him. In early 1644 King Charles commissioned him lieutenant-general of the royal forces in Scotland – not that there were any at that time. Montrose's entry into Scotland, with two companions and no troops, was not auspicious.

His luck turned when he met Alasdair Macdonnell, who had come with a small force from Antrim in the king's cause.

The River Don Whereas the Dee is rushing and wild, the Don is a much more pastoral river, winding through fertile coun-tryside and through agricultural towns and villages. It is a very beautiful river and easily followed from Cockbridge seawards, with plenty to see on the way.

Beaches and seashore

Cruden Bay (south of Peterhead) Although a major oil pipeline runs ashore here, the bay – with its high dunes and semicircle of sand – is unspoilt. At the northern end a tiny

Montrose won his first victory against the Covenanters at Tippermuir in August 1644, sacked Aberdeen and disap-peared into the Highlands. In the winter, he descended on Argyll with a force of clansmen happy to pillage the lands of Clan Campbell. In January 1645, by an astonishing flank march through the snowbound glens beside Loch Ness, he took the pursuing force of Campbells by surprise at Inverlochy. Throughout the spring of 1645 Montrose was in Aberdeenshire, beating the Covenanters at Auldearn and Alford, and, when he finally descended on the Lowlands, he shattered another Covenanting army at Kilsyth. But it could not last. The Scottish troops in England hurried home, yet Montrose got no support from the weakened king. In September he was outmanoeuvred for the first time, and his army routed at Philiphaugh. At the beginning of 1646 Montrose was still trying to continue his campaign, but on 25 April King Charles surrendered to his enemies and Montrose was forced abroad.

He returned in 1650, commissioned by King Charles II, raised troops in Orkney, but was soundly defeated at Carbisdale in Sutherland and captured a few days later. Taken to Edinburgh, Montrose was tried, condemned and executed on 21 May.

harbour and a few cottages make it positively photogenic. An enormous hotel was once built here, with tennis courts, croquet lawns and a golf course, for Cruden Bay was to be the resort to beat them all. The project was a mammoth flop; nothing remains save the golf course.

Sands of Forvie (north of Aberdeen) According to geologists, the River Ythan was once much bigger, running over what is now the North Sea. The estuary still seem bigger than today's river deserves. Among the dunes and rough heath of the river mouth is the Nature Reserve of the Sands of Forvie, a stopping point for both bird-watchers and botanists. Huge numbers of eider duck concentrate here in the breeding season.

ABERDEEN

The 'Silver City' was for many years a mixture of port, fishing town, and regional centre. The discovery of North Sea Oil transformed it, virtually overnight, into the centre of the offshore supply industry. Fears that the old city would become a brash, northern version of Houston have not been realised, though prices are generally higher, and the fast food a lot better, than elsewhere in the area.

Aberdeen is a mixture of St Andrews and Glasgow, with the academic and seaside atmosphere of the former, and something of the bustle of the latter. It spreads out between the Rivers Don and Dee, with the tranquil, academic area to the north and the busy seaport to the south. The links behind the magnificent curving seashore remain undeveloped, providing an open aspect in the heart of the city and a good blow of sea air for the inhabitants.

It is a big place, with long streets which can be hard on the feet, so a bus map will be useful.

Most of the activity happens on the ruler-straight Union Street. The modern Bon Accord Centre has chain stores under cover. Tourist information is to be found in nearby Broad Street, while the streets running towards and round the harbour make the best area for casual wandering. The harbour authorities are fairly relaxed about visitors who want to gaze at the comings and goings of the pipeline barges and the ferries to Shetland.

Getting around

Bus routes connect all the central parts of the city. Timetables are available during office hours Monday to Friday from the travel office in King Street [☎ (01224) 650065] and at all times from the portacabin in Union Street. During the summer season, Grampian Coaches runs an open-air city tour [☎ (01224) 650000], which makes a comfortable way to get your bearings.

Top sights

Aberdeen Art Gallery

✓ *Very fine collection of British paintings*

The collection here, little known outside Aberdeen, is magnificent and beautifully displayed. The tone varies from the formal melancholy of the War Memorial Court to the bright spaciousness of the upper rooms. The gallery's strength lies in its collection of British painting through three centuries, but the decorative arts section, with much local material, is almost as good. The wide range of paintings and drawings includes Blake's *Raising of Lazarus*, Piper's *Dunnottar Castle*, Millais' wonderful portrait of a self-confident young girl, entitled *Bright Eyes*, Paul Nash's windswept *Wood on the Downs*, Augustus John's sensuous *The Blue Pool*, and, among local painters, James Cowie's *Two Schoolgirls* and James McBey's simple and precise capturing of *Ythan Mouth*. Look out also for the ridiculously melodramatic *Flood in the Highlands* by Landseer. [*Mon–Sat 10–5, Sun 2–5;* ☎ *(01224) 523700;* ☝ *www.adgm.co.uk*]

Aberdeen Maritime Museum

✓ *Detailed museum, especially good on the oil industry*

✓ *Good, modern interpretation*

Partly housed in an ancient building with a neat modern

extension, the museum traces Aberdeen's history as a port, from the building of the harbours to the advent of the oil industry. A huge scale model of an oil platform half fills the new extension, and there are sequences of videos and displays about life on oil rigs, including a mock-up of an accommodation unit. The photographs and models from earlier days can barely compete, although there is plenty here about Aberdeen's past as a fishing port. There's a good tea room in the basement too. *[Mon–Sat 10–5, Sun 12–5;* ☎ *(01224) 337700;* ✆ *www.adgm.co.uk]*

Provost Skene's House
✓ *Furniture through the ages*
The oldest domestic house in Aberdeen, dating from 1545, has been restored and turned into a museum of domestic life from Cromwellian to Victorian times. As you move from room to room, you shift from one period to the next. A rather well-acted film brings to life some of the characters who made their mark on the house over the years, and there is excellent furniture as well as painted ceilings to look at. There's also an Edwardian nursery, with an excellent collection of old toys. *[Mon–Sat 10–5, Sun 2–5;* ☎ *(01224) 641086;* ✆ *www.adgm.co.uk]*

The next best sights

Duthie Park Winter Gardens (Polmuir Road)
Two whole acres of plants lie under cover in the winter garden to top them all. There are cacti, bromeleiads and succulents from all over the world. In summer, the roses in Duthie Park outside are famous, and people time their trip to Aberdeen in order to be able to see them. *[Dec to Mar, Oct and Nov, 9.30–4.30; Apr 9.30–8; May to Sept, 9.30–9;* ✆ *www.treasuresofbritain.org/Duthie]*

King's College (Old Aberdeen)

The crowned tower of King's College, which was founded in 1495, dominates the university area south of the River Don. A visitor centre takes you through the university's long history. Afterwards, take time to have a look at the venerable chapel. *[Mon-Sat 10–5, Sun 12–5;* ☎ *(01224) 273702]*

St Machar's Cathedral (Old Aberdeen)

Only the nave and aisles of this largely fifteenth-century building remain, so it appears unbalanced from every angle except at the west front. It is imposing all the same, with twin spires and a magnificent heraldic roof in the interior, which dates from 1520. The 48 shields that compose the ceiling provide a kind of visual guide to the spiritual and secular hierarchies of sixteenth-century Scotland and Europe. *[*☎ *0131–668 8800]*

Satrosphere

In its new home down by the beach, this hands-on science museum ought to make an excellent outing. There are experiments to perform and exhibitions to look at, plus a good shop. The place is obviously designed with children and school trips in mind, but this is not to say that adults won't enjoy it. *[Mon–Sat 10–4, Sun 1.30–5; closed Tue in winter;* ☎ *(01224) 213232;* 🖱 *www.satrosphere.net]*

The Tolbooth (Castle Street)

The long civic history of the city is explored in the seventeenth-century prison. The development of local government and of crime and punishment are lovingly outlined against the background of the cells of the former prison. *[Apr to Sept, Mon–Sat 10–5, Sun 12.30–5.30;* ☎ *(01224) 621167]*

Also in the area

Brig o' Balgownie The bridge, north of St Machar's Cathedral, is Scotland's oldest, built in 1320. It is a massive, single-arched construction over a deep pool. You can go across, unless you happen to be an only son riding a mare's only foal. Thomas the Rhymer (see page 42) predicted the bridge would fall in these circumstances, and Lord Byron – as an only son – remembered the 'awful proverb which made me pause to cross it'.

Fittie Exploring the streets down towards the mouth of the Dee will bring you to this tiny ancient fishermens' village, now swamped by the surrounding city. The old houses with their little courtyards are still inhabited.

Marischal College (Broad Street) The college has a wonderful frontage of rippling granite ribs, like a complicated fishing net. The college was founded in 1593, but the frontage was built in 1906. Inside, the Marischal Museum holds an anthropological collection which has assembled bits and pieces of human culture from all over the world. *[Mon–Fri 10–5, Sun 2–5;* ☎ *(01224) 274301;* ✆ *www.abdn.ac.uk/marischal-museum]*

Entertainment and nightlife

Aberdeen isn't the world's greatest spot for clubbing or the arts, but there's usually something going on, especially during the university terms. Check out what is on at His Majesty's Theatre – the main venue for plays and musicals – and also the Arts Centre, which puts on smaller productions and concerts *[for details of both venues* ☎ *(01224) 641122].* The Lemon Tree in West North Street is a genial arty place, with a small theatre, good bar meals and occasional live music from up-and-coming artistes *[information line* ☎ *(01224) 642230].*

THE MORAY FIRTH AND SPEYSIDE

The southern coast of the Moray Firth is just as beautiful and varied as that of Cornwall, yet it sees many fewer visitors. It is also an area which attracts good weather, and a fair amount of sunshine too. There is a well-signed coastal trail to lead you from village to village, and a good mixture of sandy bays and dramatic cliff scenery.

Inland, the fertile plains of Moray and Banff gradually give way to the northern foothills of the Grampians. Where the great River Spey passes along their western edge, many of Scotland's best-known malt whiskies are made, using barley from the land, peat from the moors and water from the many springs. Several distilleries have combined together to form a Whisky Trail, but there are others to visit too.

Top sights

Brodie Castle (east of Nairn)

✓ *Attractive mix of castle and stately home*

There have been 25 Brodies of Brodie since the thirteenth century, and Brodies have been living at Brodie Castle since 1567. Today they share it with the National Trust for Scotland. It is a well-polished place, with some fascinating interiors, some dating from Victorian times and others from much earlier. The Renaissance pillars in the entrance hall are actually Victorian, and the same period produced the cosy library and the spectacularly successful Gothic fireplace in the red drawing-room. But the star piece is the seventeenth-century ceiling of the dining-room – a riot of mermaids, fruit and flowers, which is so ornate and heavy-looking that visitors may well fear for their lives. The collection of twentieth-century paintings (notably watercolours) assembled by the twenty-fourth Brodie should be seen, while the same laird's interest in daffodils turns the well-landscaped grounds into a picture in spring. Children will have more fun spotting the many security alarms than in filling out the rather worthy quiz sheets. [*NTS; Apr to Sept, Mon–Sat 11–5.30, Sun 1.30–5.30; October, Sat 11–5.30, Sun 1.30–5.30;* ☎ *(01309) 641371;* 🖱 *via www.nts.org.uk*]

Cawdor Castle (south-west of Nairn)

✓ *Ancient castle, one of the best in the country*

✓ *Fascinating, mildly eccentric interior*

✓ *Terrific gardens*

This castle is a joy to visit; its history is leavened with home-liness, its dignity modified by mild eccentricity. The notes which guide you round are witty and fascinating. To add to the bargain, the two gardens are delightful. Forget Macbeth – this is a place well worth travelling to for its own sake.

An early Thane of Cawdor had a dream in which he was told to load a donkey with gold, let it wander around and watch where it lay down, for this would be the best spot for his new castle. The donkey proceeded to lie down under a thorn tree, which still stands (now long defunct) in the middle of the vaulted guardroom of the fourteenth-century tower. This same room contains a dungeon which was discovered only in 1979. It is typical that everything found in it is displayed without regard to its worth – there are sawn-off bits of moulding, chicken and horse bones, pieces of crab and lead.

On a more cultivated level, the paintings are especially worth looking at – notably the portraits (brought to life by Lord Cawdor's notes) and the more serious pieces, such as several by John Piper and a Stanley Spencer, as well as some fine watercolours. The tapestries are also good, helped again by suitable (or unsuitable) notes on their subjects.

It is hard to know what to pick out from the rest. The tour takes you through the Modern Kitchen as well as the old one, past the collections of Victoriana, the Pet's Corner, the Stones, a model of the castle and a model of a man-o'-war, not to mention the drawing-room, several bedrooms and various cubby-holes. After all this, the gardens may seem a haven of normality. The sheltered walled garden has huge climbing shrubs, and the more open herbaceous garden is a mass of colour. *[May to mid-Oct, daily 10–5.30;* ☎ *(01667) 404615;* ✆ *www.castles.org/Chatelaine/CAWDOR]*

Huntly Castle
✓ *Ruin of magnificent palace*
The first castle on the steep bank of the River Deveron was built in the time of Robert the Bruce. It was replaced by a tower-house, and then by the palace, a building designed to impress the world with the power of its owner, the first

Marquess of Huntly. The doorway still achieves its purpose. You are confronted by the arms of Huntly, the royal arms of Scotland, the five wounds of Christ and finally the risen Christ in Glory all mounting in sequence above your head. Oriel windows, French in inspiration and probably craftsmanship, jut out high over the south front. Above and beneath them runs a giant frieze, inscribed with the names of the first Marquess and his wife in letters a couple of feet high.

The interior has some further examples of heraldry; this time, the mantelpieces above the elaborate fireplaces remind you whose home you are in. The wall walk on top of the great round tower gives you a bird's-eye view of Huntly and the Deveron Valley beneath. Up here you find the most human feature of the palace – a tiny turret room built above the main staircase where the first Marquess liked to escape from all the magnificence and enjoy the view. *[HS; Apr to Sept, daily 9.30–6.30; Oct to Mar, Mon–Sat 9.30–4.30, Sun 2–4.30, closed Thur pm and Fri;* ☎ *(01466) 793191;* ✆ *via www.scottish-culture.about.com]*

Pluscarden Abbey (south-west of Elgin)

✓ *Uplifting example of monastic restoration*
✓ *Peaceful and beautiful setting*

In bald terms, this is a thirteenth-century monastery which is now owned and being restored by a community of Benedictine monks. Yet Pluscarden is more than this: it is an ancient piece of Scotland's religious tradition which has been resurrected from decay, and is being made beautiful again.

Parts of the abbey still look like a building site, for at the time of writing the monks have a long way to go, though what has been achieved since 1948, when the fraternity took up residence, is impressive. The choir, the transepts and the tower of the old church have been fully restored. The nave exists merely at foundation level.

Pluscarden is a mish-mash of architectural styles. One side of the choir is lit by large windows with fine tracery, the other has only a few small lights, the outline of the larger arches being firmly blocked in. The glory of the place lies in its modern stained glass, much of it made in the abbey work-shops. It is difficult to forget the searing reds which illuminate the chancel. The abbey is lucky in its setting – nothing disturbs the peace of the valley it sits in, apart from the birdsong. You can buy various mementos of the visit in the monks' small shop. *[Daily 4.45–9.45; ☎ (01343) 890257]*

Speyside Cooperage (Craigellachie)

✓ *Close-up view of an ancient craft*

Barrels are important to the whisky industry. After visiting this sight, you may be convinced they are even more important to the whisky itself. Certain mysteries about where whisky gets its colour and flavour from are revealed here, which you may not hear too much about in the distilleries.

A big viewing platform allows you to watch the craftsmen beneath as they dismantle old Bourbon and sherry casks and assemble them into new ones. It is fascinating and well explained, and the skill with which the workers carry out their trade is obvious. Staves are gathered together, metal hoops slipped on, and the barrels tapped and hammered into shape. Outside, the cooperage sells barrels that have run their course – transformed into planters, garden ornaments and other wooden items. *[Mon–Fri all year, 9.30–4.30, plus Sats at Easter and June to Sept; ☎ (01340) 871108; ✑ www.scoot.co.uk/speyside_cooperage]*

The next best sights

Buckie Drifter (Buckie)

A genial modern museum down among the fish processing sheds of this busy fishing town, the Buckie Drifter explores the herring boom that swept the coast in the early twentieth century, and examines the lives of the thousands of men and women who spent their days in the industry. There are photographs, films, and lots of herring made out of stuffed fabric. *[Apr to Oct, Mon–Sat 10–5, Sun 12–5; ☎ (01542) 834646; ✑ via www.moray.org]*

Dallas Dhu (south of Forres)

Deep in the countryside lies a distillery which has been turned into a museum by Historic Scotland, allowing visitors more time than they would have on a guided tour, and also allowing children under eight (not allowed by law into some parts of working distilleries – see Speyside Malt Whisky Trail, below) to see what happens.

The distillery has been arranged to let you poke and prod at your leisure, with a trail of painted footmarks to follow, and some good explanatory boards. It comes as close to the real thing as a museum possibly could, and would make either an excellent introduction to distillery-visiting or a fitting finale. *[HS; Apr to Sept, daily 9.30–6.30; Oct to Mar, Mon–Sat 9.30–4.30, Sun 2–4.30, closed Thur pm and Fri;* ☎ *(01309) 676548;* ⬦ *via www.moray.org]*

Duff House (Banff)

The great baroque mansion, built by William Adam, dominates the outskirts of Banff. It has been rescued from a state of decay and turned into an outstation for the National Galleries of Scotland. The ornate plasterwork has been restored, and the building now looks much as it did in its heyday. It is not a sight for everyone, as the paintings are chosen to fit the house rather than for their intrinsic merit (though there are one or two good ones among them). A nearby play area provides for children, who would otherwise be bored rigid. *[Daily 10–5; Oct to Mar, closed Mon–Thur;* ☎ *(01261) 818181;* ⬦ *via www.natgalscot.ac.uk]*

Elgin Cathedral

The story of Elgin's thirteenth-century cathedral shows Scotland at its best and at its worst. It was constructed as a building which in scale, elaboration and beauty could compete with any in medieval Europe; it was destroyed by piracy, religious fervour, avarice and neglect. For all this, it is still possible to catch something of the scale and magnificence of what used to be the 'Lanthorn of the North', either by contemplating the well-preserved chapter house with its jerky vaulting and ceiling bosses (look for the dragon with folded wings) or by gazing at the splendour of the western doorway. *[HS; Apr to Sept, daily 9.30–6.30; Oct to Mar, Mon–Sat 9.30–4.30, Sun 2–4.30, closed Thur pm and Fri;* ☎ *(01343) 547171;* ☝ *via www.darkisle.com]*

Macduff Marine Aquarium

A splendid modern aquarium on the edge of the sea, with a kind of water tower as the central point, in which dwell lobsters and fish of all kinds. As well as the main aquarium, there are touch pools and smaller tanks imitating rock pools. It's an excellent place in which to learn about marine life – small, friendly and full of information. *[Daily 10–5;* ☎ *(01261) 833369;* ☝ *www.marine-aquarium.com]*

Museum of Scottish Lighthouses
(Fraserburgh)

A converted castle became Scotland's first lighthouse in 1787, and the museum is appropriately sited alongside the old building at Kinnaird Head, at the extremity of the Moray Firth (you can get a joint ticket to see the old lighthouse too). The modern museum focuses on the lives led by the men who manned the isolated lights, and of Robert Louis Stevenson's family, who designed so many of the lighthouses. Huge lenses are on display, good use is made of modern media, the guides are knowledgeable and there is a tea-room. *[Apr to Oct, Mon–Sat 10–6, Sun 12–6; Nov to Mar, Mon–Sat 10–4, Sun 12–4;* ☎ *(01346) 511022]*

Speyside Malt Whisky Trail

Seven working distilleries have linked together to make up a whisky trail along the banks of the Spey *[* ☝ *via www.moray.org]*. The process is much the same in all, but the presentation, and of course the whisky, varies greatly. Gone are the days when all distilleries were happy to show you round for nothing but goodwill: most now charge (you get your money back if you buy a bottle), although three distilleries on this route happily still cling to the old custom.

Note that children under eight are not allowed into parts of the working distilleries. If you have young children in tow, go to Dallas Dhu (above) instead.

Cardhu (Knockando) The only malt distillery founded by a woman. *[Nov to Apr, Mon–Fri 9.30–4.30; May to Sept, Mon–Fri 9.30–4.30, Sat 9.30–4.30; ☎ (01340) 810204]*

Glenfarclas (Ballindalloch) Founded in 1838 by the Grants, who still run it. *[Nov to Apr, Mon–Fri 9–4.30 (10–4.30 winter); June to Sept, Mon–Fri 9–4.30, Sat 10–4 and Sun 12.30–4.30; ☎ (01807) 500245/257]*

Glenfiddich (Dufftown) Comes complete with its own bottling plant (great fun to watch). *[Free; Mon–Fri 9.30–4.30, plus Easter to mid-Oct, Sat 9.30–4.30, Sun 12–4.30; ☎ (01340) 820373]*

Glen Grant (Rothes) A pleasant garden complements the distillery tour. *[Mid-Mar to Oct, Mon–Fri 9.30–4, plus mid-June to mid-Sept, Sat 9.30–4, Sun 12.30–4; ☎ (01542) 783318]*

Glenlivet (Glenlivet) In a lovely setting. *[Free; mid-Mar to Oct, Mon–Sat 10–4; July and Aug, Mon–Sat 9–6; ☎ (01542) 783220]*

Strathisla (Keith) The malt here is used in the Chivas Regal brand. *[Mon–Fri, 9.30–4; plus July and Aug, Sat 9.30–4; ☎ (01542) 783044]*

Tamnavulin (Tamnavulin) Another good setting. *[Free; Mar to Oct, Mon–Fri 9.30–4.30; plus Apr to Sept, Sat 9.30–4.30; ☎ (01807) 590285]*

Also in the area

Boath Doocot (Auldearn) The village was the site of one of Montrose's victories over the Covenanters in 1645. You can climb up to the old doocot, where a plan shows how the battle was fought. It is worth the short diversion from the main road as a viewpoint rather than a battlefield site.

Burghead Well (Burghead) The big, grey fishing town of Burghead may once have been a major Pictish settlement. Carved stones have been found, and more may be built into the harbour. Burghead Well is a relic of those far-off days, an underground chamber with a still pool of water in the middle. The well may have been some kind of ritual centre, perhaps even built by followers of St Columba in the sixth century. [Access from keykeeper]

Culbin Sands (north-west of Forres) These huge dunes, six miles long and two miles wide, were known as the Scottish Sahara. The shifting sands are supposed to have buried a whole estate in 1694, and it is said that the steeple of the old church occasionally emerged from the dunes as they shifted. Now the whole area has been stabilised by tree-planting. Networks of walking and cycle paths run through the trees towards the wild sea. It is a great place on a fine day.

Lochindorb This lonely stretch of water above Grantown-on-Spey is notable for having been the strategic lair of the robber-baron known as the Wolf of Badenoch, who haunted the routes north in the fourteenth century. From his castle on an island in the loch he mounted a raid to burn down Elgin Cathedral in revenge for being outlawed by the church. His old castle, taking up every spare foot of an island in the loch, was demolished on James II's orders, but you can still see the walls, and the old gate is to be found in Cawdor Castle.

Moray Firth Wildlife Centre (Spey Bay) The Moray Firth is home to a school of bottlenose dolphins, which have become a favourite sight for visitors. This centre researches them and provides a lot of useful background. In addition to dolphins, information is provided about other local wildlife including ospreys, seals and otters. *[Mar to Oct, daily 10.30–5, July and Aug, 10.30–7;* ☎ *(01343) 820339;* ✆ *via www.moray.org]*

Sueno's Stone (Forres) Just by the bypass stands one of the best Pictish stones in Scotland. It is a monlith over 20 feet high, decorated with a huge battle scene, dotted with footmen, cavalry and headless bodies. It is harder to make out the detail now that the stone is enclosed in a protective glass box, but it is still well worth stopping for. For more on Pictish stones, see the box on pages 302–3.

Towns and villages to explore

Dufftown

This is a planned village, laid out in 1817 in the form of a cross, at the very centre of distillery country. The Glenfiddich Distillery (see page 345) is Dufftown's main attraction, followed by the ruined Balvenie Castle *[Apr to Sept, daily 9.30–6.30;* ☎ *(01340) 820121].* The Keith and Dufftown railway *[*✆ *via www.moray.org]* runs steam trains on summer Sundays. Half a mile south, Mortlach Church is thought to be one of the earliest places of Christian worship in the north of Scotland. Two very old carved stones – the Battle Stone and the Elephant Stone, with inscribed Christian symbols – can be seen.

Findhorn

The B9011 past RAF Kinloss takes you to this exposed village on the edge of Findhorn Bay, a stretch of water which is very beautiful when the tide is in, but not when it is out. Small sailing boats dot the bay, and there is a watersports centre and a tiny heritage museum among the old cottages. Behind the village, the dunes reach aridly into the hinterland.

Findhorn is also known for the **Findhorn Foundation**, a self-sustaining community, dedicated to building a spiritually based, holistic planetary culture. It was founded in 1962 and has come a long way since. You can go to the visitor centre *[Apr to Oct, Mon–Fri 9–12.30 and 2–5, weekends 2–5; Oct to Mar,* *daily 2–5;* ☎ *(01309) 690311;* ✆ *www.findhorn.org]* or wander past the dwellings, some of which have been constructed out of huge wooden casks once used by the whisky industry. Details about the village are on the Internet at ✆ *www.findhornbay.net*

Huntly

The broad square, the great archway spanning the street to the north and the careful layout all speak of an eighteenth-and nineteenth-century town deliberately designed to reflect the magnificence of the local magnate. In this case, the local magnates were the Gordon family – Earls and later Marquesses of Huntly before they became Dukes of Gordon.

Huntly is a quiet agricultural town in the middle of wooded countryside, safely bypassed by the main A96. Its convenient position for touring Speyside and the Banff coast makes it a good place to stop for a night or two. For recreation there is a swimming-pool, a golf course, and opportunities to fish the Bogie, Isla and Deveron rivers.

Lossiemouth

The beach is what draws visitors to this grey, grid-plan fishing town. Apart from some of the quainter cottages with gable ends facing the sea and a half-buried look about them, Lossiemouth is ugly. Its attractions are not enhanced by the rumble of aircraft from the nearby RAF base. Yet the beach redeems the place, as do the golf course, the flourishing harbour where seine-netters lumber out on the tide, and the cram-full little **museum** *[Easter to Sept, Mon–Sat 10–5;* ☎ *(01343) 813772]* down by the harbour, complete with a reconstruction of Ramsay Macdonald's study – for Lossiemouth has produced a British prime minister.

Nairn

Nairn is a small, genteel seaside resort, with a comfortable sandy beach. It is a restrained town, where the back streets are lined with substantial stone villas, each with its own rose garden, and where every second house does bed and breakfast.

Golf, walks and exploration of the countryside are the town's attractions. [☞ 🖥 *via www.cali.co/HIGHEXP]*

Tomintoul

Tomintoul is another planned village, squatting on the very edge of inhabitable country at the top of Strath Avon. The rolling plateaux of the Ladder Hills start just beyond the village, while the great tops of the Cairngorms lie to the south. There's a small **visitor centre** *[Apr, May and Oct, Mon–Fri 10–4; June to Aug, Mon–Sat 10–4.30; Sept, Mon–Sat 11–4; always closed 12–2;* ☎ *(01309) 673701;* 🖥 *www.tomintoul-glenlivet.org]* to introduce you to the village and its surroundings. It makes a good base from which to explore this side of the Grampians, in particular the nearby Glenlivet estate (the web site has full details).

The fishing towns and villages

Banff The silting up of its harbour put a stop to Banff's days as a fishing town, though old fishers' cottages remain. Some fine architecture exists here, for the local gentry chose it as their wintering spot in the eighteenth century, and built some rather fine dwellings. Nearby, the **Colleonard Sculpture Garden** *[by appointment;* ☎ *(01261) 818284]*, where you can walk through woodland dotted with figurines, provides a mildly eccentric outing.

Buckie is an industrious place, full of seafood processing factories, fish-selling agencies, container lorries, ice-factories, ship chandlers and repair yards. All the action is down by the harbour. The Buckie Drifter (see page 342) is the main attraction.

Cullen The town gave its name to an excellent smoked haddock soup (the recipe is on the web site below). It is not an attractive town but it is blessed with a long stretch of sand and a fine golf course, both of which draw visitors. The old church is fourteenth–century. [☞ 🖥 *via www.moray.org]*

Findochty and Portknockie are typical of the quiet fishing burghs whose inhabitants now work out of Buckie. Look for the rather fine modern statue of the fisherman in Findochty. Dramatic cliff scenery intervenes between the two.

Gardenstown and Pennan As the coast rises to imposing cliffs, these fishing villages have had to squeeze in where they could. The road down to **Gardenstown** is on the precipitous side of steep, and there is barely room to turn a car. Spare a minute or two to wander round the harbour and observe how many modern facilities this place manages to cram into its tiny space. Further round the bay, tucked under the cliffs of Troup Head, lies the even more dramatically situated **Crovie**. Don't even think of taking a car – walk instead. Beyond the headland lies **Pennan**, the one village on the coast that starts tourist literature off on superlatives. Pennan is not so much a village as a single row of cottages squeezed on to a shelf between an overhanging cliff and the sea. There is absolutely nothing to do here except walk from one end of the street to the other and to take photographs, or drop into the pub and read the cuttings about the film *Local Hero*, much of which was shot here.

Portsoy exudes a greater air of antiquity down by its harbour than neighbouring villages, with some of the houses going back to the early eighteenth century. There is a leaflet to guide you round. Portsoy marble is a species of locally quarried serpentine, which once provided two chimneypieces for the palace at Versailles; now it provides pretty souvenirs, on sale by the harbour. A short walk westwards brings you to a tidal swimming pool amongst the rocks, and to a serpentine outcrop, where you can pick up colourful, sea–washed pebbles.

Suggested walks

Glenlivet Estate This large expanse of moorland and forest, owned by the Crown, is well set up for visitors with networks of walks and trails. *[⌃🔋 via www.tomintoul-glenlivet.org]*

Speyside Way A long-distance riverside path linking Spey Bay to Ballindalloch using minor roads and old railway tracks. Short sections are easily accessed. [🖰 *via www.moray.org*]

WHERE TO STAY

£ – under £70 per room per night, incl. VAT

££ – £70 to £110 per room per night, incl. VAT

£££ – over £110 per room per night, incl. VAT

ABERDEEN
Ewood House
12 Kings Gate, Aberdeen AB15 4EJ
☎ /🖰 (01224) 648408
This large Victorian granite house, set in prize-winning gardens, offers spacious and tasteful *en suite* accommodation. Breakfasts can be either full cooked versions or a buffet of cereals, fruit and yoghurts.
£ *All year (phone to check at Christmas and New Year)*

The Marcliffe at Pitfodels
North Deeside Road, Aberdeen AB15 9YA
☎ (01224) 861000
🖰 (01224) 868860
🖰 *www.marcliffe.com*
Stylish, business-oriented hotel on the leafy outskirts of Aberdeen. Comfortable, spacious bedrooms. The split-level conservatory restaurant is less formal than the grandly traditional Invery Room; contemporary, locally sourced food is served.
£££ *All year*

ABOYNE
Hazlehurst Lodge
Ballater Road, Aboyne AB34 5HY
☎ (01339) 886921
🖰 (01339) 886660
This restaurant-with-rooms doubles as an art and crafts gallery. The interior of this converted Victorian coachman's lodge is minimalist, stylish and clean-cut. Imaginative food combines simple Scottish fare with European style.
££ *All year*

Struan Hall
Ballater Road, Aboyne AB34 5HY
☎ /🖰 (01339) 887241
Imposing detached house in two acres of garden with three well-furnished *en suite* bedrooms. Guests can use a roomy lounge and a drying room; the dining-room overlooks the front garden.
£ *Mar to Oct*

AULDEARN
Boath House
Auldearn, Nairn IV12 5TE
☎ (01667) 454896
🖰 (01667) 455469
🖰 *www.boath-house.com*
This lovely Regency house, rescued from dereliction, offers stylish bedrooms with antique French beds. Stately public rooms, a basement health and beauty

spa, a modern art exhibition, and
excellent food.
*£££ Closed 3 weeks from end Jan (See
Where to Eat)*

BALLATER
Balgonie Country House
Braemar Place, Ballater AB35 5NQ
☎ /🖷 (01339) 755482
Arts and Crafts house with Mackintosh-
style stained-glass panels and lovely
views. The interior is comfortable and
unpretentious with modern bedrooms.
Classic four-course dinners have choices
at all but the fish stage.
*££ Closed mid-Jan to mid-Feb (See Where
to Eat)*

BANCHORY
The Old West Manse
71 Station Road, Banchory AB31 5UD
☎ /🖷 (01330) 822202
Attractive cream-painted former manse
in mature gardens with views over the
Dee Valley. The three comfortable
bedrooms are on the ground floor with
the living rooms above. Quality food
uses local produce where possible.
£ All year

BANFF
Eden House
By Banff AB45 3NT
☎ (01261) 821282
🖷 (01261) 821283
Tennis and a games room with billiards
attract guests in this smart Georgian
house overlooking the Deveron Valley.
Most bedrooms are *en suite*; guests may
bring their own wine at dinner.
£££ All year exc Christmas .

Links Cottage
Inverboyndie, Banff AB45 2JJ
☎ /🖷 (01261) 812223
200-year-old one-storey cottage,
rescued from neglect. Three large
bedrooms in the Victorian wing have
original pine panelling and fitted
cupboards. Breakfast is served in a
separate dining-room.
£ Mar to Nov

ELGIN
The Croft
10 Institution Road, Elgin IV30 1QX
☎ /🖷 (01343) 546004
Large, elegant guesthouse in attractive
gardens with three comfortable and
spacious bedrooms. Guests have use of a
roomy lounge; packed lunches can be
provided.
£ All year

FYVIE
Meikle Camaloun
Fyvie AB53 8JY
☎ /🖷 (01651) 891319
A large stone farmhouse with a well-
tended garden. The two bedrooms are
light and bright, one *en suite* and the
other with private bathroom; traditional
breakfasts are served. Guests can enjoy a
pleasant lounge as well as the garden.
£ All year exc Christmas

GARTLY
Faich-Hill Farmhouse
Gartly AB54 4RR
☎ (01466) 720240
Remote granite bed and breakfast
offering two comfortable bedrooms. The
twin is *en suite* and the double has sole

use of a private bathroom. Cosy sitting room.

£ May to Oct

KEITH
The Haughs
The Haughs, Keith AB55 6QN
☎ /📠 (01542) 882238
The Haughs, on a working farm, dates from 1614. All the large bedrooms have private bathroom facilities. Guests are welcome to bring their own wine to dinners served in the conservatory-style dining-room.

£ Easter to Oct

KILDRUMMY
Kildrummy Castle Hotel
Kildrummy, Alford AB33 8RA
☎ (01975) 571288
📠 (01975) 571345
🖳 www.kildrummycastlehotel.co.uk
Classic country-house hotel by an atmospheric ruined castle. The nineteenth-century castellated baronial hotel is set in superb gardens; guests have 'proper sheets, large comfortable rooms and clean smart bathrooms'.

Menus are a mix of Scottish and European dishes.

£££ Closed Jan

NAIRN
Greenlawns
13 Seafield Street, Nairn IV12 4HG
☎ /📠 (01667) 452738
This large Victorian detached house is bright with hanging baskets and climbers. The eight *en suite* bedrooms are clean and comfortable; three are suitable for wheelchair users. Dinner is available if booked by 2pm.

£ All year exc Christmas

OLDMELDRUM
Cromlet Hill
South Road, Oldmeldrum AB51 0AB
☎ (01651) 872315
📠 (01651) 872164
A handsome white-painted Georgian mansion with a large secluded garden. Three well-decorated, spacious *en suite* bedrooms; communal rooms include a conservatory. Breakfast is served at one large table.

£ All year exc Christmas

WHERE TO EAT

ABERDEEN
Silver Darling
Pocra Quay, North Pier, Aberdeen AB11 5DQ
☎ /📠 (01224) 576229
This bright, cheerful first-floor dining-room has panoramic views of the harbour entrance, the North Sea and Aberdeen foreshore. Barbecued seafood from the market is a speciality,

served in restrained classic dishes and more experimental ones.

Sun–Fri L 12–2, all week D 7–9.30; closed Sun Oct to April, 2 weeks Christmas/New Year (exc 31 Dec)

ABOYNE
White Cottage
Dess, Aboyne AB34 5BP
☎ /📠 (013398) 86265

The Cottage is a restaurant-with-a-room (just the one). Dinner can be served in a small conservatory extension with a glass-fronted stove and garden view. Well-sourced ingredients in traditional, flavourful dishes.

Tue–Sat 11.30–2.30 and 7–9; closed 4 days Christmas

ARCHIESTOWN
Archiestown Hotel
Archiestown AB38 7QL
☎ (01340) 810218
📠 (01340) 810239
Eccentric 'junk shop' interiors provide an informal background. A daily-changing blackboard menu specialises in seafood; dishes use first-class produce, served simply in large portions. Standard desserts and a well-chosen short wine list.

All week 12.30–1.45 and 7–8.45; closed 1 Oct to 9 Feb

AULDEARN
Boath House
Auldearn IV12 5LE
☎ (01667) 454896
📠 (01667) 455469
✓ www.boath-house.com
The dining-room of this Georgian mansion overlooks lawns and an ornamental lake. A well-balanced menu makes good use of locally sourced ingredients in flavoursome dishes and desserts. Large wine list, reasonably priced.

Thur–Sun L 12.30–2, Wed–Sun D 7–9 (See Where to Stay)

BALLATER
Balgonie Country House
Braemar Place, Ballater AB35 5NQ
☎ /📠 (01339) 755482

Edwardian house in four acres, furnished period-style. The pastel dining-room offers a straightforward four-course dinner menu based on fine ingredients. Herbed sauces enhance flavours, and desserts are rich.

All week 12.30–2 (reservations only), 7–9; closed 5 Jan to 10 Feb (See Where to Stay)

Darroch Learg
Braemar Road, Ballater AB35 5UX
☎ (01339) 755443
📠 (01339) 755252
✓ www.darroch-learg.demon.co.uk
Views from this stylish conservatory-style dining-room extend over Ballater and Deeside. Three courses at dinner, each with half a dozen choices. Well-sourced ingredients in the expertly cooked, classic European food.

All week 12.30–2, 7–9; closed Christmas, Jan (open New Year)

Green Inn
9 Victoria Road, Ballater AB35 5QQ
☎ /📠 (01339) 755701
Big cottagey dining-room offering a traditional Scottish menu with contemporary touches. Unexpected treatments of classic dishes made with good, locally sourced ingredients.

All week D only 7–9; closed 2 weeks Oct, Sun and Mon Oct to Mar

NAIRN
Clifton House
Viewfield Street, Nairn IV12 4HW
☎ (01667) 453119
📠 (01667) 452836
Theatrical Victorian town house; dramatic colours extend from the drawing room. The dinner menu utilises fresh

ingredients in a combination of trendy, complex flavours and simpler dishes.
All week 12.30–1 and 7.30–9.30; closed mid-Dec to mid-Jan

NETHERLEY
Lairhillock Inn
Netherley AB39 3QS
☎ (01569) 730001
The conservatory with its fine views caters for families, and there is a snug plus a formal restaurant with a gallery. Food is international and versatile. Traditional, locally sourced Scottish food is served in unusual dishes, cooked to order.
12–2.30 and 5–11 (midnight Fri and Sat), Sun 12–2.30 and 6.30–11; bar food

12–1.45 and 6–9.15 (10 Fri and Sat); restaurant Sun L 12–1.45, all week D 7–9; closed 25 and 26 Dec, 1 and 2 Jan

STONEHAVEN
Tolbooth
Old Pier, Stonehaven AB39 2JU
☎ /📠 (01569) 762287
Attractive dining-room above the harbour, with a free-ranging 'eat what you like in the order you like it' menu. The strength is fresh native seafood supplemented with exotic imports; dishes range from the simple and homely to the gourmet.
Tue–Sat D only 6–9.30; closed 3 weeks after Christmas, 1 week Oct

The Central and Northern Highlands

Urquhart Castle

- Mountainous, thinly populated countryside cut by deep glens
- Traditional holiday areas around Speyside and the Great Glen
- Inverness – capital of the Highlands
- The wilderness of central Sutherland
- Gentle, fertile country and old towns in Easter Ross
- The remote, beautiful north coast of Scotland

THE CENTRAL AND NORTHERN HIGHLANDS

At a glance

✓ Good for family holidays with emphasis on outdoor activities

✓ Excellent for extensive touring holidays

✓ Wildlife, birdwatching, fishing, hill-walking

✗ Touring involves long drives

✗ Very limited facilities in the most remote areas

The central and northern Highlands are marked by a change of scale – mountainous country becomes more extensive, roads fewer, the glens longer and the population sparser. It can be a mysterious, sometimes awesome country: wild, bleak and beautiful in fine weather, dismal in the rain. Parts of this landscape are tamed – Speyside and the Great Glen bustle with holiday-makers. Parts are not – the rust-coloured bogs of Sutherland contain scarcely a house. Parts – the gentle country of Easter Ross, for example – are outposts of Lowland countryside in the middle of the Highlands.

The emptiness of the countryside is comparatively recent. The glens were once full of settlements, whose crumbled remains are marked by heaps of bracken-covered stone. The Clearances, when people were evicted from their houses to be replaced by sheep, were only a part of the long-running process of depopulation which swelled the Lowland cities and forced so many families on to the emigrant ships. Over 22,000 Scots went to Nova Scotia between 1815 and 1838; by 1840, Glasgow had absorbed more than 30,000 Highlanders. The box on pages 388–9 covers the Clearances in more detail.

The sheep that replaced the Highlanders in the glens eventually proved equally unprofitable. The sheep farms gave way to the deer forests, and huge tracts of once-populated land became the province of the deer, the ghillie and the gentleman with the rifle. Much of the Highlands remains divided into sporting estates covering several thousand acres, and the big Edwardian shooting-lodges still stand, surrounded by sheltering trees and game larders. The subject of land ownership in the Highlands is a touchy one, and you get drawn into an argument about it at your peril.

Another characteristic building of the northern Highlands is the croft house. A croft, famously defined as a piece of land surrounded by legislation, is a smallholding, the house usually ringed by a couple of fields. Few crofters have enough land from which to make a full-time living, and most supplement their income by fishing, forestry or from tourism.

Key web sites

www.host.co.uk The area tourist board's website. Covers a massive area, but has some useful information and links

www.hi-ways.org A really useful collection of links to community web sites and public services

---

Good bases in the Central and Northern Highlands

Aviemore, Kingussie and Newtonmore

✓ *Small towns, well-located for exploring Speyside and the Cairngorm mountains*
✓ *Good range of accommodation*
✓ *Plentiful outdoor activities*

These three small towns by the River Spey are well used to summer tourists and to skiers. Since the development of Aviemore as a 1960s purpose-built resort, a wide range of sights and activities has sprung up. Aviemore badly needs redevelopment, but has ample accommodation. Kingussie and Newtonmore are traditional, quieter places.

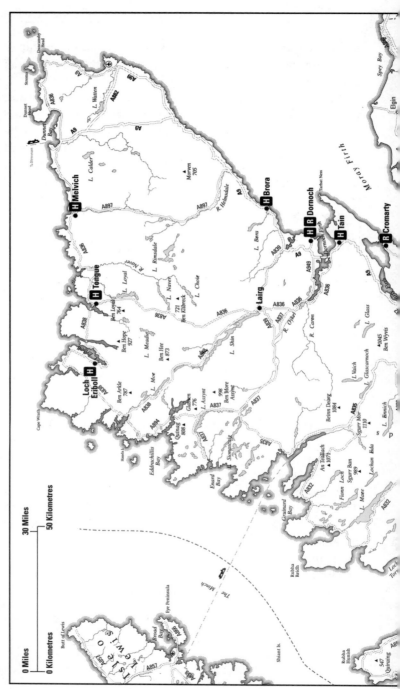

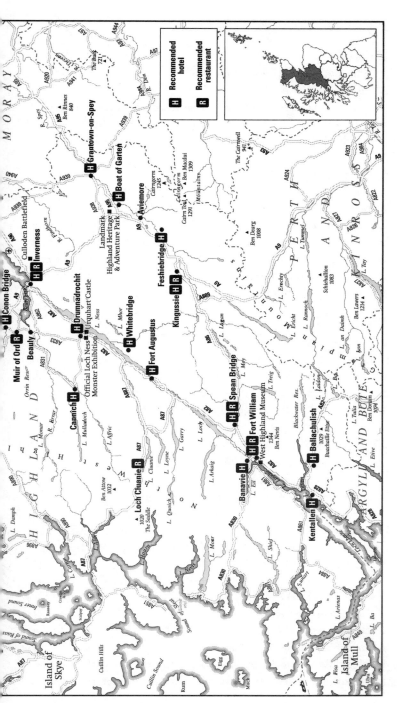

MORAY

Recommended hotel ⊞

Recommended restaurant ℞

The Buck 721

Ben Rinnes 840

R. Spey

A95 A920 A941

A97

A939

A941

Grantown-on-Spey ⊞

A95

Boat of Garten ⊞

A939

Aviemore ⊞

A9

A938

Landmark Highland Heritage ■ & Adventure Park

Cairngorm 1245

Coylum ▲ Ben Macdui 1309

Cairn Toul 1291

Meigstalm

A9

A86

Feshiebridge ⊞

Culloden Battlefield

Inverness ■

⊞ ℞ Conon Bridge

A9

R. Findhorn

A862

Drumnadrochit ⊞

Urquhart Castle ■

L. Mhor

L. Ness

Official Loch Ness ■ Monster Exhibition

Muir of Ord ⊞ ℞

Beauly ●

A862

A831 A833

Orrin Res.

R. Beauly

R. Farrar

Cannich ⊞

L. Mullardoch

L. Affric

R. Glass

L. Beinn L. Monar

H I G H L A N D

Ben Attow 1032

Loch Cluanie ℞

A87

L. Cluanie

The Saddle 1020

L. Loyne

L. Quoich

L. Garry

L. Arkaig

Whitebridge ⊞

Fort Augustus ⊞

A82

A887

Ben Dearg 1008

L. Erechy

L. an Daimh

L. Tummel

A9

A924

P E R T H

Kingussie ⊞ ℞

A889

A86

Schiehallion 1083

L. Rannoch

L. Ericht

Ben Lawers 1214 ▲

A9

A827

K I N R O S S

A923 A984

A9

A93

A826

L. Tay

A827

Spean Bridge ⊞ ℞

A86

L. Lochy

L. Laggan

L. Treig

L. Moy

Laidon

A82

A86

Fort William ⊞ ℞

West Highland Museum ■

Ben Nevis 1344 ▲

Banavie ⊞

L. Eil

A830

A82

A861

Blackwater Res.

L. an Daimh

Loch Ossian

Ballachulish ⊞ ●

A82

Buachaille Etive

L. Tulla

Ben Doran 1074 ▲

Kentallen ⊞

A828

A861

L. Linnhe

L. Shiel

L. Sunart

A884

L. Shiel

L. Arienas

A K G Y L L A N D B U T E

L. Creran

L. Etive

L. Ba

A849

Island of Mull

Ulva

Muck

Eigg

Rum

Cuillin Sound

Island of Skye

Sound of Sleat

Sound of Eigg

Inner Sound

Sound of Raasay

Raasay

Scalpay

Cuillin Hills

A87

A890

A896

L. Carron

L. Damph

L. Kishorn

Beauly

✓ *Attractive small town close to Inverness*
✗ *Limited accommodation*

This very small, red sandstone town to the west of Inverness is ideal if you do not want to get bogged down in the city itself, and well sited for exploration of Glen Affric and Easter Ross.

Cromarty

✓ *Very pretty ancient burgh*
✗ *Isolated position*

Marooned on the tip of the Black Isle, Cromarty is a handsome town which has avoided the worst effects of tourism, while managing to provide a choice of places to stay. It is too far away from the through-routes to be a sensible centre for touring, but would be ideal for a few days in a small town by the sea.

Dornoch

✓ *Good for golfers and beach-lovers*

This is a very pretty small town, famous for its golf course and for its good sands. The old cathedral in its centre is beautiful. Dornoch is a seaside resort of a quiet and restrained kind, perfect in good weather, and not badly placed for touring either.

Durness

✓ *Remote, wild beaches*
✓ *Perfect for those who really want to escape*
✗ *About as far from the bright lights as you can get*
✗ *Extremely lengthy drives needed to get anywhere else*

The most north-westerly community in Scotland, blessed with relatively fertile land and deserted, sandy beaches. The wilderness of Sutherland laps all around.

Fort William

✓ *Wide range of accommodation*
✓ *Beautiful country within easy reach*
✗ *Not an inspiring town, and can be very wet*

The excellence of the location and the proximity of first-class mountain country go some way to counteract this town's fundamental dreariness. There is a large range of guesthouse accommodation and reasonable facilities.

Grantown-on-Spey

✓ *Good for exploring the Spey valley*
✓ *Walks*

Grantown is sedate and Victorian in tone, elegant in layout and with easy communications up and down the River Spey. It has a number of solid hotels.

FORT WILLIAM AND THE GREAT GLEN

The Great Glen, which contains the renowned Loch Ness in its depths, runs from Fort William in the south-west to Inverness in the north-east. Mountainous country rises on either side, with long, beautiful glens stretching to the west. Britain's highest mountain, Ben Nevis, looms above Fort William, with the gloomy heights and depths of Glen Coe to the south.

Top sights

Official Loch Ness Monster Exhibition Centre (Drumnadrochit)

✓ *Good, modern objective exhibition*

Do not be put off by the endless 'Nessie' souvenirs which infest Drumnadrochit. This exhibition is dispassionate and well presented. It is a walk-through audio-visual experience – rooms come to life in turn, with lights and commentary to highlight the photographs, statistics and scientific gadgets used in the hunt for the monster. A lot of money has been spent to this end – a whole fleet of boats making a sonar trawl, for example – but nothing has been proved. While the technology is impressive, it seems even more impressive that all the electronic wizardry has been unable to pierce the murky depths of Loch Ness precisely enough to reveal more (or less) than a few ambiguous traces. *[Easter–May, 9.30–5.30; June to Sept, 9.30–6.30, July and Aug, 9–8.30; Oct 9.30–6; Nov to Easter, 10–4; ☎ (01456) 450573; ⁀🖳 www.lochness.co.uk]*

The Loch Ness monster

The first recorded mention of a monster in the Loch Ness area is by St Columba's biographer, way back in 565 AD. He describes the Saint's encounter with a giant beast in a river, clearly the River Ness, but does not mention the Loch.

The modern craze for the monster dates only from 1933, when the local newspaper, the *Inverness Courier*, described the sighting of an unknown creature by the loch. The story was taken up by the national press, and has refused to die ever since. Many of the best-known photographs have turned out to be fakes, or to be photographs of boats or waves, but there are also plenty of eyewitness accounts by ordinary people with no obvious reason to make things up.

Scientific investigations have included the use of sonar and of underwater cameras, but, so far, the monster has remained elusive. A whole branch of the tourist industry now depends on Nessie for its existence. The best collection of dispassionate information on the web is at ⁀🖳 www.ness-monster.com

---

Urquhart Castle (south of Drumnadrochit)

✓ *Old ruin in good setting*

This ruined fortress on the bank of Loch Ness is an enduringly popular sight. The castle itself is actually fairly boring, for much has been destroyed over the centuries. However, the setting is magnificent, for the ruin stands on a promontory jutting into the loch, and its walls drop sheer into the water. This stretch of the loch is where numerous sightings of the monster have been made, so the walls are manned by hopeful monster-gazers. To cope with the crowds, Historic Scotland was building a new car park and visitor centre at the time of writing. *[HS; Apr to Sept, daily 9.30–6.30; Oct to Mar, daily 9.30–4.30; ☎ (01456) 450551; ⁀🖳 www.aboutscotland.com/ness/urquhart]*

West Highland Museum (Fort William)

✓ *Fascinating small museum*

This is an excellent museum – serious, modest, and deliberately rather old-fashioned. The Jacobite section's star offering is a secret portrait of Charles Edward Stuart, which looks like a splodge of paint until you hold a curved mirror to it. There are also many local stories, including one describing the first ascent of Ben Nevis by car in 1911.

[June to Sept, Mon–Sat 10–5; also Suns in July and Aug, 2–5; Oct to May, Mon–Sat 10–4; ☎ *(01397) 702169]*

Best scenery and local sights

Glen Coe

At the head of Glen Coe stands one of Scotland's best-known mountains, Buachaille Etive Mor, the Great Shepherd of Etive. It is a shapely triangle of precipitous rock, gleaming with ice in winter, pearly grey in summer, which stands like a lighthouse on the western extremity of Rannoch Moor.

Behind it the road begins to drop into Glen Coe. The glen is famous for its notorious massacre, which, unlike the many massacres which took place in the ceaseless feuds between clans, was inspired by politics. It is this, and the abuse of hospitality that went with it, that has made it notorious.

The road runs parallel with the jagged height of the Aonach Eagach ridge on one side and passes the three massive buttresses of Bidean nam Bian, known as the Three Sisters, on the other. When cloud hangs on the tops and the buttresses are glistening with rain, Glen Coe is at its most sinister and oppressive. *[* 🖳 *www.glencoe-scotland.co.uk]*

Excursion to Glen Etive Many drivers racing down Glen Coe miss the road down Glen Etive. It leads nowhere, but the glen is greener, brighter and less threatening than Glen Coe. The narrow road winds beside the River Etive down to a lonely pier at the head of the loch. There are plenty of grassy spaces for picnics (though beware midges).

Glencoe and North Lorn Folk Museum Exhibits of Highland life in a clump of old thatched cottages in Glencoe village. *[Easter and May to Sept, Mon–Sat 10–5;* ☎ *(01855) 811664]*

Glen Coe Visitor Centre At the foot of the Glen, the National Trust for Scotland's visitor centre is a good stopping point, and also an excellent place to learn about the local history and environment. There are multi-media programmes about the massacre, displays on the history of mountaineering, and much information about local wildlife. *[Mar to Apr and Sept to Oct, daily 10–5; May to Aug, daily 9.30–5.30;* ☎ *(01855) 811307]*

Highland Mysteryworld An indoor purpose-built attraction which uses actors and multi-media displays to bring some of the gory myths and legends of the area to life. Good for a wet day. *[Mar to Oct, daily 10–4.30;* ☎ *(01855) 811660;* 🖳 *www.freedomglen.co.uk/mworld.html]*

Suggested walk Most of the Glen Coe mountains are the province of the experienced hill-walker only, while a summer

---

The Glen Coe massacre

In the 'Glorious Revolution' of 1688, the Catholic James VII of Scotland and II of England fled the country to avoid being deposed. The English Parliament offered the crown of England to the Protestant William of Orange. The Scots, after some hesitation, offered the Scottish crown too. The rising in support of James, started by Graham of Claverhouse (Bonnie Dundee), petered out after Dundee's death at the Battle of Killiecrankie (see pages 269–70) but certain clans remained in opposition. All chiefs were required to take an oath of loyalty to King William by 1 January 1692, but it was not until the last minute that the chief of the MacDonalds of Glen Coe went to sign at Fort William. No one there was authorised to receive his oath, and he had to go to Inveraray, which put him technically in breach of the deadline.

climb into the **Lost Valley** of Coire Gabhail is demanding but less dangerous. This hanging valley between two of the Three Sisters is approached by a steep path up from the River Coe, which winds among great tangles of boulders and trees. The open expanse at the top comes as a welcome surprise after the constricted path; on a still day, this is a sheltered spot, with only echoes from the surrounding cliffs to disturb the peace. [*via www.b-mercer.demon.co.uk*]

Glen Nevis

Just south of Fort Willam, this narrow glen traverses the southern flank of Ben Nevis. This close to Fort William, the glen sees quite a lot of activity, including the Glen Nevis water race (August) when a host of airbeds and other inflatables rush down the torrent at the bottom of the glen. *Braveheart* was mostly filmed in the glen, and the car park at the foot is named after the film. [*www.fort-william.net*]

Glen Nevis Centre A useful visitor centre with lots of information on history, geology, flora and fauna, together with

---

The purpose of the orders which were thereafter issued to Campbell of Glenlyon, telling him to 'fall upon the Rebells, the McDonalds of Glenco, and putt all to the sword under seventy' was simply *pour encourager les autres*. The orders reached Campbell on 12 February 1692, after he and his 128 men had been billeted on the MacDonalds for two weeks, and the massacre began at five the following morning. Some 40 MacDonalds were slain.

Queen Victoria piously hoped that King William had known nothing about it. This seems unlikely, although the chief agent in the massacre was Sir John Dalrymple, Master of Stair. There was an inquiry, but although the Scottish parliament agreed that the killing had been murder, Stair suffered only dismissal and the involvement of King William was glossed over.

ranger-led walks in summer. *[Easter to mid-May and Oct, daily 9–5; mid-May to Sept, daily 9–6;* ☎ *(01397) 705922]*

Suggested walk The best walk in the glen is along the path which follows the river through its gorge. Two magnificent waterfalls are to be seen. The path is well-laid-out and not very difficult.

Rannoch Moor

From Tyndrum the A82 to Fort William runs north-west into the hills, flanked by the scree-littered cone of Ben Dorain. Across the expanse of Loch Tulla you look at the mountains which run down the south-eastern side of Glen Etive. Here, as you approach the West Highlands, there is a stepping up in the scale of grandeur and roughness of the scenery.

Rannoch Moor is a huge, watery desolation. The network of small burns and lochans filling a hollow among the hills was a lake of ice as recently as 10,000 years ago. Now it is Scottish bog at its most uncompromising; walking here without a compass in bad conditions is potentially lethal. Great stumps jutting from the peat hags show that this area, like so much of what is now treeless wilderness, once carried a forest.

Rannoch Moor is best seen from the train. Between 2,000 and 5,000 men took almost five years to build the railway which crosses the very heart of the wilderness – it runs for miles without sight of house or road. Corrour Station, near the foot of Loch Ossian, lies entirely on its own – you can walk from here back to Rannoch Station.

The westward glens

Glen More, also known as Glen Albyn or the Great Glen, is the remarkable geological fault which almost severs Scotland. Running from Loch Linnhie in the south-west to Inverness in the north-east, this ruler-straight declivity is filled by deep lochs, linked by Telford's Caledonian Canal. The Great Glen is too monotonous to be called beautiful, but the glens which lead westward from it are a different matter. Exploring the narrow dead-end roads leading up them is rewarding, if time-consuming, for the scenery here is on a big scale.

Glen Affric Despite hydroelectric works, Glen Affric has that particular combination of water, hillside and ancient pine forest which is unmatchable on a fine day. The road up is narrow and winding, but there are parking places, often with walks striking off from them into the old pine woods. Dog Fall is a popular spot – it got its name after a shepherd tried to dispose of his old dog here, but was later woken by her pathetic scratching at his door. Remorse overcame him and he allowed her to live out her days in peace. Loch Affric has been left in its natural state, and is a suitably beautiful climax to the drive.

Glen Cannich The road up Glen Urquhart to the modern village of Cannich is the quickest way into this glen and neighbouring Glen Affric. Glen Cannich is more enclosed and wilder than Glen Affric, the road up it winding over hummocks of rough ground and through woods of birch and alder to arrive at the dam, behind which toss the waters of Loch Mullardoch. You are almost certain to see deer somewhere on the way.

Loch Arkaig An attractive deserted road runs along the northern shore of this loch, with occasional patches of forestry. Scenes from *Rob Roy* were filmed here.

Loch Quoich The road here is recommended for its isolation and its views of distant mountains. It eventually brings you to Kinloch Hourn, where you have the satisfaction of being on the edge of nowhere before making the 21-mile return trip. A shorter expedition involves taking the A87 up to **Loch Cluanie** and returning down Glen Moriston. A viewpoint on the way up allows you a marvellous panorama of Loch Garry and the hills beyond. A memorial beside the A887 commemorates Roderick Mackenzie, who drew pursuit away from Prince Charles Edward Stuart after Culloden and was shot in mistake for him.

Strathfarrar is the northernmost of the glens, accessible only on foot. It is a long 14-mile plod to Loch Monar at the top.

The life of the Highland clans

Before the coming of the sheep or the shooting-lodge, Highland life, deep in the mountains, centred around the extended family — the clan. The chieftain was father to his clansmen, possessing a power over them verging on the absolute, but with an equally absolute responsibility for their welfare. Where the hierarchies of Lowland society were defined by rank or wealth, the clansman defined himself by his genealogy. He might acknowledge a difference in seniority to others in his clan, but none in quality.

The truth of what clan life was like has become so obscured by romance that it is difficult to gain a clear picture. It was certainly bloody: feuds between clans were continuous, and the 'tail' of fighting men that a chieftain could raise was the most important measure of his power. Life was also pastoral, revolving around the rearing of black cattle, but there was always poverty, and raiding the neighbouring clan or joining a Lowland struggle in the hope of plunder were popular ways of relieving it. The clansman was always his own man, and one of the frustrations of generals from Montrose to Prince Charles Edward was the tendency of their Highland allies to return home when they had amassed enough loot or when it was time for the harvest.

Highland culture was, and in a few places still is, subtler than the bagpipes-and-Highland-games spectacular which is happily thrust at tourists. The history of the clan was in the custody of bards who transmitted it orally from one generation to the next, and of the piper whose duty it was to inspire the clan to battle or recall its dead in sonorous laments. Before the Battle of Culloden in 1746 there were few outsiders to record this Gaelic culture, and afterwards its mainspring had been broken. It lives on in the work of modern Gaelic poets, of whom Sorley Maclean is the most renowned, in the expertise of pipers, and in the festivals of song and music called 'Mods'.

After two centuries of emigration, the clans are now dispersed in a worldwide diaspora. Yet beneath the fashion for clan gatherings, clan museums, clan tartans, or tracing ancestors — which a cynic may see as an attempt to glue together something which is irrevocably broken — there are echoes of old loyalties which refuse to die away.

Towns and villages to explore

Drumnadrochit

If you are not put off by the traffic and the model Nessies which fill the place, Drumnadrochit is excellently situated for exploring Loch Ness, Inverness, and the glens of Cannich and Affric. The main village stands at the head of a sheltered inlet of Loch Ness but scattered houses extend up Glen Urquhart, which rises gently behind.

Corrimony Chambered Cairn in Glen Urquhart is a prehistoric burial mound, surrounded by 11 standing stones. A passage, part of which is still roofed, leads to the central chamber [☎ *0131-668 8800*].

Fort Augustus

The original fort at the foot of Loch Ness was built after the Jacobite rising of 1715 and named after William Augustus, Duke of Cumberland – later to be called 'Butcher' after the Battle of Culloden. What remains of the fort is incorporated into the buildings of the Victorian abbey (scheduled to re-open to the public at the time of writing), which has a beautiful lochside setting.

Try an excursion up **East Loch Ness**. Drive up the B852 (the old military road) on the east bank of Loch Ness, which is less traffic-ridden than the main road. At Foyers the waterfall used to be a great draw and was praised by Burns, but now loses much of its water to hydro-electricity. The narrow gorge at Inverfarigaig is another good stopping point. Return on the B851, through Clan Fraser territory, where there is pretty, deserted scenery.

Fort William

Squashed between Loch Linnhe and the mass of Ben Nevis, Fort William's location at the crossroads of the only through-routes in this part of the world, together with its easy access to Glen Nevis and Loch Ness, has turned the town from a military outpost into a holiday resort.

Fort William is neither attractive nor particularly historic, and is often drenching wet into the bargain. Even so, the gift shops and tea-rooms do a thriving trade in summer, while model Nessies of every shape and size line the shop windows. Short of Oban, Inverness, Aviemore or Portree, you will not find anywhere else with as many shops or so much choice of places to stay or eat. Look up information about the town at ✆ *www.fort-william.net*

Several good excursions from Fort William are to be had. Seven miles north of town, the slopes of Aonach Mor are a winter playground for skiers. The cable cars of the **Nevis Range Gondolas** will carry you up to the high summits with no effort. If the weather is clear, the views are magnificent *[daily 10–5 (July and Aug, 10–7);* ☎ *(01397) 705825]*.

Glen Roy (off the A86, east of Spean Bridge) is an otherwise ordinary, lonely glen which has been made famous by the 'Parallel Roads of Glen Roy', a geological freak which you see clearly as the road turns into the upper glen. Three level stripes follow the contours of the hills about 600 feet above the floor of the glen, looking exactly as if someone had carved roads in the side of the mountains. These were once the shorelines of the deep loch that filled Glen Roy at the end of the last Ice Age; the water was unable to escape because of an ice dam in Glen Spean. The three levels reflect different stages in the melting of the ice.

SPEYSIDE AND INVERNESS

The valley of the River Spey forms the most important north-south route in the Highlands. The main A9 road runs along its upper course, as does the railway to Inverness. To the east, the mass of the Cairngorm mountains is one of the most important wilderness areas in Scotland. Cairn Gorm itself has been developed for skiing, and the small towns by the Spey have become the bases for much holiday activity, summer and winter.

Inverness, capital of the Highlands, is a substantial town, with good all-round facilities.

Top sights

Culloden battlefield (near Inverness)

✓ *Evocative and moving site*
✓ *Well-presented background*

The ground where the 1745 Jacobite rising was snuffed out is well signposted from all the southern and eastern approaches to Inverness. The National Trust has restored Drumossie Moor to something nearing its state on 16 April 1746. With flags fluttering above the barren ground, and the wind whipping over the heather, the field of Culloden is by far the most evocative of Scotland's battlefields.

The visitor centre is the obvious starting point and has an excellent audio-visual introduction to the battle, as well as succinct displays about why the battle was fought, why the Hanoverians won, and what weapons were used on both sides. Thereafter, paths lead over the moor to the headstones which bear the names of all the clans who fought in the battle, and to the graves where over a thousand of them fell. Few of the wounded were spared, and the battle ushered in an era of savage repression, which did much to destroy the Highland way of life.

In summer there are often live historical enactments of one kind or another, which help bring the history to life. But for all that, Culloden is at its best on a day of cold sleet carried on the wind – the conditions under which the battle was fought. *[NTS; Visitor centre: daily, Feb to Mar and Nov to Dec, 10–4; Apr to Oct, 9–6; Battlefield: all year; ☎ (01463) 790607; ✆ via www.nts.org.uk]*

Landmark Highland Heritage and Adventure Park (Carrbridge)

✓ *Excellent outdoor family sight, with plenty to do*
✓ *Good exhibitions on forestry and live events*

This is a curious mixture of nature centre, theme park and showcase for the forestry industry, reflecting the somewhat haphazard nature of its growth over the years. The old 'treetop'

The battle of Culloden

The aura of tragedy which surrounds Culloden is the result of the inevitability of the Jacobite defeat. After its long and dispiriting retreat from Derby, a half-starved, under-strength army, exhausted after an abortive night march on Nairn, faced a body of disciplined troops on ground which its most experienced officer considered utterly unsuitable.

In such circumstances, the charge of the clans was a gamble almost bound to end in failure. For half an hour they had suffered under an artillery bombardment to which they were powerless to reply. The charge, when it came, was an ill-coordinated act of courage, its only chance of success being to break the opposing troops by its ferocity. At Prestonpans and Falkirk, the Hanoverians had broken; at Culloden, sustained by their artillery and by their three ranks of bayonets, they held. At times the clansmen, powerless to reach the redcoats with their broadswords, were reduced to throwing stones.

All along the line, the Jacobite front rank was thrown back – the Macdonalds on the left, Clan Chattan, Frasers, Camerons and Stewarts of Appin on the right. Hanoverian casualties were given as 50 dead; well over 1,000 of the Highland army died and Prince Charles Edward was led from the field to begin months of fugitive existence before he made his final escape to France.

The aftermath was savage – most of the wounded were killed where they lay, and the prisoners, being 'rebels', were ill-treated. But the real savagery was to come. The victorious Duke of Cumberland, recognising, perhaps rightly, that this military defeat was not enough to put an end to Jacobite dreams, resolved to make an example of the Highlands. Burnings and summary arrests were followed by the banning of Highland dress.

nature trail, an imaginatively constructed catwalk through ancient pine trees, remains at its heart, supplemented by a working sawmill, huge log-moving tractors and Clydesdale horses. There's also a log flume to keep children happy and a good play area. There are indoor attractions too, but they are much more conventional, so pick a fine day to come. *[Daily, summer 10–6 (7 mid-Jul and Aug); winter 10–5;* ☎ *(0800) 7313446;* ☞ *via www.aviemore.co.uk]*

The next best sights

Fort George (east of Inverness)

No enthusiast of military architecture should miss this completely intact example of an eighteenth-century stronghold. Fort George was started in 1748, with the aim, after Culloden, of ensuring an impregnable base in the Highlands. The result is a network of glacis, ditches, ravelins and bastions on the neck of a small peninsula jutting into the Moray Firth.

Through the gateway, the eighteenth-century barracks with their parade-ground in front look much like an upmarket housing estate. There was room here for two battalions. Some rooms have been reconstructed to show standards of accommodation in 1780 and 1868. Fort George also contains the Regimental Museum of the amalgamated Seaforth, Cameron and Gordon Highland regiments. It is filled with some fine displays. *[HS; Apr to Sept, daily 9.30–6.30; Oct to Mar, Mon–Sat 9.30–4.30, Sun 2–4.30;* ☎ *(01667) 462777]*

Highland Folk Museum (Newtonmore and Kingussie)

A split-site folk museum, with its older section in Kingussie, where the Highland life of the past is brought vividly to life. At Newtonmore, reconstructed buildings from Highland life throughout history form the centrepiece. A visit will make you see both the ingenuity of the people living in a land with few resources and uncertain climate, and the grinding poverty which so many of them endured. *[Apr/May to Oct; telephone for times ☎ (01540) 661307; ◌ www.highlandfolk.com]*

Highland Wildlife Park (near Kincraig)

Run by the Royal Zoological Society, this is a novel kind of safari park in that the animals are those which inhabit, or once inhabited, the Highlands. Deer, otter and pine marten are here, but so too are beavers and European bison. Part of the park is drive-through, part walk-through, and it is informative and sensibly organised (there is a free kennel for your dog, for example). *[Apr to Oct, 10–6; June to Aug, 10–7; Nov to Mar, 10–4; last entry 2 hrs before closing; ☎ (01540) 651270; ◌ via www.kincraig.com]*

Best scenery and local sights

Glen More

The great bowl which extends eastwards from Aviemore to the foot of Cairn Gorm is part forest park and part nature reserve (the reserve extends over much of the Cairngorm range). At its heart lies Loch Morlich, fringed by beaches of coarse granite sand. The Scots pines here form one of the largest remaining fragments of the old Caledonian forest, and are being carefully husbanded. Glen More is one of the last strongholds of the rarer species of Scottish wildlife – the capercaillie, the blackcock, the pine marten, the red squirrel and the wild cat.

Because of its proximity to the holiday towns of Speyside, there is more organised activity here than in many parts of the Highlands, but there is also plenty of room to be alone, or to get up on to the high tops of the Cairngorm mountains. A new funicular railway up Cairngorm was the subject of much controversy, but it will make an easy ascent into fine scenery for visitors on completion in December 2001.

Cairngorm Reindeer Centre The only free-range herd of reindeer in Britain can be seen by taking a guided walk up to where the animals graze on the hillside. *[Easter to Oct, tours at 11 and 2.30; Visitor Centre: 10–5;* ☎ *(01479) 861228;* 🖱 *via www.newtonmore.com]*

Glen More Visitor Centre A useful central point for those wishing to walk in the forest park. Displays, guided walks and off-road cycling are on offer. *[All year;* ☎ *(01479) 861220]*

Rothiemurchus Estate A Highland estate which has thrown itself into outdoor activities for visitors. Guided walks, landrover safaris, fishing, clay–pigeon shooting and off-road driving are all available. *[Daily 9–5.30;* ☎ *(01479) 812345;* 🖱 *www.rothiemurchus.net]*

Strathspey Steam Railway From Easter to October, a daily service under steam runs from Aviemore to Boat of Garten (an ideal way to reach the Osprey Centre). *[* ☎ *(01479) 810725;* 🖱 *via www.newtonmore.com]*

Touring routes The modern road running through Glen More exists to bring skiers to the slopes of Cairn Gorm. In summer, '**The Ski Road**' makes a worthwhile detour, both as an easy way of seeing Loch Morlich, and as a scenic route. Even if you do not wish to ascend the mountain by chairlift (or the new funicular), the road takes you high enough to enjoy excellent views back over Speyside.

The **B970 Kingussie–Aviemore** is well away from the heavy traffic of the A9. This narrow route winds through birch woods and past tiny settlements. Stop at Feshiebridge to admire the river (and walk up the track beside it) and at Jack Drake's Alpine nursery at Inshriach – a must for garden-lovers.

Walks A classically beautiful small loch in the middle of the pine forest is **Loch an Eilein**: it is easy to walk round, with relatively gentle going. In contrast, **Lairig Ghru** is a tough, full day's walk right through the heart of the Cairngorms to Linn of Dee (see page 332). The route runs through a narrow pass below some of the highest mountains in Scotland, under the shoulders of Braeriach and Ben Macdui (whose summit is haunted by a dimly perceived grey man). Full hill-walking precautions are needed for this route, which should not be attempted in bad weather.

Towns and villages to explore

Aviemore

In its heyday as Scotland's closest approach to a package resort, Aviemore had a certain buzz, and was filled with families, both winter and summer. The original 1960s buildings of the Aviemore Centre outlived their sell-by date, however, and many have been demolished, leaving the town lacking the infrastructure to match its remaining accommodation. Various schemes for regeneration are under consideration, but, at the time of writing, it is all a bit grim. As the closest base to the activities in Glen More, however, the town need not be written off as somewhere to stay. Web site details are at ☞ *www.aviemore.co.uk*

North-east of Aviemore is the **Loch Garten Osprey Centre**. The reintroduction of the Sea Eagle and Red Kite to Scotland have rather eclipsed memories of the excitement that surrounded the first breeding ospreys, whose chosen nesting site was at Loch Garten. At the centre in summer, you can see the osprey's nest in its tree top, or watch the activity in it relayed by CCTV. *[Apr to Aug, daily 10–6;* ☎ *(01479) 831694;* ☞ *via www.boatofgarten.com]*

Grantown-on-Spey

Grantown is a solid, dignified small town, a little too far from the slopes of Cairn Gorm to be able to capitalise on the skiing boom. Consequently, it has made do with its traditional clientele – those who come to fish on the Spey and those who prefer gentle walks by the river to flogging through the mountains.

Grantown is staid and Victorian in its architecture, with a large central square and a long street of shops. If you intend to explore the Spey, Grantown is better placed than Aviemore, and the immediate surroundings are more enticing. [🖱 *www.granton-on-spey.co.uk*]

Inverness

All the main routes through the Highlands pass through Inverness sooner or later, making it almost impossible to avoid. For the inhabitants of Sutherland, Caithness and the Northern Isles, Inverness is the great southern metropolis. If you come from anywhere else, you will find it a small, rather ordinary town – a bit of industry here and there, quiet residential estates and a compact centre with unexceptional shops. The banks of the River Ness where it runs through the town form the most attractive area, and a stroll here is rewarding on a fine day. The influx of summer visitors colours the streets, but Inverness can be dull off-season and pretty dead on Sundays.

The oldest houses are to be found in Church Street, notably Abertarff House, which dates from 1592. The Victorian Gothic cathedral of St Andrew is worth a glance on a wet day, while the modern Eden Court contains a theatre and gallery. Above the town rises its battlemented nineteenth-century mock castle.

The **Inverness Museum and Art Gallery** (near the castle) has a comprehensive regional collection from all over the Highlands, with a particularly good collection of silverwork *[Mon–Sat 9–7;* ☎ *(01463) 237114]*. In the castle itself, **The Castle Garrison Encounter** portrays the life of the eighteenth-century soldier with the help of actors, backed by a few exhibits. New recruits (you) are conducted through the Quartermaster's Store and are introduced to the Sergeant of the Guard and a female camp follower before being let loose in the Garrison shop. *[Mar to Nov, Mon–Sat 10.30–5.30]*

Look up details about Inverness at 🖱 *www.inverness-scotland.com*

Newtonmore and Kingussie

These two small towns are the first you come to in Speyside if you are driving over the Drumochter pass from the south. Typical of the area, they are neatly-planned villages of grey stone houses, quiet and unassuming, but within range of the Cairngorms.

Newtonmore is Macpherson territory (the clan museum is here) and also a stronghold of shinty – a game like hockey but even more vicious – which has fanatical adherents throughout the Highlands, but especially on Speyside. For details of fixtures (and the rules) see ☎ *www.shinty.com*, or look up the latest on Newtonmore at ☎ *www.newtonmore.com*

Near Kingussie stand the shattered remains of **Ruthven barracks**, built by the Hanoverians after the Jacobite rising of 1715, then taken by the Jacobites in 1746 and blown up by them after the defeat at Culloden.

You'll either love or hate **Waltzing Waters** – illuminated fountains dancing to music – but it is a popular attraction located between the two towns, good for children and perhaps a haven in wet weather *[Feb to Dec, daily; telephone for show times* ☎ *(01540) 673752].*

Loch Insh Watersports is nearby at Kincraig. Loch Insh is a broadening of the Spey, now a popular place for watersports of all kinds; the Centre here has lots of facilities and runs instruction courses. There are also dry-land activities. *[Apr to Oct, daily 8.30–5.30;* ☎ *(01540) 651272]*

NORTH OF INVERNESS

Much of Scotland north of Inverness is deserted wilderness. This is not immediately apparent on the East Coast, where the gentle district of Easter Ross is dotted with historic small towns and fertile farmland. If you head north from Lairg however, you rapidly arrive in the bog lands of Sutherland, a landscape at once bleak and beautiful; while by driving north-west, you arrive in an even wilder country, where mountains of shattered quartzite rise from a rocky landscape that is almost scraped bare of soil. Most of the small communities are clustered by the sea, not necessarily from choice, for this was one of the regions where the Highland Clearances were at their most devastating. The road along the north coast winds between tiny settlements. It is a remote and enthralling place.

Local sights

Dunrobin Castle

The only stately home north of Inverness regularly open to the public is one of the very few sights in Sutherland to be firmly on the tourist trail. The castle is a rather ponderous nineteenth-century version of a French chateau, with Scottish baronial overtones.

Dunrobin has passed through hard times since the days when the wealth of the Dukes of Sutherland drove the railway north (the Duke's private station can still be seen). The best things inside are the paintings – some fine portraits of diaphanously clad duchesses and some Canalettos. Wander down to the gardens for the best view of the castle, and go to the museum to see the very fine collection of Pictish stones (for the background on the stones, see box on pages 302–3). *[Apr/May and Oct, Mon–Sat 10.30–4.30, Sun 12–4.30; June to Sept, Mon–Sat 10.30–5.30, Sun 12–5.30;* ☎ *(01408) 633177; via www.great-house-scotland.co.uk]*

Smoo Cave (Durness)

This impressive cavern, east of Durness, is a result of the local outcrop of limestone which has allowed the water to penetrate and hollow it out. A path leads down to the entrance, out of which rushes a small burn. The cave's outer chamber is massive, and the drips fall at speed. The roar of a waterfall comes from an inner chamber, which you penetrate on a neat wooden bridge, deafened by noise and blinded by spray where the burn plunges 70 feet from the sinkhole above. If there is not too much water, a rubber inflatable will sometimes take you into a further chamber. An unusual form of grafitti is the rule here: visitors leave their messages picked out in stones on the slope in front of the cave.

Timespan Heritage Centre (Helmsdale)

An excellent heritage centre for the Helmsdale area, including material about the herring industry and the Highland Clearances. There is also the Barbara Cartland room – for the romantic novelist had a holiday home nearby. If your taste for incongruity needs further sharpening, have a snack in 'La Mirage' café in the village, where both owner and décor are cast in the Cartland mode. *[Apr to Oct, Mon–Sat 9.30–5, Sun 2–5 (2–6 in July and Aug);* ☎ *(01431) 821327;* 🖰 *www.timespan.org.uk]*

Best scenery and touring routes

Easter Ross and the Black Isle North of Inverness, three firths push inland towards the mountains, enclosing two isolated peninsulas, the so-called Black Isle and the Tain Peninsula. The countryside at the head of the firths where the Rivers Beauly, Conon and Oykel flow down from the glens is hilly and wooded. It seems a manageable, tame landscape, yet the bulk of Ben Wyvis rising above it is a reminder that you are still in the Highlands. The combination of the sea, the fertile landscape and the hills makes for very picturesque exploration, moving between the small, historic towns in this patch of coast. High spots are the sea views from the cliffs behind Cromarty on the Black Isle, the wooded country around Strathpeffer and the valleys of the Conon and the Oykel.

Touring routes The following routes are worthwhile. **Strathcarron** is not to be confused with the better-known Glen Carron to the west. This gentle valley runs down to join the Kyle of Sutherland opposite Bonar Bridge. Roads run on either side of the light, open strath, while fragments of old pine forest remain up towards its head. The combination of river and heathery scenery is very fine. In the churchyard of Croik, where the road ends, people from neighbouring Glencalvie took shelter after being evicted from their homes in May 1845. Scratched on the glass of the church windows are the graffiti which are their only memorial.

Strath Oykel Drive up the Oykel from Bonar Bridge and turn up Glen Cassley to see the Cassley Waterfall, which plunges into a rocky pool surrounded by pine trees and boulders. There will probably be salmon fishermen, up to their chests in waders, to watch for entertainment. Just beneath the falls lies an old graveyard with tombstones under the pines.

Falls of Shin The River Shin pours into the Oykel by the power station at Inveran. Take the B864 from here through Achanay Glen to visit the Falls of Shin. These form the best salmon leap in the country, where facilities include a large car park, a visitor centre and a well-maintained path down through the trees to a platform above the falls. The river plunges in a peat-coloured chute into a black pool, from which the salmon hurl themselves upwards into the force of water. An early evening in summer when there is plenty of water is said to give you the best chance of seeing them – take anti-midge precautions. *[Visitor centre: Mar to Oct, daily 10–6; Nov to Chr, weekends only 10–5;* ☎ *(01549) 402231]*

The Flow Country North of the Dornoch Firth lies Sutherland, a huge tract of the bleakest wilderness in Scotland. The west coast is a jumble of rock; the straths of the centre are empty of people and the small settlements of the east and north cling to the rough coasts. The strangest scenery is the Flow Country, in the far north-east of the area. This is a massive expanse of blanket bog, with unique flora and fauna. It can be unrelentingly bleak, or astonishingly beautiful – much depends on the weather *[☐ www.habitat.org.uk/flow].*

The best way of seeing the Flow Country without spending a day up to your knees in peat mire is to visit the RSPB's visitor centre at Forsinard *[Easter to Oct, 9–6;* ☎ *(01641) 571225],* located on the A897 north from Kinbrace (in the railway station). There is a short path out into the bog with an explanatory leaflet and occasional guided walks further afield.

Another, unsurpassable, way of seeing the Flow Country is to take the train. The railway first runs up the Strath of Kildonan, then loops eastward from Forsinard towards Wick, running over mile after mile of wilderness.

The north coast The area confronting the turbulent waters of the Pentland Firth is a remote place, and the narrow road skirting it is slow, winding and unfrequented. The steep cliffs are broken here and there by perfect beaches, and by the long fingers of sea – the Kyles of Durness and Tongue, and Loch Eriboll – that reach inland. Those who come here are rewarded by the short summer nights, the wildness of the sea and the dunes, and the relaxed pace of life in the small communities.

Loch Eriboll is a very beautiful sea loch, which you have plenty of time to admire as the road winds round it. It was here that the Norse ships gathered before sailing south to their defeat at Largs in 1263 and here, in 1945, that the remnants of the German U-boat fleet surfaced to surrender.

As you come over the rise beyond Loch Eriboll, the multi-peaked Ben Loyal lies before you, and will dominate the view henceforth.

A causeway crosses the **Kyle of Tongue**, which is pleasant when the tide is in, but very muddy when it is out. Just before you cross it, a road northwards takes you to the small township of Melness. This area of indented coastline, with a little pier, offshore rocky islets and rumours of Jacobite gold, may tempt you into staying. Tongue itself, a semi-rural town with a ruined castle rising above it, is a good alternative.

The settlement of **Bettyhill**, 12 miles east of Tongue, was established for evicted crofters at the time of the Clearances and named after the first Duchess of Sutherland. It is wind-blown, but there is beautiful seashore nearby. Part of Torrisdale Bay is a nature reserve, especially good for botanists, while Farr Bay to the east has a lovely beach. The **Strathnaver Museum** in the old church at Bettyhill is the place to absorb the history of the locality. The sections on the Clearances and on post-Clearance life are particularly strong. *[Apr to Oct, Mon–Sat 10–1 and 2–5;* ☎ *(01641) 521418]*

Towns and villages to explore

Beauly

'Quel beau lieu', Mary Queen of Scots is reputed to have said, looking at this small russet town 14 miles west of Inverness.

Beauly has a couple of hotels, an old-fashioned woollen and tweed shop (Campbell and Company) with a country-wide reputation, and a pleasant, wide main street. Information about the town is at ☏ *www.cali.co.uk/HIGHEXP/Beauly*

The remains of **Beauly Priory**, a beautiful thirteenth-century building, stand close to the centre. The windows, with fine decoration, are especially notable *[☎ (01463) 782141 for opening hours]*.

Cromarty

Out at the tip of the Black Isle Peninsula, the ancient royal burgh is still not much more than a village, but contains some of the most beautiful late eighteenth-century buildings in Scotland. Substantial red sandstone dwellings line some of the streets and old fishermen's cottages cling to the shore. You can visit a quiet little church with three separate lofts, and the restored buildings of an old rope works.

Cromarty Courthouse Museum explains the history of the town with neat displays *[Apr to Oct, daily 10–5; ☎ (01381) 600418]*. Cromarty was the birthplace of the renowned geologist and naturalist Hugh Miller, who did much of his research on the local old red sandstone cliffs. **Hugh Miller's Cottage** is now a simple museum with dislays about the man and his work *[May to Sept, Mon–Sat 11–1 and 2–5, Sun 2–5; ☎ (01381) 600245; ☏ via www.nts.org.uk]*.

A good local walk goes to **South Sutor**. This is one of the twin precipitous headlands guarding the narrow entrance to the Cromarty Firth, easily reached on a short uphill stroll from the town. From the rubble of old military emplacements here, the view stuns. Northward, white-streaked cliffs and a green sea; southward, on a clear day, the whole of the Moray coast stretching into the haze.

Dingwall

Bypassed by all the main-road traffic, Dingwall, at the head of the Cromarty Firth, is a pleasant small town, well worth stopping at. **Dingwall museum** is an excellent local museum, with a good selection of local relics, including a monstrous clock mechanism. Giant jigsaws on display keep children happy [*May to Sept, Mon–Fri 10–5;* ☎ *(01349) 865366*].

Dornoch

The town's repuation is built on golf, but as well as the golf courses, there is an excellent sandy beach. Dornoch is a handsome old burgh, with a little cruciform cathedral, greenery and flowers. Look up Dornoch at ◗ *www.dornoch.org.uk*

Dornoch Cathedral was started in 1224, and the bishop's palace rose alongside. The cathedral was burnt in 1570 during a clan feud and restored (with much butchering) by William Burn in 1835. A better restoration in 1924 has left it a very beautiful church indeed: the thirteenth-century work at the crossing – all in deep-red sandstone – is wonderful. Do not miss the gargoyles peering from the eaves. [*All year, 9–dusk;* ☎ *(01862) 810357*]

Durness

One of the most remote places on the Scottish mainland, Durness, in the far north-west of Sutherland, is blessed with beautiful beaches and an outcrop of limestone, which turns the surrounding country green. Hardy caravanners come here, drawn by the sand dunes around Faraid Head; regulars will tell you of the pleasure of swimming from Balnakeil beach with only seals for company. For more information check out ◗ *www.sangomore.co.uk*

Balnakeil Craft Village nearby is a group of vile concrete blocks, built in the days of the Cold War as an early-warning station. Later an enterprising council let them to craftspeople at peppercorn rents, and the village now thrives. It is usually marked on windy days by colourful kites, and you can buy candles, knitwear and other craftwork.

An excellent excursion is to **Cape Wrath**. Getting to the most north-westerly tip of mainland Britain is an adventure: there is no road from the south, and no bridge across the Kyle of Durness. Instead, a ferry shuttles across, connecting with a minibus on the far side (to no particular timetable). When the Kyle is too rough, the operation comes to a halt. Once across the Kyle, the minibus bumps along ten miles of deserted track – the whole of this area is a naval bombardment range – until the lighthouse at Cape Wrath comes into view. You look at the cliffs to the east and the cliffs to the south, and at the skerries of the Pentland Firth being creamed by the waves. If it rains you take shelter in the old engine room of the lighthouse among some ancient diesels. And that is it – a far cry from the tourist trappings of John o' Groats.

Fortrose and Rosemarkie

Two quiet seaside towns in the Black Isle, on either side of a headland, Chanory Point, which sticks out into the Beauly Firth. Chanonry Point is a good place to try to see the Moray Firth's school of bottle-nosed dolphins, which you can learn about at the Tourist Information Centre on the A9 two miles north of Inverness. Dolphins apart, Fortrose is a genteel-looking place, where copper beeches and yew trees stand by the fragmentary remains of the cathedral, and substantial Victorian villas with ball and spike finials on their gables line the quiet streets.

Fortrose Cathedral is a lovely early medieval building, with only the south aisle and the sacristy having survived the centuries. The warm, buttery sandstone and the simplicity of the early Gothic vaulting are exceptional.

In Rosemarkie, **Groam House Museum** has been turned into a centre for those in search of the Picts *[Easter and May to Sept, Mon–Sat 10–5, Sun 2–4.30; Oct to Apr, weekends only 2–4;* ☎ *(01381) 620961]*. There is a wonderful Pictish symbol stone and a good deal of information. You will also find out about the Brahan Seer, a famous local prophet who came to a sticky end in a barrel of boiling tar on Chanory Point.

Portmahomack

The little village lies right out on the tip of the Tain Peninsula, and is one of the oldest planned villages in Scotland, dating from the early eighteenth century. It has become a tiny seaside resort with a little golf course, a semicircle of sand, some rocks to climb over and a couple of streets of cottages. On a fine day, it is perfect. The old church here has a slightly oriental-looking dome instead of a spire – it was possibly once used as a lighthouse.

Strathpeffer

Strathpeffer is said to be Scotland's answer to Bavarian mountain resorts. Its outcrop of Germanic-looking hotels and villas denotes that the place was once a spa, with a branch railway line from Dingwall. You can still sample the waters. In keeping with the spa atmosphere there are plenty of undemanding walks in the surrounding countryside. One such leads to the Eagle Stone, a Pictish monument on the outskirts

---

The Highland Clearances

'… the entire population were then compressed into a space of three thousand acres of the most barren land in the parish, and the remaining one hundred and thirty thousand acres were divided among six sheep farmers.' (Evidence to the Napier Commission, 1883)

There are few corners of Scottish history as emotionally and politically charged as the Clearances. Throughout the nineteenth century, landlords evicted Highland tenants from their homes, replacing the pattern of marginal smallholdings with extensive sheep farms. It was not until 1886, in the face of growing civil disobedience such as the Battle of the Braes on Skye, that the Napier Commission's report resulted in the passing of the Crofting Act. This gave crofters security of tenure and brought the Clearances to an end, but did nothing to restore land already cleared.

The methods of eviction were often harsh, in some cases involving violence, and the burning of croft houses. Some of those evicted from their homes were resettled by the sea to work in the kelp industry, to take up fishing, or to try to wrest a new living from even more marginal land. But many thousands more emigrated. The Clearances were the most significant factor in the depopulation of the Highlands, but not the only one. Not every ruin you see has an eviction behind it.

---

of the town. It is said that ships will moor to it if it falls three times. It has fallen twice so far.

In the old station buildings, the small **Highland Museum of Childhood** throws a particular light on the life led by Highland children in past times. Toys, games and dress are all distinct. *[end Mar to Oct, Mon–Sat 10–5, Sun 1–5; July and Aug, Mon–Fri 10–7, Sat 10–5, Sun 2–5;* ☎ *(01997) 421031]*

The left-wing view of the Clearances is to see them as part of a capitalist drive to maximise gain at the expense of the people. Much the best popular expression of this interpretation remains John McGrath's 1973 play *The Cheviot, the Stag and the Black, Black Oil.* The right-wing view sees the Clearances as an unnecessarily harsh but inevitable process, justified at the time by the fashionable theory of political economy (satirised by Dickens in *Hard Times*) and in retrospect by the success of many of the emigrants' descendants. The view today's visitor gets is most likely to be the fashionable 'heritage' approach to the topic, which concentrates clearly on the dispersed communities and their lifestyle, but is apt to simplify the underlying issues.

The first Duke of Sutherland is a key figure in the demonology of the Clearances. Sir Ian Moncrieff (quoted in a guide to Dunrobin Castle) sums him up as a man willing 'to dedicate his life and fortune to making other folk do something they found desperately disagreeable for the sake of what he believed to be their future good'. On the other hand, Rob Donn, the Gaelic poet (quoted by John McGrath in *As an Fhearann*) wrote: 'First Duke of Sutherland, for your deviousness and collusion with the Lowlanders, the depths of hell are what you deserve. I would rather have Judas by my side than you'. Despite periodic pressure to demolish it, the Duke's statue still stands on Ben Vraggie; its subscribers include his 'grateful tenants'.

WHERE TO STAY

£ – under £70 per room per night, incl.
VAT

££ – £70 to £110 per room per night,
incl. VAT

£££ – over £110 per room per night,
incl. VAT

BALLACHULISH
Home Farm
Ballachulish PA39 4JX
☎ /📠 (01855) 811792
Modern farmhouse surrounded by fields
and with views of Loch Leven and Ben
Vair. Guests are welcome to roam the
farm and can use a putting green. Three
large, well-equipped bedrooms; spacious
lounge.
£ Easter to Oct

Lyn-Leven Guest House
West Laroch, Ballachulish PH49 4JP
☎ (01855) 811392
📠 (01855) 811600
Modern, one-storey guesthouse in well-
maintained gardens near Loch Leven,
with twelve en suite bedrooms. The
dining-room, with superb loch views, has
a residents' table licence and daily-
changing dinner menu.
£ All year exc Christmas

BANAVIE
Rhiw Goch
Top Lochs, Banavie, Nr Fort William
PH33 7LX
☎ /📠 (01397) 772373
All three bedrooms in this modern
detached house overlook the
Caledonian Canal and Ben Nevis. Each is

en suite and has a sitting area. The
breakfast room is on the first floor, and
the garden leads down to the towpath.
£ All year exc Christmas

BOAT OF GARTEN
Old Ferryman's House
Boat of Garten PH24 3BY
☎ /📠 (01479) 831370
This pleasant stone house offers a warm
welcome and home baking. Four
comfortable bedrooms; home-made
preserves are served at breakfast, and
evening meals are imaginative.
£ All year exc owner's holidays

BRORA
Tigh Fada
18 Golf Road, Brora KW9 6QS
☎ /📠 (01408) 621332
Visitors are greeted with tea in the
welcoming lounge. Three comfortable en
suite bedrooms; extensive breakfasts
include regional specialities. The large
garden has a four-hole pitch-and-putt
and croquet green.
£ All year exc Christmas (open Nov to Mar
by arrangement only)

CANNICH
Mullardoch House
Glen Cannich, Beauly IV4 7LX
☎ /📠 (01456) 415460
Remote converted hunting lodge. There
is lovely oak panelling in this simple,
traditional and cosy small hotel with six
cheerful bedrooms. Classic four-course
dinners.
££ Closed New Year to Easter

CONON BRIDGE
Kinkell House

Easter Kinkell, Conon Bridge, Dingwall
IV7 8HY
☎ (01349) 861270
📠 (01349) 865902
🖥 www.kinkell-house.co.uk
Neat white house on a ridge above
Cromarty Firth with stunning views of
Ben Wyvis, transformed into a
surprisingly spacious and immaculate
hotel. Three lounges and smart, cottagey
bedrooms. Confidently cooked four-
course dinners.
£££ All year

DORNOCH
Highfield

Evelix Road, Dornoch IV25 3HR
☎ (01862) 810909
📠 (01862) 811605
🖥 www.highfieldhouse.co.uk
Set in beautifully maintained lawns and
overlooking Dornoch Firth, this
guesthouse has three attractive en suite
bedrooms. Public rooms include a
breakfast room, sunny conservatory and
sitting room. Hearty and varied
breakfasts.
£ All year exc Christmas

DRUMNADROCHIT
Glenkirk

Drumnadrochit, Inverness IV63 6TZ
☎/📠 (01456) 450802
Converted former church with three
pleasant en suite bedrooms. Children
and babies welcome; packed lunches can
be provided.
£ Mar to mid-Dec

Polmaily House

Drumnadrochit, Inverness IV63 6XT
☎ (01456) 450343
📠 (01456) 450813
Plenty of activities for children at this
friendly, comfortable hotel; some public
areas are off-limits to under-10s. The
sunny conservatory acts as daytime
lounge, bar and restaurant; the more
formal dining-room uses local
ingredients.
£££ Closed Nov to Mar exc New Year

FESHIEBRIDGE
Balcraggan House

Feshiebridge, Nr Kincraig PH21 1NG
☎ (01540) 651488
Afternoon tea greets guests at this
friendly rural bed and breakfast – a
simple, modern house with two en suite
bedrooms. Dinner served at a time to
suit guests; vegetarian options available.
£ All year

March House

Feshiebridge, Nr Kincraig PH21 1NG
☎ (01540) 651388
A modern Alpine-style house in Glen
Feshie, surrounded by tall trees. Six
simple, comfortable bedrooms (five en
suite). Breakfast is served in the large
pine conservatory; dinner can be
provided. One-night bookings are not
accepted in July and August.
£ All year exc Christmas

FORT AUGUSTUS
Old Pier House

Fort Augustus PH32 4BX
☎ (01320) 366418
📠 (01320) 366770

A warm and friendly place at the southern end of Loch Ness. The double and twin rooms are *en suite*, and the family room is suitable for self-catering. Three nights' minimum stay in July and August.

£ Apr to Oct

FORT WILLIAM
Glenlochy Guest House
Nevis Bridge, North Road, Fort William PH33 6PF

☎ (01397) 702909

Substantial 1930s building in grounds overlooking the River Nevis. Twelve bedrooms, a comfortable sitting room and drying facilities. Packed lunches can be provided.

£ All year exc Christmas

The Grange
Grange Road, Fort William PH33 6JF

☎ (01397) 705516

📠 (01397) 701595

🖰 *www.grangefortwilliam.com*

Upmarket bed and breakfast in a turreted Victorian villa above the loch. Luxurious bedrooms with lovely views; one has its own garden terrace and antique Louis XV bed. Varied breakfasts are ordered in the evening.

££ Closed Nov to Feb

Inverlochy Castle
Torlundy, Fort William PH33 6SN

☎ (01397) 702177

📠 (01397) 702953

🖰 *www.inverlochy.co.uk*

A cedar-lined drive leads to this baronial pile in landscaped grounds beneath Ben Nevis. Laid-back grandeur in magnificent public rooms is carried through to

luxurious bedrooms. Extravagant four-course dinners are served in the opulent red dining-room.

£££ Closed 3 Jan to 12 Feb (See Where to Eat)

GRANTOWN ON SPEY
Culdearn House
Woodlands Terrace, Grantown on Spey PH26 3JU

☎ (01479) 872106

📠 (01479) 873641

🖰 *www.culdearn.com*

Warm, cheerful and welcoming small hotel, with smart pastel bedrooms and an ornate drawing room. Enjoyable dinners use locally sourced produce; try a wide range of whiskies.

£££ Closed Nov to Feb

Kinross House
Woodside Avenue, Grantown on Spey PH26 3JR

☎ (01479) 872042

📠 (01479) 873504

🖰 *www.kinrosshouse.freeserve.co.uk*

The traditional Scottish décor of this Victorian guesthouse belies the modern facilities within: a gymnasium, sauna and cycles. Spacious, tasteful bedrooms. Wide-ranging breakfasts; five-course dinners.

£ All year

INVERNESS
Dunain Park
Inverness IV3 8JN

☎ (01463) 230512

📠 (01463) 224532

🖰 *www.dunainparkhotel.co.uk*

Friendly country-house hotel perched high above Culloden, a hybrid of

Georgian and Victorian styles. Comfortable, roomy lounges and enjoyable food; smart, restful bedrooms. **£££** All year (See Where to Eat)

Glenmoriston Town House Hotel

20 Ness Bank, Inverness IV2 4SF

☎ (01463) 223777

🖷 (01463) 712378

An Italian influence at this central yet peaceful riverside spot. Lunch is served in the casual Terrazza; La Riviera restaurant is stylish and crisp. Individual, stylish bedrooms.

££ All year

Sealladh Sona

3 Whinpark, Canal Road, Muirtown, Inverness IV3 8NQ

☎ /🖷 (01463) 239209

Peaceful bed and breakfast by the final locks of the Caledonian Canal. Three comfortable bedrooms, and a lounge full of literature on the area. Excellent breakfasts.

£ All year

KENTALLEN
Holly Tree

Kentallen, Nr Glencoe, Argyll PA38 4BY

☎ (01631) 740292

🖷 (01631) 740345

ʻ🖢 www.hollytreehotel.co.uk

Converted railway station by Loch Linnhe – a curious hybrid of smart hotel, roadside inn and historic building. The Mackintosh-style dining-room has lovely views. Fresh local fish and seafood are on the menu; roomy bedrooms face the loch.

££ Closed end Nov to end Jan

KINGUSSIE
The Cross

Tweed Mill Brae, Ardbroilach Road, Kingussie PH21 1TC

☎ (01540) 661166

🖷 (01540) 661080

ʻ🖢 www.thecross.co.uk

Former tweed mill beside a brook, now a restaurant-with-rooms. The upstairs lounge is light and minimalist; bedrooms are cheerful and pleasing.

£££ Closed 1 Dec to 28 Feb (See Where to Eat)

Rowan House

Newtonmore Road, Kingussie PH21 1HD

☎ /🖷 (01540) 662153

Smart, detached modern home with views over the Spey Valley and Cairngorms. Attractive accommodation; breakfast time is flexible.

£ All year exc Christmas

LOCH ERIBOLL
Port-na-Con House

Loch Eriboll IV27 4UN

☎ /🖷 (01971) 511367

Former customs house on the unspoilt loch shore, by a private beach. Small, spotless bedrooms have loch views, shared by the conservatory and lounge. 'Excellent' dinners and breakfasts.

£ All year

MELVICH
The Sheiling

Melvich KW14 7YJ

☎ /🖷 (01641) 531256

Welcoming, comfortable guesthouse on a hill croft near the coast. Three en suite bedrooms and two lounges, one with wonderful views over Melvich Bay.

£ *Apr to Oct*

SPEAN BRIDGE
Invergloy House
Spean Bridge, By Fort William
PH34 4DY
☎ (01397) 712681
Stay on a 50-acre estate with wonderful views and a private shingle beach for fishing. The drawing room overlooks the loch. Attractive, comfortable bedrooms.

£ *All year exc Christmas*

Old Pines
Spean Bridge, By Fort William
PH34 4EG
☎ (01397) 712324
🖷 (01397) 712433
🖥 www.oldpines.co.uk
Restaurant-with-rooms in a low-slung, Scandinavian-style chalet. Open-plan eating in the informal, pine-clad conservatory. After 7.30pm children are banished to a playroom in readiness for the excellent food. Simple bedrooms.

£££ *All year (See Where to Eat)*

STRATHPEFFER
Craigvar
The Square, Strathpeffer IV14 9DL
☎ (01997) 421622
🖷 (01997) 421796
Small stone guesthouse with three comfortable and attractive *en suite* bedrooms. Guests can also use a cosy lounge and breakfast at separate tables.

£ *All year exc Christmas and New Year*

Inver Lodge
Strathpeffer IV14 9DL
☎ (01997) 421392
Victorian house with relaxed atmosphere, two comfortable bedrooms and a guest lounge. Home-cooked dinners.

£ *Mar to mid-Dec*

TAIN
Aldie House
Tain IV19 1LZ
☎ /🖷 (01862) 893787
Large stone Victorian house in wooded grounds near Dornoch Firth. Handsome bedrooms; 'excellent' home-cooked dinners.

£ *All year*

Mansfield House
Scotsburn Road, Tain IV19 1PR
☎ (01862) 892052
🖷 (01862) 892260
🖥 www.mansfield-house.co.uk
Splendid Victorian folly in lovely grounds with a grand fountain. Opulent and ornate public rooms, and spacious bedrooms. The well-cooked food is spiced with Eastern touches and unexpected combinations.

£££ *All year*

TONGUE
Rhian Guest House
Tongue IV27 4XJ
☎ (01847) 611257
Set in attractive countryside with views of Ben Loyal, this whitewashed house offers six *en suite* bedrooms. 'Excellent' breakfast and dinner.

£ *All year*

WHITEBRIDGE
Knockie Lodge

Whitebridge, Inverness IV2 6UP

☎ (01456) 486278

📠 (01456) 486389

🌐 www.knockielodge.co.uk

Former shooting lodge in a wonderfully isolated spot, with private sailing and fishing rights on Loch Knockie, and stalking on the Knockie estate. Creature comforts indoors continue in the bright modern bedrooms. Expert five-course dinners are Scottish-European in style. *£££ Closed mid-Oct to Apr*

WHERE TO EAT

CROMARTY
Royal Hotel

Marine Terrace, Cromarty IV11 8YN

☎ (01381) 600217

📠 (01381) 600813

🌐 www.royalcromartyhotel.co.uk

Molluscs gathered from the beach across the road by a local worthy appear as 'Mussels Albert'. Scottish fare dominates in this three-storey black-and-white house. Imagination and variety in the menu and specials board; crêpes are a speciality. *11–11; bar food and restaurant Mon–Fri 12–2 and 6–9, weekends 12–2.30 and 6–9.30*

DORNOCH
2 Quail

Castle Street, Dornoch IV25 3SN

☎ (01862) 811811

🌐 www.2quail.co.uk

Intimate restaurant-with-rooms where warm Mediterranean colours predominate; the food continues the pattern. Hearteningly simple cooking with plenty of seafood and local ingredients. 'Memorable' puddings. *Tue–Sat D only 7.30–9.30; closed 2 weeks Feb to Mar*

FORT WILLIAM
Crannog

Town Pier, Fort William PH33 7NG

☎ (01397) 705589

📠 (01397) 705026

🌐 www.crannog.net

'Spick and span' seafood lovers' restaurant at the head of Loch Linnhe, with its own boat and smokehouse. Straightforward menu supplemented by blackboard specials and desserts. *All week 12–2.30, 6–9.30 (10.30 in summer); closed 25 and 26 Dec, 1 and 2 Jan*

Inverlochy Castle

Torlundy, Fort William PH33 6SN

☎ (01397) 702177

📠 (01397) 702953

🌐 www.inverlochy.co.uk

Classy hotel in landscaped grounds. Traditional four-course dinners employ locally sourced ingredients and more unusual items. The impeccable wine list is expensive. *All week 12.30–1.45 and 7–9.15; closed 7 Jan to 12 Feb (See Where to Stay)*

INVERNESS
Culloden House

Culloden, Inverness IV2 7BZ
☎ (01463) 790461
📠 (01463) 792181
🖥 www.cullodenhouse.co.uk
Grand Georgian mansion with its
spacious, high-ceilinged rooms. Rather
old-fashioned cooking prevails among
tourist favourites, locally sourced
seafood and rich desserts. Somewhat
expensive, wide-ranging wine list.
All week 12.30–2 and 7–8.45

Dunain Park

Inverness IV3 8JN
☎ (01463) 230512
📠 (01463) 224532
🖥 www.dunainparkhotel.co.uk
Unpretentious Georgian house in
extensive grounds just outside Inverness.
The food is modern without losing its
traditional identity. Centre stage is
Aberdeen Angus steak, alongside fish,
seafood and game.
All week D only 7–8.30 (See Where to Stay)

KINGUSSIE
The Cross

Tweed Mill Brae, Ardbroilach Road,
Kingussie PH21 1TC
☎ (01540) 661166
📠 (01540) 661080
🖥 www.thecross.co.uk
Former water-powered tweed mill in
semi-wilderness beside the Gynack burn.
Five-course dinners typically start with
seafood, followed by soup, meat and
game. Dishes sound simple but are skilful
and appealing. The affordable world wine
list excludes France.

*Wed–Mon D only 7–8.30; closed 1 Dec to
28 Feb (See Where to Stay)*

LOCH CLUANIE
Cluanie Inn

Loch Cluanie IV3 6YW
☎ (01320) 340238
Remote, cosily furnished whitewashed
inn set in an area of outstanding beauty.
Choose from simple, sustaining pub fare
or a salad bar. A more formal three-
course menu is served in the restaurant.
*11–11; bar food and restaurant 12–2.30
and 6–8.30*

MUIR OF ORD
The Dower House

Highfield, Muir of Ord IV6 7XN
☎ /📠 (01463) 870090
🖥 www.thedowerhouse.co.uk
Intimate Victorian bungalow where
straightforward food is served in a three-
course menu; unusual ingredients are
seamlessly incorporated.
*All week D only 8–9.30 (L by
arrangement); closed 25 Dec*

SPEAN BRIDGE
Old Pines

Spean Bridge, By Fort William
PH34 4EG
☎ (01397) 712324
📠 (01397) 712433
🖥 www.oldpines.co.uk
Local, organic and seasonal produce.
Modern Scottish dishes employ rich
sauces; local lamb is a summer speciality.
Attractive wines are reasonably priced.
*All week D only 8 (one sitting, occasionally
7.30 in winter), April to Sept Sun D
residents only (See Where to Stay)*

The North-West

Suilven

- The best mountain scenery in the country
- Beautiful sea lochs
- Large wilderness areas, with only a few small settlements
- Skye and the Small Isles

THE NORTH-WEST

At a glance

✓ Good for lengthy seven- to ten-day tours
✓ Isolated, stay-put holidays
✓ Hill-walking and climbing for the experienced
✓ Fishing, birdwatching, beaches
✗ Touring involves long drives, sometimes slow
✗ Public transport is very limited throughout
✗ The heaviest rainfall in Britain

In a spell of clear, warm weather, the beauty of Scotland's north-western coastline is unrivalled. The interlacing of mountains, islands and sea becomes a study in blues and greens, picked out in a pure, northern light. Geological upheavals have left the coast broken by sea lochs from Mull to Kinlochbervie, and have created mountains unlike any others in Scotland. From the map, it might seem monotonous country for touring, but this is not so: the complexities of the geology have left a landscape where vegetation and rocks change radically between one area and the next, from oak woods where mosses and lichens proliferate, to the bare gneiss desert of Sutherland, where bog myrtle, coarse grass and bell heather are all that grow. Even the sea lochs have individual characters, from the gloomy waters of Loch Hourn to the sunny openness of Loch Torridon.

The North-West has many remote places where single-track roads wind round stony outcrops to end in tiny crofting townships. Wilderness still exists where you must carry all that you need to survive on your back. It is in the North-West that you are most aware of how thinly populated the Highlands now are. With the exception of Ullapool there are no towns, and even the larger villages seldom run to more than a few rows of houses and a simple shop or two.

Then there is Skye. This is the most popular of all the Scottish islands, sold as heavily for its romantic connections with Flora Macdonald and Bonnie Prince Charlie as for its scenery of mountain and sea. The romance is overdone but the scenery is hard to beat. To experience Scotland at its best, you should travel on a steam train from Fort William to Mallaig, and then cross the Sound of Sleat to Armadale, with the mountains of Knoydart blue on one side and the outlines of Eigg and Rum rising from the sea on the other.

Key web sites

www.gael-net.co.uk Small but important collection of links to Highland sites

www.undiscoveredscotland.co.uk A brilliant assembly of links to community and activity sites throughout the Highlands

www.celticfringe.org.uk A good general site for Wester Ross

www.skye.com An ambitious but admirable site which provides links to almost every community in Skye

www.road-to-the-isles.org.uk Good general guide to Arisaig, Mallaig and the Small Isles

---

Good bases in the North-West

Achiltibuie

✓ *Superb location with terrific views*
✓ *Good beaches nearby*
✗ *A long, slow drive to anywhere else*

This straggling township is blessed with superb views, a nearby sandy beach, some fishing, and easy access to the Sutherland mountains. It is a slow drive to or from it and there are few facilities, so it is especially suited to stay–put self-catering holidays.

Arisaig

✓ *Good base for trips to islands*
✓ *Beaches, views*

Good beaches and a variety of boat trips make this small village worth considering.

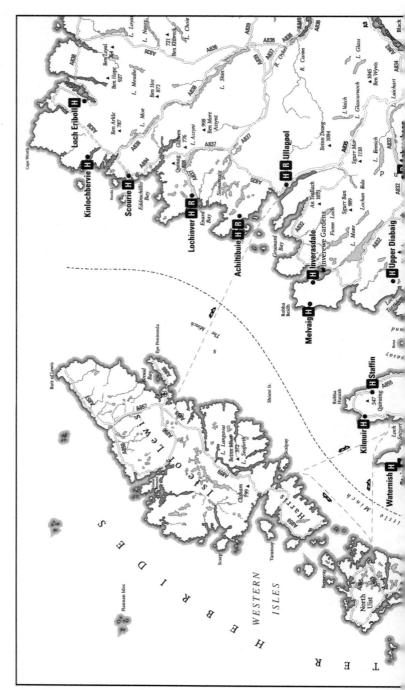

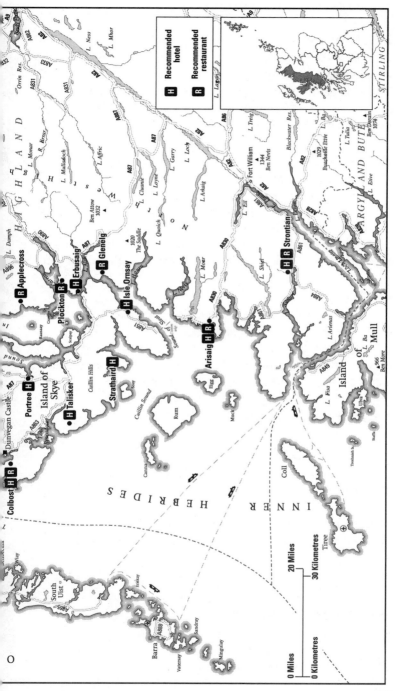

Recommended hotel H
Recommended restaurant R

STIRLING

HIGHLAND

ARGYLL AND BUTE

INNER HEBRIDES

Island of Skye

Island of Mull

Colbost H R
Portree H
Taliskar H
Strathaird H
Dunvegan Castle
Applecross R
Plockton H R
Erbusaig R H
Glenelg R H
Isle Ornsay H R
Arisaig H R
Strontian H R
Fort William
Ben Nevis 1344
The Saddle 1020
Ben Attow 1032
Ben Dearg 1074
Ben More 966

Cuillin Hills
Cuillin Sound
Sound of Sleat
Rum
Eigg
Muck
Canna
Coll
Tiree
Barra
South Uist
Eriskay
Vatersay
Sandray
Mingulay
Raasay

L. Ness
L. Mhor
Orrin Res.
L. Monar
R. Farrar
L. Mullardoch
L. Affric
L. Beanie
L. Duich
L. Damph
L. Cluanie
L. Loyne
L. Garry
L. Quoich
L. Arkaig
L. Moar
L. Shiel
L. Eil
L. Loch
L. Treig
Blackwater Res.
L. Ba
L. Etive
Loch Linnhe
L. Laggan
L. Tulla
L. Arienas
L. Fiisa
L. Sunart

A9
A82
A832
A831
A833
A835
A890
A896
A87
A861
A851
A863
A830
A82
A86
A84
A845
A884
A828

0 Miles   20 Miles
0 Kilometres   30 Kilometres

Lochinver

✓ *Good base for hill-walkers*
✓ *Beaches nearby*

The village itself is rather ordinary, but the surrounding country is splendid, with sandy beaches to the north and mountains to the east.

Portree

✓ *Best and most convenient base for Skye*
✓ *Attractive small town*

Skye's capital is a neat little town built around its sheltered harbour. It can get busy with visitors, but never quite loses its peacefulness. Well located for touring Skye, it has plenty of accommodation and is very much the centre of the island's life.

Ullapool

✓ *Wider range of facilities than anywhere else in the region*
✓ *Welcoming and even cosmopolitan in season*

This friendly fishing town was planned in the eighteenth century and has worn well. Boat trips and fishing expeditions are popular and there is plenty of accommodation.

THE MAINLAND

The ragged coastline of the North-West, where the sea has filled the great gashes created by the glaciers of the last Ice Age, provides the most stunning scenery in all of Scotland. To travel this coastline is to make a journey of infinite variety. Mountains lurk just inland, and isolated, barely-populated peninsulas thrust into the sea. Villages are few and far between.

Top sight

Inverewe Gardens

✓ *Fine garden in a wonderful setting*

That a sub-tropical garden exists here on the same latitude as Siberia is thanks to the mild climate created by the North

Atlantic Drift, and to the efforts of one man – Osgood Mackenzie – to transform a barren patch of ground on which only a single stunted willow grew. The project was started in 1862 with shelter belts to protect the site from the salt-laden gales. Estate workers carried in soil in creels and the first plantings were made. By the time Inverewe was given to the National Trust for Scotland in 1952 by Osgood Mackenzie's daughter, it was already famous. The size of the coach and car park testifies to its popularity.

Inverewe is a woodland garden, its winding paths dotted with rarities from the southern hemisphere and China. It has an enormous *Magnolia stellata*, superb rhododendrons, primulas and azaleas. At its heart lies a sheltered walled garden full of interesting plants. All the time you sense what a fragile place this is, for its luxuriance is surrounded by boggy moorland and distant mountains. Inverewe is at its most colourful in spring, but also has superb autumn colouring. July and August do not find it at its best, except for the hydrangeas, but there is always something to admire. Plant lovers should aim to spend the better part of a day here. Seeds are on sale and there is an extensive gift shop. [NTS; mid-Mar to Oct, daily 9.30–9; Nov to mid-Mar, daily 9.30–5; ☎ (01445) 781200; 🖥 via www.nts.org.uk]

Best scenery and local sights

Applecross and Torridon

Loch Carron marks a divide in the landscape. Northwards, the land becomes harsher. The mountains change radically: the jumbled peaks and ridges giving way to isolated mountains of red sandstone, often topped with shining quartzite, whose sides drop in precipitous terraces gouged with gullies.

The Applecross peninsula is barren moorland for the most part, isolated from the east by the mountain peaks of Beinn Bhan. Through these is threaded a road that is the closest Britain comes to an alpine pass. On the far side, the views over to Skye and Raasay are what make Applecross worth visiting. There was once a monastery out here, founded in 673 by St Maelrubha. Now, as the road picks its way north, there are only crofts and sheep.

Torridon introduces itself dramatically, with its three great mountains – Beinn Alligin, Liathach and Beinn Eighe – towering above Glen Torridon. Liathach is the queen, its castellated ridge running parallel to the glen 3,400 feet beneath, dwarfing the cottages of Torridon into insignificance. On a grey day, with the clouds hiding the battlements of the ridge, Liathach loses little, for then the layered terraces of stone and grass disappear into the grey swirl, to unguessable heights.

Most of Beinn Eighe is a National Nature Reserve. The mountain does not loom above the road as menacingly as Liathach, but its southern face, streaked with quartzite screes, is forbidding enough to deter thoughts of a casual climb. Stop at the visitor centre at the head of Loch Maree for a full introduction to the area. [👣 *www.torridon-mountains.com*]

Torridon NTS Visitor Centre Discover masses of useful information and pictures here and learn about the wildlife and geology of the area. Do not ignore the deer museum, which was originally set up by a local man with a lifetime's experience of deer management, and explains, with little sentimentality but much sympathy, the life of the red deer on the Scottish hills. *[NTS; May to Sept, Mon–Sat 10–5, Sun 2–5;* ☎ *(01445) 791368]*

Suggested walks At **Coire Duibh Mhoir** a tough, low-level walking route strikes up the cleft of the Coire Duibh Mhoir burn between Liathach and Beinn Eighe. On reaching the northern side of these mountains, you see them in a different aspect – hollowed by enormous, echoing corries. You can make for Loch Coire na Caime under the highest tops of the Liathach ridge, which is spectacular enough, or you can contour round the flank of Beinn Eighe to Loch Coire Mhic Fhearchair. Screes rise steeply above the dark lochan, and a sheer triple buttress, split by dark gullies, looms above the far end. Go well equipped; the ground is rough and wet. The distance is approximately eight miles. Details are on 👣 *www.btinternet.com/~thestorm/walks_in_torridon*. The **Beinn Eighe trails** are also worth trying. From a car park just west of Kinlochewe (signed), two separate trails lead into the Beinn Eighe reserve. The woodland trail is short and relatively easy. The mountain trail, which comes within range of the summit, is a lot steeper, but very well engineered. Details are via ✒ *www.b-mercer.demon.co.uk*

Best route to the area Take the A890 from Kyle of Lochalsh or the A832 from Inverness.

Ardnamurchan

Ardnamurchan is a low, bare peninsula jutting westward into the Atlantic, just north of Mull *[✒ www.ardnamurchan.com]*. The vestigial remains of volcanic craters crown its end, crumbled into low hills. All the beauty is on the coast, where, to the south, the still waters of Loch Sunart reflect yachts and trees, while the north coast looks out to Eigg, Muck and the mountains of Rum. This is isolated country; only the small villages of Strontian and Kilchoan are big enough for shops. The roads are very slow indeed, and not for those prone to car sickness.

Make for the beaches of Sanna Bay, where white sand and fabulous views are to be found on a clear day, or visit Ardnamurchan point, the westernmost point of mainland Britain. Seals are to be found close to the lighthouse.

Ardnamurchan Natural History Centre (west of Salen) A modern 'living' building with very good displays about local wildlife. *[Easter to Oct, Mon–Sat 10.30–5.30, Sun 12–5.30;* ☎ *(01972) 500209]*

Ardnamurchan Point Visitor Centre Housed in the lighthouse right on the sea's edge, the centre combines information about the lighthouse and its builders with a general background on Ardnamurchan. Views are wonderful *[Apr, May and Oct, daily 10–5; June to Sept, daily 10–5.30;* ☎ *(01972) 510210]*

Best route to the area Take the Corran Ferry across Loch Lhinnie, the A861 to Salen, then the B8007. Consider returning via the ferry from Kilchoan to Tobermory on Mull.

Assynt

The coastal road north from Achiltibuie winds tortuously through a labyrinth of rocky hummocks and river valleys. It is not a road to take a caravan on, nor is it a road for careless drivers. But it leads you to some remarkable scenery [*www.assynt.co.uk*].

Assynt is a loch-speckled district, dominated by the isolated peaks of Suilven, Canisp and Ben More Assynt. These rise out of flat sheets of gneiss like icebergs above pack ice. Suilven is the queen of them, its massive domed western peak looming over the moors. An excellent family web site with climbing details for local peaks and stunning photos is at *www.members.aol.com/barbersasa*

As well as mountains, beaches abound, notably on the Stoer Peninsula, where the best sand is at Achmelvich, Clachtoll and Clashnessie. There are also small coves to explore, On the north coast of the peninsula, Drumbeg, with its loch and its view, is worth pausing at, and Nedd, a little further on, is also attractive.

Ardvreck Castle The stubby ruins sit on a little headland in Loch Assynt, easily reached from the A837. There is not much of it left, but it has gone down in history as the place where Montrose was finally captured after his defeat at Carbisdale (see box, pages 332–3). A small beach nearby on the loch shore makes a good spot from which to contemplate the ruin.

Boat trip to Eas Coul Aulin From Kylestrome (on A894) a boat runs up Loch Glencoul to the highest waterfall in Britain. The Eas Coul Aulin is four times higher than Niagara.

Suggested walks Strike inland alongside the **Kirkaig River** from Inverkirkaig to see the dome of Suilven rising above you. There is a good waterfall to see too. Another walk from the lighthouse at the end of the Stoer Peninsula takes in the **Old Man of Stoer** – a dramatic sea stack – and some fine cliff scenery.

Details of both walks are on *www.b-mercer.demon.co.uk*

Coigach

North of Ullapool, the west-coast scenery becomes even more the stuff of fantasy. Isolated dull red or silvery mountains rear out of a wilderness of grey-white tumbled rock. Cotton grass, bog myrtle and bell heather cover the peat, except where it has been trenched for drainage or dug for fuel. On still evenings, you can scent the peat-smoke from the tiny communities clinging to the coastline

Coigach is the district between Loch Broom and Cam Loch. The fast A835 runs through it to the Ledmore junction, where the A838 provides an escape route back to Lairg and the east coast, but for the best of the scenery, take the minor road west of Drumrunie towards the Inverpolly National Nature Reserve (there's a visitor centre on the A835 at Knockan). The remarkable mountain of Stac Pollaidh, with its ridge eroded into spiky pinnacles and towers, is reflected photogenically in Loch Lurgainn.

Stop at the stunning sandy beach at Achnahaird before arriving at the straggling crofting township of Achiltibuie (see page 414). From here, you can enjoy wonderful views south and south-west to all the tangled mountains of Ross, with the Summer Isles lying on the sea in the foreground.

A good local sight is the **Achiltibuie Hydroponicum** (see page 414).

Suggested walk Inverpolly To see the forest, stop at the cottage at Linneraineach and take the track north. This is a low-level walk, leading you into a cirque of peaks, floored by lochs with sandy beaches. Cul Mor rises above Loch an Doire Duibh, which you can walk round before returning. Climbing Cul Mor, either from here or from the duller approach from Knockan, reveals the full beauty of the pattern of lochs, notably Loch Sionascaig and Loch Veyatie.

Best route to the area On the A835 from Ullapool, turn left to Achiltibuie at Drumrunie.

Glenelg and Loch Hourn

This is a hidden area of Scotland, unknown to most visitors who take the main road to Skye *[⌒◗ via www.skye.com]*. Turn west from Shiel Bridge and you come to a country of small farms, with the village of Glenelg at its centre. You can cross by ferry to Skye from here, a more romantic journey than by the bridge on the main road, and costing only slightly more.

South of Glenelg, on the coast at Sandaig, stood the house Gavin Maxwell wrote about as Camusfearna. It is a steepish climb to reach the spot, but readers of *Ring of Bright Water* may want to persist to see the bay that Maxwell describes. The web site above contains photographs.

Views across to Skye as you continue south are wonderful, until the road swings east into the fastness of Loch Hourn, a brooding, shadowy sea loch, at its best when silvered by the evening sun. Behind the pretty lochside village of Arnisdale, the scree slopes of Beinn Sgritheall rise into the mists that usually crown its top.

Glenelg brochs The two brochs in the next glen south of the village are the best-preserved on the mainland and are little-visited (for an explanation of brochs, see box below). **Dun Telve** stands on flat ground on the right of the road, and **Dun Troddan**, rather more fragmentary, on a hillside a little further

---

Brochs

Brochs are a type of fortress unique to Scotland. They were tall, circular towers, not unlike modern cooling towers in shape. They had no windows and the walls were double to allow galleries and stairways to run between the inner and outer skins. The interior of the broch was open to the sky, but roofed galleries probably ran round the walls, allowing the inhabitants some shelter.

The remains of about 500 brochs are visible, many of them close to the sea. For many years arguments raged about who built them and what they were used for. The Picts were popular

up the glen. The walls of the former rise to 33 feet, and the double skin of the wall and the series of galleries passing between the two skins are clearly visible.

Best route to the area From Glen Shiel, turn west at Shiel Bridge and follow the road to its end.

Glen Shiel and Loch Duich

The great trench running westward from Loch Cluanie is the smoothest and fastest route to Skye, and thunders with tour coaches. Glen Shiel is too hemmed in on either side by high ridges and peaks for the views to be up to much; the peaks of the Five Sisters of Glenshiel are better seen from further away. Turn west at the hamlet of Shiel Bridge and drive to the viewpoint at the top of the Ratagan Pass (about ten minutes' drive) for the best prospect of them.

Loch Duich is best seen from the quiet road on its western shore. From Totaig at the end, a good view can be had over the meeting of three lochs (Duich, Alsh and Long), with Eilean Donan Castle almost opposite.

For walks, turn off the A87 to Morvich, or else continue to Kyle of Lochalsh and Skye.

---

candidates at first, but it now seems certain that brochs are Iron Age constructions, dating from around 100 BC. The skill of the construction can be seen in the better-preserved examples: the inner and outer walls are pinned together by stone cross-slabs, stairways run up towards vanished parapets, and doorways have impressive lintels. The need for such fortresses seems to have disappeared by about AD 200. Thereafter, old brochs often became the centre of a small settlement, perhaps with little houses being built inside. The best-preserved broch of all is to be found at Mousa on Shetland (see page 471); those in Glenelg come a close second.

Eilean Donan Castle Eilean Donan has been used so extensively as an image to sell Scotland, that you are bound to recognise its familiar outline. It is ironic that the building is a total restoration, completed only in 1932. It is an obligatory stop on the road to Skye, its setting on an islet in Loch Duich being the main attraction, though several rooms and an extensive souvenir shop are open.

The original castle was destroyed by Hanoverian bombardment during the abortive 1719 Jacobite uprising, but in truth, its modern incarnation as a film director's backdrop is more interesting than its history. Chat to the custodians on a quiet day and you will hear gossip about who came to advertise what, and how the rain and the midges drove everyone crazy.

Walks Two walks from Morvich are recommended. The first takes in the **Falls of Glomach**, the second highest in Britain, although is a long haul to reach them. The start − through conifers − is not attractive, but the views improve as you approach the saddle of Bealach na Sroine. From here it is a quick downhill lope to the falls. Unless you are blessed with a head for heights, you will have to make do with the view of the upper part of the falls as they plunge 500 feet into a narrow ravine. At **Gleann Choinneachain** a slow, fairly steep and wet path carries you beneath the peaks of the Five Sisters with glimpses of towers and pinnacles above you. Eventually you come to the windswept pass of Bealach an Sgairne, the watershed between North Sea and Atlantic. Beneath you lie the boggy beginnings of Glen Affric.

Best route to the area From Fort William via the A82 and A830.

Gruinard and Little Loch Broom

The scenery in this corner of Wester Ross is dominated by the serrated peaks of An Teallach, guarding the northern edge of the Letterewe forest. The road runs round the coast beneath it. Gruinard Bay, with a stretch of pink granite sand, is a peaceful place on a fine day. Take the minor road up the western side of it to Mellon Udrigle, where there is a sandy beach, a cluster of cottages, a campsite and a lovely view.

A neck of land separates Gruinard Bay from Little Loch Broom. Stop at the top for views of the Summer Isles out to sea to the north-west. A further stopping point beside Little Loch Broom is the waterfall at Ardessie. You can see some of it from the road, but must walk to see the best sections.

From the head of Little Loch Broom, the A832 winds up the valley of the peaty-yellow Dundonnell River and debouches on to bare open moorland at the top – a spectacular and lonely drive, at its best from west to east – where you gaze into the tangle of mountains above Loch Fannich. Look back to see the peaks of An Teallach. Just when this road seems to be running into the mountains it takes a dog-leg north-east along a small glen scented with bog myrtle and joins the A835 from Garve to Ullapool at the head of the Corrieshalloch Gorge. [www.celticfringe.org.uk/gruinard]

Corrieshalloch Gorge This is among the most accessible of Scotland's gorges [via www.nts.org.uk]. You reach it from either the A832 or the A835. A quick walk down a wooded path takes you to the chasm, spanned by a bouncy suspension bridge. There is a nasty drop to a river enclosed between vertical walls of black rock, on which ranks of ferns thrive in such footholds as they can find. The Falls of Measach, at the head of the gorge, are more a chute than a waterfall proper and provide appropriate thunder only in heavy spate.

Walks The following routes are at www.b-mercer.demon.co.uk. The track at **Gruinard River** is well-maintained but sometimes wet. It runs up beside this beautiful river as far as Loch na Sealga, about five miles inland. Even if you don't want to walk that far, this route is ideal for a short stroll (it is used by vehicles, so don't obstruct it). An alternative walk is to **Loch Toll an Lochain**. A steep and sometimes indistinct track leads uphill from the A832 opposite the turning to Badrallach. Eventually it brings you to Loch Toll an Lochain, underneath the peaks of An Teallach. The precipices and tumbled screes of the mountain are faithfully reflected in the black water cupped under its cliffs. It is an awesome place, surrounded on three sides by bare rock or steep grass.

Loch Maree and Loch Ewe

Loch Maree, with the peak of Slioch reflected in its silver-blue, island-dotted waters, is rivalled for beauty only by Loch Lomond. The A832 runs along the south-western shore; much of the north-eastern shore can be explored on the path leading through Letterewe Forest. North of Slioch lies a tract of remote deer forest, bog and precipitous mountain, empty of human habitation and savage in bad weather.

Boats containing intent fishermen drift on Loch Maree, for it is a renowned sea-trout loch. Ask at the Loch Maree Hotel about fishing possibilities.

At the western end of the loch, the road runs down the River Kerry to the coast. Turn left to Redpoint through a secluded landscape of water, birch and oak. Badachro is a tiny village by the shore, its pub ideally situated on the sea's edge, with views of rocky islets in the bay. Continue south to get to three beaches of reddish sand (one accessible only on foot). They are all fairly exposed, so do not expect to do much basking in the sun.

Loch Ewe, over the hill from Gairloch, is another beautiful inlet of the sea. Take the minor road along its western shore for the best views of it.

Local attractions include **Inverewe Gardens** (see pages 402–3) and the **Gairloch Heritage Museum** (see page 415).

Best route to the area Take the A832 from Achnasheen.

Moidart and Arisaig

Loch Moidart, cutting inland from the sea, is island-studded, heavily wooded and may have seals lying on its skerries. It is a picture of loveliness at high tide in fine weather, and desolate at low tide in the rain. The low ground to the south round Acharacle is an attractive tangle of little-visited inlets.

www.geocities.com/Heartland/Bluffs/8449]

Arisaig, a strung–out sequence of bays, rocks and cottages, is more popular. The beaches are the draw, as are the wonderful views out to Eigg, Rum, and Skye, which are best at sunset. Make for the bay at Back of Keppoch for the most perfect views.

Loch Morar, to the north, is far deeper than the sea which lies a quarter of a mile distant, and is said to have a monster to rival that of Loch Ness. It is an attractive walk along the northern shore.

Castle Tioram (Acharacle) On a tidal island stand the ruins of the impregnable stronghold of Macdonald of Clanranald [*www.tioram.org.uk*]. The castle survived for four centuries until it was burnt by the fourteenth chief as he set off for the 1715 uprising, to prevent his Campbell enemies from occupying it.

Glenfinnan Monument (on A830 at the head of Loch Shiel) The monument commemorates the raising of Prince Charles Edward Stuart's standard on 19 August 1745 and is keenly visited by all would–be Jacobites. Inside, there is a first–class explanation of the complex events leading to the '45', including a clear chart of Stewart genealogy which makes it plain why the Old Pretender was the legitimate claimant to the throne of Britain. Once you have grasped the background, climb the tower for the view. *[NTS; Apr to mid-May and Sept to Oct, daily 11–5; mid-May to Aug, daily 9.30–6;* ☎ *(01397) 722250; via www.road-to-the-isles.org.uk]*

Glenfinnan Station Museum A small museum of the West Highland railway line, where steam train excursions still run from Fort William to Mallaig. *[June to Sept, 9.30–4.30;* ☎ *(01397) 722295]*

Best route to the area Take the A830 from Fort William, passing Loch Eil and the head of Loch Shiel. Turn south on A861 into Moidart, or continue to Arisaig. Consider continuing by crossing from Mallaig to Skye.

North-West Sutherland

This area is too much of a desert for some visitors, for walking through the hummocks of bare rock and picking your way around the boggy lochans can be work rather than pleasure, while the steep, loose screes of the mountains may deter thoughts of casual hill-walking. For others, the far north-west corner of Scotland is pure magic. The scenery here is bleak and beautiful, with the quartzite summits of Ben Stack, Arkle and Foinaven glimmering in the sunshine like snow.

Handa Island Off the coast north of Scourie, the cliff-girt island has a massive seabird colony, notable for its guillemots. Ferries from Scourie run *[Apr to Sept, Mon–Sat;* ☎ *(01971) 502340]*

Sandwood Bay This is everyone's ideal beach, with its long curve of empty white sand, a small river and a loch. It is empty because access is difficult. The track runs in from Oldshore Mor (with its own lovely beaches). Look up 🐭 *www.b-mercer.demon.co.uk* for details.

Towns and villages to explore

Achiltibuie (off A835)

A straggling crofting community on the south coast of Coigach, notable for its wonderful views *[*🐭 *www.summerisles.com]*. It is popular for family holidays as there are trout in the lochs, a good beach at Achnahaird, the mountains of Inverpolly and the rocky coastline along to Reiff to explore. Achiltibuie's tourist attraction is the **Achiltibuie Hydroponicum**. Tours round this huge glasshouse reveal strawberry plants, banana trees, oranges, lemons and figs all growing happily without the aid of soil. Downstairs, apples and peaches ripen, and courgettes grow in fat ranks. The contrast with the barren surroundings outside is remarkable. *[Apr to Sept, daily 10–6;* ☎ *(01854) 622353]*

Gairloch (A832)

After miles of sparsely populated country, the clusters of cottages round Loch Gairloch come as a surprise. Gairloch is popular because of the sandy beaches in the area, and there are numerous guesthouses and caravan sites. The **Gairloch Heritage Museum** has a splendid collection of objects salvaged from houses and cottages in the area, including an illicit still. It gives an excellent impression of West Highland life. *[Easter to mid-Oct, Mon–Sat 10–5; mid-Oct to end Oct, Mon–Fri 10.30–1;* ☎ *(01445) 712287;* *www.ghmr.freeserve.co.uk]*

Mallaig (A830)

This is a utilitarian ferry and fishing port, with little charm as a place to stay in but plenty as a place to visit *[via www.road-to-the-isles.org.uk]*. In summer, Mallaig is crowded with cars waiting for ferries, passengers from steam excursions on the railway, fish lorries and tourists who have simply arrived at the end of the road and are wondering what to do next. It is the natural junction point for travellers to Skye and to the islands of Eigg, Rum, Muck and Canna (boats to these go from Arisaig too). You can also get to Inverie on the coast of Knoydart – the remote, trackless area to the north. Mallaig can be dismal in the rain, but the excellent **Heritage Centre** *[Apr to June and Oct, Mon–Sat 11–4; July to Sept, Mon–Sat 11–5, Sun 1–4;* ☎ *(01687) 462085;* *www.mallaigheritage.org.uk]* and **Mallaig Marine World** *[Oct to May, Mon–Sat 9–5, Sun 10–5; June to Sept, Mon–Sat 9–9, Sun 10–6; Nov to Mar, closed Sun;* ☎ *(01687) 462292]* are excellent diversions.

Lochinver (A837)

The only settlement of any size in Assynt, Lochinver is a mixture of grubby fishing harbour and clean, cottage-lined street. Tucked into a sheltered inlet, Lochinver suffers from a lack of views but is the only place for miles with a decent choice of accommodation or anywhere much to eat. You can visit beaches in the area or climb Suilven and Canisp.

Plockton (off A890)

Built on the edge of a sheltered bay of Loch Carron, and with spindly palm trees to prove that Scotland is sub-tropical after all, Plockton is a picturesque small village, popular with artists. It is a useful stopping place, but can become crowded. [☛ *www.plockton.co.uk*]

Scourie (A894)

This sheltered village at the head of a cove is a centre for trout fishermen who like nothing better than to pursue their quarry through the myriad lochans that dot the gneiss desert inland. Scourie is not particularly distinguished, but it has an hotel and a rocky coastline to explore, and is generally a haven in the wilderness.

Shieldaig (A896)

The village is an early nineteenth-century planned community, as lovely as Plockton but less obviously postcard material. Offshore views are blocked by an island which is a sanctuary for a stand of ancient Caledonian pines. Sheep munch grass on Shieldaig's little waterfront.

Ullapool (A835)

This is the only real town in the north-west, and a genuinely pleasant one [☛ *via www.inverness-scotland.co.uk*]. It was established in 1788 by the British Fisheries Society to take advantage of the huge catches of herring in Loch Broom, and is laid out in a neat grid plan of streets and cottages. Now it fills with tourists in summer, bringing it to life. This is about the only place north of Stirling where you can enjoy watching the street life. The car park for the ferry to Stornoway is sometimes used by a pipe band or Highland dancers when not occupied by queues for the Western Isles. Ullapool is a good place to look for sea-fishing trips, or you can **cruise to the Summer Isles** [☎ *(01854) 612472;* ☛ *www.summerqueen.co.uk*].

Ullapool Museum is situated in a refurbished kirk, where many of the town's relics such as photographs, quilts and tapestry are supplemented by electronic gadgets, putting everything into context. *[Apr to Oct, Mon–Sat 9.30–5, July and Aug, 9.30–8; Nov to Mar, Wed and Sat 11–3;* ☎ *(01854) 612987]*

THE ISLANDS

The northern inner Hebridean islands are dominated by Skye. It is by far the largest island and easily the most visited – indeed, Skye tops the list for most visitors to these parts. Now that a road bridge links it to the mainland, access is fast and easy, though not cheap. But it is still possible to catch a ferry over to Skye, which is a more romantic and pleasanter way of travelling. In contrast to Skye, the island of Raasay, which lies just offshore, is little visited. It has its own considerable charm, however.

The smaller islands which lie off the coast of Arisaig are harder to get to. Their tiny populations form close-knit communities, and accommodation and facilities are both limited. Some visitors love them, returning year after year. For other people, they are just too isolated. In summer, day excursions are possible. This method is probably the best bet if you want a glimpse of what life is like on them.

Skye

✓ *Big island with reasonable facilities*
✓ *Striking mountain scenery*
✓ *Easy access*
✗ *Can be crowded in high season*

Skye exerts a hypnotic appeal, reflected in the number of coach tours that have the island as their destination. On a clear windy day, with the ridges of the Black Cuillin exposed in all their starkness and the Sound of Raasay dotted with white combers, the island is magical. However, few parts of Scotland are so disappointing in the rain or sea mist. If the weather turns against you on your way to Skye, change your plans and try again later.

As Scottish islands go, Skye is well endowed with facilities for visitors and, although there are few tourist sights as such, they are all given the hard sell. The island has plenty of places to stay, and you even have a choice of shops and places at which to eat. So, while Skye only occasionally feels overcrowded, do not expect to find yourself alone. If you need some solitude, you only have to make the short crossing to Raasay.

The best walks are long, difficult, or both, while the Black Cuillin is the preserve of the rock-climber or experienced rock-scrambler. However, if you are neither fit nor experienced, there are several enjoyable short walks, usually by the coast. The tourist office in Portree has a first-class selection of leaflets on walks. Almost all the areas and sights mentioned can be found described in detail on 🖱 *www.skye.com*

Top sight

Dunvegan Castle
✓ *Interesting history*
✓ *Good walks in the grounds*

The large car park and the numerous coaches signal that this, Skye's only substantial tourist sight, is extremely popular. It is pricey if all you want to do is visit the castle, but if you take advantage of the fine gardens and grounds for a walk it becomes better value. The castle, the seat of Macleod of Macleod, has been continuously inhabited for about 750 years.

The castle's exterior belies its age, for the Victorians added pepper-pot turrets and a battlemented gatehouse. The antiquity reveals itself in the interior, where the old barrel-vaulted kitchen goes back to 1360, and an unpleasant dungeon lurks. There are Jacobite relics which once belonged to Flora Macdonald, a portrait of Dr Johnson, who stayed here, and a very beautiful fifteenth-century silver cup. There is also Rory Mor's horn, a massive drinking vessel, which the chief's heir must drain to the dregs on his coming of age.

The greatest curiosity in Dunvegan is the Fairy Flag. Enclosed in protective glass, this almost colourless piece of fabric looks like a dishcloth in the last stages of decay. It has been dated to between the fourth and seventh centuries, while its silk is of Near-Eastern origin. This banner, Am Bratach Sith, was given to a MacLeod chief by a fairy and it has the power to ensure victory for the clan in battle. It is known to have been used twice successfully.

Popular boat trips to see seals run from the castle jetty. *[Mar to Oct, 10–5.30; Nov to Feb, 11–4;* ☎ *(01470) 521206;* 🖱 *www.dunvegancastle.com]*

Best scenery and local sights

Elgol and Loch Coruisk

At Broadford, take the A881 south. This dead-end road skirts the eastern edge of the black Cuillin mountains, running under the shoulder of Bla Bheinn. There are views of mountain and sea the whole way down. From the cluster of cottages at Elgol, right at the end, you look across Loch Scavaig into the whole semicircle of the mountains. This is the best view of the Cuillin to be had from any road. From Elgol, Bella Jane Boat Trips run sailings to Loch Coruisk, at the very heart of the hills. *[Regular sailings Apr to mid-Oct, booking essential;* ☎ *(01471) 866244 before 10 or after 7.30;* 🖱 *www.bellajane.co.uk]*

Enthralled nineteenth-century painters came to Coruisk and left impressions of a gloomy Gothic sanctuary whose overwhelming scale diminished man to a mere speck. It is not quite like that, though the wilderness of tumbled scree and layers of bare glaciated slabs beneath sheer cliffs cut by gullies leave an indelible impression.

Glen Brittle (off A863)

The drive down Glen Brittle gives you another excellent view of the Black Cuillin on the western side of their semicircle. Emerging from forestry plantations, you gaze straight into the black recesses of Coire a' Mhadaidh. The road runs on down the glen, with splendid views of the mountains, until you reach the campsite and shore at the bottom. This is a hive of activity for climbing expeditions, and much entertainment is to be had from watching the climbers loading up.

Talisker distillery If the clouds hide the mountains, turn west off the B8009 to Skye's only distillery. Tours of the Talisker distillery are pleasantly relaxed. *[Apr to June and Oct, Mon–Fri 9–4.30; July to Sept, Mon–Sat 9–4.30; Nov to Mar, Mon–Fri 2–4.30;* ☎ *(01478) 640314]*

Sleat

On the sheltered side of Skye's southern peninsula, the island is wooded and fertile. Cottages lie strung out along the shore as you follow the road north. Views over to the mainland are terrific. Take the minor road up the Ord river to Toakvaig. The landscape is much bleaker, but views over to the Cuillin mountains, with a ruined castle in the foreground, are wonderful.

Armadale Castle Gardens and Museum of the Isles Fine gardens, about the only ones on Skye, surround the derelict castle, which was once a Macdonald seat. There are walks in the extensive grounds. The exhibitions inside the museum *[Apr to Oct, daily 9.30–5.30;* ☎ *(01471) 844305;* ⓘ *www.highlandconnection.org]* explore the complex history of Clan Donald – especially its long tenure of the Lordship of the Isles. This is also the base for **West Highland Heavy Horse Tours** *[*☎ *(01478) 660233]* which will take you in a horse-drawn dray to nearby scenic spots.

Trotternish

The east coast of the Trotternish Peninsula is famous for its rock scenery. A slow-motion landslip, caused by basalt lava on top of less stable rock sliding gradually downhill, has resulted in an escarpment of sheer cliffs, with broken-off fragments as outriders. The best views are from the minor road which links Uig to Staffin, and then southward. Of particular interest are the Quirang (see below), the sea cliff known as Kilt Rock, from its tartan-like stripes, and the cigar-shaped detached pinnacle of the Old Man of Storr.

Flora Macdonald Memorial (Kilmuir) The girl who rowed Bonnie Prince Charlie over to Skye came back to the island after an eventful life, and is buried in the churchyard here. The memorial carries Dr Johnson's tribute: 'A name that will be mentioned in history, and if courage and fidelity be virtues, mentioned with honour.'

Skye Museum of Island Life (Kilmuir) A folk museum housed in a group of thatched cottages, with a cluster of domestic artefacts from bygone times and some period furniture. *[Apr to Oct, Mon–Sat 9.30–5.30;* ☎ *(01420) 552206]*

The Quirang From the road between Uig and Staffin, a rough track leads to this enclosed hollow, where the rock scenery is at its most dramatic. The various rock features of the Quirang – the Prison, the Table and the Needle – are eroded squares and pinnacles of rock, farrowed from the main cliffs in picturesque confusion.

Towns and villages to explore

Broadford

A straggling village on the north-facing coast. It has no great scenic virtues, but is well-located for exploring Sleat and the lumpish mounds of the Red Hills to the west. Like the Black Cuillins, these mountains are volcanic, but otherwise they are utterly different, being rounded mounds of pinkish granite with scree-covered flanks. In Broadford, the **Skye Sepentarium** with its collection of snakes, frogs and tortoises, may prove a useful diversion. *[Easter to Oct, Mon–Sat 10–5 plus Suns in July and Aug;* ☎ *(01471) 822209]*

Portree

Skye's little capital bustles with visitors on a hot summer's day, to the extent that you begin to wonder whether there are any local people left. It is an attractive place, set above a perfect blue-green inlet of the sea. The row of painted cottages by the harbour beautifully offsets the elegant main square. Apart from the Royal Hotel where Prince Charles Edward Stuart said goodbye to Flora Macdonald, there is not much to see in the town itself. However, with its pubs, shops, banks and selection of places to eat, Portree is a natural hub, the starting point for many of the island's bus services and for most of its bus tours.

The **Aros Heritage Centre**, south of town, is an excellent place to learn about the history and scenery of Skye, told through display boards and an audiovisual. *[Apr to Sept, daily 9–9; Oct to Mar, 10–5; ☎ (01478) 613649]*

Stein

This village on the Waternish peninsula north of Dunvegan is traditionally the place from which to watch the sun setting over the Western Isles on the horizon. It has Skye's oldest pub, a place with lots of character.

Uig

The terminal for the link between Skye and the Western Isles, much of Uig's life seems to revolve around ferry timetables. It is an attractively situated village at the end of a pretty sea loch, with a fair amount of accommodation.

Raasay

✓ *Peaceful contrast to neighbouring Skye*
✓ *Coastal and rock scenery*
✓ *Walks*
✗ *Limited facilities, no public transport*

The island of Raasay lies off Skye's eastern coast *[🖱 via www.skye.com]*. It is secluded and gentle, even when Skye is bustling. Its lack of mountains is made up for by the excellent sea views and there are coastal walks, some quite strenuous, with the cliff scenery of the east coast rivalling that of Trotternish. The curious, flat-topped Dun Caan is a volcanic hill, made famous as the place where Boswell danced a highland dance while visiting the island with Dr Johnson in 1773. Raasay was the birthplace of Scotland's best-known modern Gaelic poet, Sorley Maclean. His poems (many of which he translated into English himself) contain many references to the island.

There are many small curiosities to be found on the island: the old iron ore mine at Suisnish that was worked by German prisoners during World War I, and the mermaids lying outside the perilously dilapidated Raasay House (now an outdoor centre), whose cost drove the last MacLeod chief into bankruptcy. Brochel Castle, a vegetatious ruin, stands picturesquely on the east coast, and makes a good goal for a short drive. Beyond, the road to Arnish was built single-handedly by a local crofter over ten years from 1966, after the local authority declined to do the job itself.

The Small Isles

The Small Isles, part of the Inner Hebrides group, fill the sea between Skye and Ardnamurchan. The jagged outline of Rum and the curious profile of Eigg seen over an aquamarine sea from Arisaig suggest places of almost tropical beauty. However, these islands, with their small, precarious populations and difficult communications, are not for people who need cars or extensive facilities, and accommodation on them is limited. Short visits are possible, especially in the summer months when the year-round ferry service from Mallaig is supplemented by cruises from Arisaig, but the timetables are apt to leave you with either too little time on each island, or else too much.

Canna
✓ *Peace and quiet*
Canna is owned by the National Trust for Scotland, after years of benevolent stewardship by the Gaelic scholar Dr John Lorne Campbell. It is a small island, only five miles long, bounded by cliffs and with bright fertile patches fringing its rugged interior – a good place for birdwatchers and botanists and a very quiet refuge. Accommodation is extremely limited. [⌒ via *www.road-to-the-isles.org.uk*]

Eigg

✓ *Scenery, birds, walks*

✓ *Small, almost self-sufficient community*

✗ *No public transport*

Eigg will go down in history as the place that pioneered the community buy-out, ending decades of putting up with the whims of absentee landlords. Now the island is owned and administered by a trust, with the residents heavily represented on it. This may bring its own problems, but at least the islanders' future is in their own hands.

This is a delightful island to spend time on, although you must be prepared to walk. The strange peak of An Sgurr, a flat-topped volcanic outcrop with precipitous sides, dominates the landscape. There are singing sands at the Bay of Laig, which whisper underfoot in the right conditions. The most gruesome sight on the island is Macdonald's Cave, where 400 members of that clan were summarily suffocated by raiding MacLeods, who lit a fire at the entrance. [*www.ourworld.compuserve.com/homepages/EiggTrust*]

Muck

✓ *Day trips, walks*

Flat and fertile, tiny Muck has just over a mile of road and a beautiful shell beach. It is really too small to stay on for long (there are two small hotels, camping and holiday cottages), but the ferry from Arisaig allows you to explore it inside a day, three days a week. [*www.road-to-the-isles.org.uk/muck*]

Rum

✓ *Naturalists, walkers*

✗ *Very few facilities*

✗ *Bothy or hostel accommodation only*

✗ *Fiendish midges*

Rum is a wet, mountainous island, at its most attractive from a distance for all except the really keen and weatherproof. Its midges are notorious. The island's population was unceremoniously forced off to Canada during the nineteenth century, and Rum became an uninhabited deer forest for sporting millionaires. It was the last of these, the Lancastrian industrialist George Bullough, who built the extravagant fantasy of Kinloch Castle, importing stone from Arran and kilt-wearing craftsmen from Lancashire to create a bizarre combination of Scottish castle, Tudor mansion and Italian palazzo.

Rum is owned and managed by Scottish Natural Heritage as a huge outdoor research centre. Red deer form one of the most important areas of their work, but the island is also the scene of the successful reintroduction of the sea eagle to Scotland. Access to parts of the island is restricted – ask the warden before exploring away from the marked nature trails. One interesting walk runs across the island to Harris Bay, where the Bullough family's mausoleum – a Doric temple surmounted by crosses – stands incongruously beside the sea.

You will find information about Rum on the Internet via *www.scotland-inverness.co.uk*

WHERE TO STAY

£ – under £70 per room per night, incl. VAT

££ – £70 to £110 per room per night, incl. VAT

£££ – over £110 per room per night, incl. VAT

ACHILTIEBUIE
Summer Isles Hotel
Achiltiebuie, Ullapool IV26 2YG
☎ (01854) 622282
📠 (01854) 622251
www.summerisleshotel.co.uk
Relaxed, sophisticated farmhouse hotel with superb five-course dinners. Classy, uncluttered bedrooms. The restaurant and lounge enjoy views of the Summer Isles and beyond to Gairloch, Skye and Harris.
££ *Closed Oct to Easter (See Where to Eat)*

ARISAIG
Arisaig House
Beasdale, Arisaig PH39 4NR
☎ (01687) 450622
📠 (01687) 450626
www.arisaighouse.co.uk
Apparently austere hotel at the end of a steep, redwood-lined drive, with a tranquil and light interior. Distinctive bedrooms; excellent four-course dinners.
£££ *Closed Dec to Feb (See Where to Eat)*

Old Library Lodge
Arisaig PH39 4NH
☎ (01687) 450651
📠 (01687) 450219
This simple waterfront building is a cheerful, modern black and white bistro-with-rooms. Bedrooms are fresh and

light; two have lovely bay views. Fish and seafood on the dinner menu.

£ *Closed Nov to Mar*

COLBOST
Three Chimneys

Colbost, Dunvegan, Isle of Skye
IV55 8ZT

☎ (01470) 511258

🖨 (01470) 511358

🖳 *www.threechimneys.co.uk*

Acclaimed restaurant-with-rooms offering stylish interiors and memorable seafood. Modern, stylish bedrooms and bathrooms, many split-level. Imaginative continental breakfasts.

£££ *Closed 3 weeks in Jan (See Where to Eat)*

ERBUSAIG
Old Schoolhouse

Tigh Fasgaidh, Erbusaig IV40 8BB

☎/🖨 (01599) 534369

Pleasant, white-painted former schoolhouse in a quiet valley; three attractive *en suite* bedrooms have hill views. The restaurant, open to guests and non-residents, specialises in local produce.

£ *Easter to end Oct*

INVERASDALE
Knotts Landing

12 Coast, Inverasdale IV22 2LR

☎ (01445) 781331

Value for money in a beautiful, remote setting with views of the water and mountains. Reached by a narrow loch-shore road, this small guesthouse has three well-appointed bedrooms. Breakfast and home-cooked dinners.

£ *All year exc Christmas*

ISLE ORNSAY
Duisdale Country House Hotel

Sleat, Isle of Skye IV43 0QW

☎ (01471) 833202

🖨 (01471) 833404

🖳 *www.duisdalehotel.com*

Former hunting lodge in gardens with putting green and croquet lawn; excellent sea views to Knoydart. Graceful modern décor; attractive bedrooms. Scottish traditional cooking.

££ *Closed end Oct to Easter*

KILMUIR
Kilmuir House

Kilmuir, Isle of Skye IV51 9YN

☎ (01470) 542262

🖳 (01470) 542461

Attractive, white-painted old manse overlooking Loch Snizort. The two first-floor double rooms enjoy fine views; the ground-floor room can be a triple. Local produce features at breakfast and in the pre-booked dinners.

£ *All year exc Christmas*

KINLOCHBERVIE
Old School Restaurant

Inshegra, Kinlochbervie IV27 4RH

☎/🖨 (01971) 521383

Mostly modern accommodation – pastel rooms have loch or mountain views – and a school motif in the restaurant (a former schoolroom). Seafood is a speciality, with meat and vegetarian options.

£ *All year exc Christmas and New Year*

LOCH ERIBOLL
Port-na-Con House

Loch Eriboll IV27 4UN

☎/🖨 (01971) 511367

Former customs house on the unspoilt loch shore, by a private beach. Small, spotless bedrooms have loch views, shared by the conservatory and lounge. 'Excellent' dinners and breakfasts.
£ All year

LOCHINVER
The Albannach
Baddidarroch, Lochinver IV27 4LP
☎ (01571) 844407
🖷 (01571) 844285
Imposing gabled house with a superb panorama across the bay to Suilven, visible from the conservatory and steeply-pitched garden. Snug, richly coloured interior; five-course contemporary Scottish dinners.
£££ Closed 1 Dec to 15 Mar (See Where to Eat)

Polcraig
Lochinver IV27 4LD
☎/🖷 (01571) 844429
Modern hillside house with lounge overlooking Lochinver harbour. Five comfortable bedrooms; four en suite, one with sole use of a bathroom.
£ All year

MELVAIG
Rua Reidh Lighthouse
Rua Reidh, Melvaig IV21 2EA
☎/🖷 (01445) 771263
Fully automated lighthouse built in 1910; accommodation is in the former keeper's house, set in fine mountain and coastal scenery teeming with wildlife. Comfortable bedrooms, two lounges, a self-catering kitchen and a tea room; communal dinners.
£ All year exc 8 to 31 Jan

PORTREE
Almondbank Guest House
Viewfield Road, Portree, Isle of Skye IV51 9EU
☎ (01478) 619696
🖷 (01478) 613114
Large, modern house by the water's edge on the outskirts of Portree. The lounge and some en suite bedrooms have wonderful bay views; video players and Internet access are available.
£ All year

Viewfield House
Portree IV51 9EU
☎ (01478) 612217
🖷 (01478) 613517
🖳 www.viewfieldhouse.com
Trophies from the British Empire make this castellated country house a memorable place to stay. The Victorian atmosphere is carried through to the simple bedrooms. Delicious five-course set meals.
££ Closed mid-Oct to mid-Apr

SCOURIE
Minch View
Scouriemore, Scourie IV27 4TG
☎ (01971) 502010
White-painted house high on the west coast with wonderful sea and hill views. Four simply decorated bedrooms, two wheelchair-accessible. Guests can relax in the spacious sitting room; three-course evening meals served.
£ Easter to Oct

Scourie Lodge
Scourie IV27 4TE
☎ (01971) 502248
Four en suite bedrooms in this impeccable guesthouse. Guests may

bring their own wine to dinner; vegetarian options on request.

£ Mar to Oct

SHIELDAIG
Tigh an Eilean

Shieldaig, Strathcarron IV54 8XN

☎ (01520) 755251

🖅 (01520) 755321

Welcoming waterfront hotel on the shores of Loch Torridon; fresh, spotless bedrooms. Two lounges have views of the little loch island, and maps line the residents' bar. Unpretentious food uses locally sourced ingredients.

££ Closed end Oct to Apr

STAFFIN
Glenview Inn and Restaurant

Culnacnoc, Staffin, Isle of Skye IV51 9JH

☎ (01470) 562248

🖅 (01470) 562211

Comfortable rooms in this friendly, traditional croft in a spectacular setting. 'Excellent' dinners in the licensed restaurant involve local seafood, game and meat. Vegetarian options are always available.

£ Apr to Oct

STRATHAIRD
Strathaird House

Strathaird IV49 9AX

☎ (01471) 866269

🖅 (01471) 866320

Remote guesthouse down ten miles of undulating country road, with fine views of sea and countryside. Simple, comfortable accommodation, a sitting room and library. Breakfasters overlook the garden and croquet lawn.

£ Easter Fri to end Sept

STRONTIAN
Kilcamb Lodge

Strontian PH36 4HY

☎ (01967) 402257

🖅 (01967) 402041

🖱 www.kilcamblodge.co.uk

Isolated small hotel on the edge of Loch Sunart; the beautiful Morvern Hills are visible while dining. An unstuffy atmosphere in the convivial bar and lounge, cosy drawing room and colourful bedrooms.

££ Closed Dec to Feb (exc New Year). (See Where to Eat)

Kinloch House

Strontian PH36 4HZ

☎ (01967) 402138

🖅 (01967) 402261

Modern bungalow on the shore of Loch Sunart in 13 acres of beautiful grounds. High standards of service in a relaxing atmosphere. Well-equipped, comfortable bedrooms; local information in the lounge.

£ All year exc Christmas

TALISKER
Talisker House

Talisker, Isle of Skye IV47 8SF

☎ (01478) 640245

🖅 (01478) 640214

🖱 www.talisker.co.uk

House visited by Boswell and Johnson, a ten-minute stroll from the sea. The faded grandeur of a bygone age colours the public rooms and bedrooms. Dinners specialise in home produce.

££ Closed end Oct to early Mar

ULLAPOOL
Altnaharrie Inn
Ullapool IV26 2SS
☎ (01854) 633230
Visitors to this romantic luxury haven
must abandon their cars in Ullapool for
the little boat across Loch Broom. Crisp
Scandinavian décor and splendid views
across the water. 'Magical' five-course
dinners.
*£££ Closed Nov to Mar (exc Chr and New
Year). (See Where to Eat)*

The Sheiling Guest House
Garve Road, Ullapool IV26 2SX
☎/📧 (01854) 612947
Guesthouse with exclusive fishing rights
over 40 square miles of hill lochs, plus a
boat and equipment for hire. Non-
anglers can enjoy breathtaking scenery
from the patio.
£ Easter to Sept

UPPER DIABAIG
Upper Diabaig Farm
Upper Diabaig, By Torridon IV22 2HE
☎ (01445) 790227
Remote farmhouse in spectacular
scenery by a freshwater loch. Three
simple, comfortable bedrooms; pre-
booked dinners and packed lunches
provided.
£ Easter to Sept

WATERNISH
Lismore
Waternish, Isle of Skye IV55 8GE
☎ (01470) 592381
Restful, lovingly converted old croft.
Two *en suite* bedrooms, and a sun
lounge/breakfast room overlooking the
Outer Hebrides. Guests may bring
their own wine to varied evening
meals.
£ Apr to Oct

WHERE TO EAT

ACHILTIEBUIE
Summer Isles Hotel
Achiltiebuie, Ullapool IV26 2YG
☎ (01854) 622282
📧 (01854) 622251
🖥 www.summerisleshotel.co.uk
The blue and gold dining-room faces
west over the islands to make the most
of magical sunsets. Five-course dinners
have no choices before dessert; plenty
of seafood appears. 'Exquisitely fresh and
just-cooked' dishes and home-baked
bread.
*All week 12.30–2 and 8 (one sitting D);
closed mid-Oct to Easter (See Where to
Stay)*

ACHNASHEEN
Loch Torridon Hotel
Loch Torridon, Achnasheen IV22 2EY
☎ (01445) 791242
📧 (01445) 791296
🖥 www.lochtorridonhotel.com
Victorian baronial shooting lodge in wild
country at the head of a sea loch. Plenty
of fish and seafood on the menu,
supplemented by meat, game and
enjoyable desserts. The wine list is
somewhat expensive.
All week D only 7.15–8.45

APPLECROSS
Applecross Inn

Shore Street, Applecross IV54 8LR
☎ (01520) 744262
An enticing combination of hallmark seafood dishes and the setting lures customers to the busy bar and tiny dining-room. A predominantly fishy menu is interspersed with alternatives. Children have their own menu or small portions of the bar menu dishes.
Summer 11–11.30, Sun 12–11, winter 12–2.30 and 5–11, Sun 12–7; bar food 12–9 (no food after 2.30 Nov to Mar); restaurant D only 6–8.30; closed 25 Dec, 1 Jan

ARISAIG
Arisaig House

Beasdale, Arisaig PH39 4NR
☎ (01687) 450622
🖷 (01687) 450626
🖳 *www.arisaighouse.co.uk*
While the pace of this fine granite hotel is relaxed, the food offers a handsome, up-to-date four-course dinner menu of locally sourced produce and contemporary flavours. The wine list is global.
All week 12.30–2 and 7.30–8.30; closed Dec to Feb (See Where to Stay)

COLBOST
Three Chimneys

Colbost, Dunvegan, Isle of Skye IV55 8ZT
☎ (01470) 511258
🖷 (01470) 511358
🖳 *www.threechimneys.co.uk*
Among the local produce on the somewhat pricey menu of this relaxed restaurant-with-rooms is an enviable range of seafood. Highland beef, loin of lamb and organic salads also play their part alongside rich desserts.
Mon to Sat L 12.30–2.30 (phone to check winter times), all week D 6.30–9.30 (See Where to Stay)

GLENELG
Glenelg Inn

Glenelg, By Kyle of Lochalsh IV40 8JR
☎ (01599) 522273
Uncluttered homeliness at the closest mainland point to Skye, in a folksy inn visited by Johnson and Boswell. Bar lunches include baked potatoes and more filling fare; more formal evening meals are served in a separate dining-room.
Summer 12–2.30 and 5–11 (12 Sat, 11.30 Sun); winter Sat L 12–2.30, all week eve 5–11; bar food 12–2.30, restaurant from 7.30

LOCHINVER
The Albannach

Baddidarroch, Lochinver IV27 4LP
☎ (01571) 844407
🖷 (01571) 844285
Much of the produce served is wild or free-range, and as local as possible. The five-course format typically starts with 'beautifully fresh and superbly prepared' seafood, followed by a soup. Although there is no choice, the modern Scottish meals are well-balanced.
All week D only 8 (one sitting); closed 1 Dec to 15 Mar (See Where to Stay)

PLOCKTON
Plockton Inn

Innes Street, Plockton IV52 8TW
☎ (01599) 544222
Friendly harbour pub specialising in fresh fish. They smoke their own, which

appears on both the printed menu and the blackboard. Meat and game broaden choices, and most items can be starters or mains. A separate restaurant is also available.

Mon to Fri 11–1, Sat 11–11.30, Sun 12.30–11; bar food 12–2.30 and 5.30–10 (9 winter); restaurant 12–2.30, 5.30–10 (9 winter)

STEIN
Lochbay
1–2 Macleod Terrace, Stein, Isle of Skye IV55 8GA
☎/📠 (01470) 592235
This tiny restaurant retains the character of the original fishermen's cottages, and specialises in fresh fish. Cooking is commendably plain, without unnecessary garnishes. Hearty desserts cover traditional and Scottish favourites.

Mon to Fri 12–2.30 and 6–9; closed Oct to Easter

STRONTIAN
Kilcamb Lodge
Strontian PH36 4HY
☎ (01967) 402257
📠 (01967) 402041
🖥 www.kilcamblodge.co.uk
Outstanding views across Loch Sunart, where visitors may catch their own dinner in the hotel's small boat. Native beef, lamb, game and fish are all commendably fresh, and simple techniques make the best of excellent ingredients. Lunch is much lighter.

All week 12–2 and 7.30 (one sitting D); closed Dec to Feb exc New Year (See Where to Stay)

ULLAPOOL
Altnaharrie Inn
Ullapool IV26 2SS
☎ (01854) 633230
Tranquillity and comfort in a remote and beautiful setting. The dining-room is a combination of simplicity and pretty detail. Seafood plays the largest part in the four-course no-choice menu, with first-class ingredients expertly cooked and sauced.

All week D only 8 (one sitting); closed Nov to Apr (exc some weekends). (See Where to Stay)

The Western Isles

Harris tweed loom

- Remote islands which are the last stronghold of the old Highland way of life
- Superb beaches and desolate landscapes
- Small, tight-knit, Gaelic-speaking communities
- Great variety between one island and the next

THE WESTERN ISLES

At a glance

✓ Good for seven- to ten-day holidays, preferably in early summer

✓ Shorter three- to five-day breaks on Barra

✓ The place to go if you want to get off the beaten track

✓ Excellent fishing holidays, based on North or South Uist

✗ Ferry links can be awkward and involve a lengthy drive to Oban, Skye or Ullapool. The Mallaig service may be withdrawn

✗ Very few indoor attractions for a wet spell

✗ Total Sunday shutdown on Lewis and Harris

The islands of the Outer Hebrides (or Western Isles), which run for 130 miles parallel to Scotland's north–west coast, are unlike anywhere else in the country. Superficially they share many of the features of the north–west mainland – there are mountains, fertile coastal strips, magnificent beaches, desolate peat bogs and endless lochans. However, the Western Isles, despite the aircraft and the ferries which serve them, are remote, and for the inhabitants to climb into a car and head for the bright lights is easier said than done. Because of this, they remain in many ways the last stronghold of old Highland life. Communities are closely bound to the sea and to the soil; Gaelic is widely spoken, religious faith is strong, and hospitality is as genuine as you can hope to find in a tourist–infested world.

It is, however, a grave mistake to think that you are venturing into some unsophisticated outpost of Britain. The inhabitants of the Western Isles have seen many attempts to 'modernise' them and are correspondingly wary of outsiders' grandiose schemes to transform their way of life. They are equally aware of how easy it is for the islands to be neglected – the Western Isles did not even have their own local government until 1974. Consequently, opinions are strongly held out here. You only need to trawl the community web sites for a taste of them.

For visitors, especially those who have roots in the islands, the Western Isles exert a fascination which is difficult to justify to those who have not yet been there. The landscape of the interiors is mostly unrelenting rock, bog or water, and the long, straggling, crofting communities by the shore have no similarity to conventionally pretty villages. Even the superb beaches have their drawbacks, smelly seaweed being the commonest. Yet these are not the images that endure. Instead, it may be the blanket of wild flowers on a Uist machair, a shower clearing over the hills of Harris, a riotous evening in a Stornoway bar or simply the scent of burning peat drifting over the islands that you will remember.

During the 1990s, life was made much easier for the visitor to the Western Isles, with new causeways linking to islands that were previously only accessible by boat, and with a new direct car ferry link between Harris and North Uist. One piece of the jigsaw remains to be put in place: a dedicated ferry service between South Uist and Barra. Then, at last, it will be possible for the motorist to explore the whole chain from end to end without difficulty.

Key web sites

www.hebrides.com More an encyclopedia than a web site. Satellite maps and all kinds of background

www.witb.co.uk The tourist board's web site. Some good general background

www.w-isles.gov.uk Excellent site by the local council, especially the links to smaller communities

www.isleofbarra.com Useful directory for most services on Barra

www.uistonline.com Covers the Uists and Benbecula

LEWIS

The interior of Lewis is bare of people and bare of trees. The northern half is a flat, deserted moorland of rain-washed skies and distant horizons, where the only signs of human activity are the trenches and embankments of peat-cuttings, often marked by piles of plastic sacks.

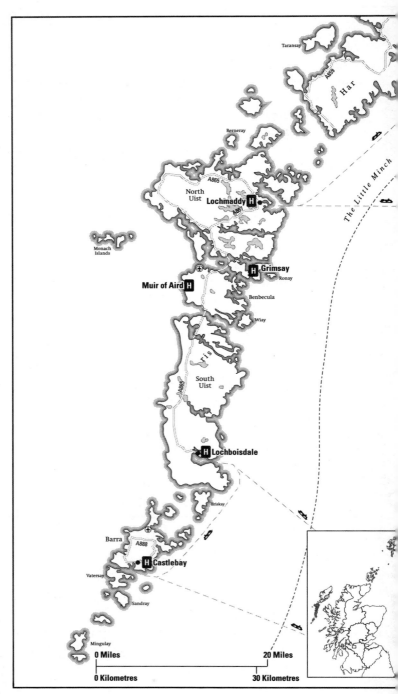

Taransay

Har

A859

Berneray

A865

North
Uist

Lochmaddy **H**

A867

The Little Minch

Monach
Islands

H Grimsay

Ronay

Muir of Aird H

Benbecula

Wiay

s

South
Uist

A865

H Lochboisdale

Eriskay

Barra

A888

H Castlebay

Vatersay

Sandray

Mingulay

0 Miles   20 Miles

0 Kilometres   30 Kilometres

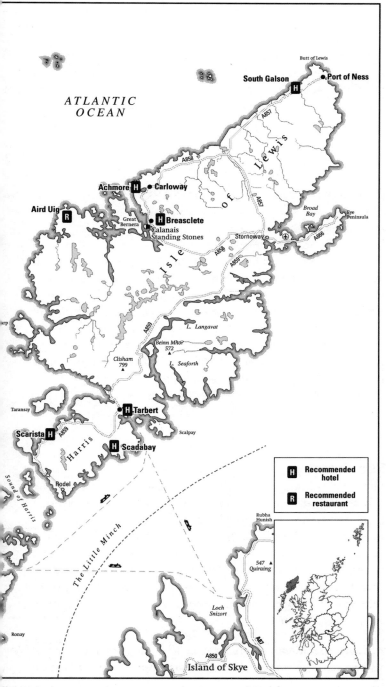

ATLANTIC
OCEAN

Butt of Lewis

South Galson **H** ● **Port of Ness**

A857

Isle of Lewis

A858

Achmore **H** ● **Carloway**

Great
Bernera

H **Breasclete**

Aird Uig **R**

Calanais
Standing Stones

Broad
Bay

Eye
Peninsula

Stornoway

A858

A859

A866

Isle

A859

L. Langavat

Beinn Mhor
572 ▲

Clisham
799 ▲

L. Seaforth

H **Tarbert**

Taransay

Scalpay

Scarista **H**

A859

Harris

H **Scadabay**

Rodel

Sound of Harris

The Little Minch

Rubha
Hunish

547 ▲
Quiraing

Ronay

Loch
Snizort

A850

Island of Skye

A87

	Recommended hotel
H	
R	Recommended restaurant

437

All the inhabitants of Lewis live by the sea, approximately 8,000 of them in Stornoway on the east coast, the only town on the islands. On the west coast, a long string of crofting townships runs the 34 miles from Ness to Carloway. Further south, settlements become sparse as rocky hills bulge out of the moor and long sea-lochs cut into the coast.

Top sight

Calanais Standing Stones (on A858)

✓ *The only stone circle in the UK to rival Stonehenge*
✓ *Freedom to wander around the stones*

Set on a lonely peninsula that is unlikely to be spoilt by crowds, the 53 stones form a pattern like a Celtic cross, with an inner circle and four arms. It is thought they date from around 3000 BC. Their function is unknown, but a lunar observatory is a popular explanation. The neighbouring visitor centre explains such facts as are known, but in truth, knowledge is not so important here as the atmosphere created by these silent grey watchers on their patch of lonely moorland. *[All year, visitor centre: summer 10–7, winter, 10–4; closed Sun;* ☎ *(01851) 621422;* 🖱 *via www.stonepages.com]*

The town

Stornoway

The small fishing town of Stornoway also happens to be the only settlement of any size in the Western Isles. There is not a great deal to see once you have bought any necessities you need (opportunities to do this will be limited elsewhere on the island), but a walk around the harbour will prove worthwhile if fishing boats are unloading. Equally, a walk in the grounds of Lews Castle (now a college) is pleasant. The woods and shrubs here would be unremarkable elsewhere, but, in the Western Isles, are exceptional.

Museum nan Eilean offers an excellent background on local history, and has some good exhibits *[Apr to Sept, Mon–Sat*

10–5.30; Oct to Mar, Tue–Fri, 10–5, Sat 10–3; ☎ *via www.witb.co.uk].* **An Lanntair** is a small but often interesting and radical art gallery, with an excellent coffee shop. At the time of writing, the gallery was about to move into a new expanded arts centre *[All year, Mon–Sat 10–5.30;* ☎ *(01851) 703307);* ☎ *www.lanntair.com].*

Look up information about the town via ☎ *www.maciain.demon.co.uk*

Best scenery and local sights

Most of the things to see lie on the west coast of Lewis. From Stornoway, the A859 and A858 carry you westward across the interior of Lewis to the road junction at Garynahine. From here you can turn south for good beaches and a visit to the island of Berneray, or north to visit the scattered communities of the coastline. All of the sights below are accessible from the A858 or A857.

Arnol Black House Museum This is a conserved example of a type of housing once common throughout the Highlands and Islands. Thick, low, double walls packed with peat for insulation support a roof thatched with heather and straw and weighed down with stones. Often there is only one door, used by both cattle and humans, and the interior is split between byre and living quarters. A peat fire smoulders on a central hearth. In a land desperately short of everything but stone and heathery peat, the black house represented an extremely effective, and energy-efficient, use of available material. *[Apr to Sept, Mon–Sat 9.30–6.30; Oct to Mar, Mon–Thur and Sat, 9.30–4.30;* ☎ *(01851) 710395]*

Butt of Lewis The lighthouse on the northernmost tip of the island was designed by the Stevensons, and is now automated. It is a stirring spot, with waves crashing against the cliffs, a little caravan selling tweed goods by day, and memorable sunsets by night.

Carloway Broch The remains of this well-preserved broch stand close to the road on a hillside overlooking the sea. Part of the wall is still 30 feet high and the collapsing stonework has exposed the interior galleries and stairs. The adjacent visitor centre, in a mini replica broch, uses multi-media effects to give you some idea of what life in a broch would have been like. See the box on pages 402–9 for more on brochs. [⌐▮ *via www.stonepages.com*]

Garenin A detour from the A858 will bring you to this small village of ruined black houses, some of which are now being restored as accommodation for holidaymakers – details are at ⌐▮ *www.gearrannan.com*

Ness Heritage Centre The district of Ness has a distinctive character (see ⌐▮ *www.hebrides.com*), not least in its relish for the gannet as a culinary delicacy. The local heritage centre is a lively place with friendly volunteers, and a wide-ranging collection of local artefacts and ephemera. *[June to Sept, Mon–Sat 9–5.30, Oct to May, Mon–Fri 9–5.30;* ☎ *(01851) 810377]*

Shawbost The folk museum here was started as a project by local schoolchildren back in 1970. It has been growing ever since, and has blossomed into a fascinating, if ramshackle, collection of artefacts and junk collected from all walks of Hebridean life. *[Apr to Nov, Mon–Sat 10–6;* ☎ *(01851) 710212]*

Best beach

Uig The best beach on Lewis is down in the south-west (via the B8011), a great bay of golden sand. It was here, in 1831, that a crofter dug up the Lewis Chessmen, 78 pieces of Scandinavian origin, carved from walrus ivory and dating from the twelfth century. The kings glower, the queens look as if they are suffering an attack of the vapours, and the pawn-warriors bite their shields in frustration. You can buy reproductions on Lewis; the originals are split between museums in Edinburgh and London.

Gaelic on the roads

The Western Isles Island Council has adopted a policy of using Gaelic place names on road signs, except in Stornoway and Benbecula, where they are bilingual. Most maps still use the English names, however. To help you find your way round, we recommend using a map (such as the one available from the Western Isles tourist board) which shows both names. We have used the English versions for this book.

Place names

Balivanich	Baile a Mhanaich
Barra	Barraigh
Benbecula	Beinn na Faoghla
Butt of Lewis	Rubha Robhanais
Carloway	Carlabhagh
Castlebay	Bagh a Chaisteil
Eriskay	Eiriosgaigh
Harris	Na Hearadh
Lewis	Eilean Leodhais
Lochboisdale	Loch Baghasdail
Lochmaddy	Loch nam Madadh
Ness	Nis
Newtonferry	Port nan Long
North Uist	Uibhist a Tuath
Rodel	Roghadal
South Uist	Uibhist a Deas
Stornoway	Steornabhagh
Tarbert	Tairbeart
Vatersay	Bhatarsaigh

GREAT BERNERA

Linked to Lewis by a bridge, the island is notable for some lovely beaches, and for a recently discovered Iron Age village, whose houses were revealed by a storm in 1992. A reconstruction of one has been built, and you can wander around the others, although much of the site has been filled in again to protect it from the elements. [⌂🖱 *via www.w-isles.gov.uk*]

HARRIS

Harris is actually part of the same landmass as Lewis, but is always considered as a separate island, although here it is mountains rather than sea that provide the barrier. Where Lewis is predominately flat moorland, Harris is largely mountain and rock. The separation of the two goes right back to Norse times, when the island was divided between the two sons of Leod. Harris remained in MacLeod hands until 1834. [⌂🖱 *via www.hebrides.com*]

Best scenery and local sights: North Harris

This, the land lying north of Tarbert, is the country for hill-walkers. None of the mountains here are as high as those on the Scottish mainland, but they are steep, rocky in places, and views from them can be marvellous. Clisham, the highest peak, is relatively easy to get to from the A859. North Harris also provides access to the island of Scalpay (see below).

Amhuinnsuidh The B887 meanders westward along the shore of West Loch Tarbert with fine views out to sea. The bombastic architecture of the turreted shooting lodge of Amhuinnsuidh Castle is a reminder of the days when much of the Western Isles was little more than a playground for millionaires. Beyond, at the end of the road, there's a small but attractive beach at Husinish.

Tarbert is a tiny place, but as it is the ferry port for Harris it has more facilities (such as a bank and a restaurant) than anywhere else. Ask at the Tourist Information Centre or the Harris Hotel if you want to fish for sea trout.

Best scenery and local sights: South Harris

You should certainly drive right round South Harris, for the change in landscape between east and west is fascinating. The road down the west coast passes the firm sandy beaches of Luskentyre and Scarista, and everywhere there are patches of fertile machair.

The single-track road up the east coast of Harris winds amongst outcrops of rock, bare of any vegetation. Crofts cling to tiny patches of level ground by the shore and boats are tied up in the many inlets. It was in this curious, inhospitable land-scape that the largest quarry in Europe was to have been built. Ten years' wrangling and extensive enquiries have eventually led to permission being refused. The battle may not be over yet, however.

The golden road This is the popular name for the road which winds up the east coast of Harris. It is a long, slow route, but very scenic. Much of the population of Harris lives here – their ancestors were cleared from the more fertile land to the west in the nineteenth century to make way for sheep. Along the road, especially near the township of Plocrapool, are several places where you can stop to watch **Harris tweed** being woven [$\curvearrowright$ *www.harristweed.com*]. The crofters are sent materials and patterns from Stornoway, and make up the lengths of tweed on clattering looms in small sheds beside their houses. You can some-times see packets of cloth left by cottage gateways for collection, where it will be taken to Stornoway for finishing. If the tweed is not hand-woven, dyed and finished in the Western Isles, it cannot be stamped with the orb symbol which marks Harris tweed.

St Clement's Church, Rodel At the very end of the A859 stands this beautifully crafted twelfth-century church, a remarkable find in what is now such a far-away spot. Inside, the tomb of Alexander MacLeod, who died in 1547, is even more remarkable. Its carvings, showing a hunting scene, a castle and many religious images, repay a close look.

A church-going society

In religion, the islands are split between the Presbyterian Lewis, Harris and North Uist, and the predominantly Roman Catholic South Uist and Barra. Benbecula has adherents of both doctrines. On Lewis and Harris, the Free Presbyterian Church of Scotland and the Free Church of Scotland (the 'Wee Frees') are both strong, and Sundays are very strictly observed. It is worth remembering that public transport will not be running and shops and petrol stations will not be open. On the Roman Catholic islands, things are more relaxed. If you want to partic-ipate in a Hebridean service, the Sunday evening service at the Free Church in Kenneth Street, Stornoway, is in held in English. Dress appropriately (women should cover their heads), and you wil be met with a little curiosity and a great deal of kindness.

Best beaches

The west coast of Harris has some of the best sand beaches in the Hebrides. Those at **Luskentyre** and **Scarista** are the best known. Backed by fertile machair, which is a carpet of flowers in spring, both these huge stretches of sand are wonderful places for a walk. Offshore lies the island of Taransay, famous as the site of the *Castaway 2000* TV programme.

SCALPAY

Linked to north Harris by a causeway, this is a small but thriving island, with a lovely harbour and a strung-out community of houses. Most of the island's activity is still based around fishing. [🖱 *www.scalpay.com*]

NORTH UIST, SOUTH UIST AND BENBECULA

These three islands are linked by causeways which cross the shallow inlets of the sea between them. There is so much water, both fresh and salt, on these islands that it is sometimes difficult to know which island you are on. One of the delights of flying over the islands is to watch the light reflected back at you from the hundreds of lochs, as if someone had shattered mirrors over a green and brown carpet. These are the islands to come to for sandy beaches, for sand runs almost the full length of their west coasts. The eastern side of the islands is where the lochs are – you can fish for trout and sea-trout until your arm drops off, but still fail to cover more than a fraction of the available water. Look up more information at ⤢🐚 *www.uistonline.com*

Best scenery and local sights

Balranald Nature Reserve (North Uist) This is a breeding site for duck and waders, and an RSPB reserve. It is one of the places in Scotland where you really do have a chance of seeing an otter, and in summer you may hear the call of the corncrake, a bird that is now extremely rare everywhere in Britain except among the crofts of the Western Isles, where traditional agricultural methods provide shelter for it. *[⤢🐚 via www.rspb.org.uk]*

Flora Macdonald's birthplace (South Uist) A cairn surrounded by sheep pens marks the spot where the girl who became part of sentimental Scottish folklore was born. It was from nearby Benbecula that she ferried Bonnie Prince Charlie 'over the sea to Skye'. The song does not mention that he was disguised as her maid at the time.

Liniclate Community School (Benbecula) In the south of the island, this school is open to the public, and has extensive facilities, including a library and small museum. It is also the site of various entertainments. It's worth knowing about if you are in search of somewhere warm and dry.

Lochboisdale (South Uist) South Uist's ferry port and chief settlement has very few facilities, but is set on a sea-loch of such singular beauty that it is well worth visiting. There is even a ruined castle on an island to greet you if you arrive by ferry.

Lochmaddy (North Uist) The village is so girdled with lochs that it almost floats. The Tourist Information Centre and the Lochmaddy Hotel are the places to enquire about fishing. For a wet day, the **Taigh Chearsabhagh** combination of museum and arts centre is an excellent small sight *[Feb to Dec;* ☎ *(01876) 500293;* ✆ *www.taigh-chearsabhagh.org].*

Best beaches

Virtually the entire west coast of these islands is uninterrupted sand. Make your way from the main road through the machair and the dunes down any one of the numerous tracks. Atlantic storms can leave piles of rotting kelp on the sand (collecting it for the potash industry was once a major source of employment on the islands), but apart from this, the beaches are pristine and unspoilt.

ERISKAY

The causeway from South Uist to Eriskay, completed in 2000, is the latest of the links to be built between the main land masses and the outlying islands. Eriskay is the spot where Prince Charles Edward Stuart first landed in 1745, the beginning of the last Jacobite uprising that was to cause so much pain and bloodshed throughout the Highlands. Eriskay's other public moment was the wreck of the *SS Politician* in 1941 – an event which was the centrepiece of Compton MacKenzie's novel, *Whisky Galore.* The place to recall this is in the island's pub, Am Politician, which preserves a couple of whisky bottles from the original wreck.

BARRA

From the map, Barra may look too small to be worth bothering with, but this is a mistake. On this self-contained island you will find a compendium of all the best parts of the Western Isles – beaches, machair, small crofting communities and peat-smothered hills. Only the lochans are missing down here – otherwise Barra makes a perfect taster for Hebridean life. [⌂ *www.isleofbarra.com*]

Best scenery and local sights

Kisimul Castle This is the castle from which Barra's main settlement, Castlebay, takes its name. Built on a rocky shoal right in the centre of the bay, it was the stronghold of the Macneils of Barra. There is nothing much inside it, but you can be taken out to see it by boat if you want to do more than gaze at it from the harbour front. [*Apr to Sept, daily, 9.30–6.30; Oct, Mon, Wed and Sat, 9.30–4.30, Thur, 9.30–12.30, Sun, 2–4.30;* ☎ *(01871) 810336*]

Tràigh Mhór The famous beach in the north of the island, which serves as Barra's airport. The 'cockle strand' once provided more than a hundred cartloads of the shellfish a day, and cockles are still raked by hand. Watching the Twin Otters from Glasgow or Benbecula coming into land is one of the island's main tourist attractions.

Tangusdale This is the best beach on Barra, a wonderful stretch of sand with wild breakers when there is any wind.

VATERSAY

A causeway links the island to Barra. There is nothing here apart from crofts, two beautiful beaches and some superb machair full of wild flowers, but on a clear day you can see the string of now uninhabited islands to the south – Sandray, Pabbay, Mingauly and Berneray, now in the ownership of the National Trust for Scotland. [⌂ *via www.isleofbarra.com – an excellent separate guide*]

WHERE TO STAY

£ – under £70 per room per night, incl. VAT

££ – £70 to £110 per room per night incl.VAT

£££ – over £110 per room per night incl.VAT

ACHMORE
Cleascro Guest House
Achmore, Isle of Lewis HS2 9DU
☎ /📠 (01851) 860302
Comfortable modern house in a quiet rural area with three light and airy *en suite* bedrooms, a lounge and library. Dinners feature local produce and home-grown vegetables; guests can bring their own wine.
£ *All year exc Christmas and New Year*

BREASCLETE
Eshcol Guest House
Breasclete, Isle of Lewis HS2 9ED
☎ /📠 (01851) 621357
The hills of Harris and Uig are seen across Loch Roag from this attractive modern house. Comfortable and pleasant bedrooms; tasty meals.
£ *All year exc Christmas*

CASTLEBAY
Ceol Mara
Nasg, Castlebay,
Isle of Barra HS9 5XN
☎ /📠 (01871) 810294
Modern hillside house close to Kiessimul Castle, overlooking the town and bay. Three spacious *en suite* bedrooms and a lounge; beautiful views from the conservatory breakfast room.
£ *All year exc Christmas*

Terra Nova
25 Nask, Castlebay, Isle of Barra HS9 5XN
☎ (01871) 810458
Welcoming modern house with panoramic bay views. Two bedrooms have sea views. Guests can relax in the spacious lounge and pleasant conservatory.
£ *Apr to Oct*

GRIMSAY
Glendale
7 Kallin, Grimsay HS6 5HY
☎ (01870) 602029
Ochre-roofed house with harbour views and three large bedrooms. Guests may bring their own wine to pre-booked dinners with fresh local shellfish.
£ *All year exc Christmas and New Year*

LOCHBOISDALE
Brae Lea House
Lasgair, Lochboisdale, South Uist HS8 5TH
☎ /📠 (01878) 700497
Lochside guesthouse with views to the hills beyond; simply furnished *en suite* bedrooms. Breakfast can be served early to those with a ferry to catch.
£ *All year*

LOCHMADDY
Stag Lodge
Lochmaddy, North Uist HS6 5AE
☎ (01876) 500364
Attractive whitewashed former village store and post office. Comfortable accommodation and a licensed

restaurant. Room service till 9.30pm.
£ *All year*

MUIR OF AIRD
Lennox Cottage
Muir of Aird, Isle of Benbecula HS7 5LA
☎ (01870) 602965
Informal, welcoming cottage with
comfortable bedrooms and a cosy
lounge. Home-baked breakfast and
dinner.
£ *All year exc Christmas*

SCADABAY
Hillhead
Scadabay, Harris HS3 3ED
☎ (01859) 511226
A warm welcome on the rugged hillside
outside this small village. The owner
produces Harris tweed in his workshop
next door. Four comfortable bedrooms;
pre-book evening meals or a dinner/B&B
package.
£ *Apr to Oct*

SCARISTA
Scarista House
Scarista, Isle of Harris HS3 3HX
☎ (01859) 550238
🖂 (01859) 550277

🖥 *www.scaristahouse.demon.co.uk*
Lovely listed Georgian house opposite a
beautiful beach. Bedrooms are individual
and full of thoughtful touches.
Adventurous gourmet dishes.
£££ *All year*

SOUTH GALSON
Galson Farm Guest House
South Galson, Ness, Isle of Lewis
HS2 0SH
☎ /🖂 (01851) 850492
🖥 *www.galsonfarm.freeserve.co.uk*
Impeccable, white-harled eighteenth-
century farmhouse by the sea, acting as
village post office. Conservative décor
and two comfortable lounges, one with
French windows to a manicured garden.
Good home cooking.
££ *All year*

TARBERT
Allan Cottage
Tarbert, Isle of Harris HS3 3DJ
☎ /🖂 (01859) 502146
Top-notch guesthouse with comfortable
bedrooms, a large but cosy sitting room
and substantial breakfasts; dinners are
served family-style.
£ *Closed Oct to Apr*

WHERE TO EAT

AIRD UIG
The Bonaventure
Aird Uig, Isle of Lewis HS2 9JA
☎ /🖂 (01851) 672474
Happy Franco-Caledonian fusion at
restaurant in former RAF block with
nautical décor and a modern retro
theme, the sometime haunt of New
Labour politicians and the odd famous
face.
Closed Nov and Feb

Caithness, Orkney and Shetland

Puffins

- Scotland's far north: gales, cliffs, seas and islands
- The best prehistoric remains in the whole of Britain
- Huge sea bird colonies and myriad other birds
- Contrasting landscapes and different lifestyles

CAITHNESS, ORKNEY AND SHETLAND

At a glance

✓ Good for really refreshing seven- to ten-day holidays

✓ Long sub-Arctic summer evenings

✓ Wildlife-watching of all kinds

✗ Expensive and/or time-consuming to reach

✗ Limited public transport on the smaller islands

A glance at a map will show the link between Caithness and the island groups to the north. The Gaelic place names common in the Highlands are replaced by a new vocabulary – peerie, geo, wick and voe. These names are relics of the time when Caithness, Orkney and Shetland were part of Norway, not of Scotland.

The Norse *jarldom* (earldom) based on Orkney lasted more than 500 years (rather less in Caithness), and the last Norse-speaking inhabitant of Shetland died in the nineteenth century. The Scandinavian influence is still strong. However, the Norsemen were far from the first inhabitants of the islands. Nowhere else in Britain is there such a density of prehistoric sites, many dating from 3500 BC. Their remains survive, together with the settlements of the Bronze Age, the brochs of the Iron Age, the houses of the Picts and the occasional Norse long house. At Jarlshof in Shetland the remains of houses spanning 2,500 years lie exposed.

In Caithness, Orkney and especially Shetland, you have the distinct impression that you are closer to the Arctic than to the south of England. This has little to do with the temperature, which is mild for a part of the world on the same latitude as southern Greenland and Alaska. It has more to do with the absence of trees, the short summer nights, the teeming birdlife, the hissing gales and the feeling that you are on the edge of the unbridled north.

Key web sites

www.caithness.org A growing community web site with a useful list of place names

www.host.co.uk The Highlands of Scotland tourist board's site. Tries to cover too much ground – rather thin

www.orkney.com A good introduction, but not enough detail to be really useful

www.orknet.co.uk Excellent community web site

www.orkneyjar.com First-class cultural and historical background from an Orcadian's site. Especially good on the prehistoric remains

www.shetland-tourism.co.uk Web site of the Shetland tourist board. Comprehensive guide to the islands seen through slightly rose-tinted spectacles

www.wildlife.shetland.co.uk Massively detailed and fascinating site, with all you need to know about Shetland's birds and mammals. Useful links too

www.shetland-music.com Detailed web site with all the latest on Shetland's famous fiddle music, and much more

www.shetland.gov.uk The Shetland Islands council site. Excellent ferry information

www.shetland-times.co.uk Useful site by Shetland's local newspaper

CAITHNESS

After the sodden moors of Sutherland, the green fields of the north-eastern tip of Scotland seem strange and exotic, the more so since there are no trees to block the views. Instead of trees, you see flagstones. Beneath the soil lie layers of horizontally bedded sedimentary rock, which split perfectly into thin slabs. Roofs, walls, fences and floors are made from this stone (so are the pavements of many of Britain's cities), and where the sea washes against cliffs of it you find extraordinary effects, from half-finished flights of giant stairs to sea-stacks like carefully balanced towers of biscuits.

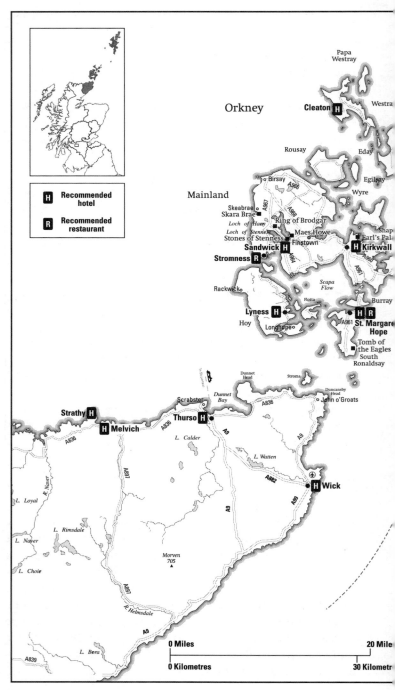

Orkney

Papa Westray

Westray

Cleaton H

Rousay

Eday

Egilsay

Mainland

Wyre

Birsay

A967

A986

Skeabrae
Skara Brae

Ring of Brodgar

Loch of Harray

Maes Howe

Loch of Stenness

Finstown

Shap

Stones of Stenness

Earl's Pal.

Sandwick H

Kirkwall H

A964

Stromness R

A961

Rackwick

Scapa Flow

Flotta

Burray

Lyness H

A961

H R

St. Margare
Hope

Hoy

Longhope

Tomb of
the Eagles
South
Ronaldsay

Dunnet
Head

Stroma

Duncansby
Head

John o'Groats

Scrabster

*Dunnet
Bay*

A836

Strathy H

A836

H **Melvich**

A836

Thurso H

A9

L. Calder

R. Naver

A897

L. Watten

A882

L. Loyal

L. Rimsdale

A9

H **Wick**

A99

L. Naver

L. Choie

A897

Morven
705
▲

R. Helmsdale

A9

0 Miles   20 Mile

0 Kilometres   30 Kilometr

L. Bera

A839

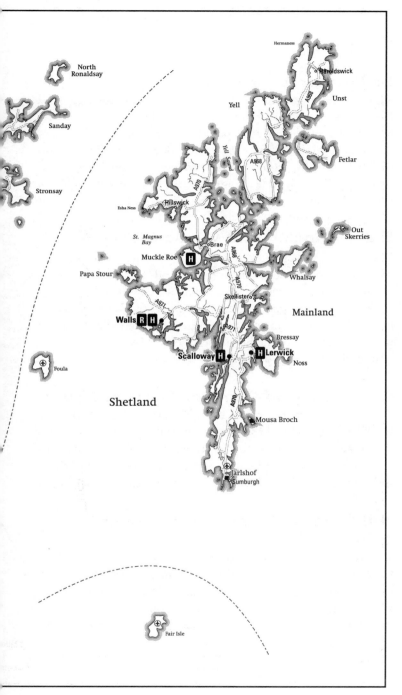

North Ronaldsay

Sanday

Stronsay

Hermaness

Haroldswick

Unst

Yell

Fetlar

Esha Ness

Hillswick

Yell Sound

A970

A968

Out Skerries

St. Magnus Bay

Brae

Muckle Roe

H

A968

Whalsay

Papa Stour

A971

Skellister

A970

Mainland

Walls R H

A971

Bressay

Scalloway H

H Lerwick

Foula

Noss

Shetland

A970

Mousa Broch

Jarlshof
Sumburgh

Fair Isle

Local sights

Badbea (north of Helmsdale)

This is where you can fully appreciate what the Highland Clearances meant to ordinary people. A few humps of stone remain of a settlement once populated by people evicted from crofts further inland. It is right on the edge of the cliffs, with no shelter and little fertile land. The village was finally deserted when the last of its folk emigrated to New Zealand. [⌃📱 *via www.caithness.org*]

Castle Sinclair and Castle Girnigoe (north of Wick)

The ruins of these twin castles stand on the narrowest of promontories, with the sea sucking at stacked layers of flagstone beneath. George Sinclair, fourth Earl of Caithness, threw his son into a dungeon here on suspicion of treachery, first starved him, then fed him on all the salt beef he could eat, and finally left him to die of thirst. [⌃📱 *via www.scottishculture.about.com*]

Grey Cairns of Camster (north of Clyth)

The three chambered cairns date from around 2500 BC, and remain as huge heaps of stones. It is worth the damp crawl into the biggest cairn at least, for the interior chamber is a spacious and sombre place (despite its concrete roof). [*Access at all times;* ☎ *0131-668 8800;* ⌃📱 *via www.stonepages.com*]

Hill O' Many Stanes (north-east of Lybster)

This is an extremely peculiar prehistoric sight. On a patch of level ground on a hillside just off the main road, 22 rows of small upright stones form a fan shape. They are mostly under knee height, and there are more than 200. No one is sure of their purpose. [*Access at all times;* ☎ *0131-668 8800;* ⌃📱 *via www.stonepages.com*]

Also recommended

Dounreay Reactor (west of Thurso) A folly in the eyes of many, Britain's prototype fast-breeder reactor still stands by the sea. Surrounded by pollution scandals and with a multi–million pound decommissioning bill on its way, the Visitor Centre *[May to Oct, 10–4;* ☎ *(01847) 802572]* somehow remains sanguine.

John o' Groats (north of Wick) Long considered 'opposite' Land's End in Cornwall, this is a curious tourist trap, for there is nothing to see. Jan de Groot was a Dutchman, whom James IV employed to start a ferry to the newly acquired territory of Orkney. He is said to have built an octagonal house with eight internal doors to solve problems of family precedence. The house is long gone, but the hotel here sports an octagonal tower in its memory. In summer, a passenger ferry runs from here to Orkney. For details, visit ⬆ *www.jogferry.co.uk*

The three follies of Auckengill (north of Wick) Three weird structures beside the road – ship's lantern, weather station and small boy's tower.

Whaligoe Harbour (north–east of Lybster) Almost 365 vertiginous steps are needed to climb down the cliff to the pier beneath. Not surprisingly, the harbour has long gone out of use, but its very existence is testimony to the wealth to be had from the herring boom; 24 boats once operated from this harbour, and the catch was carried up those terrible steps on the backs of the fishermen's wives. Great care is needed on the steps. *[⬆ via www.caithness.org]*

Towns and villages to explore

Thurso

This town used to be Scotland's chief trading port with Scandinavia and is still the largest town on the mainland north of Inverness [☎ *via www.caithness.org*]. Much of the modern town was planned by Sir John Sinclair, one of the best-known 'Improvers' of the eighteenth century. The **Thurso Heritage Museum**, with Pictish stones and a collection left by the Victorian naturalist Robert Dick, is a useful spot in which to linger if waiting for the Orkney ferry from nearby Scrabster. *[June to Sept, Mon–Sat 10–1 and 2–5;* ☎ *(01847) 892692]*

Wick

Wick [☎ *via www.caithness.org*] was once the centre of the local herring industry. By 1862, 1,122 boats were using the new harbour, and a whole new town had been constructed. Today, Wick is quiet again, the herring gone, the fishing fleet much reduced in number. It is a grey-stone town – stark, like many other Scottish fishing ports, as if its energies were focused entirely on the sea beyond the harbour wall. A port of call for most visitors is **Caithness Glass** where, in a remarkably informal factory with roaring furnaces, you can follow the making of glass from ingredients to finished article *[All year, Mon–Sat 9–5; Easter to Dec, also Sun 11–5;* ☎ *(01631) 563386]*. A small heritage museum, open in the summer months, displays records of Wick's fishing industry.

Best scenery

Dunnet Head and Duncansby Head The first is the north-ernmost point of mainland Britain, the second the north-east-ernmost point. Dunnet Head gives fine views of the Orkneys on a clear day, and of the dangerous waters of the Pentland Firth. Duncansby Head is notable for its cliff scenery. High flagstone towers, caves, inlets and offshore stacks are surrounded by clouds of birds. [☎ *via www.caithness.org*]

ORKNEY

It is Orkney's good fortune to be prosperous, beautiful and endowed with world-class sights at the same time as being far enough away from major population centres for there to be little threat from the unpleasant side-effects of mass tourism. Deserted beaches are two-a-penny, custodians have time to chat to you, the wildlife is undisturbed and tour coaches are rarely bigger than minibuses. Mostly flat and fertile, the Orkney islands are cattle-farming country. Evidence of the distant past lies everywhere. The great prehistoric sights would be worth travelling to see anywhere; their setting against the stark sea or sky here adds hugely to their appeal.

Top sights

Earl's Palace (Kirkwall)

✓ *The ruin of a magnificent Renaissance palace*

This is the ruin of a magnificent Renaissance building which speaks of power and luxury. Huge oriel windows once flooded it with light, and enormous fireplaces held promise of roaring warmth. Yet its owner was a ruthless tyrant who needed a bodyguard of 50 men when he went to the cathedral only a few yards away, and whose eventual execution had to be postponed until he had been taught the Lord's Prayer. This was Patrick Stewart, Earl of Orkney, the son of one of James V's bastards. His palace was constructed by local people via what amounted to slave labour. The ground floor is evidence of the Earl's priorities, for it consists of a series of enormous vaulted storerooms, and a giant kitchen. Upstairs, the hall's beautiful windows are complemented by some severely practical loopholes for muskets. Close by, the **Bishop's Palace** is a much older, but more complicated and less inspiring sight. *[HS; Apr to Oct, daily 9.30–6.30;* ☎ *(01856) 875461]*

Maes Howe (west Mainland)

✓ *Awe-inspiring prehistoric tomb*

✓ *Tour of interior*

Of the four great prehistoric sights grouped by the Loch of Stenness (including Skara Brae, Stones of Streness and the Ring of Brodgar – see pages 461–2), Maes Howe is the most fabulous. It is a giant chambered cairn standing on a levelled platform, with a rock-cut ditch running round it. The entrance passage and much of the interior of the tomb are built from gigantic slabs of stone, slotted together with the neatness of a Lego building.

A stooping shuffle along a passage takes you to the dim central chamber, where the guide shows off the details of the ceiling corbelling, the three side-cells and the massive block-stones which would have closed upon the last remains of the deceased. You are told how, on the shortest night of the year, a shaft of light from the setting sun will turn the entrance passage to gold and throw a splash of light on to the back wall of the chamber.

You also see the graffiti scratched here in the twelfth century by Norsemen. There is a lion and what could be a walrus and a lot of runes. It is curious to think of those Norse warriors scratching on the walls only 800 years ago, while the time that separated them from the people who dragged the massive slabs over the moors to build this astonishing place was closer to 4,000 years. *[HS; Apr to Sept, daily 9.30–6.30; Oct to Mar, Mon–Sat 9.30–4.30, Sun 2–4.30, closed Thur pm and Fri;* ☎ *(01856) 761606]*

St Magnus Cathedral (Kirkwall)

✓ *Beautiful and ancient building*

The twelfth-century cathedral bears the name of Orkney's own martyr, and dates from the time when Orkney was the centre of a powerful Norse earldom. This huge and splendid building is constructed from lucent red sandstone with occasional interleavings of yellow, and propped by massive nave columns like sea stacks. The Gothic clerestory lets light into the building, so that on sunny days it seems to glow throughout its interior. St Magnus' skull, bearing a great gash from the axe blow that felled him, was found in the cathedral in 1919. *[Apr to Sept, Mon–Sat 9–6, Sun 2–6; Oct to Mar, Mon–Sat 9–1 and 2–5;* ☎ *(01856) 874894]*

Skara Brae (west Mainland)

✓ *Uniquely well-preserved prehistoric village*
✓ *Houses, furniture and streets 5,000 years old*
✓ *Beautiful setting on sea's edge*

This is Orkney's second extraordinary prehistoric sight after Maes Howe. It is a complete Neolithic village, buried for millennia until unearthed by a storm in 1850. It is hard to see until you are standing almost on top of it, for the village was semi-subterranean, built deliberately in the middle of a great heap of decayed household refuse – the midden. Skara Brae is 5,000 years old – older than the Egyptian pyramids or Stonehenge. Considering its age, the state of preservation is stunning, down to the furniture and the drainage system.

This curious little community, where cramped, tortuous passages lead between spacious houses, with the local stone-working workshop set a little apart, irresistibly recalls a suburban housing estate. All the houses have the same design, with cupboards, stone-sided beds and central hearths, and all have stone dressers arranged opposite the doorways. All that is missing is the television. Current theories suggest that Skara Brae was a self-sufficient, egalitarian community of farmers and fishermen. Everything they had was made from stone, bone, wood or skin – there is no evidence of metal or cloth. Yet some of the things they produced – especially the intricately carved and decorated stone objects of unknown purpose – and some of their building techniques (notably the strong possibility that the village had a sanitation system flushed by running water) make it impossible to dismiss the inhabitants of Skara Brae as primitive. For six centuries or so they lived in their village, then abandoned it – no one knows why.

The new visitor centre provides useful background to what is known about Skara Brae, and there is a reconstruction of one of the houses which you can explore (you can only peer down into the genuine ones). *[Apr to Sept, daily 9.30–6.30; Oct to Mar, Mon–Sat 9.30–4.30, Sun 2–4.30;* ☎ *(01856) 841815]*

Stones of Stenness and Ring of Brodgar (west Mainland)

✓ *Atmospheric stone circles*

Only four great monoliths survive out of the original 12 which made up the stone circle of Stenness, poised where the Loch of Harray flows into the Loch of Stenness. Grey, gaunt and lonely, the huge slabs seem to have been frozen in place. It is easy to imagine them lumbering down to drink at the loch on some midsummer's night, and indeed one seems to have been caught in the act, for as you cross the causeway, a single menhir – the Watch Stone – stands on the very edge of the water. At Bamhouse, just beside the stones, recent excavations have uncovered houses and ritual buildings which must have been linked with the stones. A short walk from the road brings you to the partially reconstructed remains.

The time to be at the nearby **Ring of Brodgar** is at sunset, preferably when the sky boils with cloud and burning light. The 27 stones (there were once 60) stand still and lonely in a perfect circle silhouetted against the hills of Hoy, with water on both sides and a great sweep of sky above. *[Access at all times]*

Tomb of the Eagles (South Ronaldsay)

✓ *Friendly, family-run prehistoric sight*
✓ *The chance to see and handle some of the finds*

The Neolithic chambered cairn gets its popular name from the many bird carcasses found in the 4,000-year-old burial chamber. The site was excavated by its owner, farmer Ronald Simison. At Liddel Farm, you are taken on a most entrancing journey back in time. You are handed a prehistoric axe, which moulds perfectly into your hand, then a shiny black ring (the two halves found ten years apart) and then the cool, smooth skulls of a woman and a man, dead at 35 and 26. You will also encounter a row of wellies ready for visitors on the porch, and a trolley, knee patches and torch by the tomb entrance. *[Apr to Oct, 10–8; Nov to Mar, 10–12;* ☎ *(01856) 831339]*

Except where noted, the best web sites for all the above are 📱 *www.orkneyjar.com* or 📱 *www.orknet.co.uk*

The next best sights

Birsay and Brough of Birsay (north-west Mainland)

Birsay was the old ecclesiastical centre of the islands before St Magnus Cathedral was built, and is now an exposed straggle of a village, dominated by the remains of the Earl's Palace *[Access at all times;* ☎ *0131-668 8800]*, another work of the deplorable Stewart earls. Off the coast lies the tidal island of Brough of Birsay, reached across a slippery causeway. Check the tide tables in *The Orcadian* before coming: Birsay is one hour before Kirkwall. On the island lie the remains of the most substantial complex of Norse buildings on Orkney, and there is also a copy of a Pictish stone showing two dignified warriors marching behind their chief. *[Times depend on the tide; for information* ☎ *(01856) 721205]*

Broch of Gurness (north-east Mainland)

The broch (a prehistoric circular dry-stone tower) lies on the edge of the sea, facing the island of Rousay. It is a complicated site (though much of it has vanished into the ocean) with a jumble of Iron Age houses surrounding the substantial remains of the broch at their centre, a surrounding ditch and rampart and the relocated remains of a Pictish house and what may have been a Norse hall. Explanations are clear and convincing, and artists' impressions help to give you an idea of what it was once like. *[HS; Apr to Sept, daily 9.30–6.30;* ☎ *(01831) 579478]*

Corrigall and Kirkbister Farm Museums (north-west Mainland)

Between them, these old Orkney farms give a clear impression of life in the last century. At Kirkbister, you will find an unaltered example of an old Orkney kitchen, with its free-standing hearth, smoke hole in the roof and tiny bed built into the thickness of the wall. Corrigall is more fully restored, complete with implements, hens and cheese but, while there is more to see, it is rather less evocative. *[Mar to Oct, Mon–Sat 10.30–1 and 2–5;* ☎ *(01856) 771411 and* ☎ *(01856) 771268]*

Dwarfie Stane (North Hoy)

This strange prehistoric sight lies off the road that leads across the north of the island to Rackwick. A huge block of sandstone has been hollowed out to contain a tomb. Only stone tools were used and there cannot have been room for more than two people to work at a time. Why did they go to this enormous effort? No one knows. *[Access at all times]*

Knap of Howar (Papa Westray)

More or less in the centre of the island, past a muddy farmyard, stands the oldest house in north-west Europe. If you have visited Skara Brae, you will recognise the structure you find here – a semi-subterranean house built into a midden. Unlike Skara Brae, this is not a village but an independent farmhouse, complete with a barn next door. *[HS; access at all times;* ☎ *0131-668 8800]*

Midhowe Broch (Rousay)

The walls of the Iron Age fort still stand 13 feet high, making it an impressive ruin, and narrow passages or galleries run between the inner and outer walls. Take a torch. Nearby, the chambered cairn called **Traversoe Tuick** is worth a visit, for here two separate tombs were built one on top of the other and you can explore both. *[HS; access at all times;* ☎ *0131-668 8800]*

Midhowe Chambered Cairn (Rousay)

Like Maes Howe, this is about 5,000 years old, but of a very different design, with a long passage partitioned by pairs of upright slabs. It is housed in a modern hangar, which has a gantry allowing you to walk above the tomb and look down into it. *[HS; access at all times;* ☎ *0131-668 8800]*

Noltland Castle (Westray)

This sixteenth-century Z-plan fortress is studded with gunloops, and is a place of extraordinary strength for a remote island. It was built by an incomer from Fife, of dubious reputation, called Gilbert Balfour. It is not just a grim, damp fortress, for the main staircase with its great stone newel is a spacious and beautiful piece of building. *[HS; access at all times;* ☎ *0131-668 8800]*

Orkney Museum (Kirkwall)

Close to the cathedral, this museum makes a good starting point for learning about prehistoric Orkney, and is best seen before visiting the sites. The permanent exhibition leads you round the life and times of Orkney's earliest settlers, via pottery, carved stones, reconstructions of stone furniture and rows of skulls. Keep an eye open for the delicate and beautiful bone combs. *[May to Sept, Mon–Sat 10–5, Sun 2–5; Oct to Apr, Mon–Sat 10.30–12.30 and 1.30–5;* ☎ *(01856) 873191]*

Scapa Flow Visitor Centre (Lyness, South Hoy)

The car ferry from Houton docks under the shadow of the rusting naval guns which stand watch over the visitor centre. Much of the display has been salvaged from the depths of Scapa Flow, and a mass of information is provided about wartime Orkney. The enormous propeller and drive shaft of HMS *Hampshire*, which went down off Marwick Head in 1916 taking Lord Kitchener with her, is the largest exhibit. An old oil storage tank now makes a spendid echoing tap–dancing arena. *[Mon–Fri 9–4.30; mid-June to mid-Aug, also Sat 9–4.30, Sun 10–6; mid-Aug to mid-Sept, Sat 9–4.30, Sun 10.30–4;* ☎ *(01856) 791300]*

Stromness Museum

The wonderful clutter of photographs and objects, mostly donated by local people, can absorb you for hours. The most fascinating story told by the museum is that of the scuttling of the German fleet in Scapa Flow in 1919. The fleet had been interned at the end of the First World War and was deliberately scuttled in a final act of defiance. Seventy-four ships went to the bottom. The subsequent salvage operation was extremely complicated. Three battleships and four battle-cruisers remain on the sea bed and they form an excellent sight, in clear waters, for scuba-divers. *[May to Sept, daily 10–5; Oct to Apr, Mon–Sat 10.30–12.30 and 1.30–5;* ☎ *(01856) 850025]*

Also in the area

The Churchill Barriers On top of a foundation of haphazardly piled concrete blocks, a ribbon of road links Mainland to the islands of Lamb Holm, Glimps Holm, Burray and South Ronaldsay. The concrete and the sunken wrecks offshore were built to protect the naval anchorage of Scapa Flow from German U-Boats, after an enterprising submarine captain had slipped in on 14 October 1939 and torpedoed the battleship *Royal Oak* with the loss of 800 lives. The Churchill Barriers were built with the labour of 550 Italian prisoners of war.

Italian Chapel (Lamb Holm) The Mediterranean facade of this tiny church, with its columned portico and surmounting belfry, seems incongruous in the steely northern light. The POWs put it together from two Nissen huts, moulded concrete and whatever scrap came to hand. Inside, a Madonna and Child is painted above the altar, and there is an elaborate wrought-iron rood screen. *[All year during daylight hours;* ☎ *(01856) 781268]*

Orkney Wireless Museum (Kirkwall) An extensive and erudite collection of radio and communications gear from wartime Orkney, together with masses of other relics from the early days of wireless communication. *[Apr to Sept, Mon–Sat 10–4.30, Sun 2.30–4.30;* ☎ *(01856) 871400/874272]*

Towns and villages to explore

Kirkwall

Orkney's capital has been in existence since the eleventh century, and has much restrained dignity. Beside the magnificent red sandstone twelfth-century **cathedral**, old houses line the single main street, while the ruined **Bishop's Palace** and **Earl's Palace** add Renaissance grandeur. Pottering around the shops and looking at the silverwork inspired by Norse designs does not take long, and a day will serve to cover the sights. Nevertheless, Kirkwall makes a congenial base. Roads radiate from it all over Mainland, and there is a distillery to visit, a small theatre and a swimming-pool.

Stromness

Only the gulls and the arrival of the ferry from Scrabster disturb the quiet of this town. It was a livelier place in the days when the Hudson Bay Company's ships called on their fur-trading run to northern Canada. The main street meanders for a mile between the seafront and the steep slope of Binkie's Brae. At the start of Victoria Street, the complex of buildings by the pier has been converted into the **Pier Arts Centre** *[Tue–Sat 10.30–12.30 and 1.30–5;* ☎ *(01856) 850209]*. Displayed here is a permanent collection of twentieth-century works by Barbara Hepworth, Ben Nicholson, Naum Gabo and Eduardo Paolozzi. There are also temporary exhibitions, children's workshops, lectures and poetry readings.

Best scenery

The Cliffs at Yenaby (west Mainland) Dramatic cliff scenery, exposed to the full force of the Atlantic. Beware crumbling rock and strong winds.

Lochs of Stenness and Harray These are the best-known fishing lochs of Orkney, but are very attractive, even for non-anglers.

The Old Man of Hoy (North Hoy) This is one of the most famous sea stacks in Britain. You reach it by a path from Rackwick. At first you see only the green top of the Old Man level with the cliff edge, but as you draw near, the plunging layers of rock which make up the stack become apparent.

Rackwick (North Hoy) This bay is held by some to be the most beautiful spot on Orkney. It is a sheltered green breach in a rampart of red sea-cliffs. It would be perfect if it had a sandy beach, but alas there are only boulders.

The outer islands

Eday This island has much more heather moorland than most of the islands, and used to export peat widely. The outstanding monument is the prehistoric Stone of Setter, a standing stone fully 15 feet high, superbly situated.

Egilsay If you look over Rousay Sound towards Egilsay, the prominent round tower belongs to the twelfth-century St Magnus Church, which stands on the site where St Magnus is supposed to have prayed before his murder.

Flotta The island is dominated by its huge oil terminal, and is best viewed from a distance.

Hoy The island is unlike the rest of Orkney, being hilly, peat-covered and sparsely populated. It has the finest cliff scenery in the islands, culminating in the huge precipices of St John's Head, and the Old Man of Hoy.

North Ronaldsay This is the smallest and most remote of the northern islands. The seaweed-fed sheep are a unique breed and roam the shore in a communal flock, confined by a dry-stone dyke. There is the much-ruined Broch of Burrian by the shore to visit and rare migrant birds to spot.

Papa Westray If you are coming from Westray, it may prove irresistible to splash out on the shortest scheduled flight in the world, which takes two minutes. Papa Westray is small, and uninhabited at its northern end, where the fields give way to maritime heath. This is North Hill, now a nature reserve inhabited by bonxies (skuas) and thousands of Arctic terns. The former will buzz you ferociously if you intrude, and a stout hat is a good idea for protecting your head. The east coast is a good place to see seals, both common and grey, which haul themselves up on to the reefs at low tide and bask with head and flippers in the air. [www.norsecom.co.uk/papawestrayschool]

Rousay Next to Mainland, this is the best island for prehistoric remains, and some accommodation is available if you want to take more than a day over them. The single road runs around the perimeter and the chief sights are close to it, so hiring a bicycle is the most pleasant way of getting around.

Sanday This is a big, low-lying island, and if you want to explore it thoroughly you will need a car, unless you are a very fit cyclist. Sanday is ideal for beach-lovers for the coastline is indented with one bay after another. The Bay of Lopness, with miles of dunes, is one of the best, and the beaches on either side of the Els Ness peninsula are also attractive. You are certain to see seals somewhere as you prowl the coastline. This is also a good island for birds: the marshy areas in the north-east are the places to look. At Tafts Ness, one of the biggest prehistoric sites in Europe remains unexcavated. Over 500 burial mounds dot the landscape. The best, open, prehistoric sight on Sanday is Quoyness chambered cairn. This is the same type of tomb as Maes Howe, and, although not on the same scale, is impressive enough in its lonely isolation.

Shapinsay A flat, gentle island dominated by the Victorian pile of Balfour Castle, which it is possible both to visit and stay in. Its accessibility makes it a popular place for an outing.

Stronsay If you want to leave fellow tourists behind, Stronsay is probably the least visited of all the islands. There's nothing much to see, but a beautiful coastline with good beaches.

Westray This is a large island with a long flat tail stretching to the south-east, a range of low hills to the west, the cliffs of Noup Head to the north-west and an area of sand dunes and machair in the north. It is an attractive place to visit. Pierowall is the main settlement, strung out round the edge of a bay. Noup Head is the place to watch birds. Westray's chief sight is Noltland Castle (see above). A walk across the sandy turf of the golf course reveals wild flowers – and hosts of rabbits.

Wyre This tiny, arrow-shaped island has the remains of Scotland's oldest stone castle on it. There is also a partly restored twelfth-century chapel.

SHETLAND

According to Tacitus, the Romans sighted Shetland on their expedition round Britain and named it Thule after the mythical island on the edge of the world. And this is what it feels like. Shetland is an acquired taste. The climate is, at best, uncertain and the landscape has little of the welcoming fertility of Orkney. Yet Shetland can be addictive in much the same way as strong black coffee. A draught composed of Arctic wind, luminous skies and tearing seas can stimulate and revive. If all you want is to relax in comfort in the sun, leave it well alone.

In early summer the cliffs teem with sea birds, while rare waders breed on its lochs and desolate moorlands. To come to Shetland without doing a spot of birdwatching is a waste. The sea bird colonies in the full cacophony of the breeding season are not lightly forgotten. Nor is being dive-bombed by skuas, harassed by aggravated terns, or simply sitting watching the puffins at their burrows. Bring binoculars.

Top sights

Jarlshof (south Mainland)
✓ *Amazing collection of dwellings stretching from prehistory to the seventeenth century*
Walter Scott coined the name in his novel *The Pirate*, long before the existence of a Norse settlement here was confirmed.

But there is a profusion of buildings from even earlier times. From the Bronze Age there is a metal–worker's workshop; from the Iron Age, earth houses and the remains of a broch. The best-preserved houses, however, are wheel houses from the third to the eighth centuries. These are comfortable-looking designs, with a series of individual rooms radiating round a central hearth, giving everyone privacy and warmth. The Norse settlement would seem to have spanned the next 500 years, and the foundations of a number of long houses remain. Then there is a medieval farmstead and finally the shell of a seventeenth-century house. A platform here gives an aerial view of the jumble of buildings, with clear explanations. *[Apr to Sept, daily 9.30–6.30;* ☎ *(01950) 460112]*

Mousa Broch (Island of Mousa)

✓ *Complete Iron Age fortress*
✓ *Setting*

The best-preserved broch in Scotland is just visible from the main road, but to see it properly you must take the boat from Sandwick, which runs between May and September. The walls of the broch stand 45 feet high, probably to within a few feet of the original top, and, from inside, the impression is of standing in the base of an enormous chimney. Galleries run up the middle of the massively thick walls, and you can get to the top of the tower via one of them. Mousa (or Moseyjarborg, as the Norsemen called it) leapt into written history in the *Orkneyinga Saga* as the scene of an elopement: the absconding couple took refuge in the broch from their pursuer, Earl Harald, and forced him to negotiate. *[For details visit* 🖱 *www.mousaboattrips.co.uk or* ☎ *(01950) 431367 in advance]*

The next best sights

Shetland Croft House Museum (south Mainland)

A charming evocation of the days before fast roads and oil executives. Almost all the furniture in the house is made from driftwood, for Shetland has no trees to speak of, and even the cabbages have to be salt-resistant. The old farmstead has its separate water mill and corn-drying kiln, well restored. *[May to Sept, daily 10–1 and 2–5;* ☎ *(01595) 695057]*

Shetland Museum (Lerwick)

An old-fashioned but lovingly kept museum of Shetland life in its entirety. It includes masses of material about fishing, finds from ancient sites, geological specimens, and curiosities enough to keep anyone happy. *[Mon, Wed, Fri 10–7, Tue, Thur, Sat 10–5;* ☎ *(01595) 695057]*

Towns and villages to explore

Lerwick

Shetland's capital, sheltered by the offshore island of Bressay, exists by and for the sea. In the narrow Bressay Sound, ships of every description lie at anchor while their crews roam the shops. You will hear northern languages at every turn. Consequently, Lerwick's shops are a step up on Kirkwall's, despite being much further north. You can spend a pleasant half-day in the shops, fingering the knitwear, thumbing through the books about Shetland – look especially for short stories in the local dialect – or simply browsing. All the action takes place on Commercial Street, a flagstoned alleyway which runs parallel to the seafront. Some of the old houses rise straight out of the water. As well as the **Shetland Museum** (see above), you can visit the Cromwellian **Fort Charlotte** *[Apr to Sept, Mon–Sat 9–6.30, Sun 2–6.30;* ☎ *0131-668 8800]* and the **Up-Helly-Aa exhibition** *[mid-May to mid-Sept, Tue and Fri 7–9, Sat 2–4;* ✆ *www.up-helly-aa.org.uk].*

Clickhimmin Broch *[Access at all times;* ☎ *0131-668 8800]* is situated in the centre of a small loch in suburban Lerwick. The walls still stand 18 feet thick and 15 feet high. Together with the broch and the muddle of walls from various periods around it, there is the remains of an intimidating Iron Age gateway.

Scalloway

Scalloway used to be Shetland's capital before Lerwick, but now it is small in comparison. It is a town of narrow streets and ancient cottages, attractively situated on the edge of a curving bay looking over to the island of Trondra. The ruins of Earl Patrick's castle loom over the town. It was built in 1600 by labour exacted from the locals, but the castle was abandoned when the notorious Stewart earl was executed. Scalloway is a good place to find knitwear bargains, and has its own local museum.

Best scenery

St Ninian's Isle This is a place of remarkable beauty where a small near-island is linked to the mainland only by a double oxbow of white shell sand, like two parentheses back to back. This unusual formation is known as a tombolo, and this is the only sandy one in Britain. The island is the site of a ruined twelfth-century church where a treasure of silver objects from the eighth or ninth centuries was found buried beneath a slab. There are replicas in the Shetland Museum.

Sumburgh Head From Sumburgh Head you look out over the tide-race of Sumburgh Roost to the angular profile of Fair Isle on the horizon. There is a colony of seabirds, and a cluster of sandy beaches.

Suggested excursions

West Mainland Travelling from Scalloway to Walls takes you through scenery which grows ever wilder as you head west. Bleak moorland gives way to patches of green as you loop round the head of the voes. White cottages stand out against the dazzling sea or vanish into the grey gloom of heavy showers. Shetland sheep are everywhere, their colours ranging from deep chocolate to pure white, their knowing, pinched faces gazing at you with goat-like intensity. Their wool used to be gathered by plucking rather than shearing, and the finest Shetland shawls could be drawn through a wedding ring. Shetland ponies graze beside the road; in the past they were bred as pit ponies, their small stature making them ideal for underground work.

North Mainland Like the rest of Shetland, north Mainland is a country of sheep, birds, cottages, sea and wind. However, there is one difference: oil. Sullom Voe terminal is the biggest in Europe, but also the least conspicuous. The effect on landscape and wildlife has been minimal. Only the flickering flares at night, like something from Norse mythology, or the huge tankers threading their way between islands, tell you that it is there.

A diversion east takes you to **Lunna Ness**, where Lunna House was the headquarters of the Norwegian resistance in World War II. Brae is a village which has expanded with the coming of the terminal; there is a swimming-pool here. A trip across the bridge to the island of **Muckle Roe** is worthwhile for views and beach walks. A little further north, at **Mavis Grind**, the land is pinched into an isthmus between (somewhat fancifully) the North Sea and the Atlantic. After this, head west again, looking out for the spiny sea-stacks called the Drongs, half-hidden in spray, the oldest pub in Shetland at Hillswick (now a vegetarian restaurant), the natural arch off the coast beyond Brae Wick, and finally the cliffs at **Esha Ness**, where the road ends beside the chasm of Caldersgeo.

The northern islands

Yell

Yell is an island of desolate peat and rusting cars dumped behind crofts. Its charms are hidden very deep. The Loch of Lumbister, an RSPB reserve, is the best area for wildlife, and otters haunt the inlets on the east coast. [✎ *www.yell-tourism.shetland.co.uk*]

Fetlar

Fetlar is small, largely green, and full of interesting nooks and crannies. Start by visiting the Fetlar Interpretative Centre [*May to Sept, Tue–Sun 12–5;* ☎ *(01957) 733206]*, which has plenty of information on the history and birdlife of the island. The rare red–necked phalarope, red–throated divers and whimbrel are all to be found on Fetlar (the Loch of Funzie at the east of the island is the place to look). The Wick of Tresta has a lovely beach, bounded by the reddish moor-topped cliffs of Lamb Hoga where stormy petrels come ashore at night to breed. Look up information about the island at 🖱 *www.zetnet.co.uk/sigs/fetlar*

Unst

Up here, where summer nights are never dark (the long twilight is called simmer dim), it is easy to persuade yourself that this is the edge of the world. Unst is not quite tundra country, but often looks or feels Arctic. The most scenic part of this rather bleak island is the far north-west corner, and here too is the sea bird colony of Hermaness (notable for puffins), at the edge of an extensive reserve of maritime heath. From the cliffs at Hermaness, you can gaze out on the rock islet of Muckle Flugga, the last piece of land before the Arctic Circle. There is a visitor centre, with information about the reserve, and a warden to answer questions, in the old lighthouse buildings at Burrafirth.

Haraldswick is a scattered cluster of houses where the northernmost post office in the United Kingdom will stamp your letters with a special postmark. Muness Castle, in the south-east of Unst, is also the northernmost British castle. More information about Unst is on the Web at 🖱 *www.unst.shetland.co.uk*

The outer islands

Bressay

Bressay lies offshore opposite Lerwick, and apart from having good views of the town is of little special interest except as a stepping stone to Noss (it is about an hour's walk across the island, so it may be worth taking your car). Noss is the home of one of Shetland's biggest seabird cities, and is a National

Nature Reserve. It is not open on Monday or Thursday, but at other times you can be ferried across the narrow Noss Sound from Bressay in a perilous-looking inflatable.

Fair Isle

Rising out of the sea, more or less halfway between Orkney and Shetland, Fair Isle is paradoxically more isolated than Shetland's other outliers yet more accessible. It is a place which is well used to visitors, but which has retained all its genuine hospitality. The residents put it simply – by the end of winter they are longing for some new faces, and then, just when they are getting fed up with visitors, they all go away and they are left to themselves again. It is birds – especially those rare migrants – which bring most visitors to Fair Isle, and in spring or autumn your fellow guests are likely to be 'twitchers'. The enthusiastically run Bird Observatory [☎ *(01595) 760258]*, which doubles as a comfortable guesthouse, can be intimidating if you cannot tell a blackbird from a thrush, but there is no need to join in if you do not want to.

Fair Isle is just the right size to wander around in a day, with enough variety in its scenery, inland as well as round its wild coast, to keep you happy for longer. The locals are happy to chat, and you can poke round the little museum in the George Waterston Memorial Centre, join half the island in waiting for the *Good Shepherd IV* on its voyage from Mainland, or track down Fair Isle sweaters. Look up details on the Internet at 🖱 *www.fairisle.org.uk*

Foula

Scarcely populated, wild and mountainous, Foula sees few visitors. The sea crossing is rough and the island often gets cut off. If you want to explore, take your own supplies, for the island has no shop.

Out Skerries

This cluster of three tiny islands, two of them linked together by a bridge, still supports a community of over 80, largely dependent on fishing. Few visitors make it out here, so you can be certain of a friendly welcome. Out Skerries are good for migratory birds; otherwise carpets of flowers in spring and the sense of being miles from anywhere are the attractions.

Papa Stour

This is a peaceful island of caves and flowers with a population of about 40. Ferries leave from West Burra Firth, or you can fly. [⌂ *www.papastour.shetland.co.uk*]

Whalsay

The island is an important base for part of Shetland's fishing fleet, which explains its comparatively large population and the size of the harbour at Symbister. It has always been an important place of trade. Hanseatic merchants from the north German coast had booths here in the Middle Ages, and one has been fully restored, with an explanation of the trade between Bremen, Hamburg and Whalsay.

WHERE TO STAY

£ – under £70 per room per night, incl. VAT

££ – £70 to £110 per room per night, incl. VAT

£££ – over £110 per room per night, incl. VAT

CLEATON
Cleaton House Hotel

Cleaton, Westray KW17 2DB
☎ (01857) 677508
📠 (01857) 677442
  *www.orkneyislands.com/cleaton*
Charming country-house hotel in a beautiful, remote location. Comfortable bedrooms with good facilities; excellent meals use local produce. Packed lunches can be provided.
£ *All year*

KIRKWALL
Briar Lea

10 Dundas Crescent, Kirkwall KW15 1JQ
☎ (01856) 872747
Pleasant old stone house in the centre of Kirkwall. Two spacious twin-bedded and two single rooms. Children are welcome, and the atmosphere is relaxed. Lunch and dinner are not available, but there are several restaurants in the town.
£ *All year*

Leckmelm

Annfield Crescent, Kirkwall LW15 1NS
☎ (01856) 873917
Modern house with simple but comfortable accommodation. Guests can use the patio, a games room and

lounge; breakfast includes Orkney specialities and home-made preserves.

£ All year exc Christmas

LERWICK
Whinrig
12 Burgh Road, Lerwick ZE1 0LB
 (01595) 693554

Well-maintained guesthouse in a quiet residential area. Three comfortable smallish bedrooms and a separate lounge. Dinner is not served, but packed lunches can be provided. Breakfast includes vegetarian options and Scottish fare.

£ All year exc Christmas and New Year

LYNESS
Stoneyquoy Farm
Lyness, Hoy KW16 3NY
 (01856) 791234

Beef farm in an idyllic location overlooking Longhope Bay. The single-storey house is open-plan, with a real fire in the sitting-room, a kitchen with a range, sunroom and sheltered garden. The two *en suite* bedrooms are in an extension. Excellent home-made evening meals.

£ All year exc Christmas and New Year

MELVICH
The Sheiling
Melvich KW14 7YJ
 (01641) 531256

Comfortable guesthouse at the centre of a 15-acre hill croft. Each bedroom is *en suite*; one lounge has a TV and views over Melvich Bay, while a second overlooks the garden. 'First-class' breakfasts.

£ Apr to Oct

MUCKLE ROE
Westayre
Muckle Roe, Brae ZE2 9QW
 (01806) 522368

Muckle Roe, connected to the mainland by a narrow bridge, enjoys magnificent scenery and coastal views. This modern home is on a working croft, with three comfortable bedrooms. Guests may bring their own wine to dinner.

£ Mar to Nov

ST MARGARET'S HOPE
The Creel
Front Road, St Margaret's Hope, South Ronaldsay KW17 2SL
 (01856) 831311
www.thecreel.co.uk

Delightful place to stay on the seafront, more a restaurant-with-rooms than a guesthouse. Three large, attractive *en suite* rooms overlook the bay; guests can use a small sitting room.

£ Apr to Oct; weekends Nov and Dec (See Where to Eat)

SANDWICK
Netherstove
Sandwick KW16 3LS
 (01856) 841625

The roomy lounge of this farmhouse has views of fields and the Bay of Skaill. Two bedrooms share two bathrooms. Guests may bring their own wine to the family-style dinner.

£ May to Nov

SCALLOWAY
Hildasay Guest House
Upper Scalloway ZE1 0UP
(01595) 880822

All the roomy ground-floor bedrooms of this purpose-built guesthouse are split-level; one is suitable for disabled visitors. A separate sitting room adjoins the breakfast room. Packed lunches can be provided.

£ *All year*

STRATHY
Sharvedda

Strathy Point, Strathy KW14 7RY

 (01641) 541311

Modern house on a working croft overlooking Strathy Bay. Plainly furnished, comfortable bedrooms and a roomy lounge. Breakfast and dinner are served in the kitchen/dining-room.

£ *All year*

THURSO
Forss House

Thurso KW14 7XY

 (01847) 861201

 (01847) 861301

The forbidding exterior of this fishing hotel, built to withstand the northern coastal weather, belies the friendly interior with comfortable, roomy bedrooms. Dishes in the light, formal dining-room are traditional and

substantial, with a vegetarian menu.

££ *Closed Chr and New Year*

WALLS
Burrastow House

Burrastow, Walls, Shetland ZE2 9PD

☎ (01595) 809307

 (01595) 809213

Those lured to this remote corner of Scotland by the wildlife and Viking remains find a friendly welcome and excellent food in this handsome and civilised house by the sea. Ingredients are locally sourced; bedrooms are spacious and minimalist, with lovely views.

£££ *Closed Jan and Feb (See Where to Eat)*

WICK
Bilbster House

Bilbster, Wick KW1 5TB

☎ / (01955) 621212

Handsome country house in attractive grounds, with an imposing driveway and neat lawn. 'Very spacious' bedrooms are well-equipped, and guests can watch TV in the drawing room. Breakfast is served in the attractive dining-room.

£ *All year exc Christmas (Oct to Easter, by prior arrangement only)*

WHERE TO EAT

ST MARGARET'S HOPE
The Creel

Front Road, St Margaret's Hope, South Ronaldsay KW17 2SL

☎ (01856) 831311

 www.thecreel.co.uk

Although the house is unprepossessing,

the food served is excellent and the range of fish impressive. The short menu uses outstanding ingredients in large portions of simple dishes. Desserts, for those who still have room, are light and flavoursome.

All week D only 7–9.30; closed 2 weeks Oct, Jan and Feb (See Where to Stay)

STROMNESS

Hamnavoe

35 Graham Place, Stromness, Orkney
KW16 3BY

 (01856) 850606

A small restaurant with a homely
ambience, only open for dinner. The
short carte offers plenty of well-cooked
fish and seafood; Orkney steaks and a
vegetarian option are also available.
Desserts include European and
traditional Scottish choices.

Open D Tue–Sun

WALLS

Burrastow House

Burrastow, Walls, Shetland ZE2 9PD

 (01595) 809307

 (01595) 809213

The peat fire in the oak-panelled dining-
room welcomes visitors to this friendly
establishment. Good locally sourced
ingredients include enormous lobsters,
halibut and sea trout as well as lamb and
beef; vegetarian options also appear on
the short daily-changing menu.

*Tue–Sun L 12–2.30, Tue–Sat D 7.30–9;
closed 24 Dec to early March (See Where
to Stay)*

Scotland for everyone

Glen Nevis

Ruthwell Cross

Royal Yacht Britannia

Mary, Queen of Scots

SCOTLAND FOR EVERYONE

Many visitors to Scotland arrive with the intention of sampling as much as possible of the country in a limited period of time. It is not an easy country in which to do this, partly because of its diversity, partly because of the time it takes to get to and from the furthest-flung areas, and partly because of the uncertain weather. The vagaries of the climate in particular may mean that a tour of the Highlands which would be unforgettable in fine weather, turns out to be a damp and disappointing experience.

The way the Scottish Tourist Board is currently set up encourages visitors to think of the country in terms of its different regions. Brochures and booklets focus on the sights and activities of particular areas, which is ideal if you already have a particular region in mind or want to get to know one area well, but less useful if you want to sample the best that the country as a whole has to offer.

As an alternative to the regional focus, this chapter contains some suggestions for themed tours, which will take you to, or through, some of the most attractive areas of the whole country. Some general recommendations are given on other types of holiday too.

The number of days given for the tours are minimum esti-mates, assuming relatively slow driving and time to see the sights mentioned.

SCENERY

Lochs and mountains

Scotland's best mountain scenery is to be found in the far north-west of the country, so this is a tour that inevitably involves a lot of driving, sometimes on slow, tortuous, but very beautiful roads. In bad weather it will be a disappointing expe-rience, so if your holiday coincides with a wet spell, change your plans. In good weather, however, the route we outline will show you why the Scottish Highlands are considered some of the most beautiful landscape in Europe.

If possible, we would recommend this tour for May/June or mid–October. The early summer swathes the mountains in green; autumn turns the whole landscape into wonderful shades of orange, tan and maroon.

Route

Day 1 → Edinburgh/Glasgow → Aberfoyle → Crianlarich → Fort William

Day 2 → Glen Shiel → Shieldaig → Gairloch → Ullapool

Day 3 → Inverkirkaig → Lochinver → Inverness

Day 4 → Kingussie → Perth → Edinburgh

Variations

- By driving straight to Inverness on the A9, and picking up the route at Torridon, you can save time.
- From Glen Shiel, cross to Skye to see the Cuillin Hills (pages 419–20) and the rock scenery of the Quirang (page 421) (add one day).

Notes

Aberfoyle sits at the centre of the Trossachs scenery (pages 260–1), with a picturesque combination of lochs and mountains in the surrounding area. There are good views from the A821 north of here, but traffic can be heavy.

A84/A85 to Crianlarich Not the most attractive section of the route, but detours to **Loch Voil** and **Loch Earn** (take the south bank road) are rewarding.

Tyndrum Take the A82 north, heading up to Rannoch Moor. Rather sinister mountains close in on the road as you climb to Bridge of Orchy.

Rannoch Moor (A82) (page 368) A huge glacial basin, now an open wilderness ringed by mountains. Spectacular and lonely.

Glen Coe (A82) (pages 365–6) The famous spot where the notorious massacre of the local Macdonald clan took place. The road plunges between high, rocky ridges. There can be

LOCHS AND MOUNTAINS

0   20 miles
0   30 km

nchnadamph
tronechrubie
admore

A837

A836

Kincardine

Moray Firth

Black Isle

A9

Inverness

L. Ness

A9

Carrbridge

Aviemore

A9

Kingussie

Cairngorm

Mountains

Invergarry

A9

anoch Moor

Pitlochry

A82

A9

Sidlaw Hills

A85

Crianlarich   Lochearnhead

L. Earn

A84

Perth

M90   M85

Ochil Hills

A821

Aberfoyle

M90

L. Lomond

Firth of Forth

M9

M80

M876

M9

M8

M73

M8

EDINBURGH

GLASGOW

485

considerable sightseeing traffic, and there are few places to stop. For a quieter scenic drive, detour down the (dead-end) Glen Etive road.

Fort William Scotland's highest mountain, Ben Nevis, rises just to the east. Drive up Glen Nevis to get in among its foothills.

Fort William to Loch Duich (A82/A87) The route takes you past Loch Lochy in the depths of the Great Glen, then branches westwards past Loch Garry, Loch Loyne and Loch Cluanie (all somewhat bleak) before entering **Glen Shiel** (pages 409–10). The shapely peaks of the 'Five Sisters' fringe the glen to the north. The best views of them are looking back from the minor road which branches west from Shiel Bridge.

Loch Carron/Loch Kishorn Turn north on A890 before reaching Kyle of Lochalsh (or continue on A87 to visit Skye). Both Loch Carron and Loch Kishorn (take the A896) are beautiful sea lochs, with views over to Skye from the road which fringes them.

The Torridon Mountains Liathach and Beinn Eighe are precipitous sandstone mountains capped by quartzite. You can see tremendous views of the looming bulk of Liathach dominating upper Loch Torridon from the A896 as it passes south of the loch before skirting the slopes of Beinn Eighe (pages 404–5. Stop at the visitor centre outside Kinlochewe to learn more about these mountains and the Nature Reserve here, or to embark on a walk (a variety of lengths and difficulty available).

Loch Maree One of Scotland's prettiest inland lochs. From the A832 you see it with the isolated mountain of Slioch reflected in its waters.

Kinlochewe to Little Loch Broom One of the most spectacular sections of the route. The A832 takes a wide circle around the trackless wilderness of the Letterewe forest, pinned between sea and hills. Inverewe Gardens (described on pages 402–3, for location see map on page 400) are an obvious stopping point from which to enjoy the scenery. Gruinard bay, with its pinkish strip of sand, is another beautiful spot. Stop at the top of the hill north of here for views out to sea and to the clustered Summer Isles offshore (page 411).

Dundonnell to Ullapool The mountain of An Teallach dominates the southern shore of Little Loch Broom (pages 410–11). The best views of its rocky pinnacles are from the A832 climbing eastward away from the sea. Ahead, the peaks of the Fannich mountains block the eastern horizon. Stop before the Braemore road junction to visit the Corrieshalloch Gorge, then head north west to Ullapool.

Ullapool to Inverkirkaig This is the wildest section of the route, with single-track roads winding past small lochs and through rocky defiles. The driving is slow and requires concentration, so stop to look at the scenery rather than try to see it on the move. Turn west off the A835 at Drumrunie. Ahead is the remarkable mountain of Stac Pollaidh, whose shattered summit ridge is reflected in the waters of Loch Lurgainn beneath. Turn north towards Lochinver, through some pretty, rough country. The tiny village of Inverkirkaig lies beneath the extraordinary twin-peaked Suilven. Walk up the track by the River Kirkaig to see its rounded western dome rising above the moorland (page 406).

Lochinver to Inverness The A837 runs alongside Loch Assynt, with views of Suilven and its sister mountain, Canisp, in the distance. Ben More Assynt, another beautiful mountain, lies to the east. The trip back east on the A837 passes through the heavily wooded Strath Oykel, with the country becoming more fertile as you come down towards Bonar Bridge and the long sea inlet of the Dornoch Firth. From here it is a relatively quick road south to Inverness.

Inverness to Edinburgh The A9 provides a fast route south, but not through especially spectacular scenery. The exception is the section from Carrbridge to Newtonmore, where the massif of the Cairngorms lies to the east. They are very different mountains from those further west, with rounded summits rising from a high, sub-Arctic plateau. For a closer look, detour up the road into Glen More (the 'ski' road) which takes you right up to the slopes of Cairn Gorm (pages 376–8). A funicular is currently under construction to supplement the chair lifts and get you close to the summit.

Island-hopping

We have chosen the southern Inner Hebrides and Arran for this tour. They are reached with relative ease and provide enormous variety. In fact, if you cover every island suggested, you will have visited large and small, fertile and barren, mountainous and flat.

Other island-hopping possibilities exist, of course. For those for whom time is more important than money, Orkney, Shetland and the Western Isles have good inter-island air links as well as their ferries (and flying over the archipelagos in tiny aircraft is an experience in itself). The 'Small Isles' group of Eigg, Rum, Muck and Canna is a further option, especially for those who are drawn to small, isolated communities. Hopping between Oban, Mull, Coll and Tiree is less easy, although rewarding if you can manipulate your plans to fit the ferry departures.

The chief requirement for an island-hopping jaunt is flexibility. Ferry departures are often at frustrating times and on frustrating days. Taking a car on every ferry is not necessary, and can prove expensive. Consider hiring a car on the larger islands or a bicycle for the smaller ones.

Most of the ferries to Scottish islands are operated by Calmac, whose timetable is posted on their web site (see below). Consulting ferry timetables and planning the trip is part of the fun. Make certain, however, that your deadlines are not too rigid: bad weather or mechanical breakdown can disrupt sailings.

Our tour allows time for some exploration of each island, with a night spent on Arran, two nights on Islay, and one on

Gigha. We also recommend a third night on Islay, which allows for a day trip to Colonsay (*must* be on a Wednesday).

This route is for summer, when Calmac operate their full timetable (usually mid-April to mid-October). Reservations for vehicles must be made as noted below. Some sailings attract peak-time supplements. Discounts are available on some routes for 'early bird' sailings.

Calmac usually offer 'hopscotch' tickets for different route combinations, which give worthwhile discounts. At the time of writing, tickets of this sort exist to cover the main crossings on our route.

Route

Day 1 → **Glasgow** → **Ardrossan** → **Ferry to Brodick (Arran)**
Day 2 → **Lochranza (Arran)** → **Ferry to Claonaig** → **Tarbert**
Day 3 → **Kennacraig** → **Ferry to Port Ellen (Islay)**
Day 3 → **Port Askaig** → **Ferry to Jura** → **Ferry back to Port Askaig (Islay)**
Day 4 → **Ferry to Kennacraig** → **Tayinloan** → **Ferry to Gigha**
Day 5 → **Ferry back to Tayinloan** → **Glasgow**

Variations

- Visit Bute instead of Arran, cross to the mainland and drive round Loch Fyne to pick up the route at Tarbert.
- From Islay, visit Colonsay on a day trip (at the time of writing, only possible on Wednesday). You have about six hours on the island.
- Fly from Glasgow to Islay, saving 1–2 days.

Notes

Arran (pages 81–4) Six weekday crossings from Ardrossan (four on Sun). Car reservation required. The Lochranza-Claonaig ferry operates until mid-September only (8/9 crossings daily, no reservation).

Islay (page 228) Stay in or near Tarbert to catch the earliest ferry. (Kennacraig itself is little more than a pier.) Up to three crossings daily. Car reservation is required. This is a lovely journey in good weather.

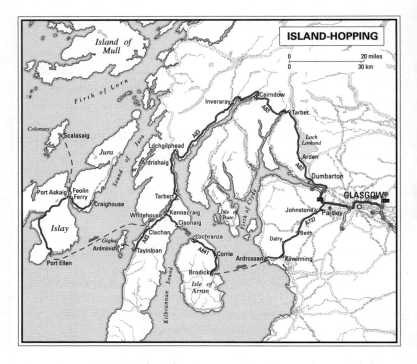

Jura (pages 231–2) The Islay-Jura crossing is very short and the service is frequent (but in a very small vessel). Unless you wish to stay on Jura, check the time of the last ferry back to Islay, and leave extra time, especially on busy weekends.

Colonsay (page 233) The Islay-Colonsay journey is beautiful, with marvellous views of Jura on the way. Beware: there is only one return crossing per week (Weds, car reservation required). The alternative is to stay on Colonsay for at least two nights, continuing to Oban.

Gigha (page 234) Up to ten ferry crossings per day. No reservation. You could return from Islay and visit Gigha inside a day, but spending the night is preferable. Hire a bicycle – the ideal way to see this tiny island.

For full details of ferry timetables and fares telephone ☎ *(01475) 650100* or look up 🕮 *www.calmac.co.uk*. The information above is based on the 2000 summer timetable.

GREAT SCOTTISH GARDENS

Scotland is renowned for its gardens, especially those on the west coast, where the benign climate allows sub-tropical shrubs to flourish, and where rhododendrons grow to Himalayan proportions. The eastern side of the country should not be ignored, however; here you will find gardens which are just as colourful, sometimes rather more formal, and often within the grounds of some ancient house or castle.

It is difficult, without a lot of driving, to visit gardens on both the east and west coasts within a single holiday. We have therefore chosen two routes, designed to visit the best on either coast. The exception is the marvellous garden at Inverewe (see pages 402–3 – visit this as part of the 'Lochs and Mountains' tour, above).

We have chosen the best of the gardens which are regularly open to the public, but there are many others (usually signed) fairly close to our routes. Throughout the summer, these are supplemented by gardens open under 'Scotland's Garden Scheme'. The 'Yellow Books' which are the guides to this scheme are readily available in tourist offices or bookshops.

Our routes are designed to give you some time at each garden. But numerous other things can be seen along the way, so consider adding a couple of days to each route. Late May or early June will show these gardens at their best, although there will be something to see right through the growing season.

The Eastern Gardens

Route

Day 1 → **Edinburgh (Royal Botanic Garden)** → **Perth (Branklyn Garden)**

Day 2 → **Edzell (Edzell Castle)** → **Aberdeen (Crathes Castle, Pitmedden Garden)**

Day 3 → **Inverurie (Leith Hall, Kildrummy Castle Garden)** → **Braemar** → **Edinburgh**

Variations
- Omit Pitmedden on day 2, spend more time at Crathes.

Notes
Royal Botanic Garden, Edinburgh (pages 123–4) Well worth spending an hour or two on. The Chinese collection is renowned. See, too, the Peat and Rock gardens and the glasshouses.

Branklyn Garden (page 262) Colourful from spring (shrubs, meconopsis) to autumn (gentians). Lots of design ideas for peat

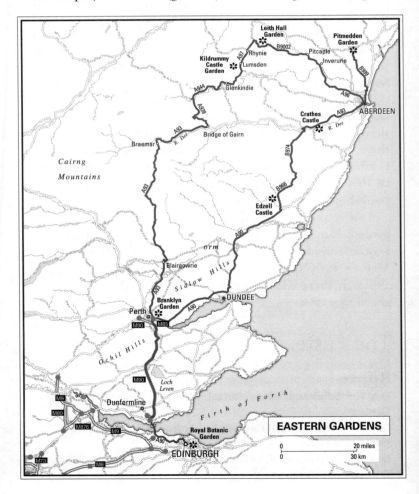

gardens and rockeries; often some interesting alpines on sale. From Perth, travel on the A90 to Brechin, then on the B966 to Edzell.

Edzell Castle (page 302) Interesting piece of formal design within an old ruined castle with a long history behind it. Very small, but attractive. Continue north on the scenic B974.

Crathes Castle (pages 322–3) The most interesting garden on the eastern side. The extensive walled garden is planted according to Gertrude Jekyll's theory of colour planting, with a woodland garden beyond. Fascinating design, especially the use of bronze, reds and greys. The castle itself is a great place to visit too. Useful plant sales area. Leave plenty of time.

Pitmedden Garden (page 329) Reached from Aberdeen by the A947 or B999. A historic, formal, sunken garden, where pattern and design are everything. It will not be to everyone's taste, perhaps, but does not take very long to visit. Stay nearby (visit Fyvie Castle) or return to Aberdeen.

Leith Hall (page 328) Wander up the Don Valley to get here, or take the A944 out of Aberdeen. The herbaceous garden is colourful, with the old house as part of the experience.

Kildrummy Castle Garden (page 328) Interesting planting in an old quarry, with Japanese ideas combining well with the setting.

Return route Take the A97, then travel up Deeside (visit Balmoral) and through Glen Shee on the A93.

The Western Gardens

Route
Day 1 ➙ Glasgow ➙ Loch Lomond ➙ Ardkinglas Woodland Garden ➙ Crarae Garden
Day 2 ➙ Achamore Gardens (Island of Gigha)
Day 3 ➙ Arduaine Garden ➙ Oban ➙ Glasgow

Variations
● Omit Gigha if time is short.

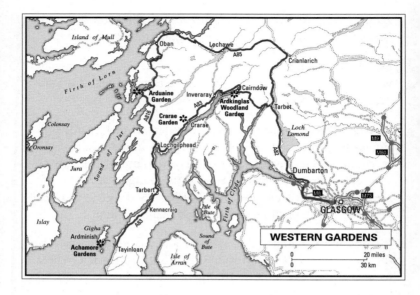

- Turn south after Ardkinglas to visit the Younger Botanic Garden (page 207) near Dunoon. Cross to Bute to visit the gardens there, and return by ferry to Gourock and Glasgow.

Notes

Ardkinglas (page 208) Travel up Loch Lomond, turning west on the A83. The garden is being restored, and is particularly good for tree-lovers. A fine setting and numerous short walks.

Crarae (pages 210–11) The best setting of any of the western gardens. Very colourful in autumn. Some steep walking. Check it is still open – at the time of writing there were financial problems.

Achamore (Gigha) (page 234) The most easily reached of the island gardens. Part of the charm is the setting. Check the ferry times and pre-book accommodation.

Arduaine (page 213) Renowned rhododendron garden by the sea. Less spectacular than Crarae, but good for specialists.

Return Route Travel on the A816 to Oban (there are several gardens open nearby, including Achnacloich, Ardchattan and Ardanaiseig), and return east on the A85.

HISTORY

Scotland abounds with ruined castles and abbeys. It is less well-known that the country is rich in remains from pre-medieval times, many of them the enigmatic traces of the Pictish people, about whom we know very little (see box on pages 290–1). The best sights are scattered far and wide throughout the land, and it is sometimes difficult to know how to organise time to take in the best. We have put together three suggestions for relatively compact routes exploring various aspects of Scottish history. They take in many of the best sights, but by no means all.

For prehistoric sights, you should make straight for Orkney (see Chapter 13), which has some of the most remarkable remains in Europe. There are several more in the Western Isles (see Chapter 12) too, and the Kilmartin area (page 211) is another rich hunting ground.

The early Christian monuments of the western seaboard, associated with the Columban church, and centred on the island of Iona (pages 225–7) make a fascinating, but more time-consuming alternative to the tour we suggest, which takes in the Border Abbeys and the sights associated with St Ninian.

Our tour of Royal Scotland covers the time span between Robert the Bruce and Elizabeth Windsor, and takes you to the chief palaces and castles used by Scotland's Stewart Kings.

Following the footsteps of some of the best-known figures from Scottish history or literature can afford a wealth of interest. Compact tours can be constructed around the figures of Robert Burns or Sir Walter Scott, while tracing the journeys of Bonnie Prince Charlie or that famous visitor to the Highlands, Dr Johnson, will carry you across great swathes of country. We have chosen a tour based around that most romantic of figures, Mary Queen of Scots. It overlaps to some degree with the Royal Scotland tour.

Early Scotland

The tour runs past the line of Roman outposts in central Scotland, and then heads east and north-east to the areas richest in Pictish and Iron Age remains. There are also several prehistoric stones and circles. Most of the sights are outdoors, and several involve walking, so take wet weather gear and wellies or boots.

Route

**Day 1 → Edinburgh → Stirling → Ardoch Roman Camp →
Scottish Crannog Centre → Aberfeldy**
Day 2 → Meigle Museum → St Vigeans → Arbroath
**Day 3 → Brechin Tower & Pictavia → Caterthuns Iron Age Forts
→ Inverurie**
**Day 4 → Archaeolink Prehistory Park and surrounding sights →
Aberdeen/Inverness/Edinburgh**

Notes

Ardoch Roman Camp (page 265) On the A822, north of Stirling. Detour to see the Pictish stone at Fowlis Wester (page 264) if time.

Scottish Crannog Centre (page 270) West of Aberfeldy at the head of Loch Tay. A reconstructed Iron Age loch dwelling. Stay overnight in the Aberfeldy area.

Meigle Museum (page 304) Drive across country via Dunkeld and Blairgowrie to reach this small village, where the museum holds one of the best collections of carved Pictish stones in the country.

St Vigeans (page 305) A smaller, but equally fascinating collection of Pictish stones is held in this hamlet just outside Arbroath. Reach it via Forfar and Arbroath (visit the abbey while you are there – see page 301).

Brechin (pages 305–6) The round tower by the cathedral is from the early Christian period. The nearby **Pictavia** is a new heritage centre which goes some way to explaining what we know of the Picts. Detour to see the sculptured stone at Aberlemno. Then head north-west into the hills to the extensive remains of the two Caterthuns Iron Age forts (page 305). Drive north on the B974 to the Inverurie area.

Archaeolink (page 159) This is partly a reconstruction of an Iron Age farm and partly a useful resource centre. Browse the many booklets and leaflets available, and put together a collection of the latter, which will guide you round the many prehistoric sites nearby. There are Pictish symbol stones to be found, and the remains of much earlier stone circles.

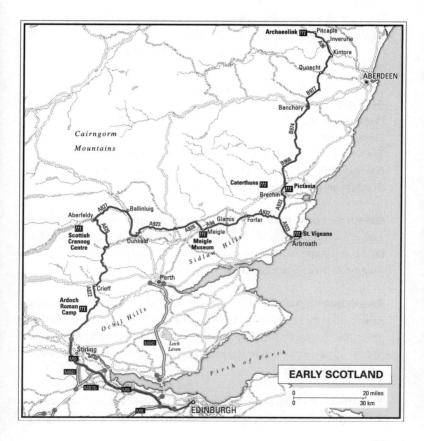

Missionaries and abbeys

This route cuts a path through south-west Scotland, via the lovely countryside of the Borders, the hills of the Southern Uplands and along the fertile coast of the Solway Firth. There are numerous sights en route, and the tour could (and should) be extended to take in some of them. Note that even the main routes in Dumfries and Galloway are slow going: leave plenty of time for the return journey (preferably most of the day).

Route

Day 1 → Edinburgh → Melrose Abbey → Jedburgh Abbey
Day 2 → Annan → Ruthwell Cross → Sweetheart Abbey →
Dundrennan Abbey → Kirkudbright
Day 3 → Whithorn Priory → St Ninian's Chapel
Day 4 → Glenluce Abbey → Edinburgh/Glasgow

Notes

Melrose Abbey (page 40) and **Jedburgh Abbey** (page 39) Travel on the A68 from Edinburgh to Melrose and Jedburgh. These are the two best of the Border Abbeys. See Dryburgh Abbey too if there's time, and maybe some of the other Borders sights (Chapter 1).

Jedburgh to Annan A lengthy cross-country haul via the A7 and A75. The A7 is not a fast road. From Annan, follow the B724 to Ruthwell, to see the famous early Christian cross (page 88). Visit Caerlaverock Castle if time.

Sweetheart Abbey The A710 south brings you to this romantic ruin (page 88). Return to Dumfries for the night, or press on to see the lonely remains of Dundrennan Abbey on the A711, ending up at Kirkcudbright, a very attractive small town (page 74).

Whithorn Priory and St Ninian's Chapel The tour now shifts from the medieval abbeys to concentrate on the sights

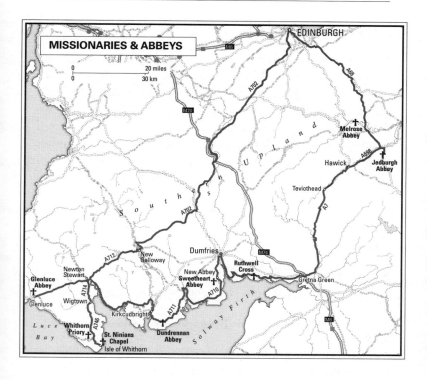

associated with St Ninian, the earliest missionary to Scotland. The countryside of the Machars Peninsula where they are found is isolated and attractive. The priory and earlier buildings were once a pilgrimage centre, and extensive archaeological work is revealing ever more of interest. St Ninian's Chapel is a small ruin by the attractive village of Isle of Whithorn (page 89). There are further sights and walks associated with St Ninian in the area.

Glenluce Abbey Reached by turning north from the A75 through Glenluce village. This is the most westerly of the abbeys. Remains are fairly fragmentary, but in a lovely setting. If time is short, omit the sight and return via the A702 (good scenery, but slow) or towards Ayr and Glasgow by the A713.

Royal Scotland

The tour begins with the three 'royal' sights in Edinburgh and takes in Linlithgow Palace and Stirling Castle, both centres for the Scottish court in medieval times. It also includes the field of Bannockburn, where King Robert the Bruce won his devastating victory, Falkland Palace, which started as a royal hunting lodge, and Glamis Castle, where the Queen Mother spent her childhood. Moving north it encompasses 'Royal Deeside', passing Balmoral Castle and visiting Queen Victoria's favourite beauty spot.

The tour is best undertaken in early summer, before Balmoral closes for the period when the Royal Family is in residence.

Route
Day 1 → **Edinburgh (Castle, Holyrood Palace and Royal Yacht** *Britannia***)**
Day 2 → **Linlithgow Palace** → **Bannockburn Heritage Centre** → **Stirling Castle**
Day 3 → **Falkland Palace** → **Glamis Castle**
Day 4 → **Braemar** → **Balmoral Castle** → **Aberdeen/Edinburgh**

Notes
Edinburgh (see Chapter 3) The three sights may take longer than a day, as there is much to see in all of them, and other attractions nearby.

Linlithgow Palace (page 159) Follow the M9 to the Linlithgow exit, or the A904, which allows you to visit Hopetoun House (pages 158–9) where George IV ate turtle soup on his visit to Scotland. Linlithgow Palace is in ruins, but well worth seeing.

Bannockburn (pages 251–2) The Heritage Centre is signed from the M9. Do not follow signs to the village of Bannockburn.

Stirling Castle (pages 250–1) The newly restored Great Hall is stunning. Leave plenty of time for this sight, aiming to spend the night somewhere nearby.

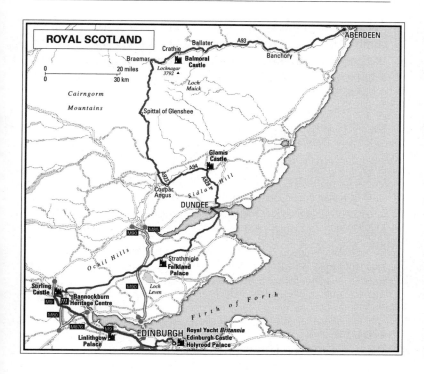

Falkland Palace (page 289) Travel here via the A91 from Stirling. Detour south to Loch Leven Castle (pages 261–2) for a royal prison (see below), but keep an eye on the time, for it is a slow drive to the next sight.

Glamis Castle (pages 300–1) Reached from Falkland via the A91/92, across the Tay Bridge, out of Dundee on A90 and then on A928. Return to Dundee for the night, or stay nearby.

Royal Deeside Head north from Blairgowrie on A93, stopping at Braemar, where the Royal Family usually attends the Highland Games. Travel down the River Dee to Balmoral (page 325) where you can see the grounds of Queen Victoria's country home and one of the rooms. Continue towards Ballater, turning right into Glen Muick. Loch Muick, at the top, was much beloved by Queen Victoria. Lengthy or short walks are possible from here. The mountain of Lochnagar (subject of a children's book by HRH Prince Charles) can be climbed from here too. Aim to stay the night around Ballater, Banchory or Aberdeen. It might be possible to return to Edinburgh on the same day, but you will have much more time to explore if you do not.

Mary Queen of Scots

This is a short two-day tour of the chief sights in central Scotland associated with the doomed Queen (see pages 254–5). We mention some others in the area to explore if you have time.

A 'second leg' to the tour could be constructed running southwards, visiting Traquair House (pages 41–2), Jedburgh (Mary Queen of Scots House (page 55) where she may have stayed, Hermitage Castle (pages 38–9) where she journeyed to visit the Earl of Bothwell and Dundrennan Abbey (page 88) where she spent her last night on Scottish soil before crossing into England.

Route

Day 1 → Edinburgh (Castle, Holyrood Palace) → Stirling
Day 2 → Stirling Castle → Port of Menteith (Inchmahome Priory) → Loch Leven Castle → Edinburgh

Notes

Edinburgh (See Chapter 3) The **castle** is where Mary gave birth to the future King James VI in June 1566; you can see the small chamber where this took place. In **Holyrood Palace**, Mary's apartments are the most interesting part of the visit. Her secretary, Rizzio, was murdered here in March 1566.

If there's time, visit the **John Knox House** (page 115) to learn about the Queen's chief religious opponent, and **Craigmillar Castle** (pages 502–3) where the murder of Darnley was plotted. Enthusiasts will want to journey to Lennoxlove House (page 149) in East Lothian to see the casket holding the letters which 'proved' Mary's involvement in the conspiracy.

Stirling On the way, you may have time to stop at **Linlithgow Palace**, where Mary was born. **Stirling Castle** is where she

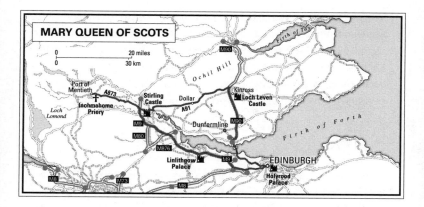

was crowned, aged only nine months. The Chapel at the castle has been extensively remodelled since then.

Inchmahome Priory (pages 255–6) Travel here from Stirling on the A873. The child Mary was hidden away on the island in the Lake of Menteith to protect her from the English invasion of 1547. A short time later she left for France.

Loch Leven Castle (pages 261–2) Take the A91. This island fortress is where Mary was held prisoner and forced to abdicate in 1567, before escaping in 1568.

ACTIVITY HOLIDAYS

There are very few places in Scotland where you cannot enjoy the activities mentioned below. These are mere pointers to the best areas in which to start looking. Detailed information is available from the regional tourist offices (see pages 16–17), and further personal recommendations or useful information can be found on a host of web sites. An excellent starting point, with extensive links, is ☞ *www.activity-scotland.co.uk*

Walking

For walks which do not involve anything too steep or too rocky, the Scottish Borders (see Chapter 1) is our chosen area. Two long-distance waymarked paths run through the area (The Southern Upland Way and St Cuthbert's Way), sections of which are easily accessed for shorter walks. The Cheviot Hills and the Lammermuir Hills offer endless opportunity for striking out on your own. Additionally, there are many quiet roads or tracks beside the lovely rivers of the area, just ideal for a morning's stroll.

Hill-walking

Most experienced hill-walkers will already have their favourite patches, and Scotland's mountains are not recommended for the inexperienced. For relatively easy walks, the hills of the Trossachs (pages 260–1) make a good destination. The Perthshire Hills, such as Schiehallion, Ben Lawers or Ben More, are not too precipitous and relatively accessible. The mountains of Glen Coe, Torridon and Assynt offer a real challenge, as do the mountains clustered around Ben Nevis. The Cairngorms, with their endless high plateaux, have their own pleasures and their own dangers.

Wherever you go, remember that Scotland's weather can change quickly. Never go hill-walking without proper clothing, a map, compass and the knowledge to go with them. Take a whistle, torch and emergency food supplies. Above all, make sure someone knows your route and your estimated time of return. And don't rely on mobile phones: reception may be bad, and batteries run down.

Wildlife watching

For the general 'green' tourist, who has been drawn to Scotland because of the wildlife, but discovers it rather hard to find, life can be difficult. Most Scottish regions tout their birds or mammals (especially otters), but the necessary infrastructure to help you see them is often rudimentary. There are nature reserves in abundance throughout, many well-equipped with hides or remote cameras, but getting from one to the next may involve lengthy journeys.

Probably the most compact area in which to consider a holiday in pursuit of wildlife is the **Island of Mull**. You are almost bound to see deer on the hills, and may well spot an eagle (or even a sea-eagle over from Rhum). There are boat trips in search of whales, and several offshore islands (such as Staffa) where you are almost certain to see puffins at the right time of year. Seals, basking in rocky bays, are common. Nearby Iona harbours corncrakes.

A growing number of web sites give information on Green Tourism. Try ✏️ *www.greentourism.org.uk*

FAMILY HOLIDAYS

Scotland still has vast areas of territory where it is possible for sensible children to roam free, with only the natural hazards posed by rocks, rivers and sea to contend with. The answer for many families is to settle on a cottage or caravan in a remote area and take advantage of whatever is available locally. **Argyll** (see Chapter 6), **Arisaig** (page 399) or around **Achiltibuie** (page 399) are good options, as are any of the smaller islands. Outdoor, waterproof clothing is, of course, vital, as are a sufficient number of activities to cope with rainy spells. Don't rely on television (reception is often bad in remote areas), or on there being a video shop nearby. Closer to the centre of the country, look at **St Andrews** (page 285) or **East Lothian** (Chapter 4), where there are good beaches and reasonable facilities to hand.

For families who want opportunities for outings, the southern half of the country is generally the most rewarding. Consider **Ayrshire** (see Chapter 2), where there are several country parks, the Big Idea at Irvine, and Vikingar! at Largs. Expeditions to Bute or Arran on the ferries should appeal, and Glasgow is within easy reach if the rain sets in. The **Oban** area (page 204) is another option, with several sights which children should enjoy, and the possibility of expeditions to the offshore islands or up Loch Etive. The area between Carrbridge and Kingussie in **Strathspey** provides more organised outdoor activity of the kind that older children will enjoy than most rural areas, and there are several interesting sights, such as the Highland Wildlife Park and the excellent Landmark Centre.

HOGMANAY

Everyone knows that Hogmanay is Scotland's New Year festival. Less commonly known is that the word is probably derived from a northern French dialect and means 'a gift', while the Gaelic for Hogmanay translates as the 'Evening of the Oatcake'. Both reflect the idea that New Year was a time for gift-giving, and this is reflected in the custom of first-footing, when Scots go round to visit friends and neighbours carrying small gifts – cake, a lump of coal for the traditionalists, as well as a bottle to share. By the time most of a small community has visited or been visited, there is not much left in the bottles. New Year's Day tends to be very quiet, in consequence.

The reason why Scots celebrate Hogmanay so ferociously goes back to the Reformation of 1560, when the new Presbyterian church put a stop to the old Catholic festivals, including 'Christ's Mass'. Well within living memory, Christmas Day was an ordinary working day in Scotland; it is only the increasing globalisation of the festival that has changed things.

Equally, it is only recently that the Scottish tourist industry has cottoned on to the fact that Hogmanay is a great excuse for pulling in thousands of off-season visitors. The Edinburgh Hogmanay festival has only been running since 1992, but shows every sign of going from strength to strength. Glasgow is rapidly catching up with its own celebrations. Stirling, Aberdeen and Inverness are also beginning to organise their own events.

Elsewhere in the country, there are older New Year festivals – some certainly tracing their origins to pagan times. These are on a much smaller scale than in the cities – but if you would rather take part in something local than in something 'put on for the visitors', they are worth tracking down.

Key web site

www.hogmanay.net Carries masses of information about what is on where, including contact details for event tickets. Worth looking at from November onwards

Edinburgh

Currently the festivities stretch over four days, ending after New Year's Day. There are few gaps left between events, and no need to hang around in the cold with nothing to do. Highlights include an open-air skating rink in Princes Street Gardens, a fairground which takes up much of a city-centre street, a torchlight procession, and a Street Party on New Year's eve. The firework displays get ever bigger and better. The craziest spectacle is the 'Loony Dook' on New Year's Day, when volunteer bathers take to the sea beneath the Forth Bridges (no wetsuits allowed). The Edinburgh Hogmanay festival is not necessarily a cheap short break – most events require tickets. In addition you will have to apply early for a street pass (free) for the Street Party on Hogmanay itself, since numbers are limited. More information is at 🖱 *www.edinburghshogmanay.org*

Glasgow

Glasgow's Hogmanay festivities are on a smaller scale than Edinburgh's, but still pretty magnificent, and mostly free and unticketed. Nothing much happens before 31st December, when there is usually a family celebration of sorts down by the River Clyde with fireworks, street theatre, and masses of music to dance to in the city centre. Find out more at 🖱 *www.glasgows-hogmanay.co.uk*

Biggar

This small town (see pages 163–4), within easy reach of both Edinburgh and Glasgow, might make an excellent alternative to city-centre festivities. The Biggar Bonfire celebrations go back to pre-Christian days. Pipe bands, Scottish dancing and the fire itself keep things going up to the stroke of midnight.

Burghead

The fishing town on the Moray Coast (see page 346) goes by an old calendar and celebrates New Year on 11 January with a fire festival that may well have its origins in Pictish times. A barrel of fire (the 'Clavie') is lit and carried around the streets of the town before being taken up to an old hill fort and used as the foundations for a bonfire.

Stonehaven

The somewhat sedate resort south of Aberdeen (see page 330) goes mad on Hogmanay when 16 men whirl cages of fire around their heads as they parade through the town before tossing the flaming balls into the sea.

Kirkwall

The chief town in Orkney holds its traditional celebration on New Year's Day, with the ba' game – one of those curious affairs where the streets of a town are filled with a heaving mass of men pursuing a football. Kirkwall's contestants are split into the 'uppies' and the 'doonies'; there is a boys' event in the morning and the men's game in the afternoon.

Distinctive Scotland

The following sections provide information on what to buy in Scotland, annual events, outdoor activities and the cultural background.

FOOD AND DRINK

Scotland produces some of the best fish, seafood, meat and game in Europe, has a long tradition of baking and confectionery, and grows some of the best soft fruit in the world. Aberdeen Angus beef and Border hill lamb are both renowned. So of course is Scottish salmon (though the advent of fish farming means the best-flavoured wild fish are seldom found on menus). If you are in Scotland during the raspberry season, make sure you find a plateful somewhere.

The reputation of both porridge and haggis has suffered at the hands of come-dians. Porridge should be made from oatmeal which has been steeped overnight. Purists insist it should be eaten with a horn spoon, standing up, and never adul-terated with sugar (salt is all right). Haggis is made from minced sheep's 'pluck' (usually heart, liver and lungs) mixed with oatmeal, suet and spices and stuffed in the sheep's stomach. It is very much more tasty than this description may suggest. Haggis is traditionally eaten with mashed potatoes and puréed turnip (called bashed neeps, and known further south as swede).

If you want to buy whisky, you can choose between a blended whisky, a de luxe whisky (a blend of particularly old or fine whiskies), a single malt whisky or a whisky-based liqueur, such as Drambuie. There is considerable variation in flavour and smoothness between the various brands of both blended and single malt whisky. Island malts (from Islay and Jura) are fiery and smoky; Speyside malts are lighter and smoother. If you have not developed your own preferences in malt whiskies, a bottle of Glenfiddich or Glenmorangie will appeal to most tastes.

Whisky connoisseurs have long maintained that whisky is just as interesting and worthy of practical study as wine. Some of the more up-market bars and restaurants are now beginning to include tasting notes with their selection of malts. For a full introduction to the mysteries of whisky tasting plus a guide to single malts, visit *www.whiskyweb.com*

SHOPPING

Tartans

For the background on tartan see page 523. Tartan gift shops of one kind or another exist in all the popular tourist haunts in Scotland. Additionally you will find kilt makers, mill shops and outfitters in most of the bigger towns; most have lists of tartans that match your name. Unless you want to buy (or hire) full Highland dress, travelling rugs and scarves make the best buys. A recent post-*Braveheart* development has been the photographic studios which will take a picture of the whole family in Highland Dress, complete with broadswords, all in tasteful sepia. It makes for a different kind of holiday postcard.

Tweed and knitwear

Shops all over Scotland specialise in these, but you are likely to find the best bargains if you look for mill shops or individual weavers and knitters. The textile towns of the Borders, especially Hawick, Selkirk and Galashiels, are fertile hunting grounds and there are mill shops too on the southern fringe of the Ochil hills. The bargains you find on Harris, source of the renowned Harris tweed, may not actually cover the cost of getting there, but you can have the satisfaction of watching the cloth being woven by hand.

Garments made from high-quality Shetland wool are sold all over the country, but the best bargains are to be found on Shetland itself. The Fair Isle jumper, with its distinctive patterns, is often imitated. The genuine article, knitted on Fair Isle, is rare. You can order one, or visit the island and see if you can persuade a local producer to put you top of the list.

Smoked produce and other foods

Smoked salmon, trout and venison can be found in shops or in the many smokeries which dot the Highlands. Many will post your order. If you can get them home fast, or can cook them on the spot, Scottish kippers, especially the lightly smoked Loch Fyne ones, are delicious. Look out too for Arbroath 'smokies'.

Oatcakes – dry, sustaining oatmeal biscuits – are easily found and easily transported. So is Scottish shortbread, sweet and crumbly. Cheese-making in Scotland is undergoing a revival and there are a number of varieties worth looking out for. Buy a black bun for New Year – highly spiced dried fruit and peel are packed into a thin pastry casing which will keep almost indefinitely until opened. Dundee cakes, light fruit cakes with a handsome topping of golden almonds, are extremely filling and good for a long day hill-walking.

Scottish cuisine may never have made it up there with the French or the Chinese, but the country has a long tradition of good home cookery, based on the fresh ingredients to be found in the seas on on the moors. It goes way beyond what you are likely to find on hotel menus, where, alas, there is a common perception that a drop of whisky or Drambuie in the pudding and something with oatmeal, salmon or venison elsewhere is enough to create an authentically Scottish menu. For a superb selection of old Scottish recipes, look at ☜🖱 *www.scotweb.co.uk/kitchen*

Silver and semi-precious stones

There is a big market in small silver items. Scottish silver-work has a long tradition behind it, and you can buy contemporary silversmiths' work in craft shops up and down the country. If you are feeling rich, a silver 'quaich' (a traditional flat drinking cup more usually made in wood or horn) makes a good present for someone. The best-known Scottish gemstone is the whisky-coloured Cairngorm.

EVENTS AND FESTIVALS

The list opposite is not fully comprehensive, but will serve to give an idea of what is likely to be happening in different areas of the country at various times of year. For a more detailed preview, visit ☜🖱 *www.rampantscotland.com*

GOLF

Scotland has the oldest golf courses and golf clubs in the world. Although the first rules were not formalised until 1744, there are records of bets on a game of golf in 1504. The home of the Royal and Ancient Golf Club which administers the game

National calendar of events

Date	Event	Location	Description
December/ January	Hogmanay	Throughout Scotland	New Year celebrations (see page 00 for details)
Last Tuesday in January	Up Helly AA	Shetland	Viking Festival
25 January	Burns Night	Throughout Scotland	Suppers in honour of Scotland's bard
January	Celtic Connections	Glasgow	Festival of Celtic music
June	Selkirk Common riding	Selkirk	Commemoration of battle of Flodden
mid-June	St Magnus Festival	Orkney	Music and other events
June/July	Border festivals	Borders	Most Border towns stage common ridings, fairs or other ancient festivals
June	Royal Highland Show	Edinburgh	Scotland's biggest agricultural show
June/ September	Highland Games	Throughout Scotland	Most towns (not just in the Highlands) and many villages hold Highland Games. In central Scotland, you will find 'galas' instead
July	T in the Park	Perthshire	Big outdoor contemporary music gig
Second week in August	Edinburgh Festival	Edinburgh	International Arts Festival
Last weekend in August	Cowal Gathering	Dunoon	Highland Games
August	World Pipe Championships	Glasgow	Musical Festival
First Saturday in September	Braemar Gathering	Braemar	Best known of the Highland Games
October	National Mod	Varies	National championship of Gaelic arts

is in St Andrews, overlooking the first tee and eighteenth green. For the holiday golfer there are over 400 courses to choose from; the most famous five play host to the British Open. Not surprisingly it is hardest to get a game on these courses. If you are less concerned with emulating golf's great players, there are an exceptional number of other superb courses where the casual visitor has a better chance of getting a game. Fees for the Open Championship courses start at around £75 to £100 a round, although £20 or so will get you a round on some of the others which are equally picturesque and challenging. For the real holiday hacker there are municipal courses where you pay £10–£15 for a round. If you are setting out to play the championship links, arm yourself with a valid handicap certificate (preferably showing a reasonable level of competence) and settle down with the phone early in the year to book your start times. If you are planning a golfing holiday, be warned that the peak months of July and August are particularly busy.

The Open Courses

St Andrews Old Course You need to book 12–18 months in advance to be assured of a tee-time, or you can put your name down for the daily ballot. A quarter of all start times are allocated by ballot. To be included, contact the starter before 2pm on the day before you wish to play – the draw is made at 4pm (your chance of being picked can be as low as 5–1 so have a back-up course in mind). Handicap certificate required; handicap limits are 24 for men, 36 for ladies [*£85 per person; closed Sun;* ☎ *(01334) 475757;* ✆ *www.standrews.org.uk*].

Carnoustie Like St Andrews, Carnoustie is a public course. Demand is not as heavy as at St Andrews but you are still advised to book at least six months in advance. A real golfing challenge, especially on a windy day. See if you can beat a 7 on the 18th hole made notorious by Jean van de Velde in the 1999 Open Championship, where he lost in a play off to local boy Paul Lawrie. Visitors not allowed before 2pm Saturday and 11.30am Sunday. Handicap certificate required; handicap limits are 28 for men, 36 for ladies. Book opens in October 2001 for April 2002 [*£75;* ☎ *(01241) 853789*].

Muirfield Home to the Honourable Company of Edinburgh Golfers, this course has some of the highest green fees in the country. Handicap certificate and proof of membership of a recognised golf club required; handicap limits are 18 for men, 24 for ladies; ladies can play only if accompanied by a man and are banned from the clubhouse [*£85 per round, £110 day ticket;* ☎ *(01620) 842123*].

Royal Troon This course has limited start times for visitors – the only days are Monday, Tuesday and Thursday. No ladies are allowed on the Championship course; a handicap certificate is required; handicap limits are 20 for men, 30 for ladies (on the Portland course) [*£135 per day, includes buffet lunch;* ☎ *(01292) 311555*].

Royal Turnberry Hotel Hotel residents can play anytime – check when you reserve a room for start times, otherwise book at least two weeks in advance. No handicap certificate required [*Non-residents: £120 Mon-Fri, £150 weekends, residents: £95;* ☎ *(01655) 331000;* ✆ *www.turnberry.co.uk*].

The best of the rest

Royal Aberdeen Handicap certificate required; handicap limits for play on the championship course are 24 or below for both men and ladies. Book six months in advance. Visitors can play only 10–11.30am and 2–3.30pm on weekdays, after 3.30pm weekends [*£60 per person weekdays, £70 weekends;* ☎ *(01224) 702571*].

St Andrews Dukes Course Opened in 1995 and managed by the Old Course Hotel. No handicap certificate needed. Book at the pro shop in the hotel or telephone *[Apr to end Oct £50 per person, £55 weekends, other times £25;* ☎ *(01334) 474371].*

Blairgowrie Handicap certificate required; handicap limits are 24 for men, 36 for ladies. Book as far ahead as possible. Wednesday and Friday are club medals so only one course will be available. At the time of writing, a ban on visitors at weekends had been proposed but not voted on *[Rosemount course: Mon–Fri £50, weekends £55; Landsdowne course: Mon–Fri £40, weekends £45; weekday ticket £70, weekends £85;* ☎ *(01250) 872622;* ✆ *www.blairgowrie-golf.co.uk].*

Cruden Bay Handicap certificate required; handicap limits are 28 for men, 36 for ladies. No visitors before 10am Monday and Tuesday *[Mon–Fri £50, weekends £60, weekday ticket £60;* ☎ *(01779) 812285;* ✆ *www.crudenbaygolfclub.co.uk].*

Royal Dornoch Handicap certificate required; handicap limits are 24 for men, 39 for ladies. Advance booking advisable *[Mon–Sat £60, Sun £70; £5 extra buys you a round on both the Struie and Championship courses;* ☎ *(01862) 810219;* ✆ *www.royaldornoch.com].*

Nairn Handicap certificate required; handicap limits are 28 for men, 36 for ladies. Advance booking advisable. Weekend visitors permitted only between 11am and 12pm *[£70 all week;* ☎ *(01667) 453208;* ✆ *www.nairngolfclub.co.uk].*

Prestwick No visitors at weekends or on Thursday. Advance booking advised. Handicap certificate required; handicap limits are 24 for men, 28 for ladies. Advance booking necessary *[Mon-Fri £80 per person;* ☎ *(01292) 477404;* ✆ *www.prestwickgc.co.uk].*

BIRDWATCHING

Much of Scotland's wildlife is of outstanding significance. Scotland holds two-thirds of the UK's most important sites for birds, making it a superb place for birdwatching. Areas favoured by birds include the Highlands and the myriad islands. You can also spot birds in the central lowlands and southern uplands, by the large firths and other coastal waters. The specialist birdwatcher visits Scotland in spring and autumn for migrants and in winter for coastal waterfowl and abundant geese; May, June or July are good for watching seabirds thronging the cliffs and for moorland and mountain birds but do not disturb breeding birds.

Birds of prey are particularly abundant in the Highlands, from the frequently encountered buzzard to the merlin, a small dashing moorland falcon. Cruising along mountain ridges may be the king of the Scottish skies, the golden eagle. Lochs in the vicinity of pine forests may attract an osprey. Scotland's most celebrated conservation success, ospreys are now widespread, though Loch Garten remains the main place to see them. The area around Loch Garten is excellent for other birds too. The ancient Caledonian forest, with its native Scots pine, hosts some unique birds including the crested tit and the Scottish crossbill, its strangely shaped beak a perfect tweezer for extracting seed from pine cones.

Various rare birds live on mountain tops, including the ptarmigan, a grouse which dons white plumage in winter. On bleak moorlands you can hear the melancholic call of the golden plover. A walk through the heather may provoke an explosion and a whirring of wings as a covey of red grouse breaks cover. Upland lochs and lochans are home for a number of birds, including elegant divers, with their eerie, wailing calls in the half-light of summer nights.

It is well worth taking binoculars on a visit to the islands as their cliffs host some of the most impressive seabird colonies in Britain, especially the rows of enchanting, comical puffins along the clifftops in June and July. Many of the islands have their own special birds such as corncrakes in the Hebrides, white-tailed eagles in the Inner Hebrides (25 years of their reintroduction to Scotland were celebrated in 2000), Fetlar's red-necked phalaropes and, on a number of islands, skuas prepared to attack unsuspecting visitors in defence of their moorland nests.

You can spot birds anywhere, but, especially for trainee birdwatchers, wildlife reserves offer the best opportunities. The Royal Society for the Protection of Birds (RSPB), whose Scotland headquarters are at Dunedin House, 25 Ravelston Terrace, Edinburgh EH4 3TP *[☎ 0131-311 6500; ✆ www.rspb.org.uk/scotland]*, has over 60 reserves in Scotland. For details of the reserves, please check the web site or write (enclose an s.a.e.) to the address above. Facilities vary; RSPB members get in free where a charge is made.

Other organisations with responsibility for natural areas include Scottish Natural Heritage *[☎ 0131-447 4784]*, the National Trust for Scotland (see page 19) and the Scottish Wildlife Trust (see page 20). Fair Isle has a bird observatory, open between May and October *[☎ (01595) 760258]*, which provides hotel-standard accommodation and the opportunity to learn more about breeding and migrant birds. There is also an observatory offering a choice of guesthouse and dormitory accommodation in a wind- and solar-powered building, on North Ronaldsay in Orkney *[☎ (01857) 633267]*.

Useful books

For identifying birds: Lars Svensson, *Collins Bird Guide* (HarperCollins, 2001).

For the best places to visit: Mike Madders and Julia Welstead *Where to Watch Birds in Scotland* (Christopher Helm, 1997).

For background information: Valerie M. Thom *Birds in Scotland* (T & A.D. Poyser, 1986).

SCOTLAND'S HISTORY

Scottish history is often baffling to the visitor. It is seldom taught beyond the borders of the country, so few outsiders have any idea of what went on before the union of the parliaments in 1707. However, some knowledge of it is useful, not simply for visiting castles, but because it helps to explain modern Scotland and some of the tensions within it.

Scottish history, read from one angle, is a litany of dashed hopes: the silence into which the Declaration of Arbroath fell in 1320; the long sequence of military incompetence at Falkirk, Halidon Hill, Flodden, Solway Moss, Pinkie, Dunbar and Culloden; the gradual realisation in the sixteenth century that the Auld Alliance with France was a double-edged sword; the sense of having been abandoned by the later Stuart kings; the terrible failure of the Darien colony and the discontent felt after the Act of Union. Add to these the devastation of the Highland way of life in the eighteenth and nineteenth centuries, the destruction of the Lowland heavy industry in the twentieth, and it would be surprising if there were not some truth behind the old clichés about the insecurity and touchiness of the Scottish character.

Looked at from another angle, the Scottish tendency to divide into factions or to put self-interest first can be held to blame for many of the country's past troubles. The endless squabbling between powerful barons and kings trying to exert their authority went on longer in Scotland than almost anywhere else. The religious sectarianism which plagued seventeenth-century Scotland was an outbreak of the same tendency. It can be argued that almost every failed enterprise undertaken by the Scots has been doomed from the start by argument and failure to work in unity. It is perhaps no surprise that Wallace and Robert the Bruce, who managed to provide Scotland with a brief flicker of united endeavour, are two of the most revered of Scotland's heroes.

Unity

The Romans

The difficulties of communication over Scotland's mountainous, boggy and sea-loch-riddled terrain long made the establishment of an effective centralising authority difficult. The Romans were the first to try, moving north from England in at least three separate campaigns between AD 81 and AD 208, defeating the inhabitants of Caledonia at Mons Graupius in AD 84. Only the area south of the Forth and Clyde was subdued for any length of time. Gibbon describes the Romans as giving up in disgust, turning 'with contempt from gloomy hills assailed by the winter tempest, from lakes concealed in a blue mist, and from cold and lonely heaths, over which the deer of the forest were chased by a troop of naked barbarians'.

The Dark Ages

The sixth century saw what is now Scotland parcelled up into four kingdoms, three of them inhabited by Celtic peoples: Picts, Scots and Britons. The Picts, in central and eastern Scotland, held the greatest area of territory, the Scots (from Ireland) had formed the kingdom of Dalriada in what is now Argyll and the Britons held Galloway and Cumbria. The Angles, from their power base in Northumbria, had extended their rule northward into Lothian. In the ninth century, the Norsemen added to the brew by extensive coastal raiding and by establishing themselves in Shetland, Orkney, the Hebrides, Sutherland and Caithness. Warfare between the rival kingdoms was constant, the battle of Nechtansmere in 685 (when the Picts defeated the Angles) being particularly notable because it stopped Anglian expansion northwards. Marriage brought some kind of unity between Picts and Scots under Kenneth MacAlpine, King of Scots, around 843 and by 1034 the old kingdoms of Britons and Angles had also been absorbed.

Several bloody conflicts took place before Malcolm Canmore emerged as king in 1057, killing Macbeth in the process (here at least Shakespeare is accurate). Two important events occurred during his reign – his marriage to Margaret, the English princess, who was a refugee from the Norman invasion, and the act of homage which Malcolm paid to William the Conqueror in 1072 at Abernethy (see Independence and Religion). Malcolm, often seen as a big barbarian married to a cultured and holy wife whom he adored, spent much time trying, and failing, to establish Scotland's southern frontier along the River Tyne.

David I and the Norman incomers

There was no Norman conquest of Scotland – the Scottish kings did the job themselves. Malcolm's successors, holding lands in England and with increasingly strong ties there, encouraged Norman families to settle in Scotland, granting land and promoting the building of castles. Many of the most famous names in Scottish history have Norman origins. David I (1124–53) hastened Norman-style feudalism by the establishment of abbeys and cathedrals and the system of royal burghs. Under David, Scotland began to develop an administrative system to match that of England, while the authority of the king was much increased.

Last of the Norsemen
Under the improbably-named Magnus Barelegs, the Norse settlers in the Hebrides had forced the Scottish crown to concede all the western islands to them (and Magnus shiftily added Kintyre to the list by dragging his boat across the Tarbert isthmus). The Norse-Hebridean chiefs were a menace to the Scottish kings, supporting rebels and making forays of their own. Somerled, ancestor of Clan Donald, was a particularly forceful character in this respect. In 1263, King Haakon of Norway assembled a huge fleet for an attack, but was routed at the battle of Largs. After this defeat, Norway gave up all her Scottish possessions apart from Orkney and Shetland under a treaty in 1266. A royal marriage with Norway in 1468 brought Orkney and Shetland to the Scottish crown.

Highlands, lowlands and islands
For centuries, the clans of the islands and glens continued a law unto themselves, sometimes allied to the crown, sometimes hostile to it. It could be argued that they never became fully part of a united Scotland. Despite expeditions mounted by various Scottish kings, it was not until the defeat of the last Jacobite rebellion at Culloden in 1746 that the power of the clans to act independently was broken. There is still a division between Highlander and Lowlander today – sometimes exaggerated, sometimes glossed over.

Independence

If there is one theme that infects Scottish history, right down to the present day, it is the independence of the nation, and in particular, independence from England. Scotland was unified by war, and fought for 300 years against ceaseless attempts by the Plantagenet and Tudor monarchs to bring their northern neighbours under control. Whatever the benefits of the subsequent union with England – first of Crown and later of Parliaments – Scots have always considered themselves as separate and distinct. The 75 per cent 'yes' vote in the 1999 referendum on the question of the re-establishment of a Scottish parliament was a manifestation of that fact.

The Wars of Independence
The conflict between England and Scotland really started in 1290 with the death of the child-queen Margaret, 'The Maid of Norway'. The blame for it must be carried almost entirely by Edward I of England, popularly known as 'Hammer of the Scots'. Edward had a clear idea that he was feudal overlord of Scotland, and was able to point to the homage done by various Scottish kings to various English kings to make his point (though what, exactly, they were doing homage for is still disputed). Edward's chance came when he was asked to judge between 13 rival claimants for the Scottish throne. He made his judgement in favour of John Balliol, but proceeded thereafter to treat this weak-minded man as such an

underling that even 'Toom Tabard' (empty coat), as he was known, was forced into revolt in 1296. Edward's response was to sack Berwick, invade Scotland, plunder the stone of Scone on which Scottish kings were traditionally crowned, depose John Balliol, and set up a government similar to the one that he had already imposed on conquered Wales. Scotland was to be a little-regarded province of England.

Revolt started almost at once, especially among the small land-owners who had no holdings in England to put in jeopardy. William Wallace defeated the English at Stirling Bridge, but was defeated in turn at Falkirk in 1298. He was captured in 1305 and executed as a traitor in London. Scottish resistance collapsed and Edward set up a new, less repressive government.

In 1306, Robert the Bruce, grandson of one of the claimants to the Scottish throne whom Edward had rejected, killed his Comyn rival in a church, thus laying himself open to charges of murder and sacrilege. His reaction was to have himself crowned King of Scotland at Scone. Edward immediately swore that he would never rest until Scotland was conquered and set about defeating Bruce. Bruce's deliverance came in May 1307 with the death of Edward, whose son, Edward II, turned back from the Scottish campaign.

Bruce proceeded to defeat his Scottish enemies, then turned on the English-garrisoned castles, until, by 1314, only Stirling remained in English hands. The Battle of Bannockburn (see page 252) put the seal on Bruce's triumph and made his kingship undisputed, but it was not until 1328 that Scotland's independence was recognised by the English king.

Further wars with the English

The conflict did not end there. By 1333 everything that Bruce had achieved had gone. John Balliol's son, with the support of Edward III of England, invaded, defeated the Scots at Halidon Hill, and promptly paid homage to the English king. His reign did not last long, but it set the pattern for the following centuries. English kings claimed feudal overlordship or supported discontented Scottish nobles, and occasionally invaded. Scottish resistance, usually marked by internal strife and military weakness, was sporadically successful, but owed its survival to the fact that English kings had more pressing tasks than subduing Scotland, notably that of maintaining their claim to France. Scotland's worst defeat by the English was entirely self-inflicted when James IV invaded England on behalf of his French ally. The result was the terrible defeat at Flodden in 1513.

Henry VIII and the Rough Wooing

James V of Scotland, the nephew of Henry VIII of England, was not inclined to follow his uncle in throwing off the Pope's authority. Rather, he chose a French bride and kept faith with the Vatican. In 1541, Henry summoned him to confer at York but James chose not to go. Henry dispatched an army northwards and James replied by sending one south, only to have it defeated at Solway Moss in 1542. James died soon afterwards, leaving the infant Mary Queen of Scots as his heir.

Henry saw his chance of bringing Scotland into his orbit by arranging for his son, Edward, to marry Mary. There were enough Protestant (and hence anglophile) lords in Scotland to make this attractive to the Scots, and a treaty was even signed at Greenwich to confirm it. But a putsch by those in favour of the old alliance with France led to Scottish rejection of the match. Henry, typically, over-played his hand by replacing diplomacy with force. The burning of the south of

Scotland in 1544 and 1545, ironically called the Rough Wooing, merely strengthened Scottish determination. Defeated at Pinkie in 1547, the Scots spirited the young queen to France and agreed to her marriage with the French dauphin, the future François II.

A French province?

The mother of Mary Queen of Scots, the redoubtable Mary of Guise, was now regent of Scotland and her response to the English invasion of the country was to bring in French troops to defend it. A military stalemate resulted, but Scotland found itself increasingly governed by French administrators. When, in 1559, a group of Protestant lords rebelled, they did so as much to rid Scotland of the French as to promote their religion. After the death of Mary of Guise in 1560, the matter was sealed: the French left.

When James VI, son of Mary Queen of Scots, inherited the throne of England in 1603 and travelled triumphantly south, he promised his Scottish subjects he would return every three years. He did not keep this promise. For a brief period during the conflict with Charles I (see Religion), the Scottish parliament asserted its independence, but the invasion of Scotland by Oliver Cromwell in 1650, the enforced, if temporary, union with England, and the absolutist policies of Charles II after the Restoration left Scotland with little independent voice. The hesitation in Scotland after the Glorious Revolution of 1688 had deposed James VII from the British throne was brief – the Scottish crown was offered to William and Mary only two months after the English one was.

The Union of Parliaments (1707)

In the years before the final union of Scotland and England, the relationship between the two countries was extremely frayed. To many Scots, union with England seemed to be the only way of avoiding bankruptcy and war. When the Scottish parliament voted itself out of existence it seemed the end at last of an independent Scotland.

The Jacobites (1715–1745)

The uprisings of 1715, 1719 and 1745, which sought to restore the Stuarts to the British throne, were not in any sense a popular struggle for Scottish independence. While the unpopularity of the Union was a factor that led some people to join the Jacobites, Lowland support for the Jacobite risings was patchy at best, and Highland support was far from solid. Nor were the ambitions of the 'Old Pretender' (James VIII) or his son, Prince Charles Edward Stuart, confined to ruling Scotland – the invasion of England in 1745 was undertaken with the purpose of gaining the British crown. Nevertheless, the uprisings showed that the old link between Scotland and France and the loyalty of many Scots to the person they saw as their legitimate king had not been entirely destroyed by union with England.

Home Rule movements (1920–2000)

The first serious attempts in modern times to regain home rule for Scotland were made between the two World Wars, at a time of economic depression and, on Clydeside, left-wing radicalism. The nationalist movement was given added fuel by the 'Scottish Renaissance' literary revival, led by Hugh MacDiarmid. All attempts to attain a measure of self-government for Scotland came to nothing, except that they eventually resulted in the formation of the Scottish Nationalist Party (SNP) in 1934. Hampered by factionalist infighting for years, the SNP made something of a breakthrough in 1974, winning seven seats and polling 21 per cent of the vote, largely because the discovery of 'Scotland's Oil' held out the prospect of independence in wealth rather than penury. An attempt to introduce a measure of devolution in 1979 ended in a controversial and inconclusive referendum, when a proposal for a form of devolution was rejected by a majority of the Scottish electorate, an abstention being held to count against.

The long sequence of Conservative election victories which followed (when Scotland consistently voted against the Tory party) revived the home rule pressure within Scotland, and led to a commitment by the Labour party to grant a measure of independence to Scotland, were it ever to be re-elected. The result was the Scotland Act of 1999, and the resounding assent to devolution in a referendum held in Scotland in the same year.

'There shall be a Scottish Parliament', the Act began, and indeed, there now is, with 129 members, a proportional representation system of election, and a structure rather different from that at Westminster. The Parliament's powers are limited, however, with questions of finance, defence, foreign relations, the constitution and many other matters reserved to Westminster.

Scotland may or may not be content with this devolution settlement, but it is noteworthy that the Scottish National Party, which seeks complete independence 'within Europe' is currently the second largest party within the Scottish parliament, and forms the official opposition.

ARCHITECTURE

Much modern Scottish domestic architecture, particularly in private housing developments, has suffered from the unimaginative, formulaic nature of housebuilders' designs – to the extent that you can even find mock half-timbering in a country which has never had any tradition of using it. Further in the past, however, Scotland had a distinctive architecture, which drew heavily on the abundance of stone. Many buildings, not just castles, reflect the country's violent history.

Just a few of the distinctive types of building (with some examples) are listed here.

Neolithic housing (Skara Brae page 461) The semi-subterranean houses unearthed in Orkney show remarkable sophistication. Well-insulated by surrounding middens, they may even have had running water to flush away waste.

The broch (Shetland page 471, Orkney page 463 Lewis page 440, Glenelg pages 408–9) Found nowhere else but Scotland, these Iron Age forts or refuges were double-walled circular structures rising to heights of 40 feet or more, with galleries running between the walls. Their exact purpose is still unknown. Later, they were adopted for domestic use. See also the box on pages 408–9.

The black house (Lewis page 439) For centuries, this single-storey, windowless house was the commonest dwelling type in the Highlands and Islands. Eighteenth- and nineteenth-century visitors (such as Shelley) condemned them as scarcely fit for human habitation, but it is now widely recognised that they were remarkably energy-efficient structures. Double-thickness walls, a central fire and the close proximity of domestic animals generated heat and kept it in. The heather thatch, impregnated with soot from the fire, could be used as fertiliser.

The medieval castle Scottish castles range from simple stone towers (Smailholm page 41) to elaborate defensive structures (Bothwell page 165, Dirleton page 148). Often they grew from the original Norman motte-and-bailey pattern, and may have been extended into Z shapes to provide better defensive protection (Menzies page 269). With the advent of artillery, they often underwent further modification, such as at Blackness (pages 159–60).

Courtly buildings The Scottish Renaissance court under James IV and James V was responsible for some fine architecture. French ideas came early to the country and French-style decoration can be seen at Falkland Palace (page 289) and Stirling Castle (pages 250–1).

The tower-house Lacking the settled peace of the Tudor and Elizabethan periods in England, the Scots were more inclined to adapt the old fortress-building habits than to turn their backs on medieval discomfort and build afresh. The result was the tower-house, where the base is often uncompromisingly defensive, but which broadens out in the top storeys to include comfortable domestic appartments. The device of corbelling outwards to provide extra space was widely used. The best examples are at Crathes (pages 322–3) and Craigevar (pages 321–2).

Neoclassicism Scottish architects were to the fore in establishing the classical revival in Britain. The Adam family are the most famous exponents of the style, although there are earlier examples, such as the courtyard at Holyrood (page 111). The best Adam house in Scotland is Mellerstain (pages 39–40), although there are numerous others.

Edinburgh's New Town is the best-known, and most inspiring example of this style, seen at its best in Charlotte Square (page 126).

Scottish baronial revival The Victorian and Edwardian love-affair with the Highlands led to a rash of building in a 'Scottish' idiom, which was partly based on the tower-house and partly pure fantasy. The shooting lodge or grand mansion, decorated with turrets and towers in every conceivable position, is a common sight; lesser buildings were sometimes similarly garnished too.

Nineteenth-century housing Rows of neat, stone Victorian villas are to be found in the small towns of Scotland, often decorated with characteristic finials. Their most distinctive feature is their high-ceilinged rooms and expansive windows. The same style was continued in the cities in the characteristic 'tenement' or town house split into several flats with a central stair. The best examples are in Glasgow (page 184). At their worst, such buildings became slums, but many tenements were built for the prosperous classes too.

Tenement life had a long Scottish tradition, arising from the buildings of the Old Town in Edinburgh (page 104) where lack of space led to ever-taller buildings with a mix of inhabitants.

Lorimer and Mackintosh The arts and crafts movement of the early twentieth century produced wonderful results in Scotland, notably through the 'Glasgow Style' pioneered by Charles Rennie Mackintosh (page 193). Lorimer's work, notably in the restoration of Dunblane Cathedral (page 250) but also seen at Hill of Tarvit (page 293) and Kellie Castle (pages 293–4) is also inspiring.

RELIGION

The Celtic Church

The first Christian missionary to Scotland was St Ninian, who, from a base in Galloway, set out to convert the southern Picts around AD 400. He was followed, in 563, by St Columba, whose foundation at Iona became a centre of learning and spirituality which was to have enormous influence throughout Scotland. The Celtic church, its gospel spread by missionaries whose names still crop up in remote place names, eventually made contact with the Roman church, whose doctrine, brought to England by St Augustine, had spread up to Northumbria. In various conflicts over practice (the date of Easter was one point at issue), the Celtic church gave way. Its influence was weakened by Norse raids on Iona and the increasing hold of Roman doctrine.

The Norman period

Just as the Anglo-Norman settlement of Scotland established feudalism, so it placed the Roman doctrine on a firm basis. The remnants of the Celtic church, many of whose priests were not celibate, could not exist within the new system. Malcolm Canmore's wife Margaret, who founded the monastery at Dunfermline, rebuilt Iona but was firm in suppressing the erroneous ways of the older church. By the time dioceses and parishes had been established, continental monastic orders invited in and great abbeys founded, the church in Scotland was almost identical in practice to that in England. The Celtic church, except perhaps in the Highland fastnesses, had vanished.

Church and Crown (1153–1560)

Just as the English kings claimed jurisdiction over Scotland, so did the English church – but in this case the Scots had an easier victory, for the Pope recognised the Scottish church as directly responsible to Rome in 1192. In 1472, St Andrews became an archbishopric. During the Middle Ages, the church, wealthier than the king and wielding immense influence, was a strong force for stability in the face of recurring crises. However, in common with the church in so many European countries before the Reformation, it grew fat and lax. When the Lutheran doctrines began to be heard in Scotland, they found fertile ground, although reformers were burnt – notably George Wishart in 1546. The energetic Cardinal Beaton, doing his best to counter the anglophile, Protestant party, was murdered in his turn at St Andrews in the same year. The regency of Mary of Guise, during the time when the young Mary Queen of Scots was in France, saw open warfare, when Protestant lords, aided by the English, confronted the government.

Reformation (1560)

In the brief period between the death of Mary of Guise in 1560 and the return to Scotland of Mary Queen of Scots in 1561, the Scottish Reformation took place. The preacher John Knox laid before the Scottish parliament a Confession of Faith, which was accepted; the authority of the Pope was denied, and the mass declared illegal. Scotland achieved, in one step, a radical transformation of her church. At the same time, the principle that the church was independent of state control was laid down and the basis for Presbyterianism established. This essential difference between the reformed Scottish church and the Church of England was to cause much anguish. The Confession of Faith was followed by the Book of Discipline, which laid out not only how the new church might be organised but envisaged a complete scheme of education from primary school to university, astoundingly in advance of its time.

Mary Queen of Scots

In 1561, Mary, a Catholic queen, returned to a country in the first uneasy aftermath of a Protestant revolution. Fear of a reimposition of the old faith was strong, and the Catholic powers of Europe encouraged Mary to undertake a counter-revolution. The religious tolerance with which Mary attempted to rule was no solution to the polarisation of attitudes within Scotland. Although she suppressed the Catholic Huntly family, she did herself no good by marrying the Catholic Darnley. Part of Mary's tragedy is that she attempted to steer a middle course between two extremes. The nobles who rebelled against her did so largely out of self-interest, but religious concerns were not far beneath the surface.

The turmoil which gripped Scotland throughout much of the seventeenth century was the result of monarchs attempting to impose their will on a church unprepared to accept interference in its affairs. James VI succeeded in reimposing bishops upon the reformed Scottish church, thereby gaining a means of exerting authority, but he achieved this only after long struggle. Charles I, in attempting to dictate particular forms of worship, went too far. The signing of the National Covenant in 1638 led indirectly to civil war in Scotland, England and Ireland, to the throwing off of the king's authority in Scotland and to the appearance of a temporary theocracy, which crumbled in the face of Oliver Cromwell's invasion. After the restoration, Charles II reimposed bishops and let loose troops to persecute the Presbyterian extremists who refused to be reconciled to his policies. The 'Killing Times' round the year 1685 saw the worst of the unequal contest. The accession of James VII, himself a Catholic, led to another swing of the pendulum. Extreme Presbyterianism would not be tolerated in Scotland, but a Catholic monarch was not acceptable in either country. The Glorious Revolution of 1688 deposed James and made way for the Protestant William of Orange and his wife, Mary.

Disruption

The Reformed Church of Scotland, now once more in the ascendant, was an austere body, with the authority to enforce its discipline at the 'repentance stool' in church if need be. One major point of dissent remained – the issue of lay patronage, or whether or not congregations had the right to choose their own ministers. Conflict over this matter led to the withdrawal of more than 470 ministers from the established church in 1843, an event known as the Disruption. During the nineteenth century, other branches of the Kirk split and rejoined. The Church of Scotland remains strong throughout the country; more extreme Presbyterian churches are found in some parts, notably Skye and Lewis.

SCOTTISH DANCING

The origins of distinctively Scottish dances are lost in the mists of time, but the fundamental dance form is the 'reel' – a set dance involving several couples tracing simple or elaborate figures.

For the visitor, Scottish dancing can easily be split into three types. Highland Dancing is seen at Highland Games throughout the country. Many of the steps and patterns have evolved from the old reels. Highland Dancing is a highly competitive and strict art form, designed for display rather then social dancing, and an immensely popular hobby, not just in Scotland, but wherever Scots have settled across the world. Classes take place throughout the country.

Scottish Country Dancing is a much more sociable affair, although it can be equally formal when being danced for display. It has very strong links with the Scottish regiments, who have created many of the tunes and not a few of the dances – some very elaborate ones amongst them. Mostly, this kind of dancing happens at big set-piece occasions, such as Charity Balls or Hunt Balls.

Of most interest to visitors may be Ceilidh dancing. This can be loosely defined as an informal night spent dancing the most popular Scottish country dances, supplemented perhaps by some barn dances and a variety of waltzes. The past two decades have seen a massive revival in Ceilidh dances, largely because of the new importation of the American habit of having a 'caller' – meaning that no one need any longer be inhibited by not knowing what to do.

Ceildih dances can happen anywhere, at any time, but you are most likely to find a convenient one in the cities, or around Burns Night or St Andrews night.

The web site ◌ *www.ceilidhs.co.uk* is a good starting point for details of what is on.

TARTAN

The distinctive check patterns of tartan were originally woven into woollen cloth, but now appear on many different materials and are exported and recognised across the globe.

The whole elaborate mythology surrounding tartan dates only from 1822, the time of George IV's visit to Edinburgh, when Highland dress suddenly became fashionable. The tartan craze received further reinforcement throughout the nineteenth century, partly because of the prominent part played by Highland regiments in the many wars of the period, and partly through the immense popularity of Sir Walter Scott's novels. Queen Victoria's love for all things Highland put the seal on tartan's desirability as leisurewear for the sporting aristocracy.

The patterns and colours which form distinctive tartans were probably originally associated with districts, rather than with individual clans, so the whole process of finding the tartan that goes with your name (and most shops have lists) need not be taken more seriously than you want. The need to have 'a tartan' has long ago spread from individals to companies and corporations, and there are also district or universal tartans which can be worn by anyone.

For more information, and a glance at the complete register of tartans, try ◌ *www.tartans.scotland.net* Several further web sites have pictures of tartans and tartan wallpaper which you can download for your PC.

BACKGROUND READING

General history
T.M. Devine *The Scottish Nation: 1700–2000* (Penguin, 2000) At once erudite and readable, the best of the modern histories

Arnold Kemp *The Hollow Drum: Scotland since the War* (Mainstream, 1993) Good, if slightly jaundiced, analysis of Scottish post-war politics

Michael Lynch *Scotland – A New History* (Pimlico, 1992) A readable general history

Tom Nairn *After Britain* (Granta Books, 2000) Scotland, Britain and Blair, by an avowed Nationalist

T.C. Smout *A History of the Scottish People 1560–1830 and 1830–1950* (Fontana, 1987) The standard social history text, full of interesting insights

Specific histories and historical novels
John Buchan *Montrose* (House of Stratus, 2000) Still one of the best biographies of the Royalist general

Antonia Fraser *Mary Queen of Scots* (Arrow, 1989) The classic biography of Mary, and still the best

George MacDonald Fraser *The Steel Bonnets* (HarperCollins, 1989) Brilliant, almost racy, account of Border warfare

Raymond Campbell Paterson *For the Lion: A History of the Scottish Wars of Independence* (John Donald, 1996) and *My Wound is Deep: A History of the later Anglo-Scottish Wars* (John Donald, 1997) Very good histories

John Prebble *The Highland Clearances/Culloden/Glencoe: the Story of the Massacre* (Penguin, 1969/1996/1968) and *Darien: The Scottish Dream of Empire* (Birlinn Ltd, 2000) Detailed accounts of disasters and misfortunes

Sir Walter Scott *Waverley* (Penguin, 1995) and *The Tale of Old Mortality* (Penguin, 1999) Two of the best of Scott's historical novels

Nigel Tranter *The Wallace* (Coronet, 1989) and *The Bruce Trilogy* (Coronet, 1985) Colourful historical fiction

Memoirs

Lord Henry Cockburn *Memorials of his Time* (Mercat Press, 1971) Post-enlightenment Edinburgh gossips and goings-on, by a very civilised writer

Elizabeth Grant *Memoirs of a Highland Lady* (Canongate, 1992) Fascinating account of old Highland life

Johnson and Boswell *A Journey to the Western Islands of Scotland* and *The Journal of a Tour to the Hebrides* (Canongate, 1996; Houghton Mifflin, 1990; Penguin, 1984) Two of Scotland's earliest tourists record their impressions of the Highlands

Novelists and poets for the regions

Poems by Robert Burns (South-West)

Derek Cooper (West Highlands and Islands)

Robert Garioch (Edinburgh)

Lewis Grassic Gibbon (Aberdeenshire)

Alasdair Gray, William MacIlvanney and Neil Munro (Glasgow)

Neil Gunn (Caithness and the far north)

George Mackay Brown (Orkney)

Compton Mackenzie *Whisky Galore* (Penguin, 1999) (West Highlands and Islands)

Ian Rankin *Knots and Crosses, Black and Blue* (both Orion, 1998) and others (Edinburgh, for lovers of the crime novel)

Sir Walter Scott *Heart of Midlothian* (Penguin, 1994) (Edinburgh) and *Rob Roy* (Penguin, 1995) (the Trossachs)

Robert Louis Stevenson *Kidnapped* (Penguin, 1994) (West Highlands and Islands)

David Thomson *Nairn in Darkness and Light* (Vintage, 1988) (North-East)

Maps

The Michelin map of Scotland (1:400,000) covers the whole country; the Ordnance Survey Routemaster series (1:250,000) is good for those on touring holidays; walkers will need the Landranger maps (1:50,000).

Index